Developability of Biotherapeutics

Developability of Biotherapeutics

Editor

Luigi Salvay

scitus academics

Developability of Biotherapeutics
Edited by **Luigi Salvay**

ISBN: 978-1-68117-688-8
Library of Congress Control Number: 2016958855

616, Corporate Way, Suite 2, 4766,
Valley Cottage, NY 10989

www.scitusacademics.com

Notice

Printed in United States of America on Acid Free Paper

Preface

Biopharmaceuticals emerge as frontline medicines to fight a number of life-threatening and chronic diseases. They are currently the fastest growing pharmaceutical group, being a treatment option for a variety of chronic and life-threatening conditions. A variety of natural products covering nucleic acids, viral particles, whole cells, proteins and vaccines are represented by biotherapy. Recently, major steps have been taken to develop safer and more efficient biotherapeutics and to adopt cost-effective, efficient and streamlined production processes. In the coming years, this trend is likely to accelerate as emerging areas relating to advanced therapies or even personalized medicine mature. In spite of these advances, you can find knowledge gaps at all stages of development, together with regulatory and technical obstacles that could stop the approval process for these items. A group of topics covering relevant biotherapeutics aspects are presented in this title.

This compilation describes the application of computer and molecular modeling techniques that improve the overall discovery and development process by eliminating empiricism. This book collectively gives a comprehensive overview of the current advances in biotherapy and the exciting challenges ahead. It should be of a valuable tool for industry research and development professionals, practitioners, scientists working with regulatory agencies and students and educators in pharmacy, medicine and life sciences.

Table of Contents

1

CHAPTER

Antibiotic-Free Selection in Biotherapeutics: Now and Forever

Charlotte Mignon Régis Sodoyer * and Bettina Werle

Technology Research Institute Bioaster, 317 avenue Jean-Jaurés, 69007 Lyon, France

ABSTRACT

The continuously improving sophistication of molecular engineering techniques gives access to novel classes of bio-therapeutics and new challenges for their production in full respect of the strengthening regulations. Among these biologic agents are DNA based vaccines or gene therapy products and to a lesser extent genetically engineered live vaccines or delivery vehicles. The use of antibiotic-based selection, frequently associated with genetic manipulation of microorganism is currently undergoing a profound metamorphosis with the implementation and diversification of alternative selection means. This short review will present examples of alternatives to antibiotic selection and their context of application to highlight their ineluctable invasion of the bio-therapeutic world.

Keywords

Antibiotic-free selection; auxotrophy; post-seggregational killing; minicircle

1. INTRODUCTION

The discovery of antibiotics, considered for several decades a major step forward in the global domain of therapy against some infectious agents, is still a very active domain of investigation. Unfortunately, the excessive and sometimes inappropriate use of antibiotics is responsible for a large-scale spreading of antibiotics in the environment. The first consequence is the emergence of resistant or even multi-resistant pathogenic bacterial strains that has become a general concern promise to even further increase [1]. The improvement of existing antibiotics and discovery of new molecules is, by definition, an endless quest [2,3]. Besides therapeutic applications, antibiotics are often used as a selection pressure to avoid bio-contamination in production processes such as fermentation. In this particular context, the problem can show two distinct facets: The antibiotic molecule itself, seen as a contaminant product in a given biological and the antibiotic resistance gene used as a selection marker.

The increasing regulatory requirements to which biological agents are subjected will hopefully have a great impact in the fields of industrial protein expression and production, live vectors for bio-therapeutic agent delivery and gene therapy. There is an expectation that in the near future, the rule becomes "zero tolerance" towards antibiotic-based selection in production and delivery systems. Besides the antibiotic itself, the antibiotic resistance gene is a major subject of consideration. The complete absence of antibiotic-resistance genes being the only way to ensure that propagation in the environment or transfer of resistance to pathogenic strains will not happen. In order to address these issues, different and complementary approaches can be applied. The first would be to design more stable host/vector couples allowing to set-up and conduct fermentation processes in the complete absence of antibiotics. A more achieved strategy would be to substitute the antibiotic-based selection by an alternative mean such as the complementation of an essential gene product, not expressed by the host, poison antidote mean of selection or sophisticated post-segregational killing mechanism.

For specific therapeutic agents or fields of application such as DNA vaccination, passive immunization using antibody gene transfer

[4] or gene therapy, the presence of an antibiotic resistant gene in the vector backbone is rightly pointed out as undesirable by health authorities. The major issue associated with DNA delivery or immunization being a possibility of horizontal transfer of antibiotic resistance to circulating microbial population. Such a consideration is emphasized by the very long persistence of DNA constructs upon injection, some published data indicates several months. Armengol *et al.* have used *in situ* hybridization and PCR to document persistence of a plasmid harboring the *cry11Bb* gene of *Bacillus* up to two years after injection in mouse muscle [5]. Other studies based on bio-distribution and safety of antibiotic-free plasmid encoding somatostatin genes delivered by attenuated *Salmonella enterica* serovar *Choleraesuis* revealed detection in several examined tissues with the exception of ovary and brain, but a rapid clearance from the body (approximately 10 days) [6]. The situation can be seen as worthwhile for long term and multiple delivery protocols currently used in the field of gene therapy. Finally, another domain of application must be included in the discussion, this domain being the use of live bacteria as delivery vehicles containing extra chromosomal elements that need to be stably maintained. Obviously, in that category, we will find commensal bacterial strains expressing plasmid borne foreign antigens.

Regulatory Concern

To date, the use of the β-lactam antibiotic family is not acceptable, in order to avoid concerns for patients showing reactivity to β-lactam antibiotics. Therefore, Kanamycin and to a lesser extent, Tetracyclin, are commonly used and still acceptable to health authorities and the development of new drugs is always more challenging [7]. Susceptibility to the antibiotic compound is the visible part of the iceberg, the most critical issue being the horizontal genetic transfer of antibiotic resistant genes to prokaryotic organisms, present in the environment or in commensal flora. It becomes clear that antibiotic-resistant bacteria are causing a global health crisis and that mechanisms behind acquisition of resistance are more and more documented [8].

Horizontal genetic transfer (HGT), an important driving force in bacterial evolution, is the passage of genetic elements between organisms [9,10]. HGT is influenced by the advantage conferred by the transferred gene, the toxicity of its product, the capacity of the transferred gene to be integrated into the host genome and to be stabilized, and a certain compatibility of codon usage between the transferred gene and the host. The probability of integration and stabilization of a HGT into a new host genome is correlated and increased by the similarity between the tRNA pools of the donor and recipient organism. Acquisition of antibiotic resistance is one example of this evolution by HGT. As early as in 1965, Datta and Kontomichalou [11] showed the widespread transfer of penicillin resistance across *Enterobacteriaceae*. A marked β-lactamase activity was also measured in various *Pseudomonas aeruginosa* resistant strains in the early seventies [12]. More recently, acquisition of the virulence factors that distinguish *Salmonella* from *Escherichia coli* has been clearly shown as the result of horizontal gene transfer [13]. Recent technological breakthroughs, such as the one that can be observed for next generation sequencing, offers unthinkable and extensive possibilities of detecting numerous HGT events, especially if the data acquisition is completed by new bioinformatics tools like nucleotide substitution rate matrixes [14]. Moreover, if we consider the situation at the microbiome level, it becomes obvious that a multitude of different bacterial species, exhibiting many types of complex interactions, are likely to use HGT as a preponderant mechanism for adaptation in difficult environment [15].

For the above mentioned reasons, health agencies and global organizations (FDA, EMEA, WHO) are all going in the same direction concerning recommendations towards the limitation in use of antibiotics and propagation of antibiotics resistance genes [16]. The principal rules to be applied can be summarized as follows:

- It is strongly advised to avoid or minimize the use of any kind of antibiotics in cell or bacterial culture.
- If antibiotics are nevertheless used, it is mandatory to minimize their amount and to monitor the presence of traces in the final product.

- The rationale for the use of antibiotics must be clearly documented in the Common Technical Document (CTD).
- Penicillin, and more generally β-lactams and streptomycin, must not be used in reason of potential concerns with hyper reactivity of some patients to antibiotics of the β-lactam family
- Kanamycin and neomycin are the preferred choice and still tolerated.
- The use of antibiotic resistance markers is generally discouraged, and if used, the *in vivo* outcome and effect needs to be evaluated.

There are specific mentions for the nature of the gene encoding resistance to kanamycin, as reviewed by Williams *et al.* [7] The gene neomycin phosphotransferase III [*npt-III, aph(3')-III*] should be avoided, since it also confers resistance to amikacin [17], a reserve antibiotic (EMEA, 2008).

As a final comment, it is easy to anticipate what the future requirements from health authorities might be: Constructs have to be completely devoid of antibiotic resistance genes in their final structure, even if in use at early stages of construction. Alternative solutions would be available and validated soon.

2. VECTOR STABILIZATION

Besides any consideration about pressure of selection obtained through antibiotic or antibiotic-free selection, natural stability of a given plasmid might be an additional source of investigation.

Several studies on natural plasmids, conducted in the 1970s or early 1980s, have highlighted that some plasmids naturally display regions necessary for their stability.

Plasmid F, which exists only as one to two copies per chromosome, is stably inherited to daughter cells during cell growth, contains stabilization sequences. Ogura; Hiraga [18], have shown that these sequences were independent from plasmid replication function.

Their work lead to the identification of three essential regions for plasmid maintenance:

SopA and *SopB* acting in *trans* and *SopC* acting in *cis* in order to stabilize the plasmid likely through interaction with, unidentified at that time, cellular components.

These authors also put in evidence that the combination *SopA*, *SopB* and *SopC* was not sufficient for a complete stabilization of mini-F plasmid, and thus identified the additional element *ccd* (control of cell death) region that seemed crucial to control cell division when copy number carrying *ccd* segment decreases [18]. The so-called *ccd* region can be split into two functional domains: *ccdB*, the product of which inhibits the host cell division and *ccdA*, able to act as an antagonist to the ccdB function. Two years after, Jaffé *et al.* [19], demonstrated that cell division is not immediately inhibited and that residual division could take place in the plasmid free-cells before finally being inhibited. Authors concluded that the *ccd*region guarantees that plasmid carrying cells could grow preferentially in a population by killing plasmid free daughter cells, introducing the concept of post-segregational killing. Plasmid R1 has also been shown to contain a stabilization system [20]. As for plasmid F, the stabilization system is based on post segregational killing due to the *parAB +* locus. This locus is composed of two genes *Hok* (Host killing) and *Sok* (suppression of killing). The translation of the *Hok* messenger, encoding a toxin lethal to the bacteria, is completely blocked by the anti-messenger *Sok*. In the absence of plasmid, *Sok*, which is less stable than *Hok*, is lost first, allowing the translation of the *Hok* mRNA and expression of the toxin lethal to the cell. Several hok mRNA paralogs have been identified in the genome of *E. coli*, and Hok protein orthologs are also found in the genomes of Enterobacteria [21,22,23].

Concerning plasmid maintenance, it has been shown that factors reducing multimerization of plasmid could increase plasmid stability [24]. ColE1 plasmid contains a region, *cer* that seems to be necessary for a recombination event converting multimers to monomers, allowing the plasmid to be more stable. Multimer resolution is achieved through action of the XerCD site-specific recombinase at the *cer* site. Precise characterization of the cer site by progressive deletions has shown the importance of its boundaries in terms of length and the apparent poorly conserved sequence among multimer resolution sites [25]. In recent work,

Rcd was even more precisely described, a small regulatory RNA encoded within *cer*, which is also required. Rcd is transcribed from the P_{cer} promoter in plasmid dimers, but not in monomers, and is a key component of the checkpoint that delays the division of dimeror multimer-containing cells [26]. It was further demonstrated that a fifth chromosome-encoded protein, FIS, binds to *cer* in a sequence-specific manner. FIS appears to have little or no influence on*cer*-mediated recombination, but, along with XerC and XerD, is required for proper regulation of the P_{cer} promoter [27]. Cloning of the *cer* locus into various expression vectors has been extensively documented and the proof of principle largely established in high-cell density cultures [28].

Multimer Resolution

The multimer resolution rule applying for plasmids has some equivalent in chromosome duplication during cell division. In Prokaryotic microorganisms, cell division can be completed only after segregation of newly replicated monomeric chromosomes. The presence of dimeric chromosomes, often due to homologous recombination between replicated chromosomes must be precisely controlled and resolved before correct completion of the cell division.

In *Escherichia coli*, dimeric chromosome segregation has been shown to be mediated by a site-specific recombination between two small sequence elements termed *dif* sites (deletion-induced filamentation). Functional *dif* site was identified as contained into a DNA fragment of 32 bp which is sufficient to allow Xer-mediated plasmid multimerization and dimer resolution. A core recombination site containing two 11 bp half-sites, flanking a 6 bp central region is the current definition of the *dif* site, and dimer resolution is achieved through action of the XerCD site-specific recombinase at the *dif* site in a similar way as *cer*.

The structural organization of *dif* is similar to that of related lambda integrase family site-specific recombination loci, e.g.,*P1 loxP*, and Saccharomyces cerevisiae *FRT*.

In the context of DNA vectorization for genetic immunization or gene therapy the productivity is a major consideration and it seems useful to consider the induced metabolic stress and plasmid stability during production. Silva *et al.* have suggested possible evolution of fermentation methods towards online bioprocess monitoring to circumvent metabolic burden and plasmid instability [29]. Process optimization is a way to improve productivity, nevertheless the nature and design of the construct and recent innovations in strain and vector engineering or alterations of the host genome or vector backbone are more likely to dramatically increase production of plasmid DNA [30].

An ultimate evolution or simplification can be provided by so-called minicircle vectors that are genetic constructs devoid of plasmid bacterial sequences. The intrinsic small size of minicircles, combines safety and improved resistance to the shearing forces associated delivery methods using pneumatic devices [31].

3. ANTIBIOTIC-FREE SELECTION AND PLASMID MAINTENANCE

To fulfill new regulatory constraints, to develop marker-less expression hosts or to produce safer gene delivery vectors, antibiotic-free selection systems and plasmid addiction mechanisms have been developed.

All these systems can be classified according to their mechanism of action. The different types of systems, as described inTable 1, are based on (i) complementation of auxotrophic marker, (ii) post-segregational killing (PSK), (iii) RNA-interference, (iv) de-repression of an essential gene, (v) chromosomal integration, (vi) minicircles and (vii) non antibiotic resistance.

The first systems investigated were based on the complementation of auxotrophic markers. Among these the one established by Degryse *et al.* [32] uses an *E.coli* strain mutated in the DAP (Diaminopimelic acid) pathway due to a mutation or deletion in *DapD* gene. The plasmid carries *DapD* gene to complement the stain DAP auxotrophy. As a consequence, only bacteria containing the plasmid will grow when cultivated without DAP supplementation in the culture medium (Scheme 1A). As DAP is implicated in cell wall synthesis and mutation in the DAP pathway

Table 1. Antibiotic-free selection systems: Mechanisms of action; Applications. Abbreviations used in the table: R: Resistance; Tet: Tetracycline; Cm: Chloramphenicol; Amp: Ampicillin; Kan: Kanamycin resistance; bla: Beta-lactamase; Neo: Neomycin; Rif: Rifampicin.

Strain	Strain Modification	Plasmid Maintenance Gene	Antibiotic Resistance Gene Used for Selection	Application	Reference
		Complementation of an essential gene			
Escherichia coli	*dapD* mutation → DAP auxotrohpy	*dapD*	No	DNA and protein expression	Degryse, [32]
Salmonella typhimurium	Δ*asd* → DAP auxotrophy	*asd*	No	Live vaccine	Galan *et al.* [33]
Salmonella typhi	Δ*asd* → DAP auxotrophy	*asd*	No	Vaccin delivery	Tacket *et al.* [34]
Salmonella typhimurium and S.typhi	*thyA* mutation → Thymidine auxotrophy	*ThyA*	No	Live vaccine	Morona *et al.* [35]
Vibrio cholerae	*glnA* with an internal deletion → Glutamine auxotrophy	*glnA*	No but presence of TetR and CmR genes on plasmid	Vaccine delivery	Ryan *et al.* [36]
Salmonella enterica serovar Choleraesuis	Δ*asd* → DAP auxotrophy	*asd*	No	Live vaccine expressing somatostatin	Liang, *et al.* [6]
Escherichia coli	Δ*ProBA* → Proline auxotrophy	*proBA*	Yes, CmR	protein expression	Fiedler *et al.* [37]
Escherichia coli	Δ*TpiA* →no growth on glycerol	*TpiA*	No but presence of AmpR and KanaR genes on plasmid	protein expression	Velur Selvamani, et al. [38]
Escherichia coli	*ArgE* amber mutation + *pir116* → arginine auxotrophy	*Phe sup tRNA* + ori γ	No	DNA (pCOR)	Soubrier *et al.* [39]
Escherichia coli	*ThyA* amber mutation → thymidine auxotrophy	*His sup tRNA*	No	DNA (pFAR)	Marie, *et al.* [40]
Salmonella enteritidis	Δ*asd* → DAP auxotrophy	*asd*	No	Ghost vaccine, live vaccine	Jawale lee, [41]
Escherichia coli	Δ*glyA* → Glycine auxotrohpy	*glyA*		protein expression	Vidal *et al.* [42]
Escherichia coli	Δ*QAPRTase* → NAD auxotrophy	*QPARTase*		protein expression	Dong, et al. [43]
Bacillus amyloliquefaciens	Δ*gspA* → G3P auxotrophy	*glycerine-3-phosphate dehydrogenase*	No	protein expression	US2010/0248306A1
Escherichia coli	Δ*araD*	*araD*	No	protein expression	US2007/0036822
		Post Segregational Killing			
Escherichia coli	-	hok/sok (*parB* locus)	Yes, bla	DNA and protein expression	Gerdes *et al.* [44]
Escherichia coli	-	hok/sok, *parDE*	Yes, KanR, AmpR	DNA and protein expression	Pecota *et al.* [45]
Escherichia coli	-	hok/sok (*parB* locus)		DNA and protein expression	Schweder *et al.* [46]

are lethal, several systems based on DAP complementation were investigated in other gram negative bacteria, especially *Salmonella* strains. Avirulent strains of*Salmonella* with a deletion of *asd* gene were developed to be used as live vaccines expressing a recombinant protein using a plasmid maintained with the asd complementation. Tacket *et al.* [34] constructed a *S.typhi* vaccine strain expressing the core protein of Hepatitis B virus. More recently, Liang, *et al.* [6], adopted the same strategy to express somatostatin in a *S.enterica serovar Choleraesius*. in a particular application of the same complementation, an antibiotic-free system to generate “ghost”*Salmonella* enteritidis bacteria as a vaccine. To do so, they express *PhiX174* lysis gene E in *Salmonella* enteritidis. By using another auxotrophic marker in combination with DAP auxotrophy, Wang, *et al.* [71] propose a recombinant attenuated salmonella vaccine with dual plasmid delivery system.

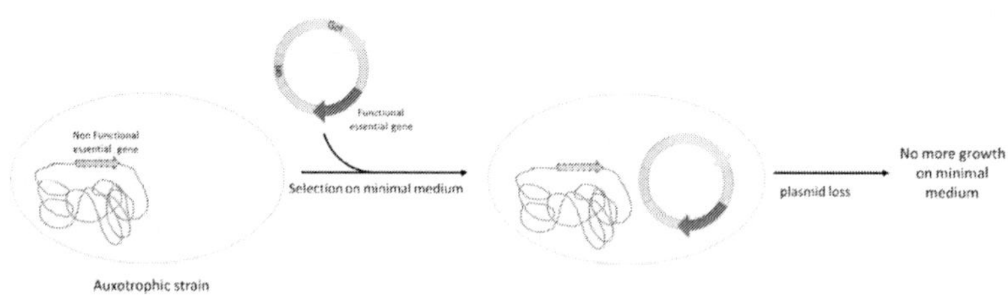

(A)

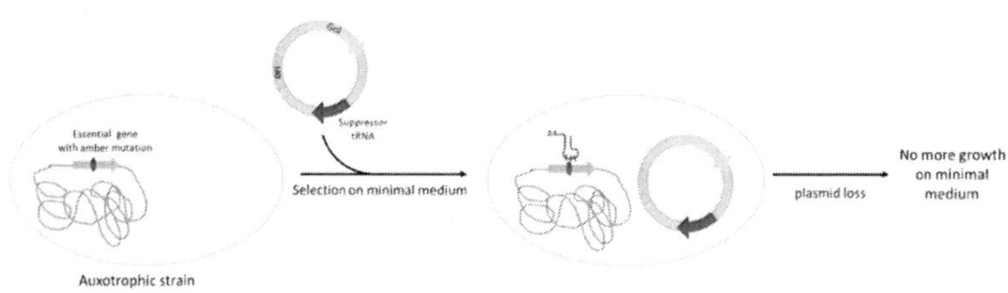

(B)

Scheme 1. Plasmid selection and maintenance by auxotrophy complementation. (**A**): Strain auxotrophy is due to an essential gene mutation or deletion. The auxotrophy is complemented by the plasmid-born expression of the functional gene. (**B**): Strain auxotrophy is due to an amber mutation in an essential gene. Expression of the suppressor tRNA correcting amber mutation can complement the auxotrophy. GoI: Gene of Interest; ori: Origin of replication.

The ORT® technology (Scheme 2) uses also DAP as a central element, but in this case the regulation is based on a plasmid-mediated repressor titration driving the expression of the chromosomal *dapD* gene. The engineered host strain contains*dapD* under control of the *lac* operator/promoter *(lacO/P)*. In the absence of IPTG as inducer, cell growth is blocked by *dapD*repression. The presence, in the host, of a high copy number plasmid containing the lac operator *(lacO)* releases the repression of *dapD* expression through titration of LacI from the operator [59]. In addition to plasmid DNA production, the ORT® system has been adapted for vaccine delivery using *Salmonella enterica* live bacterial vectors [72]. The system has been completed by a very elegant mean of excision of the selectable marker used for the vector cloning steps and strain engineering. The antibiotic resistance gene is flanked by dif sites that are the recognition sequence for the native Xer recombinases responsible for chromosome dimer resolution. Upon transformation and chromosomal insertion, the recombinases resolve the two directly repeated dif sites to a single site, excising the antibiotic resistance gene [73].

DAP auxotrophy and more generally the use of auxotrophic markers should have some influence on the overall productivity of a given host strain. It is nevertheless difficult to evaluate the real cost of compensating for auxotrophy [74]. The analysis would have to include the impact on specific amino acid biosynthesis pathways, the composition of the media and the additional metabolic burden associated with the expression of the plasmid-borne essential gene.

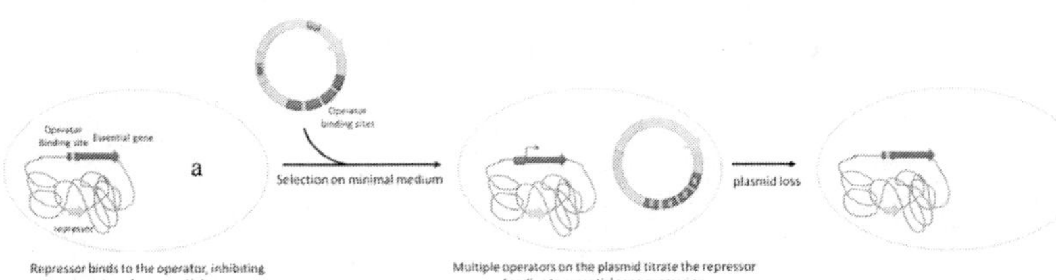

Scheme 2. Plasmid selection and maintenance by Operator Repressor Titration. Note of a: An essential gene is repressed by a genome encoded repressor. Plasmid containing several sequences of the operator can titrate this repressor by competition, allowing essential gene expression. GoI: Gene of Interest; ori: Origin of replication.

The most recently developed complementation system is based on tpiA auxotrophy in *Escherichia coli* [38]). Authors use a strain *ΔTpiA*, which presents a low growth rate with glucose as carbon source and no growth with glycerol. Only the strain carrying the plasmid expressing *tpiA* gene can restore normal growth behavior to a medium with glycerol as sole carbon source. Even if the plasmid used in the study still carries ampicillin and kanamycin resistance genes, authors show that the TpiA auxotrophy complementation is efficient enough to allow bacterial selection, plasmid stability and recombinant protein production in a 2L-batch fermentation process.

More elegant systems express a tRNA suppressor to restore an amber mutation in an essential gene. The pFAR plasmids (Marie, *et al.* [40]) allows the expression of histidine suppressor tRNA to suppress an amber mutation in the *thyA* gene. Only bacteria carrying a plasmid can grow in absence of thymidine (Scheme 1B). Plasmids called pCOR [39] use the same mechanism with a phenylalanine suppressor tRNA that suppress an amber mutation in *ArgE*. The plasmid maintenance of pCOR is improved by a conditional replication origin on the plasmid that needs *pir116*, added on the *E.coli* chromosome. Both plasmid and chromosome are in a mutually dependent, leading to a safer DNA vector that is unable to replicate in environmental bacterial strains [39].

An improved version of the system, with increased copy number, was obtained through genetic engineering in *Escherichia coli*. The bacterial gene encoding the pi initiator-protein, which plays a pivotal role in pCOR replication, was mutagenized to identify novel copy-up mutations. A particular combination of copy-up mutations was shown to produce a 3-5-fold increase in plasmid DNA per biomass unit [75].

These two systems have been mainly used for DNA vector preparation, and their applications in pre-clinical and clinical studies have been reviewed by Vandermeulen, *et al.* [76].

The second kind of system is based on a mechanism initially discovered by studying natural plasmids, called PSK. PSK consist of a plasmid locus that encodes a toxin and its own antidote, or antitoxin. In most cases, the toxin expressed is generally more stable than the antitoxin, the bacteria losing the plasmid after segregation will therefore be killed. Among the numerous toxin/antitoxin identified and recently referenced into the TADB database [77], two have been investigated for applications in biotechnology. the *parB* locus, also identified as *hok/sok*, is used for plasmid maintenance since 1986 [44] and have also been combined with *parDE* [45]. *Hok* is a messenger encoding a toxic protein, inhibited in its expression by the *Sok*anti-messenger. In case of plasmid loss, *Sok* due to shorter half-life disappears first and allow translation of the Hok protein inducing cell death (Scheme 3A). Combination of *parB* and *parA*, also showed a real improvement in plasmid maintenance [78], for a live vaccine application.

The ccdB/ccdA toxin/antitoxin pair is also used by several authors [48,79], by cloning the entire locus on the plasmid to allow its stabilization in *E.coli*. If this system is efficient for maintenance, it cannot allow a real antibiotic-free selection. For this reason, Szpirer *et al.* developed a "separate component" system where toxin is carried by the chromosome and the antidote is brought by the plasmid [49] (Scheme3B). This system, using the same genes, allows for an efficient selection of transformed bacteria. To further improve this, Peubez, *et al.* [28] proposed a way to completely eliminate the antibiotic resistant gene necessary for the construction of the vector, with a positive selection. In their strategy, the antibiotic resistant gene is flanked by both 5' and 3' ends of the *ccdA* gene containing a small homologous region. Upon transformation the two*ccdA* moieties associate through homologous recombination and give a fully functional gene, ensuring complete elimination of the antibiotic resistance gene (patent WO2010007246).

Toxin/antitoxin pairs that play an important role in plasmid maintenance and evolution in the bacterial world are numerous, and still need to be explored for future biotechnological applications [80], adjustable killing activity can even be transferred to higher eukaryotic systems [81].

Interestingly, separated components toxin/antitoxin stabilization systems have been developed for protein production in*Streptomces lividans*, using *YoeBsl* gene on the chromosome and *YefMsl* gene on the plasmid [50].

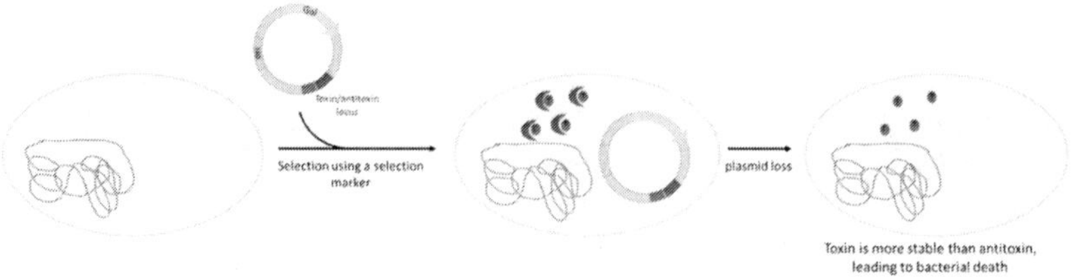

(A)

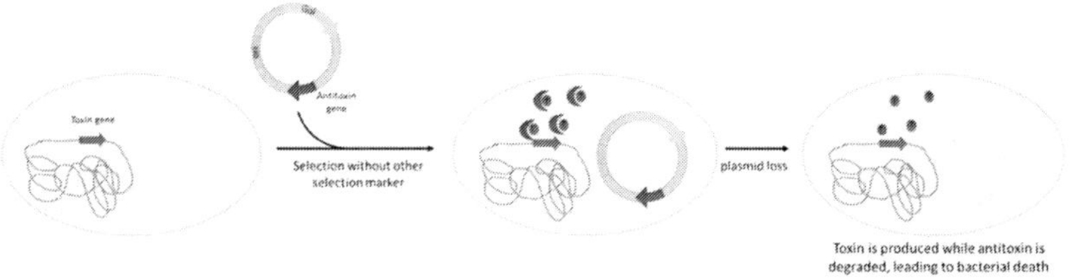

(B)

Scheme 3. Plasmid selection or/and maintenance by post-segregational killing. (**A**): Both toxin and antitoxin genes are on the plasmid allowing plasmid maintenance. Another marker (*i.e.*, antibiotic resistant gene) is still needed to allow strain selection. (**B**): As the toxin gene is inserted into bacterial genome and antitoxin is plasmid-born, this system allows both selection and plasmid maintenance in absence of any antibiotic. GoI: Gene of Interest; ori: Origin of replication.

An alternative and novel plasmid addiction model, based on ColE1 derived RNAI properties was suggested by Pfaffenzeller *et al.* [55]. The replication inhibitor RNAI of ColE1 based plasmid can serve as an antisense to bind mRNA of an engineered toxic gene, encoded by the bacterial chromosome. This system was proposed in a fine-tuned version by using the same "selection marker" serving as an antisense to alleviate the repression of an essential gene. The essential gene *murA*, implicated in cell wall synthesis, is under control of the Tet operator, repressed by the Tet repressor that integrate a complementary sequence of RNAI. In absence of plasmid, *murA* expression is repressed by *TetR*, leading to cell death (Scheme 4A). In bacteria carrying a replicating ColE1 based plasmid, RNAI interfere with its complementary sequence, repressing *TetR*, resulting in de-repression, expression of murA and cell growth [56]. By integrating other RNA/AS-RNA sequences, a system not restricted to ColE1-derived plasmids, was developed. In this system, Vectors express a RNA-OUT antisense RNA. RNA-OUT represses the expression of a chromosomally integrated, constitutively expressed counter-selectable marker (*sacB*). The expression of *sacB*, derived from *Bacillus subtilis*, induce a susceptibility to sucrose. In a culture medium containing sucrose, bacteria that lack the RNA-out plasmid will not keep growing (Scheme 4B) (Luke, *et al.* [57,82]).

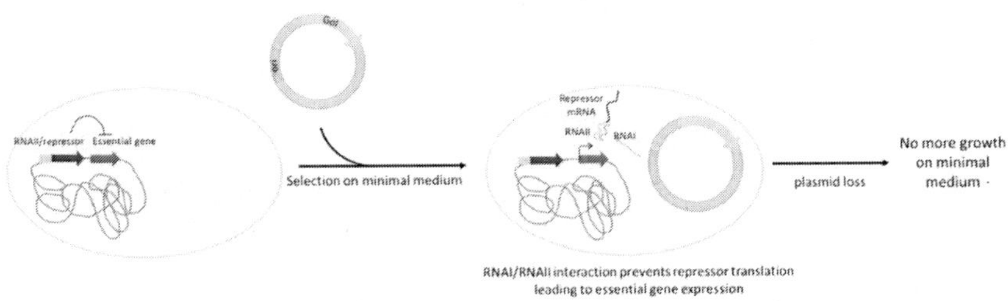

(A)

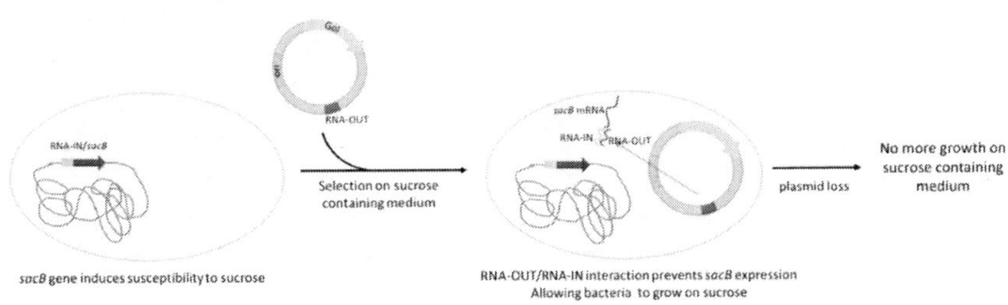

(B)

Scheme 4. Plasmid selection and maintenance by RNA/RNA interaction. (**A**): An essential gene is under control of a repressor fused to RNAI homologous sequence. RNAI, produced from plasmid ori (ColE1 derived), binds to this homologous RNA, inhibits the repressor translation and restores the essential gene expression. (**B**): *sacB*gene is inserted into the genome, fused to RNA-IN sequence. RNA-OUT, encoded by the plasmid, binds to RNA-IN, inhibiting sacB translation, restoring ability of the strain to grow on sucrose containing medium. GoI: Gene of Interest; ori: Origin of replication.

The counterselectable marker *sacB* is also described in a patented but unpublished system (patent WO2010/135742). In this system, *sacB* is inserted into *E. coli* chromosome, under control of the λ *Pr* promoter. Plasmids expressing the λ *cI* 857, temperature sensitive repressor lead to the controlled inhibition of *sacB* which allows bacteria growth in presence of sucrose. The major advantage of this system is the reduction of vector size and plasmid produced can be used for protein expression as well as for DNA vector production for gene therapy.

To produce a recombinant protein, a way to avoid the antibiotic resistance marker is to integrate the gene of interest into bacterial chromosome [83]. With the development of seamless genomic integration by lambda red integrase [84], this kind of system is more and more accessible to easy establishment but cannot be considered for plasmid-based applications.

Striedner *et al.* [62] developed a plasmid-free, T7-based *E. coli* expression system in which the target gene is stably integrated into the chromosome of the host at a specific site (Scheme 5). The system, validated in real fermentation conditions, might suffer from some weaknesses due to relatively complex cloning procedure and it is also, important to consider that single copy integration might be a disadvantage for protein over-expression. One possibility to overcome the single-copy drawback might be to take advantage of a position effect, Bryant *et al.* [85] have shown that expression of gfp may vary by around 300-fold depending on its precise position on the chromosome of *E. coli* K12.

In contrast, chromosome integration is a technology of choice for some applications, such as the one described by Baumgartner *et al.* [64]. Using a chromosomal integration of recombinant genes and altering the copy number and expression of 2'-FL and intracellular GDP-L-fucose levels, the authors were able to construct and improve the first selection marker-free *E. coli* strain producing 2'-FL without the use of expression plasmids.

Another example is provided by Lemuth *et al.* [63], using a plasmid-free *Escherichia coli* strain to produce the xanthophyll astaxanthin, a high-value compound with applications in the nutraceutical, cosmetic, food, and animal feed industries.

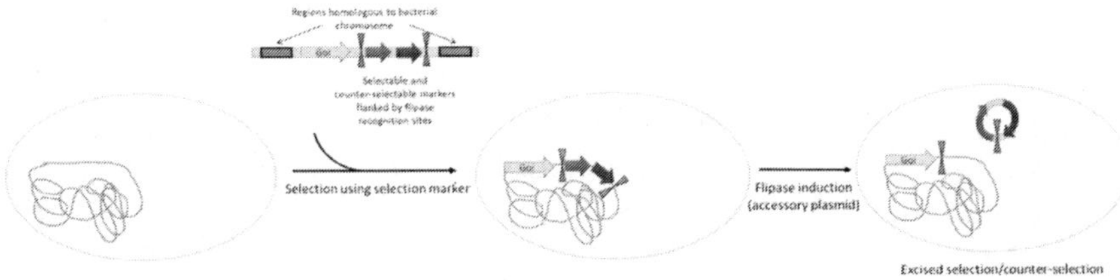

Scheme 5. Plasmid-free expression after genomic integration. The gene of interest (GoI) is inserted into the genome to avoid antibiotic resistance gene in the production strain.

It is also important to consider that single copy integration might be a disadvantage for protein over-expression.

For plasmid DNA production, development of minicircle is more and more considered as an obviously interesting option. Minicircle consists of a circular DNA sequence devoid of bacterial backbone. The major advantage of these vectors is their safety due to absence of antibiotic resistance gene, bacterial replication origin and un-methylated immunogenic CpG sequence. To produce minicircle, a producer plasmid has first to be constructed. This plasmid contains a transgene expression cassette flanked by integrase or recombinase recognition sequences and all the bacterial sequences needed for selection and amplification. To propagate the producer plasmid, antibiotic selection is still used but the bioprocess is generally conducted in absence of any antibiotic to avoid minute amounts of antibiotics in the final product and to lower the process cost. After amplification of the producer plasmid, recombination at specific recognition sites lead to the production of minicircles and plasmid backbone (Scheme 6). Minicircles are more difficult to produce than conventional plasmids due to the recombination and purification steps. Minicircle generation can be done using lambda integrase [86], Cre recombinase [87] or ΦC31 integrase [65,68]. In the first production system using ΦC31 integrase, the produced plasmid contained a gene encoding homing endonuclease I-SceI and two copies of the gene encoding ΦC31 integrase and an I-SceI recognition site. ΦC31 integrase expression allows recombination of producer plasmid into minicircles and backbone plasmids. I-SceI, located in the backbone plasmid after recombination, allows the cleavage and the degradation of this plasmid. To optimize the minicircle production process, multiple copies of I-SceI and ΦC31 integrase have been integrated into the bacterial chromosome. This strategy allows for the improvement of production yields by increasing recombination efficiency and reducing contaminant backbone plasmid, facilitating minicircles' purification.

The development of a totally antibiotic-free minicircle generation process could be considered by implementing a producer plasmid selection system using auxotrophy complementation.

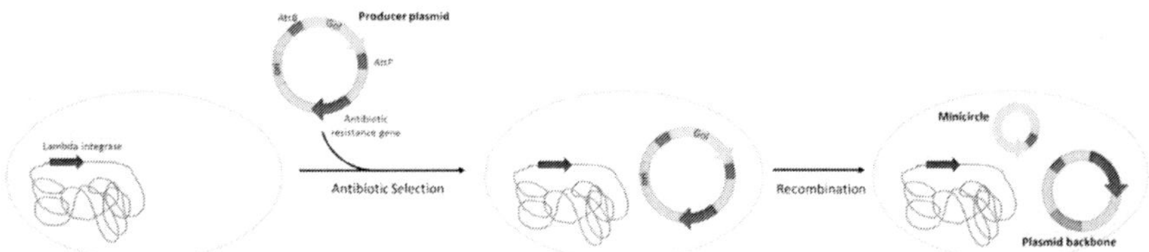

Scheme 6. Minicircle production. The producer plasmid is selected using an antibiotic resistance gene. Cleavage and recombination leads to the formation of circular plasmid backbones and minicircles. Minicircles do not contain any antibiotic resistance gene. Strategies of *in vivo* degradation of plasmid backbone are developed to facilitate minicircle purification.

Another way to avoid the antibiotic resistance is to use resistance to other chemicals. Based on this strategy, resistance to Triclosan can be provided by the expression of the plasmid-born *FabI* gene Goh and Good [53]. Even if the chemical used is not considered as an antibiotic, this kind of antibiotic-free system presents the same limitations than antibiotic-based systems and same regulatory issues.

The toxicity of triclosan was evaluated in a rat model through exposure to aerosol inhalation [88] and its potential effect on DNA damage and reproduction was also demonstrated [89]. The results showed that the reproduction of earthworms were significantly reduced ($p < 0.05$) after exposure to triclosan concentrations ranges from 50 to 300 $mg{\cdot}kg^{-1}$. Finally, triclosan, widely used as a biocide, was also shown to induce resistance in *Aeromonas salmonicida*, a pathogen bacteria for fish [90].

Among all the systems classified in Table 1, some of them can fit two classes. For example, pFAR and pCOR plasmids, based on auxotrophic marker are categorized in Table 1 as "complementation of auxotrophic markers" but could also belong to RNA-based systems as they use t-RNA suppressor. To better understand the mechanism of action of all the antibiotic-free selection and maintenance systems, reviews including schematic have been recently published [28,76,91,92].

4. GENE THERAPY; DNA IMMUNIZATION

For different reasons, including efficiency, easier access to proof of concept and validation in the target species, DNA immunization has proven to be more successful in the domain of animal health. Various DNA vaccines for animal health have been approved.

The Fort Dodge's West Nile DNA vaccine was approved in 2005 by the US department of agriculture. This plasmid DNA-based vaccine contains gene sequences coding WNV surface antigens prM and E within a vector background pCBWN containing an ampicillin resistance gene. The Novartis licensed DNA vaccine Apex-IHN was approved in 2005 for use in salmon in Canada to prevent from infection of hematopoetic necrosis virus (HNV). The plasmid vector expressing viral glycoprotein of HNV contains an ampicillin resistance gene. A canine melanoma vaccine (Merial, Duluth, GA, USA) was approved in the US in 2007 for the treatment of canine malignant melanoma. This vector background encodes human xenogenoic tyrosinase and contains a kanamycin resistance gene. LifeTide® SW 5 is the first DNA therapy for food animals approved in Australia in 2008 (VGX animal Health, TX, USA). A swine injectable plasmid encoding porcine Growth Hormone Release Hormone carrying a kanamycin resistance gene has been approved in sows of breeding age to increase the number of piglets weaned.

Although these animal DNA vaccines are still based on antibiotic marker selection, very recently the first antibiotic free produced vaccine was approved by USDA in December 2013. The Merial's Porcine Rotavirus vaccine based on expression of NSP4, VP4 and VP6 rotavirus antigens that prevents pigs from gastroenteritis (US 2013/0209507A1). This antibiotic free selection system uses the stabilization system StabyExpress based on the use of toxin-antitoxin genes [28,93] and anticipates future regulatory requirements.

4.1. DNA Vaccines for Human Application

For human applications, 365 clinical assays were initiated or completed using naked or plasmid DNA [94]. Approaches to develop antibiotic-free plasmid DNA are recommended by regulatory agencies (FDA, USDA, EMEA) for more than 15 years in order to reduce risk of allergic reactions and decrease risk of selection of antibiotic resistant pathogenic bacteria.

Although kanamycin selection marker remains allowed for gene therapy clinical trials [95,96] the first steps to increase biosafety have been performed using antibiotic-free plasmids in clinical models [76]. However, evaluation of a DNA dengue-1 vaccine in a phase I trial by an naval medical research center was still based on a VR1012 plasmid backbone containing kanamycin resistance [97].

First human phase I and II clinical trials using plasmid pCOR encoding fibroblast growth factor 1 have suggested an improvement of perfusion and an increase in amputation free survival in patients with critical limb ischemia [98]. This pCOR plasmid is an antibiotic free selection DNA vector based on complementation of amber mutation tRNA suppressor [39]. The pORT vector was chosen to develop a HIV-1 DNA vaccine, and its delivery induced a specific immune response in patients [99]. Moreover, proof of concept of gene therapy using antibiotic-free pORT plasmid AMEP coding for the recombinant desintergrin domain of ADAM 15 in disseminated melanoma has demonstrated safety and efficacy results of a phase I first-in-man study (European Society for Medical Oncology Meeting in 2012). Approval for clinical trial Phase I/II was obtained by regulatory authorities. This pORT plasmid strategy is based on "operator repressor titration" (see Table 1) [100].

A possible breakthrough technology that was not so far considered as sufficiently come to maturity, is the use of RNA-based nucleic acid vaccination [101,102]. After long and disappointing results, this technique recently entered a new era with the advent of self-replicating RNA viruses [103]. This platform has successfully entered clinical trials after encouraging pre-clinical evaluation.

4.2. Use of Viral Vectors

Since no DNA based vaccines for human applications received FDA approval today there is renewed interest on viral vector based vaccines. Although viral vectors have the same safety concern than nucleic DNA concerning integration capacity, they have the advantage not to contain selection markers. In animal health, ten viral vectors based vaccines are already on the market. Most of them are based on recombinant poxvirus as avian fowlpox, attenuated canarypox (Alvac), and vaccinia. The leader of the viral vector based vaccines is Merial with eight approvals based on recombinant Alvac vector, fowlpox and vaccinia. Avimex and Biomune developed fowlpox virus based and Newcastle disease virus based viral vectors respectively.

For human health, in the past years two products, Advexin (p53 based treatment of squamous cell carcinoma of the head and neck) and Cerepro (use of thymidine kinase for malignant glioma) failed the FDA and EMA approval, respectively. However, Amsterdam-based UniQure's Glybera (alipogene tiparvovec) was approved for the treatment of Lipoprotein Lipase Deficiency (LPLD) by the European commission on September 2012. Glybera is a replication-deficient, adenovirus associated virus type 1 (AAV1) vector, containing a CMV promoter and expressing Ser447X variant of the human LPL gene [104].

In spite of a decreasing attractiveness of DNA based vaccination in human health, some developments are nevertheless in progress. One can mention the work done by Nelson *et al.* [105] on herpes simplex virus 2 with a DNA construct incorporating the regulatory agency compliant, minimal, antibiotic-free (AF) NTC8485 mammalian expression vector.

5. LIVE VACCINE; DELIVERY SYSTEMS

Recombinant live vaccine and delivery vectors are a specific category of bio-therapeutic agents that combine the most sophisticated technologies and complex safety/regulatory constraints. This group of biological agents is clearly distinct from old live attenuated vaccines and contains diverse technologies such as genetically attenuated pathogenic strains, GRAS [106] microorganisms (Generally Recognized As Safe) used as delivery vehicles or viral strains carrying foreign antigens.

Neglected tropical diseases, such as Chagas caused by the protozoan parasite *Trypanosoma cruzi* is a good illustration of the relevant strategy of genetically engineer a complex target for which the identification of protective antigens has proven to be difficult. The protective capacity of genetically attenuated parasite is explained by a better exposition to the different components of the immune response [107].

Lactic acid bacteria and other commensal hosts are candidates of choice for the design of novel oral vaccines and possible alternatives to attenuated pathogens [108]. A recombinant version of the extensively used BCG strain is the basis of a new strategy to improve long-lasting memory response and overcome the relative lack of efficiency of the original vaccine formula [109].

Other bacteria, such as *Samonella*, capable of activating the innate, humoral and cellular immune responses at both mucosal and systemic compartments, are therefore good vehicles to present antigens from difficult targets like HIV [110].

For all these categories of recombinant microorganisms, the requirement for antibiotic-free selection mean is absolutely essential, as they are by definition live agents prone to propagation of genetic elements.

There are numerous examples of live vaccines, for instance in the domain of animal health the MM-3 *Escherichia coli* strain a candidate for the protection of neonatal piglets against diarrhea that was originally carrying the *cat* (chloramphenicol acetyltransferase) gene. The lambda-Red technology was used to replace the first cassette by the aspartate-semialdehyde dehydrogenase gene (*asd*) and the expression levels of the two antigens K88ac fimbriae and heat-labile enterotoxin B subunit (LTB) in cell lysate were proven equivalent to MM-3 [111].

In another work based on the same kind of antibiotic-free selection, Liang *et al.* [6] evaluated the efficacy, biodistribution and safety of plasmid delivered by the strain C501. The model is based on a balanced-lethal system using an *Asd(+)*expression plasmid pVGS/2SS-asd encoding two copies of somatostatin (SS) genes carried by *Δasd/Δcrp* double mutant*Salmonella enterica* serovar *Choleraesuis*.

6. CONCLUSIONS

Genetic engineering technologies and regulatory requirements are continuously improving and moving in the same direction. Better techniques are creating new challenges and it is likely that in the near future the regulatory status for antibiotic-free selection will progressively move from preferred to highly recommended and mandatory. This is particularly true if we consider that credible alternatives already exist and moreover that some non-antibiotic selection means can even be advantageous options at the industrial level. Antibiotic-free selection is a field of investigation that will benefit from accumulating knowledge of biological pathways and genetic regulation of industrial microorganisms and drive an impossible step backwards.

ACKNOWLEDGMENTS

This work has received, through BIOASTER investment, funding from the French Government through the Investissement d'Avenir program (Grant NO. ANR-10-AIRT-03).

CONFLICTS OF INTEREST

The authors declare no conflict of interest.

REFERENCES

1. Livermore, D.M. Introduction: The challenge of multiresistance. *Int. J. Antimicrob. Agents* **2007**, *29* (Suppl. S3), S1–7.

2. Bax, R.; Green, S. Antibiotics: The changing regulatory and pharmaceutical industry paradigm. *J. Antimicrobi. Chemother.* **2015**.

3. Finch, R.; Hunter, P.A. Antibiotic resistance—Action to promote new technologies: Report of an EU Intergovernmental Conference held in Birmingham, UK, 12–13 December 2005. *J. Antimicrob. Chemother.* **2006**, *58*(Suppl. S1), i3–i22.

4. Bakker, J.M.; Bleeker, W.K.; Parren, P.W. Therapeutic antibody gene transfer: An active approach to passive immunity.*Mol Ther.* **2004**, *10*, 411–416.

5. Armengol, G.; Ruiz, L.M.; Orduz, S. The injection of plasmid DNA in mouse muscle results in lifelong persistence of DNA, gene expression, and humoral response. *Mol. biotechnol.* **2004**, *27*, 109–118.

6. Liang, A.; Riaz, H.; Dong, F.; Luo, X.; Yu, X.; Han, Y.; Chong, Z.; Han, L.; Guo, A.; Yang, L. Evaluation of efficacy, biodistribution and safety of antibiotic-free plasmid encoding somatostatin genes delivered by attenuated Salmonella enterica serovar Choleraesuis. *Vaccine* **2014**, *32*, 1368–1374.

7. Williams, K.J.; Bax, R.P. Challenges in developing new antibacterial drugs. *Curr. Opin. Investig. Drugs* **2009**, *10*, 157–163.

8. Blair, J.M.; Webber, M.A.; Baylay, A.J.; Ogbolu, D.O.; Piddock, L.J. Molecular mechanisms of antibiotic resistance. *Nat. Rev. Microbiol.* **2015**, *13*, 42–51.

9. Tuller, T. Codon bias, tRNA pools and horizontal gene transfer. *Mob. Genet. elements.* **2011**, *1*, 75–77.

10. Juhas, M. Horizontal gene transfer in human pathogens. *Crit. rev. Microbiol.* **2015**, *41*, 101–108.

11. Datta, N.; Kontomichalou, P. Penicillinase synthesis controlled by infectious R factors in Enterobacteriaceae. *Nature* **1965**, *208*, 239–241.

12. Garber, N.; Friedman, J. Beta-lactamase and the resistance of Pseudomonas aeruginosa to various penicillins and cephalosporins. *J. Gen. Microbiol.* **1970**, *64*, 343–352.

13. Wiedenbeck, J.; Cohan, F.M. Origins of bacterial diversity through horizontal genetic transfer and adaptation to new ecological niches. *FEMS Microbiol. Rev.* **2011**, *35*, 957–976.

14. Hamady, M.; Betterton, M.D.; Knight, R. Using the nucleotide substitution rate matrix to detect horizontal gene transfer. *BMC bioinform.* **2006**, *7*, 476.

15. Roberts, A.P.; Kreth, J. The impact of horizontal gene transfer on the adaptive ability of the human oral microbiome. *Front. Cell. Infect. Microbiol.* **2014**, *4*, 124.

16. Sodoyer Regis, C.V.; Peubez, I.; Mignon, C. Antibiotic-free selection for: Moving towards a new "gold standard". In *Antibiotic Resistant Bacteria—A Continuous Challenge in the New Millennium*; Marina, P., Ed.; InTech: Rijeka, Croatia, 2012; pp. 531–548.

17. Georghiou, S.B.; Magana, M.; Garfein, R.S.; Catanzaro, D.G.; Catanzaro, A.; Rodwell, T.C. Evaluation of genetic mutations associated with Mycobacterium tuberculosis resistance to amikacin, kanamycin and capreomycin: A systematic review. *PLoS ONE* **2012**, *7*, e33275.

18. Ogura, T.; Hiraga, S. Mini-F plasmid genes that couple host cell division to plasmid proliferation. *Proc. Natl. Acad. Sci. USA* **1983**, *80*, 4784–4788.

19. Jaffe, A.; Ogura, T.; Hiraga, S. Effects of the ccd function of the F plasmid on bacterial growth. *J. Bacteriol.* **1985**, *163*, 841–849.

20. Gerdes, K.; Larsen, J.E.; Molin, S. Stable inheritance of plasmid R1 requires two different loci. *J Bacteriol.* **1985**, *161*, 292–298.

21. Gerdes, K.; Poulsen, L.K.; Thisted, T.; Nielsen, A.K.; Martinussen, J.; Andreasen, P.H. The hok killer gene family in gram-negative bacteria. *New Biol.* **1990**, *2*, 946–956.

22. Pedersen, K.; Gerdes, K. Multiple hok genes on the chromosome of *Escherichia coli*. *Mol. Microbiol.* **1999**, *32*, 1090–1102.

23. Steif, A.; Meyer, I.M. he hok mRNA family. *RNA biol.* **2012**, *9*, 1399–404.

24. Summers, D.K.; Sherratt, D.J. Multimerization of high copy number plasmids causes instability: CoIE1 encodes a determinant essential for plasmid monomerization and stability. *Cell* **1984**, *36*, 1097–1103.

25. Summers, D.K.; Sherratt, D.J. Resolution of ColE1 dimers requires a DNA sequence implicated in the three-dimensional organization of the cer site. *EMBO J.* **1988**, *7*, 851–858.

26. Balding, C.; Blaby, I.; Summers, D. A mutational analysis of the ColE1-encoded cell cycle regulator Rcd confirms its role in plasmid stability. *Plasmid* **2006**, *56*, 68–73.

27. Blaby, I.K.; Summers, D.K. The role of FIS in the Rcd checkpoint and stable maintenance of plasmid ColE1.*Microbiology (Reading, England)* **2009**, *155*, 2676–82.

28. Peubez, I.; Chaudet, N.; Mignon, C.; Hild, G.; Husson, S.; Courtois, V.; de Luca, K.; Speck, D.; Sodoyer, R. Antibiotic-free selection in *E. coli*: New considerations for optimal design and improved production. *Microb. Cell Fact.* **2010**, *9*, 65.

29. Silva, F.; Queiroz, J.A.; Domingues, F.C. Evaluating metabolic stress and plasmid stability in plasmid DNA production by *Escherichia coli*. *Biotechnol. Adv.* **2012**, *30*, 691–708.

30. Bower, D.M.; Prather, K.L. Engineering of bacterial strains and vectors for the production of plasmid DNA. *Appl. Microbiol. Biotechnol.* **2009**, *82*, 805–813.

31. Stenler, S.; Blomberg, P.; Smith, C.I. Safety and efficacy of DNA vaccines: Plasmids *vs.* minicircles. *Hum. Vaccin. Immunother.* **2014**, *10*, 1306–1308.

32. Degryse, E. Stability of a host-vector system based on complementation of an essential gene in *Escherichia coli. J. Biotechnol.* **1991**, *18*, 29–39.

33. Galan, J.E.; Curtiss, R., 3rd. Distribution of the invA. -B, -C, and -D genes of Salmonella typhimurium among other Salmonella serovars: InvA mutants of Salmonella typhi are deficient for entry into mammalian cells. *Infect. Immun.***1991**, *59*, 2901–2908.

34. Tacket, C.O.; Kelly, S.M.; Schodel, F.; Losonsky, G.; Nataro, J.P.; Edelman, R.; Levine, M.M.; Curtiss, R., 3rd. Safety and immunogenicity in humans of an attenuated Salmonella typhi vaccine vector strain expressing plasmid-encoded hepatitis B antigens stabilized by the Asd-balanced lethal vector system. *Infect. Immun.* **1997**, *65*, 3381–3385.

35. Morona, R.; Brown, M.H.; Yeadon, J.; Heuzenroeder, M.W.; Manning, P.A. Effect of lipopolysaccharide core synthesis mutations on the production of Vibrio cholerae O-antigen in *Escherichia coli* K-12. *FEMS Microbiol. Lett.* **1991**, *66*, 279–285.

36. Ryan, E.T.; Crean, T.I.; Kochi, S.K.; John, M.; Luciano, A.A.; Killeen, K.P.; Klose, K.E.; Calderwood, S.B. Development of a DeltaglnA balanced lethal plasmid system for expression of heterologous antigens by attenuated vaccine vector strains of Vibrio cholerae. *Infect. Immun.* **2000**, *68*, 221–226.

37. Fiedler, M.; Skerra, A. proBA complementation of an auxotrophic E. coli strain improves plasmid stability and expression yield during fermenter production of a recombinant antibody fragment. *Gene* **2001**, *274*, 111–118.

38. Velur Selvamani, R.S.; Telaar, M.; Friehs, K.; Flaschel, E. Antibiotic-free segregational plasmid stabilization in*Escherichia coli* owing to the knockout of triosephosphate isomerase (tpiA). *Microb. Cell Fact.* **2014**, *13*, 58.

39. Soubrier, F.; Cameron, B.; Manse, B.; Somarriba, S.; Dubertret, C.; Jaslin, G.; Jung, G.; Caer, C.L.; Dang, D.;

Mouvault, J.M.; *et al.* pCOR: A new design of plasmid vectors for nonviral gene therapy. *Gene Ther.* **1999**, *6*, 1482–1488.

40. Marie, C.; Vandermeulen, G.; Quiviger, M.; Richard, M.; Preat, V.; Scherman, D. pFARs. plasmids free of antibiotic resistance markers, display high-level transgene expression in muscle, skin and tumour cells. *J. Gene Med.* **2010**, *12*, 323–332.

41. Jawale, C.V.; Lee, J.H. Development of a biosafety enhanced and immunogenic Salmonella enteritidis ghost using an antibiotic resistance gene free plasmid carrying a bacteriophage lysis system. *PLoS ONE* **2013**, *8*, e78193.

42. Vidal, L.; Pinsach, J.; Striedner, G.; Caminal, G.; Ferrer, P. Development of an antibiotic-free plasmid selection system based on glycine auxotrophy for recombinant protein overproduction in *Escherichia coli*. *J. Biotechnol.* **2008**, *134*, 127–136.

43. Dong, W.R.; Xiang, L.X.; Shao, J.Z. Novel antibiotic-free plasmid selection system based on complementation of host auxotrophy in the NAD *de novo* synthesis pathway. *Appl. Environ. Microbiol.* **2010**, *76*, 2295–2303.

44. Gerdes, K.; Bech, F.W.; Jorgensen, S.T.; Lobner-Olesen, A.; Rasmussen, P.B.; Atlung, T.; Boe, L.; Karlstrom, O.; Molin, S.; von Meyenburg, K. Mechanism of postsegregational killing by the hok gene product of the parB system of plasmid R1 and its homology with the relF gene product of the *E. coli* relB operon. *EMBO J.* **1986**, *5*, 2023–2029.

45. Pecota, D.C.; Kim, C.S.; Wu, K.; Gerdes, K.; Wood, T.K. Combining the hok/sok. parDE, and pnd postsegregational killer loci to enhance plasmid stability. *Appl. Environ. Microbiol.* **1997**, *63*, 1917–1924.

46. Schweder, T.; Schmidt, I.; Herrmann, H.; Neubauer, P.; Hecker, M.; Hofmann, K. An expression vector system providing plasmid stability and conditional suicide of plasmid-containing cells. *Appl. Environ. Microbiol.* **1992**, *38*, 91–93.

47. Galen, J.E.; Nair, J.; Wang, J.Y.; Wasserman, S.S.; Tanner, M.K.; Sztein, M.B.; Levine, M.M. Optimization of plasmid

maintenance in the attenuated live vector vaccine strain Salmonella typhi CVD 908-htrA. *Infect. Immun.* **1999**, *67*, 6424–6433.

48. Wegerer, A.; Sun, T.; Altenbuchner, J. Optimization of an *E. coli* L-rhamnose-inducible expression vector: Test of various genetic module combinations. *BMC Biotechnol.* **2008**, *8*, 2.

49. Szpirer, C.Y.; Milinkovitch, M.C. Separate-component-stabilization system for protein and DNA production without the use of antibiotics. *Biotechniques* **2005**, *38*, 775–381.

50. Sevillano, L.; Diaz, M.; Santamaria, R.I. Stable expression plasmids for Streptomyces based on a toxin-antitoxin system. *Microb. Cell Fact.* **2013**, *12*, 39.

51. Nehlsen, K.; Herrmann, S.; Zauers, J.; Hauser, H.; Wirth, D. Toxin-antitoxin based transgene expression in mammalian cells. *Nucleic Acids Res.* **2010**, *38*, e32.

52. Sanchez-Romero, J.M.; Diaz-Orejas, R.; de Lorenzo, V. Resistance to tellurite as a selection marker for genetic manipulations of Pseudomonas strains. *Appl. Environ. Microbiol.* **1998**, *64*, 4040–4046.

53. Goh, S.; Good, L. Plasmid selection in *Escherichia coli* using an endogenous essential gene marker. *BMC Biotechnol.***2008**, *8*, 61.

54. Herrero, M.; de Lorenzo, V.; Timmis, K.N. Transposon vectors containing non-antibiotic resistance selection markers for cloning and stable chromosomal insertion of foreign genes in gram-negative bacteria. *J. Bacteriol.* **1990**, *172*, 6557–6567.

55. Pfaffenzeller, I.; Mairhofer, J.; Striedner, G.; Bayer, K.; Grabherr, R. Using ColE1-derived RNA I for suppression of a bacterially encoded gene: Implication for a novel plasmid addiction system. *Biotechnol. J.* **2006**, *1*, 675–681.

56. Mairhofer, J.; Pfaffenzeller, I.; Merz, D.; Grabherr, R. A novel antibiotic free plasmid selection system: Advances in safe and efficient DNA therapy. *Biotechnol. J.* **2008**, *3*, 83–89.

57. Luke, J.; Carnes, A.E.; Hodgson, C.P.; Williams, J.A. Improved antibiotic-free DNA vaccine vectors utilizing a novel RNA based plasmid selection system. *Vaccine* **2009**, *27*, 6454–6459.

58. Nuttall, S.D.; Krishnan, U.V.; Hattarki, M.; de Gori, R.; Irving, R.A.; Hudson, P.J. Isolation of the new antigen receptor from wobbegong sharks, and use as a scaffold for the display of protein loop libraries. *Mol. Immunol.* **2001**, *38*, 313–326.

59. Cranenburgh, R.M.; Lewis, K.S.; Hanak, J.A. Effect of plasmid copy number and lac operator sequence on antibiotic-free plasmid selection by operator-repressor titration in *Escherichia coli*. *J. Mol. Microbiol. Biotechnol.* **2004**, *7*, 197–203.

60. Garmory, H.S.; Leckenby, M.W.; Griffin, K.F.; Elvin, S.J.; Taylor, R.R.; Hartley, M.G.; Hanak, J.A.; Williamson, E.D.; Cranenburgh, R.M. Antibiotic-free plasmid stabilization by operator-repressor titration for vaccine delivery by using live Salmonella enterica Serovar typhimurium. *Infect. Immun.* **2005**, *73*, 2005–2011.

61. Iwanicki, A.; Piatek, I.; Stasilojc, M.; Grela, A.; Lega, T.; Obuchowski, M.; Hinc, K. A system of vectors for Bacillus subtilis spore surface display. *Microb. Cell Fact.* **2014**, *13*, 30.

62. Striedner, G.; Pfaffenzeller, I.; Markus, L.; Nemecek, S.; Grabherr, R.; Bayer, K. Plasmid-free T7-based *Escherichia coli*expression systems. *Biotechnol. Bioeng.* **2010**, *105*, 786–794.

63. Lemuth, K.; Steuer, K.; Albermann, C. Engineering of a plasmid-free *Escherichia coli* strain for improved *in vivo*biosynthesis of astaxanthin. *Microb. Cell Fact.* **2011**, *10*, 29.

64. Baumgartner, F.; Seitz, L.; Sprenger, G.A.; Albermann, C. Construction of *Escherichia coli* strains with chromosomally integrated expression cassettes for the synthesis of 2'-fucosyllactose. *Microb. Cell Fact.* **2013**, *12*, 40.

65. Chen, Z.Y.; He, C.Y.; Kay, M.A. Improved production and purification of minicircle DNA vector free of plasmid bacterial sequences and capable of persistent transgene expression *in vivo*. *Hum. Gene Ther.* **2005**, *16*, 126–131.

66. Chang, C.W.; Christensen, L.V.; Lee, M.; Kim, S.W. Efficient expression of vascular endothelial growth factor using minicircle DNA for angiogenic gene therapy. *J. Control. Release* **2008**, *125*, 155–163.

67. Huang, M.; Chen, Z.; Hu, S.; Jia, F.; Li, Z.; Hoyt, G.; Robbins, R.C.; Kay, M.A.; Wu, J.C. Novel minicircle vector for gene therapy in murine myocardial infarction. *Circulation* **2009**, *120*, S230–S237.

68. Kay, M.A.; He, C.Y.; Chen, Z.Y. A robust system for production of minicircle DNA vectors. *Nat. Biotechnol.* **2010**, *28*, 1287–1289.

69. Yi, H.; Kim, Y.; Kim, J.; Jung, H.; Rim, Y.A.; Jung, S.M.; Park, S.H.; Ju, J.H. A new strategy to deliver synthetic protein drugs: Self-reproducible biologics using minicircles. *Sci. Rep.* **2014**, *4*, 5961.

70. Zhang, X.; Epperly, M.W.; Kay, M.A.; Chen, Z.Y.; Dixon, T.; Franicola, D.; Greenberger, B.A.; Komanduri, P.; Greenberger, J.S. Radioprotection *in vitro* and *in vivo* by minicircle plasmid carrying the human manganese superoxide dismutase transgene. *Hum. Gene Ther.* **2008**, *19*, 820–826.

71. Wang, S.; Kong, Q.; Curtiss, R., 3rd. New technologies in developing recombinant attenuated Salmonella vaccine vectors. *Microb. Pathog.* **2013**, *58*, 17–28.

72. Huang, J.M.; Sali, M.; Leckenby, M.W.; Radford, D.S.; Huynh, H.A.; Delogu, G.; Cranenburgh, R.M.; Cutting, S.M. Oral delivery of a DNA vaccine against tuberculosis using operator-repressor titration in a Salmonella enterica vector. *Vaccine* **2010**, *28*, 7523–7528.

73. Bloor, A.E.; Cranenburgh, R.M. An efficient method of selectable marker gene excision by Xer recombination for gene replacement in bacterial chromosomes. *Appl. Environ. Microbiol.* **2006**, *72*, 2520–2525.

74. Raiford, D.W.; Heizer, E.M., Jr.; Miller, R.V.; Doom, T.E.; Raymer, M.L.; Krane, D.E. Metabolic and translational efficiency in microbial organisms. *J. Mol. Evol.* **2012**, *74*, 206–216.

75. Soubrier, F.; Laborderie, B.; Cameron, B. Improvement of pCOR plasmid copy number for pharmaceutical applications. *Appl. Microbiol. Biotechnol.* **2005**, *66*, 683–688.

76. Vandermeulen, G.; Marie, C.; Scherman, D.; Preat, V. New generation of plasmid backbones devoid of antibiotic resistance marker for gene therapy trials. *Mol. Ther.* **2011**, *19*, 1942–1949.

77. Shao, Y.; Harrison, E.M.; Bi, D.; Tai, C.; He, X.; Ou, H.Y.; Rajakumar, K.; Deng, Z. TADB: A web-based resource for Type 2 toxin-antitoxin loci in bacteria and archaea. *Nucleic Acids Res.* **2011**, *39*, D606–D611.

78. Galen, J.E.; Wang, J.Y.; Chinchilla, M.; Vindurampulle, C.; Vogel, J.E.; Levy, H.; Blackwelder, W.C.; Pasetti, M.F.; Levine, M.M. A new generation of stable. nonantibiotic, low-copy-number plasmids improves immune responses to foreign antigens in Salmonella enterica serovar Typhi live vectors. *Infect. Immun.* **2010**, *78*, 337–347.

79. Stieber, D.; Gabant, P.; Szpirer, C. The art of selective killing: Plasmid toxin/antitoxin systems and their technological applications. *Biotechniques* **2008**, *45*, 344–346.

80. Diago-Navarro, E.; Hernandez-Arriaga, A.M.; Lopez-Villarejo, J.; Munoz-Gomez, A.J.; Kamphuis, M.B.; Boelens, R.; Lemonnier, M.; Diaz-Orejas, R. parD toxin-antitoxin system of plasmid R1—Basic contributions, biotechnological applications and relationships with closely-related toxin-antitoxin systems. *FEBS J.* **2010**, *277*, 3097–3117.

81. De la Cueva-Mendez, G.; Mills, A.D.; Clay-Farrace, L.; Diaz-Orejas, R.; Laskey, R.A. Regulatable killing of eukaryotic cells by the prokaryotic proteins Kid and Kis. *EMBO J.* **2003**, *22*, 246–251.

82. Luke, J.M.; Carnes, A.E.; Williams, J.A. Development of antibiotic-free selection system for safer DNA vaccination.*Methods Mol. Biol.* **2014**, *1143*, 91–111.

83. Datsenko, K.A.; Wanner, B.L. One-step inactivation of chromosomal genes in *Escherichia coli* K-12 using PCR products.*Proc. Natl. Acad. Sci. USA* **2000**, *97*, 6640–6645.

84. Tuntufye, H.N.; Goddeeris, B.M. Use of lambda Red-mediated recombineering and Cre/lox for generation of markerless chromosomal deletions in avian pathogenic *Escherichia coli*. *FEMS Microbiol. Lett.* **2011**, *325*, 140–147.

85. Bryant, J.A.; Sellars, L.E.; Busby, S.J.; Lee, D.J. Chromosome position effects on gene expression in *Escherichia coli* K-12.*Nucleic Acids Res.* **2014**, *42*, 11383–11392.

86. Darquet, A.M.; Cameron, B.; Wils, P.; Scherman, D.; Crouzet, J. A new DNA vehicle for nonviral gene delivery: Supercoiled minicircle. *Gene Ther.* **1997**, *4*, 1341–1349.

87. Bigger, B.W.; Tolmachov, O.; Collombet, J.M.; Fragkos, M.; Palaszewski, I.; Coutelle, C. An araC-controlled bacterial cre expression system to produce DNA minicircle vectors for nuclear and mitochondrial gene therapy. *J. Biol. Chem.***2001**, *276*, 23018–23027.

88. Yang, Y.S.; Kwon, J.T.; Shim, I.; Kim, H.M.; Kim, P.; Kim, J.C.; Lee, K. Evaluation of toxicity to triclosan in rats following 28days of exposure to aerosol inhalation. *Regul. Toxicol. Pharmacol.* **2015**, *71*, 259–268.

89. Lin, D.; Li, Y.; Zhou, Q.; Xu, Y.; Wang, D. Effect of triclosan on reproduction. DNA damage and heat shock protein gene expression of the earthworm Eisenia fetida. *Ecotoxicology* **2014**, *23*, 1826–1832.

90. Khan, R.; Lee, M.H.; Joo, H.; Jung, Y.H.; Ahmad, S.; Choi, J.; Lee, S.W. Triclosan resistance in a bacterial fish pathogen aeromonas salmonicida subsp. salmonicida is mediated by an enoyl reductase FabV. *J. Microbiol. Biotechnol.* **2014**.

91. Oliveira, P.H.; Mairhofer, J. Marker-free plasmids for biotechnological applications—Implications and perspectives.*Trends Biotechnol.* **2013**, *31*, 539–547.

92. Williams, J.A. Improving DNA vaccine performance through vector design. *Curr.Gene Ther.* **2014**, *14*, 170–189.

93. Reschner, A.; Scohy, S.; Vandermeulen, G.; Daukandt, M.; Jacques, C.; Michel, B.; Nauwynck, H.; Xhonneux, F.; Preat, V.; Vanderplasschen, A.; *et al.* Use of Staby((R)) technology for development and production of DNA vaccines free of antibiotic resistance gene. *Hum. vaccin. Immunother.* **2013**, *9*, 2203–2210.

94. Ginn, S.L.; Alexander, I.E.; Edelstein, M.L.; Abedi, M.R.; Wixon, J. Gene Therapy Clinical Trials Worldwide to 2012.*J. Gene Med.* **2013**, *15*, 65–77.

95. Note for guidance on the quality, preclinical and clinical aspects of gene transfer medicinal products. Annex on non-clinical testing for indadvertent germline transmission of gene transfer vectors. (2001:648)

96. WHO. Guidelines for assuring the quality of non clinical safety evaluation of DNA vaccines. In Proceedings of the 56th Meeting of the WHO Expert Committee on Biological Standardization, Geneva, Switzerland, 24–28 October 2005.

97. Beckett, C.G.; Tjaden, J.; Burgess, T.; Danko, J.R.; Tamminga, C.; Simmons, M.; Wu, S.J.; Sun, P.; Kochel, T.; Raviprakash, K.; *et al.* Evaluation of a prototype dengue-1 DNA vaccine in a Phase 1 clinical trial. *Vaccine* **2011**, *29*, 960–968.

98. Nikol, S.; Baumgartner, I.; van Belle, E.; Diehm, C.; Visona, A.; Capogrossi, M.C.; Ferreira-Maldent, N.; Gallino, A.; Wyatt, M.G.; Wijesinghe, L.D.; *et al.* Therapeutic angiogenesis with intramuscular NV1FGF improves amputation-free survival in patients with critical limb ischemia. *Mol. Ther.* **2008**, *16*, 972–978.

99. Mwau, M.; Cebere, I.; Sutton, J.; Chikoti, P.; Winstone, N.; Wee, E.G.; Beattie, T.; Chen, Y.H.; Dorrell, L.; McShane, H.;*et al.* A human immunodeficiency virus 1 (HIV-1) clade A vaccine in clinical trials: Stimulation of HIV-specific T-cell responses by DNA and recombinant modified vaccinia

virus Ankara (MVA) vaccines in humans. *J. Gen. Virol.* **2004**,*85*, 911–919.

100. Cranenburgh, R.M.; Hanak, J.A.; Williams, S.G.; Sherratt, D.J. *Escherichia coli* strains that allow antibiotic-free plasmid selection and maintenance by repressor titration. *Nucleic Acids Res.* **2001**, *29*, E26.

101. Andries, O.; Kitada, T.; Bodner, K.; Sanders, N.N.; Weiss, R. Synthetic biology devices and circuits for RNA-based "smart vaccines": A propositional review. *Expert Rev. Vaccin.* **2015**, *14*, 313–331.

102. Ulmer, J.B.; Mason, P.W.; Geall, A.; Mandl, C.W. RNA-based vaccines. *Vaccine* **2012**, *30*, 4414–4418.

103. Ljungberg, K.; Liljestrom, P. Self-replicating alphavirus RNA vaccines. *Expert Rev. Vaccin.* **2015**, *14*, 177–194.

104. Melchiorri, D.; Pani, L.; Gasparini, P.; Cossu, G.; Ancans, J.; Borg, J.J.; Drai, C.; Fiedor, P.; Flory, E.; Hudson, I.; *et al.* Regulatory evaluation of Glybera in Europe—Two committees, one mission. *Nat. Rev. Drug Discov.* **2013**, *12*, 719.

105. Nelson, J.; Rodriguez, S.; Finlayson, N.; Williams, J.; Carnes, A. Antibiotic-free production of a herpes simplex virus 2 DNA vaccine in a high yield cGMP process. *Hum. Vaccin. Immunother.* **2013**, *9*, 2211–2215.

106. Mattia, A.; Merker, R. Regulation of probiotic substances as ingredients in foods: Premarket approval or "generally recognized as safe" notification. *Clin. Infect. Dis.* **2008**, *46*, S115–118, discussion S144–151.

107. Sanchez-Valdez, F.J.; Perez Brandan, C.; Ferreira, A.; Basombrio, M.A. Gene-deleted live-attenuated Trypanosoma cruzi parasites as vaccines to protect against Chagas disease. *Expert Rev. Vaccin.* **2014**, 1–17.

108. Trombert, A. Recombinant lactic acid bacteria as delivery vectors of heterologous antigens: The future of vaccination?*Benef. Microbes* **2014**, 1–12.

109. Da Costa, A.C.; Nogueira, S.V.; Kipnis, A.; Junqueira-Kipnis, A.P. Recombinant BCG: Innovations on an Old Vaccine.

Scope of BCG Strains and Strategies to Improve Long-Lasting Memory. *Front. Immunol.* **2014**, *5*, 152.

110. Chin'ombe, N.; Ruhanya, V. Recombinant salmonella bacteria vectoring HIV/AIDS vaccines. *Open Virol. J.* **2013**, *7*, 121–126.

111. Yuan, S.L.; Wang, P.; Tao, H.X.; Liu, X.X.; Wang, Y.C.; Zhan, D.W.; Liu, C.J.; Zhang, Z.S. Removal of antibiotic resistance of live vaccine strain *Escherichia coli* MM-3 and evaluation of the immunogenicity of the new strain. *Acta Biochim. Biophys. Sin.* **2006**, *38*, 844–856.

2

CHAPTER

Developments and Challenges for mAb-based Therapeutics

Sumit Goswami [1], Wei Wang [1], Tsutomu Arakawa [2,*] and Satoshi Ohtake [1]

[1]Pfizer, Pharmaceutical R&D – BioTherapeutics Pharmaceutical Sciences, 700 Chesterfield Parkway West, Chesterfield, MO 63017, USA

[2]Alliance Protein Laboratories, 6042 Cornerstone Ct West, Suite A1, San Diego, CA 92121, USA

ABSTRACT

The continuous increase in the number of approved monoclonal antibody (mAb)-based therapy suggests that mAbs, and their derivatives, will continue to be the focus of the biotherapeutics industry for years to come. Although vast improvements in our capability to manufacture, characterize, and stabilize mAbs have been achieved, there are still challenges to be overcome. These include analytical and stabilization approaches associated with the development of high concentration mAb formulations. In addition, several mAb-based modalities are under development, including antibody drug conjugates (ADCs), fusion proteins, and bispecific antibodies (bsAbs), all designed to overcome the limitations encountered with mAb therapy. The current status of their development, with emphasis on manufacturing challenges as well as preliminary clinical results, will be reviewed.

Keywords:

Monoclonal antibody; fusion-proteins; antibody drug conjugates; fragments; bi-specific

1. INTRODUCTION

Antibodies are the first line of our body's defense for fighting infectious diseases. Immunized serum and intravenous immunoglobulin (IVIG) have been widely used to treat patients suffering from immunoglobulin deficiency and infectious diseases [1,2]. The invention of monoclonal antibody (mAb) and recombinant technologies has drastically changed the therapeutic utility of antibodies. AB89 (murine mAb) was the first antibody reported to be administered to a patient in USA for the treatment of non-Hodgkin's lymphoma [3]. The development of hybridoma technology has enabled a consistent production of mAbs at large scale, paving the way for development of various therapeutic antibodies [4]. The first commercial mAb drug product was OKT3, which suffered from short half-life and immunogenicity due to its non-human nature, and was subsequently withdrawn [5]. Further progress in biotechnology has allowed the successful production of fully human antibodies.

Antibodies, like other proteins, are not very stable relative to small molecule drugs; for example, mAbs possess potential for self-association (aggregation). Because of the relatively high dose required for efficacy, they are often prepared at an extremely high concentration, which further enhances self-association, and as a consequence, may lead to high viscosity and difficulty in handling/processing. In addition, their large size and surface-exposed functional groups are a major source of several chemical degradation pathways. These are only a subset of the challenges currently encountered in the development of antibody therapeutics.

This review covers the current state of mAb development and its expansion into other mAb-based modalities, which utilizes the specificity of antibodies for antigen binding or the unique properties of antibody Fc domain. The examples include antibody-drug conjugate (ADC), fusion proteins, antibody fragments, and miscellaneous mAb-based modalities, which have been produced with the aim of greater potency, increase in circulation half-life, expanded function, specific delivery of drugs and effector proteins to the site of action, and enhanced tissue penetration. Table 1 lists the milestones of regulatory approvals of mAb-based therapeutics.

Table 1. Milestones of regulatory approval of monoclonal antibody (mAb)-based therapeutics.

Year	Molecule name	Brand name	Target antigen	Primary Indication	Antibody type	Comment
1986	Muromonab	Orthoclone®	CD3	Acute transplant rejection	Murine, IgG2a	First ever Ab approved by FDA; later withdrawn [6]
1991	Nebacumab	Centoxin®	Endotoxin (HA-1A)	Sepsis and Gm-ve bacteraemia	Human hybridoma derived IgM	First human mAb to be approved by regulatory agency (Europe); later withdrawn from the market [7,8]
1993	Abciximab	ReoPro®	GPIIb/IIIa	Cardiac ischemia, stroke, myocardial infarction	Chimeric Fab of IgG1	First approved Fab-based therapeutic [9]
1997	Rituximab	Rituxan®	CD20	Non-Hodgkin's lymphoma	Chimeric IgG1	First approved full length chimeric mAb [10,11]
1997	Daclizumab	Zenapax®	CD25	Prevention of kidney transplant rejection	Humanized IgG1	First approved full length humanized mAb [12]
1998	Etanercept	Enbrel®	TNF-receptor	RA	TNFR2-Fc fusion	First approved Fc fusion protein [9]

Table 1. Cont.

Year	Molecule name	Brand name	Target antigen	Indication	Antibody type	Comment
2000	Gemtuzumab Ozogamicin	Mylotarg®	CD33	Acute myelogenous leukaemia	Human IgG4	First ADC to be approved in US; withdrawn from the market [13,14]
2002	Adalimumab	Humira®	TNFα	RA	Human IgG1	First human mAb to be approved in USA [12]
2009	Catumaxomab	Removab®	EpCAM on tumor cells and CD3 on T-cells	Malignant ascites	CD3- and EPCAM-specific mouse–rat hybrid	First bispecific to be approved by EMA [12,15]

2. mAb

2.1. Structure, Type, and Function

Antibodies (Abs) are biological macromolecules naturally produced by the immune system. Molecular structure is composed of four polypeptide chains (two heavy chains of molecular weight ~50 kDa each, and two light chains of molecular weight ~25 kDa each). The heavy chain contains four structural domains; three constant domains (CH1, CH2 & CH3) and one variable domain (VH). On the other hand, the light chain is composed of two structural domains; one constant (CL) and one variable (VL). A detailed description of the antibody structure has been provided in the review article by Wang *et al.* [16]. Based on the sequence of the constant region of the heavy chain, antibodies are divided into five classes: IgM, IgD, IgG, IgE, and IgA [14]. IgGs are further classified as IgG1, IgG2, IgG3, and IgG4, in the order of their relative abundance in plasma. Each of these also contains different heavy chains: γ1, γ2, γ3, and γ4, respectively [16]. Ab-based therapy was first utilized for the treatment of cancer; initially focused primarily against lymphoma and leukemia, however it was also used for the treatment of solid tumors, such as melanoma [17]. The first antibody to be administered to a patient (suffering from non-Hodgkin's lymphoma) was Ab-89 [3]. Although the treatment was not successful, the study demonstrated (for the first time) the feasibility of Ab-based of therapy in the treatment of cancer that demonstrates an acceptable safety profile.

Next, the advent of hybridoma technology allowed the production of monoclonal antibody (mAb) that could be utilized for targeted therapy, owing to its increased specificity towards a target antigen. mAbs are primarily composed of two major functional units. One is the constant fragment (Fc), and the other is the fragment of antigen binding (Fab). Fab unit contains three hypervariable complementarity determining regions (CDRs), which together form the antigen binding site on the surface of the antibody. The major issue with murine mAbs is their low half-life and immunogenicity, despite achieving specific targeting [5]. In chimeric antibodies, the murine variable domain is fused with the human constant domain [12]. There are different ways by which humanized antibodies are created. One of the most common methods is to graft mouse CDRs onto human acceptor antibody framework. Fully human antibodies, on the other hand, are either naturally obtained, recombinantly expressed, or collected from transgenic mouse, in which the immune repertoire has been replaced by the human genes [18,19]. Another effective way of producing human antibody is phage display [20].

The primary mode of action for mAb-based therapeutics for the treatment of cancer has been considered to be antibody derived cell-mediated cytotoxicity (ADCC). According to this mechanism, the Fc portion interacts with FC_{γ}-receptors on the surface of the effector immune cells (such as monocyte and macrophages), while the antibody is bound to the surface antigen of the cancer cell through its Fab region, and results in ADCC response [21,22]. For example, cetuximab, which binds to the epidermal growth factor receptor (EGFR) antigen on the surface of the tumor cells, is known to mediate its anti-tumor activity through ADCC [23]. Another important mode of action is direct interference of specific cell signaling pathways. For example, bevacizumab binds to the soluble vascular endothelial growth factor (VEGF), and thus inhibits angiogenesis, which is important for the maintenance of tumor vasculature and tumor health [24]. There are also other mechanisms that are worth mentioning, including induction of phagocytosis, complement activation, and activation of T-cell immunity. A thorough description of various modes of action applicable to therapeutic antibody can be found elsewhere [25].

1986 remains a historical year, as it witnessed the first approval of mAb-based therapy by the FDA, Muromonab (Orthoclone®, anti-CD3); a murine-type mAb, which was later withdrawn by the FDA [26] (Table 1). In 1997, the first full length chimeric monoclonal antibody, rituximab, was approved by the FDA (anti-CD20 on the surface of B-lymphocytes) for the treatment of cancer [27], which is still marketed today. This drug is currently being utilized as a single agent (for induction and maintenance), or in combination with chemotherapeutic agents, for the treatment of various human lymphoma and chronic lymphocytic lymphoma [10,28]. 1997 witnessed the approval of the first humanizd mAb, daclizumab (anti-CD25 specific). The first, fully human mAb, adalimumab (anti-TNF), was not approved by the FDA until 2002 [29].

2.2. Glycosylation and Its Importance

Monoclonal antibodies are naturally available in glycoslated form. Glycosylation is an important form of chemical modification. In recent years, the scientific community has gained knowledge regarding the significance of carbohydrate moieties in therapeutic monoclonal antibodies. mAbs are known to contain N-linked glycan residues, connected through Asp (N) residue on the amino acid sequence such as Asn-X-Ser/Thr [30,31]. Asn297 in the CH2 domain (near the hinge region) is the only conserved glycosylation site in human IgG. The core sequence of the glycan connected to this residue is a heptasaccharide, comprised of $(GlcNAc)_2$-$(Man)_3$-$(GlcNAc)_2$. Presence of glycosylation in general is thought to provide structural stability to protein against stress factors, such as thermal stress, and to improve solubility [32]. In fact, the presence of oligosaccharide has been reported to improve the structural integrity of IgG1 mAb [33,34]. Loss of glycosylation may result in increased propensity towards aggregation, as was observed with IFN-β, which resulted in the formation of insoluble aggregates and loss of activity upon enzymatic deglycosylation [35]. It has been reported that the interaction site for FCγR on the Fc region is located near the hinge domain [36], and glycosylation in the hinge region is critical for mediating interaction between FCγR and the Fc region (*i.e.*, effector function) [36,37]. Activation of FCγR results in various types of immune responses including: ADCC, antibody-mediated phagocytosis, and secretion of inflammatory modulators [38,39,40]. Complete deglycosylation of IgG1 results in loss of binding capacity with FCγR and subsequent loss of effector function [41]. The absence of fucose residue in the Fc-linked glycan moiety has been reported to increase the efficacy of mAb in initiating the ADCC response at much lower concentrations, which has been attributed to the higher binding affinity of non-fucosylated mAb to the FCγRIIIa receptor [42,43,44]. High binding affinity allows non-fucosylated mAb to compete with the binding of serum IgG to the FCγRIIIa receptor expressed on natural killer cells (NK) [45]. Engineering of expression host cells has allowed the large scale production of non-fucosylated antibodies possible [46]. Recent phase-I clinical trials with two different non-fucosylated mAbs (MEDI-563, a humanized anti-IL-5 receptor IgG1, and KW-0761, a humanized anti-CCR4 IgG1) demonstrated the attainment of high efficacy at low doses [31]; this was attributed to the absence of fucosylation and enhancement of ADCC response [31]. Glycosylation is a process taking place during post-translational modification, and thus, deglycosylation is a consequence of such modification not occurring in the endoplasmic reticulum (ER) during mAb synthesis. Therefore, achievement of selective defucosylation is challenging and requires careful control of the production process. A number of processes have been proposed for selective defucosylation, including selective inactivation of fucosylation pathway in mammalian cells, enzymatic modification of the N-glycan, and chemical synthesis of the non-fucosylated form of the N-glycan [31].

2.3. Development of mAb Therapeutics and Associated Challenges

mAbs possess high level of specificity for their target, and in general, are more efficacious than their small molecule counterpart. The development of mAb-based therapeutics has its own challenges, however. mAb is a macromolecule, and in general follow similar degradation pattern as with other protein-based biopharmaceuticals [47]. Biological activity of mAb-based therapeutics is closely tied to their structural, conformational, and chemical stability. Degradation may occur at various stages of development starting from bioprocessing and purification to formulation, storage, and delivery. Successful development of mAb-based therapeutics requires a thorough understanding of possible degradation pathways. A number of review articles are available that focus on this topic for mAb-based therapeutics, or protein-based therapeutics in general [16,48,49]. Degradation can be broadly classified into two major categories, physical and chemical [50], and will be briefly described below.

2.3.1. Physical Degradation

The most common pathway of physical degradation is aggregation, by which two or more monomeric units of mAbs may bind to each other to form higher order oligomeric structures such as dimer, trimer, tetramer, *etc.*, or even larger structures. The size of aggregates can range from nanometers to hundreds of microns. Based on the size range, aggregates have been classified into the following categories: (1) submicron (<1 μm size) particles, which are conventionally referred to as soluble particles; (2) sub-visible particles (1–100 μm size), and (3) visible particles (>100 μm size) [51,52]. Sub-visible and visible particles together are referred to as insoluble particles. Particles that belong to the size range of 0.1–1 μm are at times referred to as small sub-visible particles [51]. Aggregates can be non-covalent in nature, mediated by weak forces such as hydrophobic interaction, Van der Waals interaction, hydrogen bonding, and electrostatic forces [53]. Covalent interaction (e.g., disulfide linkage and dityrosine linkage) may also lead to the formation of aggregates [54,55]. Various stress factors have been reported to induce aggregation, and the exposure to such stresses may occur during the regular life-cycle of a mAb. Common practice in the biopharmaceutical industry is to assess the relative stability of the compound of interest through its exposure to a range of stress factors in its extremity. The most common stress factors encountered during manufacturing and processing include temperature stress, mechanical stress, and freeze/thaw stress. Exposure to elevated temperature is a common cause for aggregation of mAbs. As accidental temperature excursion may occur during shipping or storage, exposure to elevated temperature is intentionally carried out during stability assessment. At elevated temperature, mAb may undergo conformational destabilization, or partial-to-complete unfolding, which may lead to the formation of aggregates via non-covalent interactions [48,56]. During frozen storage and shipping, on the other hand, accidental excursion of temperature may lead to unintentional exposure to freeze/thaw cycle. Freeze/thaw causes aggregation via a number of factors such as partitioning of the protein molecule to ice-water interface, adsorption to the container surface (solid-water interface), cryo-concentration, and change in pH due to non-uniform crystallization of buffer [57,58,59,60]. Mechanical stress can be manifested in a number of ways, including agitation, shaking, stirring, pumping, filling, and filtration. These are stresses to which a mAb may be exposed during manufacturing and transport. Formulation conditions such as pH, ionic strength, and concentration of mAb may also have significant influence on aggregation [61]. Formulation of mAb at high concentration for subcutaneous (sc) application is of great interest to the pharmaceutical industry, and thus will be described further below.

2.3.2. Chemical Degradation

Chemical degradation may occur in a number of different ways. This type of degradation affects the primary sequence and may also lead to significant changes in the higher order structure. Examples of chemical degradation include deamidation, oxidation, isomerization, clipping/fragmentation, and cross-linking [16,47,50]. Deamidation is probably the most common type of chemical degradation encountered in mAb-based biotherapeutics [62,63,64]. The reaction is favored at neutral and basic pH [63]. There are examples of deamidation occurring at lower pH, however that has been reported to occur primarily through a mechanism independent of succinimide formation [65]; for example, deamidation of Asn in the A chain of insulin is favored at pH < 5, which is mediated via the formation of cyclic anhydride intermediate [66]. There are factors other than pH that influences the rate of deamidation, e.g., sequence and local structure (steric effect). Amino acids present at the carboxyl end of Asn have been reported to influence the rate of deamidation; the decrease in rate has been correlated with increase in size and branching of the side chain [63,64]. Isomerization is another common method of chemical degradation that shares the common outcome with deamidation. It can occur directly from Asp residue or from the succinimide intermediate [67]. Similarly to deamidation, isomerization is favored at neutral and basic pH, and the rate has been reported to be influenced by the steric effect [63,67]. Hydrolysis of a peptide bond leads to fragmentation of the protein. Some peptide bonds, such as Asp-Gly and Asp-Pro, are sensitive to hydrolysis. Asp-Y sequence has been reported to be 100 times more sensitive to hydrolysis than any other peptide bonds [68,69]. At times, hydrolysis is the natural, subsequent reaction following deamidation of Asn residue, as is observed with insulin [70].

Furthermore, mAbs may contain certain residues that are sensitive to oxidation, such as Met, Tyr, Trp, His, and Cys [62,65,71]. Although not as prevalent as deamidation and isomerization, oxidation has been reported to be the major pathway of degradation for certain proteins, e.g., OKT3 (IgG2), which demonstrated oxidation at several Met residues and free Cys under 5 °C storage condition [72]. There are several external factors that have been reported to induce oxidation, including exposure to light, contamination with trace amount of transition metal ion, and the presence of degradation product of an excipient (e.g., hydrogen peroxide from polysorbate degradation) [73,74,75]. The consequence of oxidation may include increase in aggregation [76]. Oxidation is observed most commonly with the Met residue, and the major by-product of such reaction is the formation of sulfoxide and sulfone [77]. Two factors that affect the rate of oxidation are the local structure around the oxidation sensitive group (e.g., surface exposure and steric hindrance) and the solution pH [73,77]. In some cases, increase in solution pH has been found to increase the rate of oxidation [78], but pH-dependent increase in oxidation is not a general phenomenon.

Chemical degradation may also result from cross-linking, which may or may not be mediated by the formation of disulfide bond. When cross-linking is disulfide bond-mediated, the reaction occurs either by the formation of a new disulfide bond or by disulfide bond exchange. Intra-molecular disulfide linkage may lead to change in tertiary structure, whereas inter-molecular (or inter-domain) disulfide linkage may lead to change in quaternary structure or formation of covalent aggregates [16,79]. At higher pH, the formation of reactive thiolate ion (S^-), from the thiol group (–SH) of cys residue, is favored, which may increase the probability of disulfide linkage formation [80]. There are instances of covalent cross-linking that may occur between different amino acid residues besides Cys, which, unlike disulfide linkage, are non-reducible [81].

2.3.4. Importance of Controlling Degradation

Successful development of mAb-based therapeutics requires a careful assessment of the various degradation pathways possible for a molecule (both physical and chemical). Degradation of the molecule may interfere with the intended biological activity, as the site of degradation may involve a domain that is critical for biological function. There are cases in which the formation of aggregates was followed by loss of biological activity; for example, the antiviral activity of interferon-β-1b (IFN-β-1b) aggregate was found to be three times lower than that of its monomer form [35]. Another major impact of protein aggregation is immunogenicity, which may result from the multiplicity of epitope and/or change in conformation [82,83]. Immunogenicity refers to antibody formation by the indigenous immune system against the administered biologics. Antibodies formed can be neutralizing in nature and thus may simply result in the loss of efficacy of the administered therapeutic. If the level of neutralizing antibody is very high, it may result in the neutralization of the essential endongenous protein; for example, the neutralization of endogenous erythropoietin by the antibody, formed against recombinant human erythropoietin (epoetin), has been reported to cause red cell aplasia [84]. Examples of IFN-β-1b and erythropoietin have been included here to provide an analogy for mAb degradation and its possible effect on immunogenicity and biological activity, since degradation of proteins (in general) and their biological consequences follow a similar pattern. Specific example of mAb degradation (aggregation) and induction of immune response can be found in a recent article published by Joubert *et al.* [85]. In this article the author has clearly shown that presence of large number of particles in therapeutic mAb formulation to induce immunogenicity through innate immune response, which may further progress through T-cell response [85].

Aggregation of naturally occurring immunoglobulin into fibrillar or amorphous type of aggregates, followed by deposition inside the glomeruli, is known to cause renal failure [86]. Since aggregation is commonly observed with therapeutic immunoglobulin, there is a chance of potential toxicity. Thus, aggregation is a major issue in the development of biopharmaceuticals and requires careful characterization and quantification. Level of aggregates in clinical and commercial drug product is tightly controlled by the regulatory agencies [48,51]. The amount of sub-visible particles allowed in a commercial product is governed by USP <788>, which states that the amount should not exceed 6,000 particles for ≥10 μm size and 600 particles for ≥25 μm size, per container of nominal volume ≤100 mL [87]. Level of soluble aggregates in commercial product is required to be less than 5%, according to WHO standards [16]. On the other hand, injectable biologics are required to be free of visible particles and 100% visual inspection is required for releasing clinical and commercial products [51]. Besides aggregation, chemical degradation may also lead to the loss in the activity of biologics; for example, isomerized species of Herceptin® mAb (isomerization on Asp in CDR) was found to posses only 9–21% of biological activity of the native species [88]. Oxidation, on the other hand, may result in enhanced immunogenicity [82]. In fact, the oxidized form of rh-IFNα2a was reported to show increased immunogenicity compared to its non-oxidized form [89].

2.3.5. Stabilization Approaches

A thorough understanding of the mechanism, by which biopharmaceuticals degrade, has enabled the pharmaceutical scientists to propose various stabilization strategies. Some of these stabilization strategies will be briefly discussed in this section, with the primary focus on liquid formulation.

The first step in formulation development is pH optimization. The most common approach is to identify the pI of the mAb from the primary sequence, typically using a commonly available software such as ExPASy or Sednterp [90], followed by formulation of mAb at pH away from the pI. However, it is important to perform an assessment of the target pH, at which the molecule is adequately stable. pH has been reported to have an effect on conformational stability [91]. pH can alter the ionization behavior of the charged amino acid group covering the protein surface, and thus may interfere with the favorable electrostatic interaction (e.g., salt bridge) required for maintenance of the native, folded structure [92]. As described in the previous section, various pathways of chemical degradation are pH sensitive. For example, deamidation and isomerization are favored at neutral and basic pH [14,67], thus it is preferable to formulate biopharmaceuticals at slightly acidic pH. In fact, out of 28 commercially approved mAb-type biopharmaceuticals, 20 are formulated at pH $\leq$ 6.5 (data acquired through PharmaCircle [93]). The stability of mAb against CD20, which was reported to be oxidation sensitive at pH 7.5, has been improved by lowering the pH to 5.0 [94,95]. A case by case optimization may be required for pH-mediated stabilization against oxidation, as there are examples in which increase in pH was found to be stabilizing [95].

Besides pH, buffer components also play an important role in stabilizing mAbs. Sodium phosphate and histidine are the most commonly-used buffer components in commercial formulations. While sodium phosphate is more common for low concentration mAb formulations ($\leq$10 mg/mL), histidine is the primary buffer of choice for higher mAb concentrations [96]. Histidine has a pKa of ~6, which allows the preparation of mAb formulation under slightly acidic pH [96]. Moreover, histidine has been reported to demonstrate stabilizing effects [97,98], although contradictory findings have also been documented [94]. Nevertheless, histidine buffer has been found to be extremely useful in formulating several mAb-based commercial products and is suggested to be the primary buffer of choice [96].

Surfactants are also included in typical mAb formulations [96]. Surfactants are surface active agents that are amphipathic in nature (polar head and hydrophobic tail). Surfactants tend to accumulate at various interfaces, resulting in reduced interfacial tension. Interface can be air-water, ice-water, or solid-water (e.g., surface of the container and the liquid). Protein molecules are also surface active and tend to partition at the interface; complex three dimensional fold of polypeptide chains creates hydrophobic as well as charged (polar) patches along the surface, which provides proteins with amphiphilicity, the essential property of surface activity [99]. Surfactants may stabilize protein molecules from interfacial stress by preferentially accumulating at the interface, thus preventing the proteins from being partitioned onto the interface [16,47,100]. This loss can be significant, particularly in cases for formulations containing low protein concentration.

Surfactants have also been reported to directly interact with the protein and prevent it from interfacial stress. Detailed description of the various surfactant mechanisms has been discussed in detail by Lee *et al.* [100]. Polysorbates (polysorbate-20 and -80) are the most commonly used surfactants in the pharmaceutical industry [101]. Out of 28 commercially approved pure mAb-type biopharmaceuticals, 24 contain either polysorbate-20 or polysorbate-80 (data acquired from PharmaCircle [93]). Inclusion of polysorbate in biopharmaceutical formulation has been suggested to be a part of a platform formulation approach [96].

Another important constituent of biopharmaceutical formulation is a stabilizer. Stabilizers are typically small molecular entities and are added to the biopharmaceutical formulation based on the intended purpose. For example, stabilizers can be used as anti-oxidant, metal chelator, or cryoprotectant. For the protein of interest, careful assessment of possible degradation pathways must be conducted prior to selecting a stabilizer. Sugars and polyols are common stabilizers used as a cryoprotectant and/or bulking agent, of which, sucrose and trehalose are the two most widely used. The presence of cryoprotectants, such as sucrose and trehalose, may provide protection against freeze/thaw-induced degradation of drug substance which may undergo multiple freeze/thaw cycles during storage [94,102,103]. Polyols, such as mannitol and sorbitol, are commonly used as bulking agent during lyophilization. Sugars and polyols are also known to stabilize the protein conformation; analytically, this is represented by an increase in the protein unfolding temperature (T_m). For example, sucrose was found to increase the T_m of RNAse by about 10 °C [104]. Sugars and polyols have also been reported to stabilize proteins from chemical degradation. For example, the presence of mannitol or trehalose was found to increase the chemical stability of rhu anti-CD20 (recombinant human anti-CD20) mAb by minimizing the amount of acidic species [94]. Li *et al.* [105,106] demonstrated that different types of sugars and polyols, such as glucose and mannitol, stabilize the hu-relaxin protein from metal-induced oxidation. For example, mannitol was found to stabilize rhu HER2 mAb from oxidation at the methionine residue [95]. For stabilization against oxidation, methionine is typically the stabilizer of choice [95]. Metal ion-induced oxidation is prevented by the addition of a chelator type of molecule, such as EDTA.

Although EDTA is effective for most metal ions, there are certain metal ions, such Fe^{3+}, for which EDTA has been found to be ineffective at preventing metal-induced oxidation [107]. Use of salt as stabilizer in biopharmaceutical formulation is a variable. Salts are known to influence the solubility and conformational stability of proteins, and their effect is concentration dependent [108]. At high concentrations, the effect on solubility and conformational stability has been proposed to follow the Hoffmeister series [109]. For both cations and anions, the stabilizing effect has been reported to increase as one moves from left to right in the series. On the other hand, increase in salt concentration (thus ionic strength) is known to screen charge-charge interactions, and thus decrease the proximity energy. Decrease in proximity energy has been proposed to be the cause of colloidal instability, and thus increase in aggregation [110]. Therefore, the use of salt as a potential stabilizer of biopharmaceuticals requires careful assessment.

3. DEVELOPMENT OF HIGH CONCENTRATION FORMULATION

3.1. Subcutaneous Delivery and Its Limitation

Although mAb-based therapy was introduced primarily for the treatment of cancer, mAbs are reported to penetrate solid tumors poorly; in fact, only about 0.01% of the applied dose has been reported to penetrate into the tumor [111,112]. EC_{50}values are typically higher than those of globular proteins, such as cytokines [113]. Thus, there is a need for high dose delivery of mAbs.

High dose administration is made possible through intravenous (iv) infusion, however this often requires special set up and involvement of a health care provider. Although most of the commercial antibodies are administered via the iv route, there is an increasing trend towards the development of dosage forms for alternative routes of administration, in particular the subcutaneous (sc) route. For chronic diseases, such as asthma and arthritis, for which frequent administration is required, development of sc dosage form is valuable in many ways. This includes: ease of administration, patient compliance, and reduction in cost as administration is possible at home. One inherent limitation of sc dosage form is the injection volume. The maximum volume that can be administered is typically less than 2 mL [114]. The area available in the skin, under epidermis and dermis, is limited in such a way that injection of large volume creates high back pressure. Pain at injection site is another problem that is caused by a number of different factors such as individual expertise, needle size, and formulation [115]. It is also protein specific. Formulation plays an important role in controlling the pain at injection site. For example, histidine buffer is known to be less prone to cause pain upon injection compared to phosphate and citrate buffer [116,117,118]. Since mAbs are administered at high dose and the maximum injection volume is limited for sc delivery, development of stable and robust high concentration formulation is critical to enable sc administration of biopharmaceuticals.

3.2. Challenges of High Concentration Formulation Development

High concentration is defined by the solution, in which a significant portion of the solution volume (≥0.1) is occupied by the solutes [119,120]. Another definition of high concentration solution is the situation in which the molecular size and the distance between the Van der Waals surfaces are on the same order of magnitude [110]. Irrespective of the definition, high concentration refers to inter-molecular distance or molecular proximity. The primary challenge in achieving high concentration formulation is the solubility of the target protein. Solubility is controlled by its molecular property (sequence, charge distribution, *etc.*), as well as by the solution condition, such as pH, ionic strength, excipient concentration, *etc.* [121]. Solubility of a protein is defined by the maximum amount of the protein that can be present in a solution, without appearance of any visible aggregates, precipitates, *etc.* A more technical definition will be the maximum amount of protein that remains in solution, following 30min of centrifugation at 30,000 g in the presence of co-solute [122,123]. Besides solubility, there are other issues associated with the development of high concentration mAb formulation.

These include opalescence, viscosity, and aggregation. Opalescence is commonly expressed by nephelometric turbidity unit, however opalescence is not necessarily equivalent to turbidity. Typically a solution becomes turbid due to the presence of particulates. However, opalescence may result even if the solution is free of any particulates. Sukumar *et al.* [124] reported that an IgG1, demonstrating considerable opalescence at high concentration, was essentially monomeric, and the opalescence was primarily a result of Raleigh scattering. Although opalescence is not a major issue, and may occur independent of aggregation, it remains a major concern as it may fail to satisfy patient compliance due to its appearance. Reversible protein-protein and liquid-liquid phase separation may also lead to opalescence [124,125]. Protein-protein interaction at high concentration is a major factor that may influence opalescence and viscosity. When molecules are in close proximity, they can interact with each other, resulting in reversible self-association, increase in viscosity, opalescence, and even aggregation [126]. Protein-protein interaction has been explained by various theories, including molecular crowding, or excluded volume effect, and proximity energy effect, *etc.* [110,127].

Increase in viscosity at high concentration has a major impact on manufacturability and injectability. Tangential flow filtration (TFF) is one of the main technologies used for buffer exchange and concentrating proteins during large scale manufacture (clinical as well as commercial) [128]. Increase in viscosity at high concentration may create back pressure high enough to exceed the capacity of the pump. TFF process itself is considerably stressful to the mAb, as rapid pumping and continuous circulation through the narrow tubing create significant cavitation and shear stress [129]. Increase in back pressure, due to increase in viscosity, may retard the process further which can be even more destabilizing to the protein. At minimum, this increases the process time, and in turn, the cost of manufacture. Increase in viscosity has a significant impact on administration of sc dosage form. Ease of sc injection is described by the glide force, or extrusion force, which refers to the force required to push the liquid through the syringe. While there are various factors including needle gauge, length of needle, *etc.*, that are associated with glide force, one of the main contributing factors is solution viscosity. Viscosity has been reported to be directly correlated to glide force for sc injection [130,131]. Increase in viscosity increases the time of injection, and also the pain at injection site, which may lead to decrease in patient compliance [132].

Protein-protein interaction in a high concentration formulation may result in reversible self-association, which may further progress towards the formation of insoluble aggregates. At high concentration, the probability of one molecule bumping into another is much higher, and this increases the chances of formation of reversible oligomers such as dimer, tetramers, *etc.* Formation of aggregates occurs through multiple mechanisms, including the formation of covalent linkages (e.g., disulfide exchange). Even minor conformational change in the native structure may lead to the formation of aggregates. At high concentration, the probability of such occurrence is greater than that in a dilute solution [126].

3.3. Analytical Assessment of High Concentration Formulation

Most of the analytical techniques employed for the assessment of chemical degradation of mAb in a dilute solution (e.g., ion exchange chromatography, capillary gel electrophoresis, reversed phase chromatography, mass spectrometry, *etc.*) can be utilized for high concentration formulation. The primary challenge around adapting these techniques for high concentration formulation is sample preparation, which typically involves dilution of the concentrated stock. Since chemical degradation is relatively less sensitive to concentration, adaptation of these techniques for high concentration formulation is relatively straight forward [129]. On the other hand, the assessment of aggregation and particle formation (physical degradation) is much more complicated as dilution of test sample is not the most suitable option, because it may modulate specific high concentration behaviors, such as reversible self association. Direct measurement of molecular property at high concentration is extremely challenging due to thermodynamic non-ideality and high viscosity associated with high concentration [126]. Only a few techniques can be utilized for the direct assessment of high concentration formulation. These include preparative analytical ultracentrifugation (AUC), fluorescence detection system (FDS) equipped with AUC, membrane osmometry, and static light scattering, to some extent [129]. With preparative AUC, samples at high concentration are sedimented under equilibrium mode, and the content of the centrifugation tube is collected in fractions using an automated microfractionator, followed by measurement of protein concentration using UV spectroscopy [133,134]. This method is time consuming, labor intensive, and the number of data points collected is typically one-third of what is collected from a regular AUC [129]. Availability of FDS allows measurement of sedimentation behavior directly in the AUC instrument. This technique requires the fluorescent labeling of the target mAb, however. Labeled mAb is added to the unlabeled high concentration formulation to serve as a tracer molecule. Since the fluorescently-labeled mAb is present only at trace quantity and is structurally and functionally indistinguishable from the unlabeled mAb, it is expected that the labeled mAb will be part of the reaction kinetics and intermolecular interaction occurring under the high concentration condition. Thus it is extremely important to ensure that both structural and functional integrity have not been compromised by labeling of the molecule [135,136]. There are examples in which static light scattering (SLS) has been utilized for assessing the aggregation behavior of a protein at high concentration, however, the consequence of multiple scattering at higher concentration should be carefully evaluated [137]. Membrane osmometry has been utilized to measure the osmotic pressure of high concentration formulation. At high concentration, for which considerable thermodynamic non-ideality exists (due to self-association and molecular crowding), concentration gradient of osmotic pressure deviate from linearity and demonstrates concentration dependence [138]. Yousef*et al.* [139] measured the osmotic pressure of bovine IgG solution up to 424 mg/mL. Mathematical interpretation of the self-association behavior from concentration dependence of osmotic pressure data is difficult. Various models have been utilized to interpret osmotic pressure data, such as the free solvent model, leading to reversible association and non-ideal behavior [133,139].

Since the assessment of molecular behavior directly at high concentration is challenging, some alternative approaches have been proposed that utilize dilute solution properties to predict and represent high concentration behavior. Most commonly used dilute solution parameters are second virial coefficient (B22), diffusion interaction parameter (Kd), and net charge. Second virial coefficient is a measure of intermolecular interaction, and is primarily driven by electrostatic attraction or repulsion, van der Waals attraction, and repulsion from molecular crowding [140,141,142]. Positive and negative B22 in general refer to repulsive and attractive interactions, respectively [141]. For example, Saito *et al.* [143], found that the B22 value, measured by sedimentation equilibrium, demonstrated strong qualitative correlation with the viscosity and aggregation propensity of mAbs. There are different ways by which B22 value can be measured, including the composition gradient SLS, self interaction chromatography (SIC), osmometry, *etc.* [144,145,146,147,148,149,150]. Diffusion interaction parameter (Kd) is another useful, dilute solution property that can be utilized for the prediction of high concentration behavior. Kd is expressed by the slope of the linear relationship of diffusion coefficient *vs.* concentration, and can be determined by dynamic light scattering in a high-throughput manner [151]. Kd is related to B22 via an equation developed by Harding and Johnson [152], and thus can be utilized for indirect measurement of B22. Kd can be directly correlated to the viscosity and aggregation propensity of high concentration mAb solution, as reported by Connolly *et al.* [153]. On the other hand, the net charge on protein molecule plays an important role in determining the proximity energy when the intermolecular distance is <1 nm. Charge-charge interaction is repulsive in nature and increases the proximity energy. Increase in proximity energy relates to increase in activation energy barrier that needs to be overcome while two molecules are interacting with each other [110]. Thus, high charge is preferable for lowering viscosity (reduced reversible self association) and minimizing aggregation. Moreover charge measured at dilute solution is expected to be least influenced by concentration, given that the structural property of the molecule and the solution property remain unchanged [110]. A number of methods are available for the measurement of net charge. Most of these techniques utilize the principle of electrophoretic mobility; e.g., capillary zone electrophoresis (CZE), membrane confined electrophoresis (MCE) [154,155], and a new technique from Wyatt tech corporation that utilizes massively parallel phase analysis light scattering (MP-PALS) [156]. Although the above mentioned parameters are measured to predict high concentration behavior, there is another school of thought that claims prediction of high concentration behavior from dilute solution is not reliable [133,157].

4. ADC

The rapid growth in monoclonal antibody (mAb) therapeutics has recently stimulated the research and development of antibody-drug conjugates (ADCs) in different phases [158,159,160]. The key drive for the development of ADCs was to make use of the binding specificity of the antibodies for cell surface-associated antigens to bring the cytotoxic agents (small molecular drugs or toxins) to the desired cell population. Specific binding of ADCs to cell surface-associated antigens would minimize the non-specific and intolerable effects of cytotoxic agents on normal cells. The binding of ADCs to specific tumor-associated antigens (TAAs) can trigger internalization of the binding complex and release the drugs inside the cancer cells for the intended cytotoxic action [161]. In addition, the released small molecule drugs, due to its membrane permeability, are able to exert cytotoxic activity on bystander cells [162].

Another reason for the development of ADCs is to address the issue of drug resistance. It is known that P-glycoprotein (P-gp), a drug transporter, is abundantly expressed in tumors and facilitates the elimination of chemotherapeutics, a phenomenon known as multidrug resistance (MDR) [163]. Drug resistance has been observed both for anticancer small molecule drugs [164,165] and mAbs [166,167]. The concept of ADCs as magic bullets was proposed decades ago [168], however only three such drug products have been approved in the US; gemtuzumab (anti-CD33) ozogamicin (Mylotarg®) for acute myeloid leukemia (AML) in 2000 (voluntarily withdrawn from the US market in 2010), brentuximab (anti-CD30) vedotin (Adcetris®) in 2011 for Hodgkin's lymphoma or anaplastic large cell lymphoma, and ado-trastuzumab (anti-HER2) emtansine (Kadcyla®) for HER2-positive metastatic breast cancer in early 2013. The limited number of ADC approvals is due, in part, to two significant challenges: (1)

inadequate cellular uptake (likely <1%); and (2) residual off-target effects. To address the first issue, the antibody needs to be designed to target one or more surface antigens with high binding affinity and high rate of internalization. The antibody target should be highly, or overly, expressed in the target cells [169]. It is also necessary to use cytotoxic agents, which are highly effective at low concentrations, with a clear mechanism of action. The second issue is discussed in the following section.

4.1. Design and Selection of Different Linkers

One of the main reasons for off-target effects is the premature release of drugs outside of target cells. The premature release explains the faster-than-expected clearance of the conjugates of cantuzumab mertansine (huC242-DM1) in blood [170]. On the other hand, the drugs need to be readily releasable inside the cells to exert their cytotoxic effects. This requires a delicate balance in designing chemical linkers that possess high stability in the bloodstream, while allowing efficient payload release within the target cells. Various types of chemical linkers have been designed to achieve the desired properties [171,172].

The traditional linking sites in the preparation of protein conjugates are primary amines on lysines. The ε-amino group in lysine residue can be easily acylated. However, depending on the number and relative accessibility of lysine residues on the protein surface, the random acylation process would generally result in a heterogeneous mixture of conjugates. Mylotarg® (gemtuzumab ozogamicin), the first-generation ADC, is a heterogeneous mixture of 50% unconjugated antibody and 50% conjugated antibody with 1 to 8 calicheamicin moieties per IgG molecule (average of 2–3 drug molecules), randomly linked to solvent-exposed lysyl residues of the antibody [169]. The heterogeneity of the drug product requires stringent process controls to achieve product consistency, and characterization of the product mixture is a significant burden for analytical/quality control.

These challenges have led to the use of thiols for mAb conjugation, as the number of thios is limited and fixed in the different subtypes of IgGs. The commercial antibody products are primarily IgG1s, which possess 4 inter- and 12 intra-chain disulfide bonds.

Drugs can be linked to inter-chain disulfides following reduction [173]. Nonetheless, the use of disulfides for conjugation may still yield a heterogeneous population of conjugated products that contains positional isomers [174]. The heterogeneity derives from the different tendencies of disulfides for reduction during the conjugation process. Using two mAbs as model proteins, it was found that: (1) the inter-chain disulfide bonds are more susceptible to reduction than intra-chain disulfide bonds; (2) the disulfide bonds between the light and heavy chains are more susceptible than disulfide bonds linking two heavy chains; (3) the upper disulfide bonds linking the two inter heavy chains are more susceptible than the lower one, and (4) disulfide bonds in the CH2 domain are the most susceptible to reduction [175]. Heterogeneity can be minimized by preferential cleavage of particular mAb inter-chain disulfides through chemical reduction and oxidation, and isomeric homogeneity can be as high as 60–90% [176]. Another obvious option to minimize heterogeneity is to create a limited number of cyteine residues through engineering [177,178]. Indeed, much more homogeneous conjugates have been obtained through this process [178]. On the other hand, the engineering sites need to be carefully chosen to not affect the original activity of mAb and the conjugates. The solvent accessibility and spatial environment of the engineering sites have been demonstrated to influence the stability of thiol-reactive linkers and therapeutic activity [179]. Minimization of conjugate heterogeneity can also be achieved through engineering unnatural amino acids and precise control of the conjugation site and stoichiometry. For example, p-acetylphenylalanine was site-specifically incorporated into both a Fab fragment and full-length IgG, and conjugated to an auristatin derivative through a stable oxime linkage [180].

A commonly-used conjugation chemistry is the reaction between –SH and maleimide functional group, leading to the formation of cleavable thiosuccinimide in the presence of excessive thios. Several issues with this approach exist, however. First, the thioether bond formed by the reaction is unstable. It can undergo hydrolysis in dilute solutions, as demonstrated for immunoconjugates formed by the maleimide-sulfhydryl method [181]. The drug can be released in human plasma from thioether linked ADCs through sulfoxide formation and elimination [182]. Second, the ring structure is not stable and the thioether-maleimide has been reported to undergo complete hydrolysis of the maleimide ring (ring opening reaction) at pH 8 in 4 h at 37 °C [183].

These issues, along with the challenge in balancing the stability in blood and cleavability within the target cells, led to the design of many other different types of cleavable linkers, such as dipeptide linkers; valine-citrulline [184], Val-Cit, and Phe-Lys [185]. The limited *in vivo* stability of cleavable linkers in plasma led to the design and testing of non-cleavable leakers, which are generally more stable, such as maleimidocaproyl linker [186]. Presumably, due to the increased stability of the linker, reduced toxicity was observed relative to conjugates with cleavable linkers [187]. If the linkers are non-cleavable, release of the drug has to occur through degradation of the antibody protein in the lysosome, and the linker-retained drug needs to be active. Indeed, ADCs can be adequately processed to release the active form of the drug in the lysosomes of the target cells, such as mAb-maytansinoid conjugates containing either a disulfide linker or a thioether linker [188]. The superior efficacy and reduced toxicity of a trastuzumab-maytansinoid (mAb-DM1) conjugate eventually led to the approval of T-DM1 this year as the first ADC with a non-reducible thioether linker, following demonstration of both safety and efficacy [167].

4.2. Optimization of Antibody Drug Ratio

Another issue in the preparation of ADCs is to optimize drug load, or the antibody-drug ratio (ADR). Ideally, the affinity of the conjugated antibody for its target should not to be affected relative to the naked antibody. In general, the greater the number of drug molecules loaded onto an antibody, the higher the plasma clearance, and the weaker the binding strength between the antibody and antigen. Increasing the drug load may not increase the efficacy after reaching a limit [173,189].

4.3. Formulation Challenges

As discussed above, ADCs contain three components: mAb, linker, and drug. Among the three components, mAb and linkers are the first to be considered for formulation stabilization, as they are generally less stable than the small molecule drugs.

mAbs generally have reasonable stability, and approximately half of all naked mAb drug products are in liquid dosage form. Their stability can be negatively impacted during and/or following chemical modification for ADCs. Many of the small drug candidates are relatively hydrophobic, such as calicheamicin and paclitaxel, and the addition of a hydrophobic group would enhance the hydrophobicity-driven aggregation tendency. In addition, conjugation via lysine residues may lead to the reduction in the number of protein surface charges and the hydrophilicity of the protein. Thus, the addition of such molecules to antibodies may negatively impact antibody stability [190,191] or solubility [192].

Some peptide linkers are relatively hydrophobic and can negatively influence the stability of ADCs. In the preparation of a mAb and doxorubicin conjugate using Phe-Lys or Val-Cit as a linker, the formation of non-covalent dimer was observed immediately upon conjugation [185]. In another example, the addition of a hydrophilic methoxytriethylene glycol chain onto doxorubicin, via a hydrazone bond, has been reported to greatly inhibit the aggregation of final conjugates, most likely due to the hydrophobic nature of these peptides [193].

Ideally, the linkers are stable enough to prevent the generation of any amount of free cytotoxic drugs during formulation, manufacturing process, shipping, and storage. The reality is that most cleavable linkers discussed above possess limited *in vitro* stability. For example, the conjugate vaccine amAb-KLH, linked via succinimidyl 4-(*N*-maleimidomethyl)-cyclohexane-1-carboxylate (SMCC), is stable in PBS (pH 7.2) only at −80 °C, and significant release of free mAb was observed at 4 °C over 6 months of storage [194]. In addition, the linker stability can be significantly influenced by the neighboring groups [195].

Thioether oxidation was implicated in linker instability and varying rate of oxidation was observed at different pH's [182]. These examples demonstrate that the solution pH of ADCs is a critical parameter for evaluation in the development of a stable formulation. Lyophilization may have to be used if the linker instability is difficult to control. In fact, all three commercial ADC products are in lyophilized form (Table 2).

Table 2. Information on currently available commercial antibody drug conjugates (ADCs).

ADC	Linker	Drug-antibody ratio (DAR)	Dosage form	Excipients	Package system	Product storage
Mylotarg® (withdrawn in 2010)	*N*-4-(4-acetylphenoxy) butanoic acid and *N*-acetyl-γ-calicheamicin dimethl hydrazide	2–3	Lyo	Dextran 40, sucrose, NaCl and phosphate buffer	Single-use amber glass	2–8 °C
Adcetris® (approved in 2011)	Maleimidocaproyl-valine-citrulline	~4	Lyo	Trehalose, polysorbate 80, and citrate buffer	Single-use glass vials	2–8 °C
Kadcyla® (approved in 2013)	4-[*N*-maleimidomethyl] cyclohexane-1-carboxylate (MCC)	~3.5	Lyo	Sucrose, polysorbate 20, and sodium succinate	Single-use glass vial	2–8 °C (4 h limit after recon at 2–8 °C)

4.4. Challenges during Product Manufacturing and Stability Monitoring

ADCs are complex drug products. Purified drug substance intermediates include mAbs, linkers, and small molecule drugs. Several reaction steps may have to be carefully controlled to manufacture drug products consistently. Due to the high toxicity of small molecule drugs, dedicated suites for handling these agents and ADCs may be required. Isolators may be ideal, however operation may not be efficient. Prevention of cross contamination and good cleaning procedures require implementation. Due to the stringent requirement for aseptic processing and specific handling requirement for the cytotoxic agents, manufacturing processes may need to take place in different phases at different manufacturing sites. This will certainly make the manufacturing process complex and time-consuming.

5. ANTIBODY FUSION CONSTRUCT

Fusion proteins are designed to possess multiple functions, *i.e.*, site-specific delivery. The main difference between ADCs and fusion proteins is in the molecular structure. In ADCs, toxic agents are chemically conjugated to antibodies or their fragments, as depicted in Figure 1, while for fusion proteins, effector molecules (either protein or peptide) are inserted into the protein on the genetic level. Here, fusion proteins are grouped into three distinct classes depending on the mode of construct. First class (Figure 1) is composed of mAb (or fragments) and effector molecule. Fc-fusion proteins are composed of binding/functional peptides or proteins fused to the Fc-domain [12] (Figure 1). While antibody (or fragment) fusion proteins utilize specific antigen binding property of antibodies, Fc-fusions lack antigen-binding variable domains, and thus are not designed for targeted delivery. The Fc-domains are fused to either enhance the circulating half-life or confer ADCC or CDC function. Although no formal distinction exists, Fc-fusion proteins may be formally divided into Fc-protein fusion and Fc-peptide fusion.

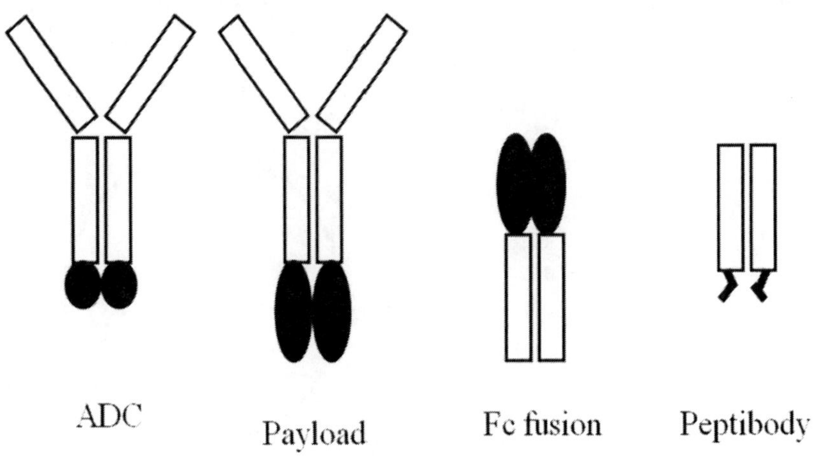

Figure 1. Illustrative comparison of the structure of ADC to those of fusion proteins. Note that although these effector molecules are shown to be fused to either the N- or C-terminus, they can also be fused to the other terminus. Though ADCs are shown to be linked to the C-terminus of antibodies or their fragments, they can also be linked to other functional groups, e.g., the N-terminus or side chains, by *in vitro* chemical reaction.

5.1. mAb-Effector Fusion Protein (Payload)

Antibodies and their fragments can be fused to various effector molecules, e.g., enzymes, toxic proteins, cytokines, and other functional proteins, on either the N- or C-terminal. In some cases, antibodies directed at tumor-associated antigens are fused to enzymes for specific delivery to tumor cells, in which the enzyme cleaves the prodrug (which has been administered separately), and penetrate the tumor cell as a cytotoxic drug (Figure 2). While the prodrug may also penetrate healthy cells, it cannot be converted to a cytotoxic form, and thus is not toxic [196]. Similar to ADCs, immunotoxins are fusion proteins designed for the targeted delivery of toxic agents. Plant or bacterial toxins are genetically fused to antibodies or their fragments and delivered to cancer cells, in which the fusion proteins are internalized and subsequently kill cancer cells [197]. Enzymes, such as ribonuclease (RNase) and granzyme B (granule-derived serine protease), can be used as a cytotoxic agent of immunotoxins [198,199,200,201]. RNase and granzyme B have been delivered to various cancers through different tumor antigens (e.g., CD22, CD32, CD64, HER2, mucin, and MEL) using specific antibodies or their fragments (e.g., scFv) [202].

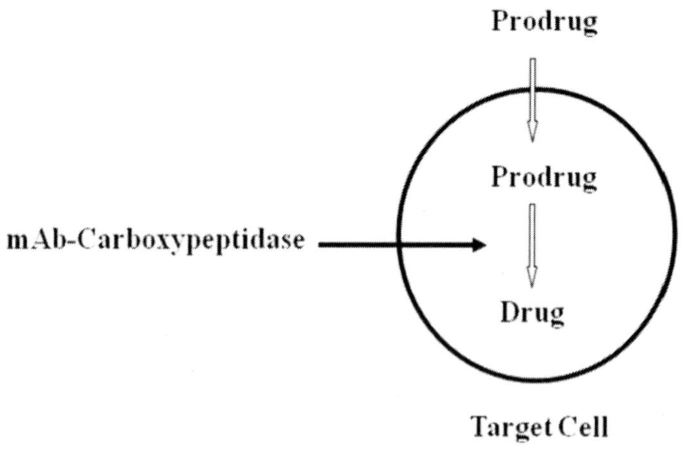

Figure 2. Illustration of the mechanism of mAb-effector fusion protein of a prodrug. The mAb is directed towards tumor-associated antigens and the enzyme is delivered to the tumor cell, within which the prodrug is cleaved, releasing the cytotoxic drug.

Another interesting construct is a mAb/avidin fusion construct. Tumor-specific delivery of cell death factors possess great potential as anti-cancer fusion proteins [202]. Although it is in itself not an antibody-effector fusion protein, it can deliver toxins site-specifically into tumors for biotin-labeled compounds. If toxins are small molecule drugs, the fusion is essentially the same as in ADC. In this case, the fusion construct is based on an antibody (or its fragment) fused to avidin. One example is anti-transferrin fusion of avidin. Transferrin plays a pivotal role in iron uptake, and transferrin receptor (TfR) has been reported to be more abundantly expressed in dividing cells [203]. Anti-TfR antibody can thus target cancer cells. In addition, TfR is expressed in blood-brain barrier and can be targeted by the same antibody or fragments [204]. In fact, neurotrophic nerve growth factor was delivered to the brain by conjugating the factor to anti-TfR antibody [205,206]. Anti-TfR antibody can thus be used for the delivery of effector proteins to the brain. Fusion process of the effector molecules can be bypassed by constructing anti-TfR fusion with avidin, as long as biotinylated effector molecules are readily generated. Avidin is a non-covalent tetramer. The covalent structure of the anti-TfR antibody/avidin fusion was found to contain two avidin molecules, as expected in a dimeric fusion molecule (see Figure 3). Size exclusion chromatography analysis demonstrated, however, a molecular weight of 400 kDa for the fusion, suggesting that this fusion is a non-covalent dimer. This is most likely due to the formation of tetrameric avidin complexes that bring two antibodies together, as depicted in Figure 3 [207]. Brain uptake of biotinylated anti-sense PNA (peptide-nucleic acid) against HIV was greatly enhanced when co-administered with the anti-TfR/avidin fusion protein [207].

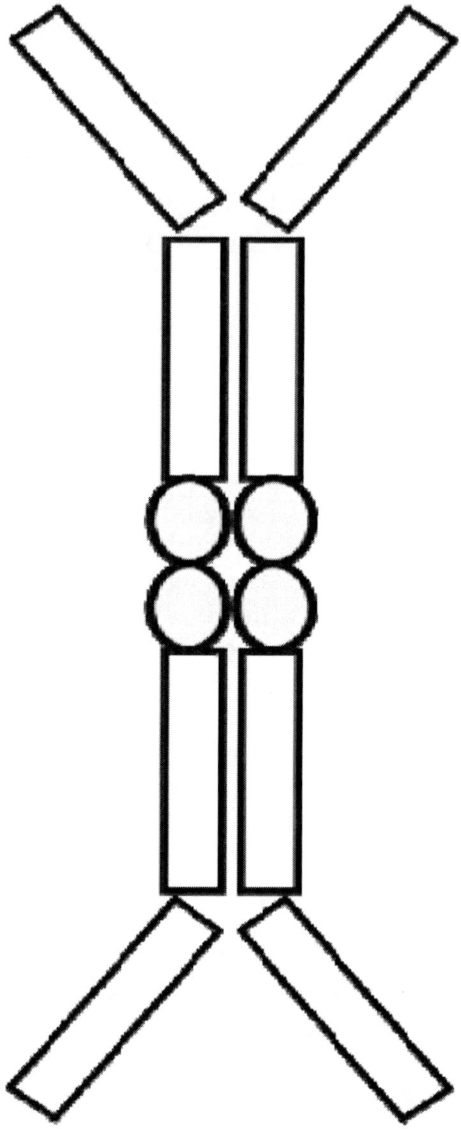

Figure 3. Illustration of a tetrameric fusion complex (anti-transferrin receptor (TfR) antibody/avidin fusion). Avidin (○) is fused to the C-terminus of the antibody.

TfR can also be used for the delivery of therapeutics into cancer cells as described above. The anti-TfR antibody/avidin fusion has been reported to deliver biotinylated glucose oxidase (MW 18.6 kDa), and even a larger protein, into cancer cells [208]. Although this construct was developed for delivery through TfR, it was accidentally observed to induce apoptosis in cancer cells [208]. It appears that both the anti-TfR antibody and avidin moieties are required to exert such apoptotic effects.

Anti-CD20 mAb (Rituxan®) has been developed to treat B-cell non-Hodgkin lymphoma. To further improve its efficacy, a cytokine fusion protein was developed [209]. Interferon-α was used as an effector cytokine, as it inhibits cell proliferation and augments immune systems. This fusion was able to recruit interferon-α at tumor sites and significantly enhance the anti-tumor effects of Rituxan®.

Neuroblastoma highly expresses disialoganglioside (GD_2). A fusion protein comprising anti-GD_2 mAb and IL2 (as a fusion) demonstrated anti-tumor responses in neuroblastoma patients [210]. This fusion construct has been reported to enhance the delivery of IL2 to tumor microenvironments and result in activation of natural killer cells, through IL2 binding to the cognate receptor, as well as tumor cell killing via ADCC mechanism [211,212].

HER2 is over expressed in certain breast cancer patients. Anti-HER2 mAb (Herceptin®) demonstrated regression of tumors, however only for some patients. GM-CSF is a cytokine that promotes growth and differentiation of granulocyte-macrophage lineages and stimulates immune responses. High local GM-SCF concentration at tumor sites should enhance its anti-tumor T-cell immunity. Thus, anti-HER2 GM-CSF fusion protein was constructed to recruit this cytokine to breast cancer cells [213]. The fusion protein was reported to bind to its antigen (cell-surface HER2) with the same affinity as for anti-HER2 mAb. Similarly, the fusion protein stimulated the cell line, whose proliferation depends on GM-CSF, at the same concentration as the free cytokine. This fusion protein exhibited tumor killing through both Fc-mediated ADCC and macrophage activation.

Endostatin demonstrates strong suppressive effects on angeogenesis and tumor growth, but demonstrated marginal therapeutic efficacy in clinical trials. Anti-HER2 IgG3 fusion of endostatin demonstrated a drastic improvement in serum half-life and stability, and increased the local endostatin concentration around HER2 expressing tumor [214].

Decay-accelerating factor (DAF) is an inhibitor of complement activation. This inhibitor was fused to the C-terminus of anti-dansyl mAb or its fragments [215]. This fusion protein bound both dansyl and anti-DAF antibody. CHO cells conjugated with dansyl were used to confirm cell surface binding of the anti-dansyl IgG/DAF fusion protein. The fusion protein has been reported to protect complement-mediated cell lysis.

5.2. Protein-Fc Fusion

This fusion construct makes no use of antibody's unique function, *i.e.*, antigen specificity, as it lacks antigen binding variable domains. Variable domains are replaced with the protein of interest, which is fused to Fc for prolonging circulation life, CDC and ADCC, or dimerization. Fc also facilitates purification, as it specifically binds to Protein-A or Protein-G. The main difference from peptibodies, described next, is that the molecule to be fused is a protein or a domain of naturally existing proteins. Although each protein in the fusion construct may be readily folded, the fusion protein is a non-natural construct, particularly in the linker region, which may cause folding problems. A blockbuster product, etanercept (Enbrel®), belongs to this group of constructs. It comprises tumor necrosis factor receptor (TNFR) fused to Fc. Mammalian expression of etanercept illustrates this folding problem. Two patents from Immunex report this folding problem when the fusion was derived from a mammalian expression system [216,217]. When Protein-A purified etanercept was analyzed by analytical hydrophobic interaction chromatography (HIC), three distinct peaks were typically observed. First peak corresponds to the clipped form, second peak to the native etanercept (N-etanercept), and the third peak (PIII) to the misfolded form. SDS-PAGE analysis of PIII mainly demonstrated the band of N-etanercept along with small amounts of aggregates and the clipped form. PIII demonstrated greatly reduced activity, perhaps reflecting its incorrect structure. Nevertheless, spectroscopic and peptide mapping analysess suggested that the misfolded structure is rather limited to the localized area, which involves SS pairing. More importantly, the amount of PIII in the culture media varied from ~10 to ~60%, depending on the fermentation conditions.

Glycosylation, in particular sialylation, can vary between different products, even if their amino acid sequences are identical. Although such difference does not appear to affect biological activity, it may alter the serum half-life, suggesting the importance of glycosylation on pharmacokinetics. At this moment, whether fusion of TNFR to Fc in etanercept affects glycosylation is unclear.

As in etanercept, the majority of Fc-protein fusions comprise an extracellular domain of receptors fused to the N-terminus of the Fc domain (Figure 4A). There are many applications of this type of construct. Triggering receptor expressed on myeloid cells (TREM-1), expressed on immune cells, is a TREM family member which is engaged in inflammation responses. TREM-1 can cause, upon bacterial infection, excessive amplification of inflammation and mediate septic shock [218]. The administration of TREM-1/Fc fusion has been reported to result in decreased septic shock [219] and improve disease symptom from collagen-induced arthritis, similar to etanercept. Similarly, anti-angeogenic vascular endothelial growth factor (VEGF) inhibitor has been developed as an Fc-fusion protein, termed VEGF-Trap [220]. It is a fusion protein containing VEGF receptor-1, VEGF receptor-2, and Fc domain of human IgG.

Hemophilia B results from a deficiency of factor IX (FIX), which is responsible for blood coagulation. Patients suffering from a bleeding disorder are treated by injection or infusion of FIX, whose short circulation life time often requires repeated treatments. Recombinant Fc fusion protein of FIX has been prepared by expressing together an FIX-Fc fusion gene and an Fc gene, resulting in FIX-Fc monomer comprising one functional FIX and two Fc domains (Figure 4B). This fusion construct demonstrated higher circulation half life, due to its binding to FcRn, and resultant recycling of the fusion molecule [221]. Factor VIII (FVIII) is also involved in the blood coagulation cascade. Hemophilia patients with low level of FVIII suffer a similar bleeding disorder. Recently, Biogen Idec filed a BLA for a longer circulating FVIII-Fc fusion protein.

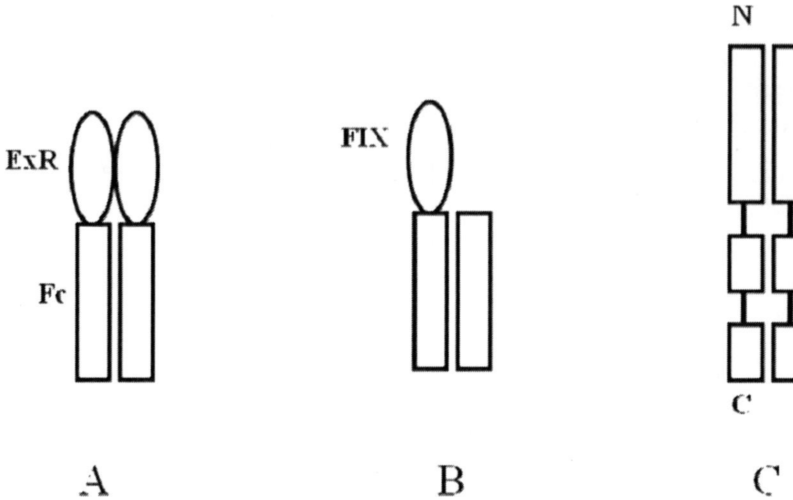

Figure 4. Illustration of various Fc-fusion proteins: (**A**) construct of extracellular domain of receptors (ExR) fused to the N-terminus of Fc, (**B**) FIX (coagulation factor IX)—Fc monomer comprising one functional FIX and two Fc domains, and (**C**) Fc fusion of the peptide, romiplostin/Nplate®, that contains two tandem repeats of the peptide. Fc is depicted as long rectangles and the peptide as short rectangles. These three constructs form dimers through the Fc domain.

5.3. Peptibody

Short peptides occupy a large portion of biopharmaceutical drugs currently available. Short peptides are significantly different from proteins in their structural properties; many short peptides are disordered, flexible, with a strong tendency for aggregation, unless structurally constrained. While a large number of short peptides are naturally present in humans, a new class of short peptides is under development that has been identified by screening peptide libraries against known disease targets. They are artificial agonistic or antagonistic peptide ligands. Peptibodies, composed of artificial peptides fused to Fc, have been primarily developed by Amgen. One such peptide was identified by screening phage display libraries based on binding to thrombopoietin receptor, to which the endogenous protein ligand, thrombopoietin, binds. This 14 amino acid peptide serves as an agonistic ligand and stimulates platelet production, and thus can be used in thrombocytopenic patients. The Fc-fusion of the peptide (romiplostin/Nplate®) contains 2 tandem repeats of the peptide, as schematically shown in Figure 4C, and thus four peptides in dimeric Fc construct. This should increase the avidity for receptor binding. It appears that fusion at the C-terminus of Fc renders the peptide more active. One potential source of such differences may be due to the structure. As in many peptides, these artificial short peptides may be disordered, flexible, and with the tendency to aggregate. These properties may be affected by surrounding the structure of Fc (and constraining the overall peptide structure) by fusion (either the N- or C-terminus of the peptides). Such structural constraint may be stronger if the peptides are inserted into the CH3 domain of the Fc, as shown in Figure 4C. Apparently, this insertion was designed to have no impact on Fc binding to the Fc receptor and recycling of the peptibody through binding to cell surface FcRn [222].

Neither structural nor aggregation propensity of the peptides by themselves, or in the peptibodies, has been reported. However, one of the functional peptides, SEYQGLCTRWPWMCPPQGWK, in a peptibody (called "peptibody A") [223] has been reported to mediate self-association by increasing the salt concentration (to 150 mM) and solution pH (from pH 5 to 7). More specifically, peptibody A demonstrated a strong tendency to self-associate, with no involvement of its Fc domain in physiological solution. Considering the high solubility of the Fc domain, the results appear to suggest that this artificial functional peptide may possess a strong tendency to aggregate, even with the structural rigidity imposed by a disulfide bridge (through 2 Cys in the sequence).

6. OTHER MAB-BASED THERAPEUTICS

Bispecific

Bispecific, monovalent antibodies were first described in 1961 by Nisonoff and Rivers [224]. The binding of at least two molecular targets with one single bispecific antibody (bsAb) is an attractive therapeutic concept. Bispecific compounds are being developed to enable: (1) simultaneous inhibition of two cell surface receptors; (2) simultaneous blocking of two ligands; (3) cross linking of two receptors; and (4) recruitment of T-cells to the proximity of tumor cells; to name a few [225]. The formats currently employed include tandem single chain Fv (scFv), diabodies, tandem diabodies, dual variable domain antibodies, and hetero-dimerization [226] (Figure 5). The most advanced bispecific antibody formats include Triomab® and BiTE®, which will be described further below. bsAb, as a single molecular entity, may provide a viable alternative to combination therapy with two mAbs (*i.e.*, mAb cocktail, as will be described further below).

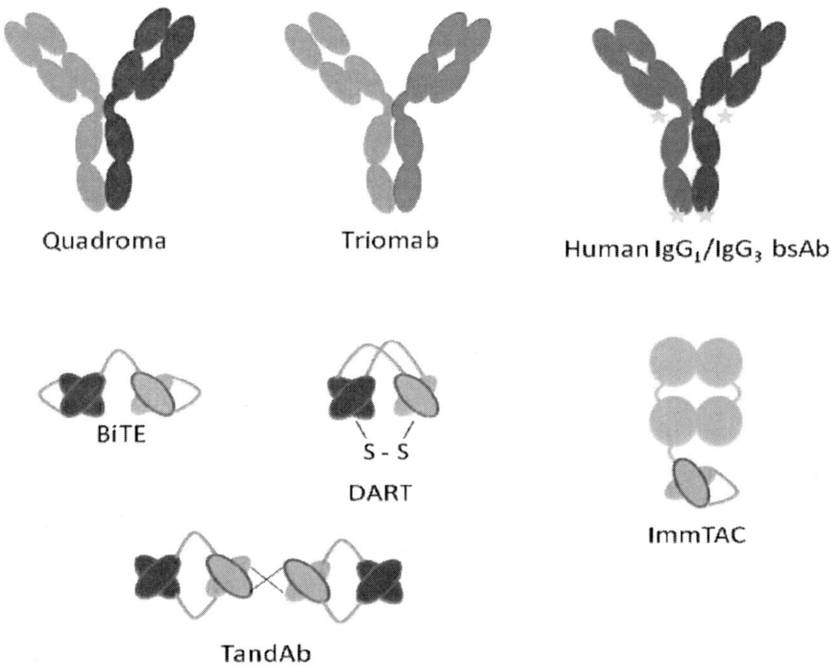

Figure 5. Illustration of various bispecific antibodies, including bispecific T-cell engager (BiTE®), Dual-Affinity Re-Targeting (DART™), tetravalent bispecific recombinant antibody (TandAb®), and Immune mobilizing mTCR Against Cancer (ImmTAC). Figure from May *et al.* [225].

bsAbs that bind two antigens on the same cell can be used to enhance specificity for cells expressing both targets relative to cells expressing only one [198,227,228]. This was validated at the preclinical level by Zu and colleagues using a single-gene bispecific diabody (bs-diabody) specific for VEGFR2 (KDR) and VEGFR3 (Flt-4) [229,230]. bsAbs enables an increase in the number of antigen targets, and potentially to overcome tumor immune escape mediated by down-regulation or loss of MHC [231]. In another application, bsAbs have been designed with one specificity directed towards a tumor antigen and the other designed for activation and retargeting of natural killer (NK) cells and myeloid effector cells [232]. Similar to redirected toxicity utility, bsAbs can also be used for rapid clearance of pathogens from the body [233,234]. Moreover, bsAbs can be used for the specific targeting of toxins [235], chemotherapeutic drugs [236], and radioisotopes to tumor cells [237]. Majority of both bispecific diabodies and bis-scFv are designed to bind to the CD3 T-cell co-receptor, and thus recruit cytotoxic T-cells to the tumor site [238]. In contrast, bispecific T-cell engagers (BiTEs®) are capable of efficiently redirecting T-cell cytotoxicity against various target cells without any requirement for pre- or co-stimulation of effector T cells [239,240].

Antibodies with a dual specificity in their binding arms usually do not occur in nature, and thus needs to be engineered using recombinant DNA or cell-fusion technology. The first approach employed to construct and produce bsAbs was the quadroma technology [241,242], which is based on the somatic fusion of two different hybridoma cell lines expressing murine monoclonal antibodies. Bispecific antibodies from quadroma cell lines closely resemble conventional mAbs; besides the dual-specific antigen binding fragment (Fab) parts, they contain an Fc_{γ} part, and thus can be considered trispecific. A major improvement to the conventional quadroma approach employed the somatic fusion of a murine and a rat hybridoma cell line, expressing monoclonal antibodies with two IgG subclasses selected for their preferential pairing [15,243]. The hybrid antibodies generated by this method incorporated binding sites for two different antigens while retaining its intact Fc. These trifunctional antibodies, termed TriomAbs, have the combined effect of redirecting T cells, along with Fc receptor expressing cells, to the tumor, and have been reported to eliminate tumor cells by a combination of T-cell mediated lysis and ADCC [15]. bsAbs without Fc regions can be prepared and may have better tissue penetration, although they will have short serum half-lives, as will be discussed later in the *mAb fragment section*. Other explored approaches include: (1) chemical conjugation of two different monoclonal antibodies or smaller antibody fragments [244], (2) 'Knobs-into-holes' strategy [245,246], and (3) strand-exchange engineered domain (SEED) [247].

Alternative recombinant strategies focused on smaller bispecific antibody constructs. In diabodies, each V_L domain is connected by a short peptide linker to the V_H domain of the other antigen specificity, and vice versa [248]. Co-expression of respective V_H-V_L fusions in the periplasm of *E. coli* resulted in stable bispecific diabodies. Further extension of diabodies, tandem diabodies [249], has also been manufactured. An alternative small format is the arrangement of two scFvs connected by a flexible polypeptide linker on a single polypeptide chain [250]. BiTE® antibodies are recombinant protein constructs created by linking two scFv molecules via a five amino acid peptide linker [251]. Some key features of BiTEs® include cell surface antigen-dependent polyclonal T-cell activation, potent T-cell mediated serial lysis, and the induction of T-cell proliferation. The short serum half-life of BiTE® antibodies (several hours) allows for rapid-clearance, which may be considered a safety feature of this highly potent class of therapeutic bsAbs. The first BiTE® developed by Micromet, blinatumomab, is a recombinant anti-CD3 × anti-CD19, and is the most advanced BiTE® in clinical trials [252,253]. Blinatumomab is being studied as a treatment of patients with relapsed NHL and acute lymphblastic leukemia. A competing recombinant format based on a covalently-linked bispecific diabody, termed DARD® (Dual-Affinity Re-Targeting), was reported by the biotechnology company MacroGenics Inc [254,255].

Several other technologies are currently being pursued, including dual-variable domain immunoglobulin (DVD-Ig™) for the generation of an Fv-bispecific molecule [256], and mAb² ™ antibodies, produced by Modular Antibody Technology platform (f-star inc., [257] and ImmTAC (immune mobilizing monoclonal TCR against cancer; Immunocore, [258]).

The vast majority of bispecific Abs developed in oncology are undergoing preclinical evaluation. HRS-3/A9 is a CD16-directed bispecific antibody already tested in clinical trials [232,259]. The compound is a bispecific $F(ab)_2$ antibody (without $F_{c\gamma}$ part) targeting the CD30 antigen on Hodgkin and Reed-Sternberg cells in patients with Hodgkin's Disease. Of the bsAbs derived using quadroma technology, the Triomab® (TRION Research GmbH, Munich, Germany) class is the most encouraging thus far [243]. Catumaxomab is the most clinically advanced Triomab® [15]. Catumaxomab combines two half antibodies of mouse anti-EpCAM IgG2a and rat anti-CD3 IgG2b [260]. In a randomized Phase II/III study involving 258 patients with malignant ascites, catumaxomab demonstrated significant improvement in survival, which led to EU approval in 2009 for the treatment of malignant ascites in patients with EpCAM-positive tumors, and was the first bispecific antibody approved for clinical use [15,261].

Despite the advantages discussed above, there are several hurdles that need to be overcome for bsAbs to be considered a viable alternative therapy. The primary challenges with bsAbs include chemical manufacturing control issues, production yield and purity, and poor clinical results associated with early formats. Although producing small amounts for *in vitro*studies and animal models may be relatively straightforward, high and affordable production yields, as needed, for clinical grade material will require major efforts.

7. MAB FRAGMENTS

Smaller recombinant antibody fragments (*i.e.*, Fab, scFv, and single variable V_H and V_L domains) and engineered variants (diabodies, triabodies, minibodies, and single-domain antibodies) are now emerging as viable alternatives to mAbs (Figure 6). These fragments retain the targeting specificity of whole mAbs while possessing additional unique properties for a range of diagnostic and therapeutic applications. For example, diffusion has been reported to play a prominent role in the transport of molecules within tumors [262]. Smaller constructs such as scFv, diabodies, triabodies, minibodies, and Fabs have been shown in xenograft systems to possess shorter half-lives and accumulate at higher tumor-to-organ ratios in comparison to corresponding Fab'$_2$ constructs [263,264]. Similarly, scFvs have been reported to efficiently penetrate certain tissue barriers due to their more efficient extravasation from blood vessels and improved diffusion in the extracellular matrix, in comparison to a mAb [265]. ESBA105, a TNF-alpha inhibitory scFv, have been reported to penetrate through ocular epithelial barriers and reach therapeutic concentrations in different ocular compartments including the vitreous humor and retina [266]. It is hypothesized that its excellent tissue penetration properties may also facilitate delivery into the CNS for the treatment of neurological disorders, following either intranasal or systemic administration. In another example, many pathogenic viruses have evolved narrow cavities in their surface antigens to escape immunosurveillance [267]. Compared to monoclonal antibodies, camelid VhH and shark V-NAR domains display long surface loops, and are thus able to penetrate cavities in target antigens [268,269,270]. Similarly, HIV-1 has evolved a number of strategies to evade humoral immunity [271]. A human dAb (domain antibody; ~15 kDa), m36, has been shown to target a highly protected structure on the HIV-1 envelope glycoprotein (Env), gp120, and exhibit exceptionally potent neutralizing activity against HIV-1 primary isolates, with higher potency on average than those of the broadly cross-reactive mAbs [272].

Fab fragments (55 kDa), obtained by proteolytic digestion of IgG, are typically composed of a single antibody light chain linked by a disulfide bond to a heavy chain fragment, which represents a single binding site for the antigen. (Fab)$_2$fragments are bivalent and retain the heavy chain hinge region. Single-chain Fvs (scFv; 25 kDa) are a popular format in which the V_H and V_L domains are joined using a flexible polypeptide linker [274]. scFv molecules can also be engineered to enable the formation of an (scFv)$_2$ fragment by virtue of disulfide bridging. Diabody is a bivalent molecule, formed by linking two scFvs non-covalently [275]. Diabodies have rigid, compact structures, which allow for lower separation of the two binding sites and possess an excellent combination of rapid tumor uptake and clearance for *in vivo* imaging [276,277]. Minibody is an alternative to diabody, in which 2 scFv fragments are linked by a component of the heavy-chain region [278]. Single-domain antibodies (dAbs, 11–15 kDa) have been engineered and selected as targeting reagents against hitherto immunosilent cavities in enzymes, receptors, and infectious agents.

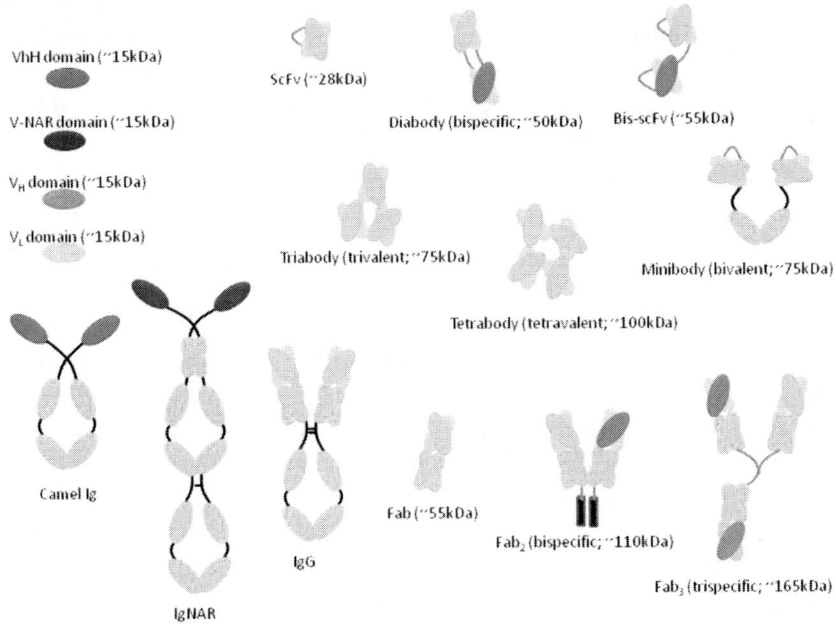

Figure 6. Schematic representation of various antibody formats, including the intact IgG molecule alongside various representations of antibody fragments. Figure from Holliger and Hudson [273].

In addition, antibody fragments have been linked or fused genetically to a vast range of molecules that provide important ancillary functions, following target binding. These include radionuclides, cytotoxic drugs, toxins, peptides, proteins, enzymes, and liposomes for improved drug delivery, and even viruses for targeted gene therapy [279,280,281]. Another concept that has been galvanized by progress in mAb-fragment engineering is antibody-directed enzyme prodrug therapy (ADEPT). In this strategy, mAb fragments (for example, a humanized scFv [282] or camelid VhH [283]) are fused to enzymes (such as β-lactamase and carboxypeptidase), which catalyze prodrug activation.

Domantis developed phage display libraries of fully human V_H- and V_L-chain dAbs to select single variable domain-based antibodies (called domain antibodies) against a variety of therapeutic targets [284]. Ablynx Inc. has used the immunization approach to generate single variable domain-based antibodies called nanobodies [285,286]. These dAbs and nanobodies are approximately 13 kDa in size, bind antigens with high affinity and express well in both microbial and mammalian cells. These functionally active dAbs and nanobodies can be reformatted into a linked dAb or CH1/CL dAb, or be attached to V_H and/or V_L chains, or the CH3 of a regular antibody to make a bispecific or multispecific molecule [287].

Efficient methods of gene delivery, with localized functional expression of the encoded product, are still in their infancy, however when successful, *in situ* expression will provide an attractive alternative to systemic administration of antibody fragments [288]. In fact, *in situ* expression and secretion of cytotoxic scFv fragments [289] or a bispecific diabody [290] (termed intrabodies) *in vivo* from just a few expressor cells have been reported to promote significant growth inhibition of established tumor xenografts. Like their extracellular counterparts, intrabodies may be engineered into multivalent and multispecific forms to enhance their efficacy [291].

The major hurdles reported with the various scFv-based formats relate to low yields, poor product quality (high aggregation propensity and product heterogeneity), poor stability, and *in vivo* loss of activity. Numerous expression systems have been evaluated and compared [292,293]; in summary, mammalian or plant cells are the favored hosts for high-yield expression of larger intact antibodies and minibodies, whereas bacterial and yeast systems are most useful for mAb fragments and V domains. The pharmacokinetics and pharmacodynamics of these agents should be carefully investigated, since their molecular structure cannot be compared with those of conventional monoclonal antibodies.

7.1. mAb Cocktail

Theoretical drawback of mAb therapy is that these reagents, by definition, target a single epitope, and provide one type of effector function corresponding to their isotype. The potent neutralizing ability of mAbs can inadvertently result in increased antigenic escape in experimental infection with highly variant RNA viruses. Indeed, treatment with a single mAb has culminated in escape variants in HIV [294], hepatitis C virus [295], and influenza A [296]. This problem may be counterbalanced by selecting mAbs that target conserved areas of viral particles or by using mixtures of mAbs that target various epitopes. For example, combination therapy with mAb cocktails has been reported to prevent escape variants for many viruses including influenza [297], hepatitis B virus [298], and rabies virus [299]. Originally a poly Ig product, RespiGam® was developed by MedImmune and approved for prophylactic use in infants. While efficacious, a humanized IgG1 mAb product (Synagis®, palivizumab) was designed to replace RespiGam®. *In vitro* and *in vivo* experiments have demonstrated that antibody combinations can not only show an additive effect, but also a synergistic effect on target cell populations [300,301,302]. As early as 1982, combinations of two mAbs against the vesicular stomatitis virus have been demonstrated to act synergistically in virus neutralization, and similar findings were subsequently reported for other viruses, including rabies [303] and HIV [304,305,306]. Synergistic or additive effects of cocktails of mAbs are not restricted to virus neutralization. In oncology and infectious diseases, cocktails of two conventionally manufactured mAbs are used for targeting HER2/neu (breast cancer [307]) and CD20 and CD22 (non-Hodgkin's lymphoma [308]). In addition, mixtures of three mAbs against botulinum toxin were demonstrated to have almost 100-fold higher potency than that reported for human polyclonal botulinum-immune globulin or individual mAbs [309]. mAb cocktail also has widened biological effector functions as it consists of multiple classes of antibodies. The ability to induce ADCC or CDC is dependent on both the isotype and glycosylation status of the antibody [310], thus the variability inherent in polyclonal preparations should provide added benefit and a protective advantage.

mAb cocktails address two major problems posed by targeting a single epitope. First, by targeting two neutralizing epitopes, at minimum, escape mutants generated from each mAb are cleared by the complementing antibody [297]. In addition, mAb cocktails further add to the 'functional specificity' of antibody therapy by selectively targeting tumor cells with the correct antigenic make-up, based on combinations of target molecules, while leaving non-tumor cells unharmed. Second, by increasing the antibody density on the viral surface, which may be the most important factor in virus neutralization [311], the neutralizing ability of the antibody is amplified considerably [312]. It is becoming evident that treatment of an infectious disease with multiple mAbs is most probably required to provide optimal protection. This concept is not novel, however. In the late 1890s Behring and Kitasato developed the first widely available and effective antimicrobial treatment by showing that transfer of immune sera could provide passive immunity to diphtheria [313]. Following the discovery, serum therapy was used against a diverse range of infectious diseases, including pneumococcal pneumonia, meningococcal meningitis, erysipelas, anthrax and others [1,314].

Several methods for the production of mAb cocktails have been documented. In one strategy, animals are genetically manipulated to harbor human immunoglobulin loci, and the animal's endogenous immunoglobulin loci are inactivated [19]. Upon immunization, these transgenic animals produce human antibodies, and the pooled sera could be used to prepare human polyclonal antibody therapeutics. However, batch-to-batch variation, risk of disease transmission, and precise control over the antibody composition of the polyclonal sera, are potential issues. Another manufacturing approach exploits a single master cell bank, comprising a mixture of clonal cell lines that each produces a single human mAb [315]. This approach requires the development of large numbers of cell lines that each stably secrete sufficient amounts of mAb to contribute to the mixture. Furthermore, individual cell lines in the mixture could have different growth characteristics, which will result in asymmetrical contribution of individual mAbs to the eventual mixture and, probably, batch-to-batch variation. An alternative approach uses a technology platform that permits the stable and high-yield production of multiple mAbs from clonal cell lines [315]. Genetic constructs encoding three to five different mAbs are inserted into a single cell, and antibody cocktails consisting of bivalent and bispecific IgG molecules are produced. The advantages of this approach are that it requires the development of only a single cell line for a cocktail of mAbs and that the requirements for production runs are similar to those for conventional mAbs.

Despite the advantages mentioned above, there must also be caution. A potentially serious complication of antibody cocktail therapy is the development of antagonistic effects. For example, should any one of the administered antibodies lose efficacy *in vitro*, then there may be antagonistic effects that need to be fully understood. With three or more antibodies formulated together, it is reasonable to assume that each will have different *in vivo* pharmacokinetics. Furthermore, mixing independently generated mAbs to concoct a more potent therapeutic may not be commercially viable due to the high cost of development [316]. In addition, clinical phase trials may be more complex due to the various mAb combinations possible (*i.e.*, combined drug product, sequential injections, *etc.*). In addition, the inclusion of multiple immunoglobulins in any therapeutic formulation is fraught with complex regulatory and licensing issues. Nevertheless, progress in overcoming these burdensome regulatory issues is evidenced by the recent development of a mAb mixture for the prophylaxis of rabies that targets several virus types [303].

8. SUMMARY

With the number of viable mAb-based therapy increasing, it is evident that the focus of the biotherapeutics industry will continue to be mAbs or their derivatives. To provide the effective dose, the currently available options are to prepare mAb formulations at high concentration, deliver a high volume, or to engineer enhanced targeting capability. The issues described in the current review for the preparation of high concentration mAb formulations include manufacturing challenges, stability, and delivery. Various mAb-based modalities are also under development, including ADCs, fusion proteins, and bsAbs, to circumvent some of the issues encountered with mAb therapies; nevertheless, similar issues may still be encountered with alternative mAb-based products. Though promising results have been obtained, there are still challenges to be overcome. Nonetheless, it is difficult to ignore the benefits of expanding therapeutic tools that have become available, as well as the improvements in our capability to manufacture, analyze, and formulate these complex biologicals.

CONFLICT OF INTEREST

The authors declare no conflict of interest.

REFERENCES

1. Casadevall, A.; Scharff, M.D. Return to the past: The case for antibody-based therapies in infectious diseases. *Clin. Infect. Dis.* **1995**, *21*, 150–161.
2. Bruton, O.C. Agammaglobulinemia. *Pediatrics* **1952**, *9*, 722–728.
3. Nadler, L.M.; Stashenko, P.; Hardy, R.; Kaplan, W.D.; Button, L.N.; Kufe, D.W.; Antman, K.H.; Schlossman, S.F. Serotherapy of a patient with a monoclonal antibody directed against a human lymphoma-associated antigen. *Cancer Res.* **1980**, *40*, 3147–3154.
4. Kohler, G.; Milstein, C. Continuous cultures of fused cells secreting antibody of predefined specificity. *Nature* **1975**,*256*, 495–497.
5. Oldham, R.K. Monoclonal antibodies as anticancer agents. *Adv. Exp. Med. Biol.* **1983**, *166*, 45–57.
6. Reichert, J.M. Metrics for antibody therapeutics development. *MAbs* **2010**, *2*, 695–700.
7. Marks, L. The birth pangs of monoclonal antibody therapeutics: The failure and legacy of Centoxin. *MAbs* **2012**, *4*, 403–412.
8. Hurley, J.C. Sepsis management and antiendotoxin therapy after nebacumab. A reappraisal. *Drugs* **1994**, *47*, 855–861.
9. Beck, A.; Wurch, T.; Bailly, C.; Corvaia, N. Strategies and challenges for the next generation of therapeutic antibodies.*Nat. Rev. Immunol.* **2010**, *10*, 345–352.
10. Coiffier, B.; Lepage, E.; Brière, J.; Herbrecht, R.; Tilly, H.; Bouabdallah, R.; Morel, P.; Van Den Neste, E.; Salles, G.; Gaulard, P.; *et al.* CHOP chemotherapy plus rituximab

compared with CHOPalone in elderly patients with diffuse large-B-cell lymphoma. *N. Engl. J. Med.* **2002**, *346*, 235–242.

11. McLaughlin, P.; Grillo-López, A.J.; Link, B.K.; Levy, R.; Czuczman, M.S.; Williams, M.E.; Heyman, M.R.; Bence-Bruckler, I.; White, C.A.; Cabanillas, F.; *et al.* Rituximab chimeric anti-CD20 monoclonal antibody therapy for relapsed indolent lymphoma: Half of patients respond to a four-dose treatment program. *J. Clin. Oncol.* **1998**, *16*, 2825–2833.

12. Reichert, J.M. Antibody-based therapeutics to watch in 2011. *MAbs* **2011**, *3*, 76–99.

13. Sievers, E.L.; Appelbaum, F.R.; Spielberger, R.T.; Forman, S.J.; Flowers, D.; Smith, F.O.; Shannon-Dorcy, K.; Berger, M.S.; Bernstein, I.D. Selective ablation of acute myeloid leukemia using antibody-targeted chemotherapy: A phase I study of an anti-CD33 calicheamicin immunoconjugate. *Blood* **1999**, *93*, 3678–3684.

14. Weiner, L.M.; Surana, R.; Wang, S. Monoclonal antibodies: Versatile platforms for cancer immunotherapy. *Nat. Rev. Immunol.* **2010**, *10*, 317–327.

15. Linke, R.; Klein, A.; Seimetz, D. Catumaxomab: Clinical development and future directions. *MAbs* **2010**, *2*, 129–136.

16. Wang, W.; Singh, S.; Zeng, D.L.; King, K.; Nema, S. Antibody structure, instability, and formulation. *J. Pharm. Sci.* **2007**,*96*, 1–26.

17. Oldham, R.K.; Dillman, R.O. Monoclonal antibodies in cancer therapy: 25 years of progress. *J. Clin. Oncol.* **2008**, *26*, 1774–1777.

18. Hoogenboom, H.R. Selecting and screening recombinant antibody libraries. *Nat. Biotechnol.* **2005**, *23*, 1105–1116.

19. Lonberg, N. Human antibodies from transgenic animals. *Nat. Biotechnol.* **2005**, *23*, 1117–1125.

20. McCafferty, J.; Griffiths, A.D.; Winter, G.; Chiswell, D.J. Phage antibodies: Filamentous phage displaying antibody variable domains. *Nature* **1990**, *348*, 552–554.

21. Clynes, R.A.; Towers, T.L.; Presta, L.G.; Ravetch, J.V. Inhibitory Fc receptors modulate *in vivo* cytotoxicity against tumor targets. *Nat. Med.* **2000**, *6*, 443–446.

22. Graziano, R.F.; Fanger, M.W. Fc gamma RI and Fc gamma RII on monocytes and granulocytes are cytotoxic trigger molecules for tumor cells. *J. Immunol.* **1987**, *139*, 3536–3541.

23. Kimura, H.; Sakai, K.; Arao, T.; Shimoyama, T.; Tamura, T.; Nishio, K. Antibody-dependent cellular cytotoxicity of cetuximab against tumor cells with wild-type or mutant epidermal growth factor receptor. *Cancer Sci.* **2007**, *98*, 1275–1280.

24. Jain, R.K. Normalizing tumor vasculature with anti-angiogenic therapy: A new paradigm for combination therapy.*Nat. Med.* **2001**, *7*, 987–989.

25. Chan, A.C.; Carter, P.J. Therapeutic antibodies for autoimmunity and inflammation. *Nat. Rev. Immunol.* **2010**, *10*, 301–316.

26. Ducancel, F.; Muller, B.H. Molecular engineering of antibodies for therapeutic and diagnostic purposes. *MAbs* **2012**, *4*, 445–457.

27. Dillman, R.O. Magic bullets at last! Finally—Approval of a monoclonal antibody for the treatment of cancer!!! *Cancer Biother. Radiopharm.* **1997**, *12*, 223–225.

28. Huhn, D.; von Schilling, C.; Wilhelm, M.; Ho, A.D.; Hallek, M.; Kuse, R.; Knauf, W.; Riedel, U.; Hinke, A.; Srock, S.; *et al.* Rituximab therapy of patients with B-cell chronic lymphocytic leukemia. *Blood* **2001**, *98*, 1326–1331.

29. Nelson, A.L.; Dhimolea, E.; Reichert, J.M. Development trends for human monoclonal antibody therapeutics. *Nat. Rev. Drug Discov.* **2010**, *9*, 767–774.

30. Wormald, M.R.; Dwek, R.A. Glycoproteins: Glycan presentation and protein-fold stability. *Structure* **1999**, *7*, R155–R160.

31. Yamane-Ohnuki, N.; Satoh, M. Production of therapeutic antibodies with controlled fucosylation. *MAbs* **2009**, *1*, 230–236.

32. Lis, H.; Sharon, N. Protein glycosylation. Structural and functional aspects. *Eur. J. Biochem.* **1993**, *218*, 1–27.

33. Mimura, Y.; Churcha, S.; Ghirlandob, R.; Ashtonc, S.; Donga, S.; Goodalla, M.; Lunda, J.; Jefferisa, R. The influence of glycosylation on the thermal stability and effector function expression of human IgG1-Fc: Properties of a series of truncated glycoforms. *Mol. Immunol.* **2000**, *37*, 697–706.

34. Kayser, V.; Chennamsetty, N.; Voynov, V.; Forrer, K.; Helk, B.; Trout, B.L. Glycosylation influences on the aggregation propensity of therapeutic monoclonal antibodies. *Biotechnol. J.* **2011**, *6*, 38–44.

35. Runkel, L.; Meier, W.; Blake Pepinsky, R.; Karpusas, M.; Whitty, A.; Kimball, K.; Brickelmaier, M.; Muldowney, C.; Jones, W.; Goelz, S.E. Structural and functional differences between glycosylated and non-glycosylated forms of human interferon-beta (IFN-beta). *Pharm. Res.* **1998**, *15*, 641–649.

36. Sondermann, P.; Huber, R.; Oosthuizen, V.; Jacob, U. The 3.2-A crystal structure of the human IgG1 Fc fragment-Fc gammaRIII complex. *Nature* **2000**, *406*, 267–273.

37. Burton, D.R.; Woof, J.M. Human antibody effector function. *Adv. Immunol.* **1992**, *51*, 1–84.

38. Anegon, I.; Cuturi, M.C.; Trinchieri, G.; Perussia, B. Interaction of Fc receptor (CD16) ligands induces transcription of interleukin 2 receptor (CD25) and lymphokine genes and expression of their products in human natural killer cells. *J. Exp. Med.* **1988**, *167*, 452–472.

39. Fanger, M.W.; Graziano, R.F.; Li, S.; Guyre, P.M. Fc gamma R in cytotoxicity exerted by mononuclear cells. *Chem. Immunol.* **1989**, *47*, 214–253.

40. Anderson, C.L.; Shen, L.; Eicher, D.M.; Wewers, M.D.; Gill, J.K. Phagocytosis mediated by three distinct Fc gamma

receptor classes on human leukocytes. *J. Exp. Med.* **1990**, *171*, 1333–1345.

41. Jefferis, R.; Lund, J.; Pound, J.D. IgG-Fc-mediated effector functions: Molecular definition of interaction sites for effector ligands and the role of glycosylation. *Immunol. Rev.* **1998**, *163*, 59–76.

42. Vugmeyster, Y.; Howell, K. Rituximab-mediated depletion of cynomolgus monkey B cells *in vitro* in different matrices: Possible inhibitory effect of IgG. *Int. Immunopharmacol.* **2004**, *4*, 1117–1124.

43. Matsumiya, S.; Yamaguchi, Y.; Saito, J.; Nagano, M.; Sasakawa, H.; Otaki, S.; Satoh, M.; Shitara, K.; Kato, K. Structural comparison of fucosylated and nonfucosylated Fc fragments of human immunoglobulin G1. *J. Mol. Biol.* **2007**, *368*, 767–779.

44. Ferrara, C.; Stuart, F.; Sondermann, P.; Brünker, P.; Umaña, P. The carbohydrate at FcgammaRIIIa Asn-162. An element required for high affinity binding to non-fucosylated IgG glycoforms. *J. Biol. Chem.* **2006**, *281*, 5032–5036.

45. Iida, S.; Misaka, H.; Inoue, M.; Shibata, M.; Nakano, R.; Yamane-Ohnuki, N.; Wakitani, M.; Yano, K.; Shitara, K.; Satoh, M. Nonfucosylated therapeutic IgG1 antibody can evade the inhibitory effect of serum immunoglobulin G on antibody-dependent cellular cytotoxicity through its high binding to FcgammaRIIIa. *Clin. Cancer Res.* **2006**, *12*, 2879–2887.

46. Shitara, K. Potelligent antibodies as next generation therapeutic antibodies. *Yakugaku Zasshi* **2009**, *129*, 3–9.

47. Wang, W. Instability, stabilization, and formulation of liquid protein pharmaceuticals. *Int. J. Pharm.* **1999**, *185*, 29–88.

48. Mahler, H.C.; Friess, W.; Grauschopf, U.; Kiese, S. Protein aggregation: Pathways, induction factors and analysis. *J. Pharm. Sci.* **2009**, *98*, 2909–3934.

49. Daugherty, A.L.; Mrsny, R.J. Formulation and delivery issues for monoclonal antibody therapeutics. *Adv. Drug Deliv. Rev.* **2006**, *58*, 686–706.

50. Parkins, D.A.; Lashmar, U.T. The formulation of biopharmaceutical products. *Pharm. Sci. Technol. Today* **2000**, *3*, 129–137.

51. Narhi, L.O.; Jiang, Y.; Cao, S.; Benedek, K.; Shnek, D. A critical review of analytical methods for subvisible and visible particles. *Curr. Pharm. Biotechnol.* **2009**, *10*, 373–381.

52. Das, T.K. Protein particulate detection issues in biotherapeutics development—Current status. *AAPS PharmSciTech.* **2012**, *13*, 732–746.

53. Karshikoff, A. *Non-Covalent Interactions in Proteins*, 1st ed.; Imperial College Press: London, UK, 2006.

54. Andya, J.D.; Hsu, C.C.; Shire, S.J. Mechanisms of aggregate formation and carbohydrate excipient stabilization of lyophilized humanized monoclonal antibody formulations. *AAPS PharmSci.* **2003**, *5*, E10.

55. Malencik, D.A.; Anderson, S.R. Dityrosine as a product of oxidative stress and fluorescent probe. *Amino Acids* **2003**,*25*, 233–247.

56. Hawe, A.; Kasperb, J.C.; Friessb, W.; Jiskoota, W. Structural properties of monoclonal antibody aggregates induced by freeze-thawing and thermal stress. *Eur. J. Pharm. Sci.* **2009**, *38*, 79–87.

57. Kreilgaard, L.; Jones, L.S.; Randolph, T.W.; Frokjaer, S.; Flink, J.M.; Manning, M.C.; Carpenter, J.F. Effect of Tween 20 on freeze-thawing- and agitation-induced aggregation of recombinant human factor XIII. *J. Pharm. Sci.* **1998**, *87*, 1597–1603.

58. Strambini, G.B.; Gonnelli, M. Protein stability in ice. *Biophys. J.* **2007**, *92*, 2131–2138.

59. Pikal-Cleland, K.A.; Cleland, J.L.; floatdoquy, T.J.; Carpenter, J.F. Effect of glycine on pH changes and protein stability

during freeze-thawing in phosphate buffer systems. *J. Pharm. Sci.* **2002**, *91*, 1969–1979.

60. Kueltzo, L.A.; Wang, W.; Randolph, T.W.; Carpenter, J.F. Effects of solution conditions, processing parameters, and container materials on aggregation of a monoclonal antibody during freeze-thawing. *J. Pharm. Sci.* **2008**, *97*, 1801–1812.

61. Schreiber, G. Kinetic studies of protein-protein interactions. *Curr. Opin. Struct. Biol.* **2002**, *12*, 41–47.

62. Cleland, J.L.; Powell, M.F.; Shire, S.J. The development of stable protein formulations: A close look at protein aggregation, deamidation, and oxidation. *Crit. Rev. Ther. Drug Carrier. Syst.* **1993**, *10*, 307–377.

63. Tyler-Cross, R.; Schirch, V. Effects of amino acid sequence, buffers, and ionic strength on the rate and mechanism of deamidation of asparagine residues in small peptides. *J. Biol. Chem.* **1991**, *266*, 22549–22556.

64. Son, K.; Kwon, C. Stabilization of human epidermal growth factor (hEGF) in aqueous formulation. *Pharm. Res.* **1995**,*12*, 451–454.

65. Daniel, R.M.; Dines, M.; Petach, H.H. The denaturation and degradation of stable enzymes at high temperatures.*Biochem. J.* **1996**, *317*, 1–11.

66. Strickley, R.G.; Anderson, B.D. Solid-state stability of human insulin. I. Mechanism and the effect of water on the kinetics of degradation in lyophiles from pH 2-5 solutions. *Pharm. Res.* **1996**, *13*, 1142–1153.

67. Cacia, J.; Keck, R.; Presta, L.G.; Frenz, J. Isomerization of an aspartic acid residue in the complementarity-determining regions of a recombinant antibody to human IgE: Identification and effect on binding affinity. *Biochemistry* **1996**, *35*, 1897–1903.

68. Li, S.; Schoneich, C.; Borchardt, R.T. Chemical pathways of peptide degradation. VIII. Oxidation of methionine in small model peptides by prooxidant/transition metal ion

systems: Influence of selective scavengers for reactive oxygen intermediates. *Pharm. Res.* **1995**, *12*, 348–355.

69. Powell, M.F. A compendium and hydropathy/flexibility analysis of common reactive sites in proteins: Reactivity at Asn, Asp, Gln, and Met motifs in neutral pH solution. In *Formulation, Characterization, and Stability of Protein Drugs*; Pearlman, R., Wang, Y.J., Eds.; Plenum Press: New York, NY, USA, 1996; pp. 1–140.

70. Brange, J.; Langkj, L.; Havelund, S.; Vølund, A. Chemical stability of insulin. 1. Hydrolytic degradation during storage of pharmaceutical preparations. *Pharm. Res.* **1992**, *9*, 715–726.

71. Manning, M.C.; Patel, K.; Borchardt, R.T. Stability of protein pharmaceuticals. *Pharm. Res.* **1989**, *6*, 903–918.

72. Kroon, D.J.; Baldwin-Ferro, A.; Lalan, P. Identification of sites of degradation in a therapeutic monoclonal antibody by peptide mapping. *Pharm. Res.* **1992**, *9*, 1386–1393.

73. Li, S.; Nguyen, T.H.; Schoneich, C.; Borchardt, R.T. Aggregation and precipitation of human relaxin induced by metal-catalyzed oxidation. *Biochemistry* **1995**, *34*, 5762–5772.

74. Lam, X.M.; Yang, J.Y.; Cleland, J.L. Antioxidants for prevention of methionine oxidation in recombinant monoclonal antibody HER2. *J. Pharm. Sci.* **1997**, *86*, 1250–1255.

75. Ha, E.; Wang, W.; Wang, Y.J. Peroxide formation in polysorbate 80 and protein stability. *J. Pharm. Sci.* **2002**, *91*, 2252–2264.

76. Knepp, V.M.; Whatley, J.L.; Muchnik, A.; Calderwood, T.S. Identification of antioxidants for prevention of peroxide-mediated oxidation of recombinant human ciliary neurotrophic factor and recombinant human nerve growth factor.*PDA J. Pharm. Sci. Technol.* **1996**, *50*, 163–171.

77. Liu, J.L.; Lu, K.V.; Eris, T.; Katta, V.; Westcott, K.R.; Narhi, L.O.; Lu, H.S. *In vitro* methionine oxidation of recombinant human leptin. *Pharm. Res.* **1998**, *15*, 632–640.

78. Fransson, J.; Florin-Robertsson, E.; Axelsson, K.; Nyhlén, C. Oxidation of human insulin-like growth factor I in formulation studies: Kinetics of methionine oxidation in aqueous solution and in solid state. *Pharm. Res.* **1996**, *13*, 1252–1257.

79. Shahrokh, Z.; Eberlein, G.; Buckley, D.; Paranandi, M.V.; Aswad, D.W.; Stratton, P.; Mischak, R.; Wang, Y.J. Major degradation products of basic fibroblast growth factor: Detection of succinimide and iso-aspartate in place of aspartate. *Pharm. Res.* **1994**, *11*, 936–944.

80. Kamat, M.S.; Tolman, G.L.; Brown, J.M. Formulation development of an antifibrin monoclonal antibody radiopharmaceutical. *Pharm. Biotechnol.* **1996**, *9*, 343–364.

81. Tous, G.I.; Wei, Z.; Feng, J.; Bilbulian, S.; Bowen, S.; Smith, J.; Strouse, R.; McGeehan, P.; Casas-Finet, J.; Schenerman, M.A. Characterization of a novel modification to monoclonal antibodies: Thioether cross-link of heavy and light chains. *Anal. Chem.* **2005**, *77*, 2675–2682.

82. Hermeling, S.; Crommelin, D.J.A.; Schellekens, H.; Jiskoot, W. Structure-immunogenicity relationships of therapeutic proteins. *Pharm. Res.* **2004**, *21*, 897–903.

83. Schellekens, H. Immunogenicity of therapeutic proteins: Clinical implications and future prospects. *Clin. Ther.* **2002**,*24*, 1720–1740; discussion 1719.

84. Casadevall, N.; Nataf, J.; Viron, B.; Kolta, A.; Kiladjian, J.-J.; Martin-Dupont, P.; Michaud, P.; Papo, T.; Ugo, V.; Teyssandier, I.; *et al.* Pure red-cell aplasia and antierythropoietin antibodies in patients treated with recombinant erythropoietin. *N. Engl. J. Med.* **2002**, *346*, 469–475.

85. Joubert, M.K.; Hokom, M.; Eakin, C.; Zhou, L.; Deshpande, M.; Baker, M.P.; Goletz, T.J.; Kerwin, B.A.; Chirmule, N.; Narhi, L.O.; *et al.* Highly aggregated antibody therapeutics can enhance the *in vitro* innate and late-stage T-cell immune responses. *J. Biol. Chem.* **2012**, *287*, 25266–25279.

86. Demeule, B.; Gurny, R.; Arvinte, T. Where disease pathogenesis meets protein formulation: Renal deposition

of immunoglobulin aggregates. *Eur. J. Pharm. Biopharm.* **2006**, *62*, 121–130.

87. USP, *General Chapters: <788> Particulate Matter in Injections*; Pharmacopeial Forum: Maryland, MD, USA, 2009; pp. SP32–NF27.

88. Harris, R.J.; Kabakoff, B.; Macchi, F.D.; Shen, F.J.; Kwong, M.; Andya, J.D.; Shire, S.J.; Bjork, N.; Totpal, K.; Chen, A.B. Identification of multiple sources of charge heterogeneity in a recombinant antibody. *J. Chromatogr. B Biomed. Sci. Appl.* **2001**, *752*, 233–245.

89. Hochuli, E. Interferon immunogenicity: Technical evaluation of interferon-alpha 2a. *J. Interferon. Cytokine Res.* **1997**, *17*, S15–S21.

90. Laue, T.M.; Shah, B.; Ridgeway, T.M.; Pelletier, S.L. Computer-aided Interpretation of Sedimentation Data for Proteins. In *Analytical Ultracentrifugation in Biochemistry and Polymer Science*; Harding, S.E., Rowe, A.J., Horton, J.C., Eds.; Royal Society of Chemistry: Cambridge, UK, 1992; pp. 90–125.

91. Hartmann, W.K.; Saptharishi, N.; Yang, X.Y.; Mitra, G.; Soman, G. Characterization and analysis of thermal denaturation of antibodies by size exclusion high-performance liquid chromatography with quadruple detection. *Anal. Biochem.* **2004**, *325*, 227–239.

92. Chiti, F.; van Nuland, N.A.J.; Taddei, N.; Magherini, F.; Stefani, M.; Ramponi, G.; Dobson, C.M. Conformational stability of muscle acylphosphatase: The role of temperature, denaturant concentration, and pH. *Biochemistry* **1998**, *37*, 1447–1455.

93. PharmaCircle. Available online: www.pharmacircle.com (accessed on 1 June 2013).

94. Lam, X.M.; Oeswein, O.J.; Ongpipattanakul, B.; Shahrokh, Z.; Weissburg, W.S.; Wong, R.P. Stabilized Antibody Formulation. US Patent CA 2292730, 1998.

95. Johnson, R.E.; Hong, Q.I.; Borgmeyer, J.R.; Kessler, R.K.; Zeng, D.L. Stable pH optimized formulation of a modified antibody. WO Patent WO/2004/019861, 2004.

96. Warne, N.W. Development of high concentration protein biopharmaceuticals: The use of platform approaches in formulation development. *Eur. J. Pharm. Biopharm.* **2011**, *78*, 208–212.

97. Lee, L.S. Stabilized Monomeric Protein Compositions. US Patent 5,656,730, 1997.

98. Worn, A.; Pluckthun, A. Mutual stabilization of VL and VH in single-chain antibody fragments, investigated with mutants engineered for stability. *Biochemistry* **1998**, *37*, 13120–13127.

99. Horbett, T.A. Protein adsorption on biomaterials. In *Biomaterials: Interfacial Phenomena and Applications*; Cooper, S.L., Peppas, N.A., Hoffman, A.S., Ratner, B.D., Eds.; American Chemical Society: Washington DC, USA, 1982; pp. 233–244.

100. Lee, H.J.; McAuley, A.; Schilke, K.F.; McGuire, J. Molecular origins of surfactant-mediated stabilization of protein drugs. *Adv. Drug Deliv. Rev.* **2011**, *63*, 1160–1171.

101. Kerwin, B.A. Polysorbates 20 and 80 used in the formulation of protein biotherapeutics: Structure and degradation pathways. *J. Pharm. Sci.* **2008**, *97*, 2924–2935.

102. Chen, B.; Bautista, R.; Yu, K.; Zapata, G.A.; Mulkerrin, M.G.; Chamow, S.M. Influence of histidine on the stability and physical properties of a fully human antibody in aqueous and solid forms. *Pharm. Res.* **2003**, *20*, 1952–1960.

103. Paborji, M.; Pochopin, N.L.; Coppola, W.P.; Bogardus, J.B. Chemical and physical stability of chimeric L6, a mouse-human monoclonal antibody. *Pharm. Res.* **1994**, *11*, 764–771.

104. McIntosh, K.A.; Charman, W.N.; Charman, S.A. The application of capillary electrophoresis for monitoring effects of excipients on protein conformation. *J. Pharm. Biomed. Anal.* **1998**, *16*, 1097–1105.

105. Li, S.; Patapoff, T.W.; Nguyen, T.H.; Borchardt, R.T. Inhibitory effect of sugars and polyols on the metal-catalyzed oxidation of human relaxin. *J. Pharm. Sci.* **1996**, *85*, 868–872.

106. Li, S.; Patapoff, T.W.; Overcashier, D.; Hsu, C.; Nguyen, T.H.; Borchardt, R.T. Effects of reducing sugars on the chemical stability of human relaxin in the lyophilized state. *J. Pharm. Sci.* **1996**, *85*, 873–877.

107. Ji, J.A.; Zhang, B.; Cheng, W.; John Wang, Y. Methionine, tryptophan, and histidine oxidation in a model protein, PTH: Mechanisms and stabilization. *J. Pharm. Sci.* **2009**, *98*, 4485–4500.

108. Gokarn, Y.R.; Matthew Fesinmeyer, R.; Saluja, A.; Razinkov, V.; Chase, S.F.; Laue, T.M.; Brems, D.N. Effective charge measurements reveal selective and preferential accumulation of anions, but not cations, at the protein surface in dilute salt solutions. *Protein Sci.* **2011**, *20*, 580–587.

109. Fesinmeyer, R.M.; Hogan, S.; Saluja, A.; Brych, S.R.; Kras, E.; Narhi, L.O.; Brems, D.N.; Gokarn, Y.R. Effect of ions on agitation- and temperature-induced aggregation reactions of antibodies. *Pharm. Res.* **2009**, *26*, 903–913.

110. Laue, T. Proximity energies: A framework for understanding concentrated solutions. *J. Mol. Recognit.* **2012**, *25*, 165–173.

111. Adams, G.P.; Schier, R.; McCall, A.M.; Crawford, R.S.; Wolf, E.J.; Weiner, L.M.; Marks, J.D. Prolonged *in vivo* tumour retention of a human diabody targeting the extracellular domain of human HER2/neu. *Br. J. Cancer* **1998**, *77*, 1405–1412.

112. Di Fede, G.; Bronte, G.; Rizzo, S.; Cervetto, C.R.; Cocorullo, G.; Gulotta, G.; Bazan, V.; Russo, A. Monoclonal antibodies and antibody fragments: State of the art and future perspectives in the treatment of non-haematological tumors.*Expert Opin. Biol. Ther.* **2011**, *11*, 1433–1445.

113. Stockwin, L.H.; Holmes, S. Antibodies as therapeutic agents: Vive la renaissance! *Expert Opin. Biol. Ther.* **2003**, *3*, 1133–1152.

114. Bookbinder, L.H.; Hofera, A.; Hallera, M.F.; Zepedab, M.L.; Kellera, G.-A.; Lima, J.E.; Edgingtonc, T.S.; Shepardd, H.M.; Pattone, J.S.; Frosta, G.I. A recombinant human enzyme for enhanced interstitial transport of therapeutics. *J. Control Release* **2006**, *114*, 230–241.

115. Gatlin, L.A.; Gatlin, C.A.B. Formulation and administration techniques to minimize injection pain and tissue damage associated with parenteral products. In *Injectable Drug Development: Techniques to Reduce Pain and Irritation*; Gapta, P.K., Brazeau, G.A., Eds.; Interpharm Press: Denver, CO, USA, 1999; pp. 401–425.

116. Yu, A.W.; Leung, C.B.; Li, P.K.; Lui, S.F.; Lai, K.N. Pain perception following subcutaneous injections of citrate-buffered and phosphate-buffered epoetin alpha. *Int. J. Artif. Organs.* **1998**, *21*, 41–43.

117. Kappelgaard, A.M.; Bojesen, A.; Skydsgaard, K.; Sjögren, I.; Laursen, T. Liquid growth hormone: Preservatives and buffers. *Horm. Res.* **2004**, *62*, 98–103.

118. Laursen, T.; Hansen, B.; Fisker, S. Pain perception after subcutaneous injections of media containing different buffers.*Basic Clin. Pharmacol. Toxicol.* **2006**, *98*, 218–221.

119. Hall, D.; Minton, A.P. Macromolecular crowding: Qualitative and semiquantitative successes, quantitative challenges.*Biochim. Biophys. Acta* **2003**, *1649*, 127–139.

120. Rivas, G.; Minton, A.P. Non-ideal tracer sedimentation equilibrium: A powerful tool for the characterization of macromolecular interactions in crowded solutions. *J. Mol. Recognit.* **2004**, *17*, 362–367.

121. Yadav, S.; Laue, T.M.; Kalonia, D.S.; Singh, S.N.; Shire, S.J. The influence of charge distribution on self-association and viscosity behavior of monoclonal antibody solutions. *Mol. Pharm.* **2012**, *9*, 791–802.

122. Schein, C.H. Solubility as a function of protein structure and solvent components. *Biotechnology* **1990**, *8*, 308–317.

123. Shire, S.J.; Shahrokh, Z.; Liu, J. Challenges in the development of high protein concentration formulations. *J. Pharm. Sci.* **2004**, *93*, 1390–1402.

124. Sukumar, M.; Doyle, B.L.; Combs, J.L.; Pekar, A.H. Opalescent appearance of an IgG1 antibody at high concentrations and its relationship to noncovalent association. *Pharm. Res.* **2004**, *21*, 1087–1093.

125. Cromwell, M.E.M.; Carpenter, J.F.; Scherer, T.; Randolph, T.J. Opalescence in Antibody Formulations is a Solution Critical Phenomenon. In Proceseedings of the 236th ACS National Meeting, Philadelphia, PA, USA, 2008.

126. Saluja, A.; Kalonia, D.S. Nature and consequences of protein-protein interactions in high protein concentration solutions. *Int. J. Pharm.* **2008**, *358*, 1–15.

127. Zhou, H.X.; Rivas, G.; Minton, A.P. Macromolecular crowding and confinement: Biochemical, biophysical, and potential physiological consequences. *Annu. Rev. Biophys.* **2008**, *37*, 375–397.

128. Shiloach, J.; Martin, N.; Moes, H. Tangential flow filtration. *Adv. Biotechnol. Processes.* **1988**, *8*, 97–125.

129. Shire, S.J.; Liu, J.; Friess, W.; Jörg, S.; Mahler, H.-C. High-concentration antibody formulations. In *Formulation and Process Development Strategies for Manufacturing Biopharmaceuticals*; Hershenson, F.J.S., Ed.; John Wiley & Sons, Inc: Hoboken, NJ, USA, 2010.

130. Friess, H.; Langrehr, J.M.; Oettle, H.; Raedle, J.; Niedergethmann, M.; Dittrich, C.; Hossfeld, D.K.; Stöger, H.; Neyns, B.; Herzog, P.; *et al.* A randomized multi-center phase II trial of the angiogenesis inhibitor Cilengitide (EMD 121974) and gemcitabine compared with gemcitabine alone in advanced unresectable pancreatic cancer. *BMC Cancer* **2006**, *6*, 285.

131. Rathore, N.; Pranay, P.; Bernacki, J.; Eu, B.; Ji, W.; Walls, E. Characterization of protein rheology and delivery forces

for combination products. *J. Pharm. Sci.* **2012**, *101*, 4472–4480.

132. Harris, R.J.; Shire, S.J.; Winter, C. Commercial manufacturing scale formulation and analytical characterization of therapeutic recombinant antibodies. *Drug Develop. Res.* **2004**, *61*, 137–154.

133. Jimenez, M.; Rivas, G.; Minton, A.P. Quantitative characterization of weak self-association in concentrated solutions of immunoglobulin G via the measurement of sedimentation equilibrium and osmotic pressure. *Biochemistry* **2007**, *46*, 8373–8378.

134. Minton, A.P. Analytical centrifugation with preparative ultracentrifuges. *Anal. Biochem.* **1989**, *176*, 209–216.

135. Kroe, R.R.; Laue, T.M. NUTS and BOLTS: Applications of fluorescence-detected sedimentation. *Anal. Biochem.* **2009**,*390*, 1–13.

136. MacGregor, I.K.; Anderson, A.L.; Laue, T.M. Fluorescence detection for the XLI analytical ultracentrifuge. *Biophys. Chem.* **2004**, *108*, 165–185.

137. Scherer, T.; Kanai, S.; Liu, J.; Shire, S. Characterization of monoclonal antibodies at high concentrations by light scattering. In Proceedings of AAPS National Biotechnology Conference, San Diego, CA, USA, 2007.

138. Ross, P.D.; Minton, A.P. Analysis of non-ideal behavior in concentrated hemoglobin solutions. *J. Mol. Biol.* **1977**, *112*, 437–452.

139. Yousef, M.A.; Datta, R.; Rodgers, V.G.J. Free-Solvent Model of Osmotic Pressure Revisited: Application to Concentrated IgG Solution under Physiological Conditions. *J. Colloid. Interface Sci.* **1998**, *197*, 108–118.

140. Paliwal, A.; Asthagiri, D.; Abras, D.; Lenhoff, A.M.; Paulaitis, M.E. Light-scattering studies of protein solutions: Role of hydration in weak protein-protein interactions. *Biophys. J.* **2005**, *89*, 1564–1573.

141. Neal, B.L.; Asthagiri, D.; Lenhoff, A.M. Molecular origins of osmotic second virial coefficients of proteins. *Biophys. J.* **1998**, *75*, 2469–2477.

142. Salinas, B.A.; Sathish, H.A.; Bishop, S.M.; Harn, N.; Carpenter, J.F.; Randolph, T.W. Understanding and modulating opalescence and viscosity in a monoclonal antibody formulation. *J. Pharm. Sci.* **2010**, *99*, 82–93.

143. Saito, S.; Hasegawa, J.; Kobayashi, N.; Kishi, N.; Uchiyama, S.; Fukui, K. Behavior of monoclonal antibodies: Relation between the second virial coefficient (B (2)) at low concentrations and aggregation propensity and viscosity at high concentrations. *Pharm. Res.* **2012**, *29*, 397–410.

144. Attri, A.K.; Minton, A.P. New methods for measuring macromolecular interactions in solution via static light scattering: Basic methodology and application to nonassociating and self-associating proteins. *Anal. Biochem.* **2005**,*337*, 103–110.

145. Alford, J.R.; Kendrick, B.S.; Carpenter, J.F.; Randolph, T.W. Measurement of the second osmotic virial coefficient for protein solutions exhibiting monomer-dimer equilibrium. *Anal. Biochem.* **2008**, *377*, 128–133.

146. Some, D.; Kenrick, S. Characterization of protein-protein interactions via static and dynamic light scattering, in rotein interaction. In *Protein Interactions*; Cai, J., Ed.; InTech.: Rijeka, Croatia, 2012.

147. Le Brun, V.; Friess, W.; Bassarab, S.; Garidel, P. Correlation of protein-protein interactions as assessed by affinity chromatography with colloidal protein stability: A case study with lysozyme. *Pharm. Dev. Technol.* **2010**, *15*, 421–430.

148. Le Brun, V.; Friess, W.; Bassarab, S.; Mühlau, S.; Garidel, P. A critical evaluation of self-interaction chromatography as a predictive tool for the assessment of protein-protein interactions in protein formulation development: A case study of a therapeutic monoclonal antibody. *Eur. J. Pharm. Biopharm.* **2010**, *75*, 16–25.

149. Deszczynski, M.; Harding, S.E.; Winzor, D.J. Negative second virial coefficients as predictors of protein crystal growth: Evidence from sedimentation equilibrium studies that refutes the designation of those light scattering parameters as osmotic virial coefficients. *Biophys. Chem.* **2006**, *120*, 106–113.

150. Tessier, P.M.; Lenhoff, A.M.; Sandler, S.I. Rapid measurement of protein osmotic second virial coefficients by self-interaction chromatography. *Biophys. J.* **2002**, *82*, 1620–1631.

151. Saluja, A.; Matthew Fesinmeyer, R.; Hogan, S.; Brems, D.N. Diffusion and sedimentation interaction parameters for measuring the second virial coefficient and their utility as predictors of protein aggregation. *Biophys. J.* **2010**, *99*, 2657–2665.

152. Harding, S.E.; Johnson, P. The concentration-dependence of macromolecular parameters. *Biochem. J.* **1985**, *231*, 543–547.

153. Connolly, B.D.; Petry, C.; Yadav, S.; Demeule, B.; Ciaccio, N.; Moore, J.M.R.; Shire, S.J.; Gokarn, Y.R. Weak interactions govern the viscosity of concentrated antibody solutions: High-throughput analysis using the diffusion interaction parameter. *Biophys. J.* **2012**, *103*, 69–78.

154. Winzor, D.J.; Jones, S.; Harding, S.E. Determination of protein charge by capillary zone electrophoresis. *Anal. Biochem.* **2004**, *333*, 225–229.

155. Durant, J.A.; Chen, C.; Laue, T.M.; Moody, T.P.; Allison, S.A. Use of T4 lysozyme charge mutants to examine electrophoretic models. *Biophys. Chem.* **2002**, *101–102*, 593–609.

156. WYATT. Available online: www.wyatt.com (accessed on 1 June 2013).

157. Minton, A.P. Molecular crowding: Analysis of effects of high concentrations of inert cosolutes on biochemical equilibria and rates in terms of volume exclusion. *Methods Enzymol.* **1998**, *295*, 127–149.

158. Janthur, W.-D.; Cantoni, N.; Mamot, C. Drug Conjugates Such as Antibody Drug Conjugates (ADCs), Immunotoxins and Immunoliposomes Challenge Daily Clinical Practice. *Int. J. Mol. Sci.* **2012**, *13*, 16020–16045.

159. Adair, J.R.; Howard, P.W.; Hartley, J.A.; Williams, D.G.; Chester, K.A. Antibody-drug conjugates—A perfect synergy.*Expert Opin. Biol. Ther.* **2012**, *12*, 1191–1206.

160. Sievers, E.L.; Senter, P.D. Antibody-drug conjugates in cancer therapy. *Annu. Rev. Med.* **2013**, *64*, 15–29.

161. Sutherland, M.S.; Sanderson, R.J.; Gordon, K.A.; Andreyka, J.; Cerveny, C.G.; Yu, C.; Lewis, T.S.; Meyer, D.L.; Zabinski, R.F.; Doronina, S.O.; *et al.* Lysosomal trafficking and cysteine protease metabolism confer target-specific cytotoxicity by peptide-linked anti-CD30-auristatin conjugates. *J. Biol. Chem.* **2006**, *281*, 10540–10547.

162. Okeley, N.M.; Miyamoto, J.B.; Zhang, X.; Sanderson, R.J.; Benjamin, D.R.; Sievers, E.L.; Senter, P.D.; Alley, S.C. Intracellular activation of SGN-35, a potent anti-CD30 antibody-drug conjugate. *Clin. Cancer Res.* **2010**, *16*, 888–897.

163. Lam, K.C.L.; Rajaraman, G. Assessment of P-glycoprotein substrate and inhibition potential of test compounds in MDR1-transfected MDCK cells. *Curr. Protoc. Pharmacol.* **2012**.

164. Krech, T.; Scheuerera, E.; Geffers, R.; Kreipe, H.; Lehmann, U.; Christgen, M. ABCB1/MDR1 contributes to the anticancer drug-resistant phenotype of IPH-926 human lobular breast cancer cells. *Cancer Lett.* **2012**, *315*, 153–160.

165. Bidwell, G.L., 3rd; Davis, A.N.; Fokt, I.; Priebe, W.; Raucher, D. A thermally targeted elastin-like polypeptide-doxorubicin conjugate overcomes drug resistance. *Invest. New Drugs* **2007**, *25*, 313–326.

166. Hughes, B. Antibody-drug conjugates for cancer: Poised to deliver? *Nat. Rev. Drug Discov.* **2010**, *9*, 665–667.

167. Barginear, M.F.; John, V.; Budman, D.R. Trastuzumab-DM1: A clinical update of the novel antibody-drug conjugate for HER2-overexpressing breast cancer. *Mol. Med.* **2013**, *18*, 1473–1479.

168. Rowland, G.F.; O'Neill, G.J.; Davies, D.A. Suppression of tumour growth in mice by a drug-antibody conjugate using a novel approach to linkage. *Nature* **1975**, *255*, 487–488.

169. Beck, A.; Lambert, J.; Sun, M.; Lin, K. Fourth World Antibody-Drug Conjugate Summit: February 29-March 1, 2012, Frankfurt, Germany. *MAbs* **2012**, *4*, 637–647.

170. Xie, H.; Audette, C.; Hoffee, M.; Lambert, J.M.; Blättler, W.A. Pharmacokinetics and biodistribution of the antitumor immunoconjugate, cantuzumab mertansine (huC242-DM1), and its two components in mice. *J. Pharmacol. Exp. Ther.* **2004**, *308*, 1073–1082.

171. Ducry, L.; Stump, B. Antibody-drug conjugates: Linking cytotoxic payloads to monoclonal antibodies. *Bioconjug. Chem.* **2010**, *21*, 5–13.

172. Dosio, F.; Brusa, P.; Cattel, L. Immunotoxins and anticancer drug conjugate assemblies: The role of the linkage between components. *Toxins (Basel)* **2011**, *3*, 848–883.

173. Hamblett, K.J.; Senter, P.D.; Chace, D.F.; Sun, M.M.C.; Lenox, J.; Cerveny, C.G.; Kissler, K.M.; Bernhardt, S.X.; Kopcha, A.K.; Zabinski, R.F. Effects of drug loading on the antitumor activity of a monoclonal antibody drug conjugate. *Clin. Cancer Res.* **2004**, *10*, 7063–7070.

174. Le, L.N.; Moore, J.M.R.; Ouyang, J.; Chen, X.; Nguyen, M.D.H.; Galush, W.J. Profiling antibody drug conjugate positional isomers: A system-of-equations approach. *Anal. Chem.* **2012**, *84*, 7479–7486.

175. Liu, H.; Chumsae, C.; Gaza-Bulseco, G.; Hurkmans, K.; Radziejewski, C.H. Ranking the susceptibility of disulfide bonds in human IgG1 antibodies by reduction, differential alkylation, and LC-MS analysis. *Anal. Chem.* **2010**, *82*, 5219–5226.

176. Sun, M.M.; Beam, K.S.; Cerveny, C.G.; Hamblett, K.J.; Blackmore, R.S.; Torgov, M.Y.; Handley, F.G.M.; Ihle, N.C.; Senter, P.D.; Alley, S.C. Reduction-alkylation strategies for the modification of specific monoclonal antibody disulfides. *Bioconjug. Chem.* **2005**, *16*, 1282–1290.

177. Dornan, D.; Bennett, F.; Chen, Y.; Dennis, M.; Eaton, D.; Elkins, K.; French, D.; Go, M.A.T.; Jack, A.; Junutula, J.R.; *et al.* Therapeutic potential of an anti-CD79b antibody-drug conjugate, anti-CD79b-vc-MMAE, for the treatment of non-Hodgkin lymphoma. *Blood* **2009**, *114*, 2721–2729.

178. Junutula, J.R.; Raab, H.; Clark, S.; Bhakta, S.; Leipold, D.D.; Weir, S.; Chen, Y.; Simpson, M.; Tsai, S.P.; Dennis, M.S.; *et al.* Site-specific conjugation of a cytotoxic drug to an antibody improves the therapeutic index. *Nat. Biotechnol.* **2008**,*26*, 925–932.

179. Shen, B.Q.; Xu, K.; Liu, L.; Raab, H.; Bhakta, S.; Kenrick, M.; Parsons-Reponte, K.L.; Tien, J.; Yu, S.-F.; Mai, E.; *et al.* Conjugation site modulates the *in vivo* stability and therapeutic activity of antibody-drug conjugates. *Nat. Biotechnol.***2012**, *30*, 184–189.

180. Axup, J.Y.; Bajjuri, K.M.; Ritland, M.; Hutchinsa, B.M.; Kima, C.H.; Kazane, S.A. ; Halder, R.; Forsyth, J.S.; Santidrian, A.F.; Stafin, K.; *et al.* Synthesis of site-specific antibody-drug conjugates using unnatural amino acids. *Proc. Natl. Acad. Sci. USA* **2012**, *109*, 16101–16106.

181. Presentini, R.; Terrana, B. Influence of the antibody-peroxidase coupling methods on the conjugate stability and on the methodologies for the preservation of the activity in time. *J. Immunoassay* **1995**, *16*, 309–324.

182. Fishkin, N.; Maloney, E.K.; Chari, R.V.J.; Singh, R. A novel pathway for maytansinoid release from thioether linked antibody-drug conjugates (ADCs) under oxidative conditions. *Chem. Commun. (Camb)* **2011**, *47*, 10752–10754.

183. Ryan, C.P.; Smith, M.E.B.; Schumacher, F.F.; Grohmann, D.; Papaioannou, D.; Waksman, G.; Werner, F.; Baker, J.R.; Caddick, S. Tunable reagents for multi-functional

bioconjugation: Reversible or permanent chemical modification of proteins and peptides by control of maleimide hydrolysis. *Chem. Commun. (Camb)* **2011**, *47*, 5452–5454.

184. Doronina, S.O.; Mendelsohn, B.A.; Bovee, T.D.; Cerveny, C.G.; Alley, S.C.; Meyer, D.L.; Oflazoglu, E.; Toki, B.E.; Sanderson, R.J.; Zabinski, R.F.; *et al.* Enhanced activity of monomethylauristatin F through monoclonal antibody delivery: Effects of linker technology on efficacy and toxicity. *Bioconjug. Chem.* **2006**, *17*, 114–124.

185. Dubowchik, G.M.; Radia, S.; Mastalerz, H.; Walker, M.A.; Firestone, R.A.; Dalton King, H.; Hofstead, S.J.; Willner, D.; Lasch, S.J.; Trail, P.A. Doxorubicin immunoconjugates containing bivalent, lysosomally-cleavable dipeptide linkages.*Bioorg. Med. Chem. Lett.* **2002**, *12*, 1529–1532.

186. Sapra, P.; Damelin, M.; DiJoseph, J.; Marquette, K.; Geles, K.G.; Golas, J.; Dougher, M.; Narayanan, B.; Giannakou, A.; Khandke, K.; *et al.* Long-term tumor regression induced by an antibody-drug conjugate that targets 5T4, an oncofetal antigen expressed on tumor-initiating cells. *Mol. Cancer Ther.* **2013**, *12*, 38–47.

187. Polson, A.G.; Calemine-Fenaux, J.; Chan, P.; Chang, W.; Christensen, E.; Clark, S.; de Sauvage, F.J.; Eaton, D.; Elkins, K.; Michael Elliott, J.; *et al.* Antibody-drug conjugates for the treatment of non-Hodgkin's lymphoma: Target and linker-drug selection. *Cancer Res.* **2009**, *69*, 2358–2364.

188. Erickson, H.K.; Park, P.U.; Widdison, W.C.; Kovtun, Y.V.; Garrett, L.M.; Hoffman, K.; Lutz, R.J.; Goldmacher, V.S.; Blättler, W.A. Antibody-maytansinoid conjugates are activated in targeted cancer cells by lysosomal degradation and linker-dependent intracellular processing. *Cancer Res.* **2006**, *66*, 4426–4433.

189. Oflazoglu, E.; Stone, I.J.; Gordon, K.; Wood, C.G.; Repasky, E.A.; Grewal, I.S.; Law, C.-L.; Gerber, H.-P. Potent anticarcinoma activity of the humanized anti-CD70 antibody h1F6 conjugated to the tubulin inhibitor auristatin via an uncleavable linker. *Clin. Cancer Res.* **2008**, *14*, 6171–6180.

190. Hollander, I.; Kunz, A.; Hamann, P.R. Selection of reaction additives used in the preparation of monomeric antibody-calicheamicin conjugates. *Bioconjug. Chem.* **2008**, *19*, 358–361.

191. Wakankar, A.A.; Feeney, M.B.; Rivera, J.; Chen, Y.; Kim, M.; Sharma, V.K.; John Wang, Y. Physicochemical stability of the antibody-drug conjugate Trastuzumab-DM1: Changes due to modification and conjugation processes. *Bioconjug. Chem.* **2010**, *21*, 1588–1595.

192. Quiles, S.; Raisch, K.P.; Sanford, L.L.; Bonner, J.A.; Safavy, A. Synthesis and preliminary biological evaluation of high-drug-load paclitaxel-antibody conjugates for tumor-targeted chemotherapy. *J. Med. Chem.* **2010**, *53*, 586–594.

193. King, H.D.; Yurgaitis, D.; Willner, D.; Firestone, R.A.; Yang, M.B.; Lasch, S.J.; Hellström, K.E.; Trail, P.A. Monoclonal antibody conjugates of doxorubicin prepared with branched peptide linkers: Inhibition of aggregation by methoxytriethyleneglycol chains. *J. Med. Chem.* **2002**, *45*, 4336–4343.

194. Kafi, K.; Betting, D.J.; Yamada, R.E.; Bacica, M.; Steward, K.K.; Timmerman, J.M. Maleimide conjugation markedly enhances the immunogenicity of both human and murine idiotype-KLH vaccines. *Mol. Immunol.* **2009**, *46*, 448–456.

195. Christie, R.J.; Anderson, D.J.; Grainger, D.W. Comparison of hydrazone heterobifunctional cross-linking agents for reversible conjugation of thiol-containing chemistry. *Bioconjug. Chem.* **2010**, *21*, 1779–1787.

196. Bagshawe, K.D. Targeting: The ADEPT story so far. *Curr. Drug Targets* **2009**, *10*, 152–157.

197. Pastan, I.; Hassan, R.; FitzGerald, D.J.; Kreitman, R.J. Immunotoxin treatment of cancer. *Annu. Rev. Med.* **2007**, *58*, 221–237.

198. Vogelzang, N.J.; Porta, C.; Mutti, L. New agents in the management of advanced mesothelioma. *Semin. Oncol.* **2005**, *32*, 336–350.

199. Pavlakis, N.; Vogelzang, N.J. Ranpirnase—An antitumour ribonuclease: Its potential role in malignant mesothelioma.*Expert Opin. Biol. Ther.* **2006**, *6*, 391–399.

200. Rosenblum, M.G.; Barth, S. Development of novel, highly cytotoxic fusion constructs containing granzyme B: Unique mechanisms and functions. *Curr. Pharm. Des.* **2009**, *15*, 2676–2692.

201. Kurschus, F.C.; Kleinschmidt, M.; Fellows, E.; Dornmair, K.; Rudolph, R.; Lilie, H.; Jenne, D.E. Killing of target cells by redirected granzyme B in the absence of perforin. *FEBS Lett.* **2004**, *562*, 87–92.

202. Weidle, U.H.; Georges, G.; Brinkmann, U. Fully human targeted cytotoxic fusion proteins: New anticancer agents on the horizon. *Cancer Genomics Proteomics* **2012**, *9*, 119–133.

203. Larrick, J.W.; Cresswell, P. Modulation of cell surface iron transferrin receptors by cellular density and state of activation. *J. Supramol. Struct.* **1979**, *11*, 579–586.

204. Kordower, J.H.; Charles, V.; Bayer, R.; Bartus, R.T.; Putney, S.; Walus, L.R.; Friden, P.M. Intravenous administration of a transferrin receptor antibody-nerve growth factor conjugate prevents the degeneration of cholinergic striatal neurons in a model of Huntington disease. *Proc. Natl. Acad. Sci. USA* **1994**, *91*, 9077–9080.

205. Granholm, A.C.; Albeck, D.; Bäckman, C.; Curtis, M.; Ebendal, T.; Friden, P.; Henry, M.; Hoffer, B.; Kordower, J.; Rose, G.M.; *et al.* A non-invasive system for delivering neural growth factors across the blood-brain barrier: A review. *Rev. Neurosci.* **1998**, *9*, 31–55.

206. McGrath, J.P.; Cao, X.; Schutz, A.; Lynch, P.; Ebendal, T.; Josephina Coloma, M.; Morrison, S.L.; Putney, S.D. Bifunctional fusion between nerve growth factor and a transferrin receptor antibody. *J. Neurosci. Res.* **1997**, *47*, 123–133.

207. Penichet, M.L.; Kang, Y.-S.; Pardridge, W.M.; Morrison, S.L.; Shin, S.-U. An antibody-avidin fusion protein specific for the transferrin receptor serves as a delivery vehicle for

effective brain targeting: Initial applications in anti-HIV antisense drug delivery to the brain. *J. Immunol.* **1999**, *163*, 4421–4426.

208. Ng, P.P.; Dela Cruz, J.S.; Sorour, D.N.; Stinebaugh, J.M.; Shin, S.-U.; Shin, D.S.; Morrison, S.L.; Penichet, M.L. An anti-transferrin receptor-avidin fusion protein exhibits both strong proapoptotic activity and the ability to deliver various molecules into cancer cells. *Proc. Natl. Acad. Sci. USA* **2002**, *99*, 10706–10711.

209. Xuan, C.; Steward, K.K.; Timmerman, J.M.; Morrison, S.L. Targeted delivery of interferon-alpha via fusion to anti-CD20 results in potent antitumor activity against B-cell lymphoma. *Blood* **2010**, *115*, 2864–2871.

210. Koehn, T.A.; Trimble, L.L.; Alderson, K.L.; Erbe, A.K.; McDowell, K.A.; Grzywacz, B.; Hank, J.A.; Sondel, P.M. Increasing the clinical efficacy of NK and antibody-mediated cancer immunotherapy: Potential predictors of successful clinical outcome based on observations in high-risk neuroblastoma. *Front. Pharmacol.* **2012**, *3*, 91.

211. Lode, H.N.; Xiang, R.; Becker, J.C.; Gillies, S.D.; Reisfel, R.A. Immunocytokines: A promising approach to cancer immunotherapy. *Pharmacol. Ther.* **1998**, *80*, 277–292.

212. Johnson, E.; Dean, S.M.; Sondel, P.M. Antibody-based immunotherapy in high-risk neuroblastoma. *Expert Rev. Mol. Med.* **2007**, *9*, 1–21.

213. Dela Cruz, J.S.; Ryan Trinh, K.; Morrison, S.L.; Penichet, M.L. Recombinant anti-human HER2/neu IgG3-(GM-CSF) fusion protein retains antigen specificity and cytokine function and demonstrates antitumor activity. *J. Immunol.* **2000**,*165*, 5112–5121.

214. Cho, H.M.; Rosenblatt, J.D.; Kang, Y.-S.; Luisa Iruela-Arispe, M.; Morrison, S.L.; Penichet, M.L.; Kwon, Y.-G.; Kim, T.-W.; Webster, K.A.; Nechustan, H. Enhanced inhibition of murine tumor and human breast tumor xenografts using targeted delivery of an antibody-endostatin fusion protein. *Mol. Cancer Ther.* **2005**, *4*, 956–967.

215. Zhang, H.; Lu, S.; Morrison, S.L.; Tomlinson, S. Targeting of functional antibody-decay-accelerating factor fusion proteins to a cell surface. *J. Biol. Chem.* **2001**, *276*, 27290–27295.

216. Fung, V.P. Method for producing recombinant proteins. US Patent 7,294,481, 2007.

217. Sassenfeld, H.M.; Remmele, R.L., Jr.; McCoy, R.E. Increased recovery of active proteins. US Patent 7,157,55, 2007.

218. Bouchon, A.; Facchetti, F.; Weigand, M.A.; Colonna, M. TREM-1 amplifies inflammation and is a crucial mediator of septic shock. *Nature* **2001**, *410*, 1103–1107.

219. Iwai, H.; Kohsaka, H. Blockade of Triggering receptor expressed on myeloid cells-1 as a new therapy of arthritis.*Nihon Rinsho Meneki Gakkai Kaishi* **2012**, *35*, 81–86.

220. Holash, J.; Davis, S.; Papadopoulos, N.; Croll, S.D.; Ho, L.; Russell, M.; Boland, P.; Leidich, R.; Hylton, D.; Burova, E.;*et al.* VEGF-Trap: A VEGF blocker with potent antitumor effects. *Proc. Natl. Acad. Sci. USA* **2002**, *99*, 11393–11398.

221. Peters, R.T.; Low, S.C.; Kamphaus, G.D.; Dumont, J.A.; Amari, J.V.; Lu, Q.; Zarbis-Papastoitsis, G.; Reidy, T.J.; Merricks, E.P.; Nichols, T.C.; *et al.* Prolonged activity of factor IX as a monomeric Fc fusion protein. *Blood* **2010**, *115*, 2057–2064.

222. Hall, M.P.; Gegg, C.; Walker, K.; Spahr, C.; Ortiz, R.; Patel, V.; Yu, S.; Zhang, L.; Lu, H.; DeSilva, B.; *et al.* Ligand-binding mass spectrometry to study biotransformation of fusion protein drugs and guide immunoassay development: Strategic approach and application to peptibodies targeting the thrombopoietin receptor. *AAPS J.* **2010**, *12*, 576–585.

223. Gokarn, Y.R.; Matthew Fesinmeyer, R.; Saluja, A.; Cao, S.; Dankberg, J.; Goetze, A.; Remmele, R.L., Jr.; Narhi, L.O.; Brems, D.N. Ion-specific modulation of protein interactions: Anion-induced, reversible oligomerization of a fusion protein. *Protein Sci.* **2009**, *18*, 169–179.

224. Nisonoff, A.; Rivers, M.M. Recombination of a mixture of univalent antibody fragments of different specificity. *Arch. Biochem. Biophys.* **1961**, *93*, 460–462.

225. May, C.; Sapra, P.; Gerber, H.P. Advances in bispecific biotherapeutics for the treatment of cancer. *Biochem. Pharmacol.***2012**, *84*, 1105–1112.

226. Scott, A.M.; Wolchok, J.D.; Old, L.J. Antibody therapy of cancer. *Nat. Rev. Cancer* **2012**, *12*, 278–287.

227. Vallera, D.A.; Todhunter, D.A.; Kuroki, D.W.; Shu, Y.; Sicheneder, A.; Chen, H. A bispecific recombinant immunotoxin, DT2219, targeting human CD19 and CD22 receptors in a mouse xenograft model of B-cell leukemia/lymphoma. *Clin. Cancer Res.* **2005**, *11*, 3879–3888.

228. Dorvillius, M.; Garambois, V.; Pourquier, D.; Gutowski, M.; Rouanet, P.; Mani, J.-C.; Pugnière, M.; Hynes, N.E.; Pèlegrin, A. Targeting of human breast cancer by a bispecific antibody directed against two tumour-associated antigens: ErbB-2 and carcinoembryonic antigen. *Tumour Biol.* **2002**, *23*, 337–347.

229. Jimenez, X.; Lu, D.; Brennan, L.; Persaud, K.; Liu, M.; Miao, H.; Witte, L.; Zhu, Z. A recombinant, fully human, bispecific antibody neutralizes the biological activities mediated by both vascular endothelial growth factor receptors 2 and 3. *Mol. Cancer Ther.* **2005**, *4*, 427–434.

230. Lu, D.; Zhang, H.; Koo, H.; Tonra, J.; Balderes, P.; Prewett, M.; Corcoran, E.; Mangalampalli, V.; Bassi, R.; Anselma, D.;*et al.* A fully human recombinant IgG-like bispecific antibody to both the epidermal growth factor receptor and the insulin-like growth factor receptor for enhanced antitumor activity. *J. Biol. Chem.* **2005**, *280*, 19665–19672.

231. Tanaka, K.; Isselbacher, K.J.; Khoury, G.; Jay, G. Reversal of oncogenesis by the expression of a major histocompatibility complex class I gene. *Science* **1985**, *228*, 26–30.

232. Hartmann, F.; Renner, C.; Jung, W.; Deisting, C.; Juwana, M.; Eichentopf, B.; Kloft, M.; Pfreundschuh, M. Treatment of

refractory Hodgkin's disease with an anti-CD16/CD30 bispecific antibody. *Blood* **1997**, *89*, 2042–2047.

233. Taylor, R.P.; Sutherland, W.M.; Martin, E.N.; Ferguson, P.J.; Reinagel, M.L.; Gilbert, E.; Lopez, K.; Incardona, N.L.; Ochs, H.D. Bispecific monoclonal antibody complexes bound to primate erythrocyte complement receptor 1 facilitate virus clearance in a monkey model. *J. Immunol.* **1997**, *158*, 842–850.

234. Reinagel, M.L.; Taylor, R.P. Transfer of immune complexes from erythrocyte CR1 to mouse macrophages. *J. Immunol.* **2000**, *164*, 1977–1985.

235. French, R.R.; Penney, C.A.; Browning, A.C.; Stirpe, F.; George, A.J.; Glennie, M.J. Delivery of the ribosome-inactivating protein, gelonin, to lymphoma cells via CD22 and CD38 using bispecific antibodies. *Br. J. Cancer* **1995**, *71*, 986–994.

236. Ford, C.H.; Osborne, P.A.; Rego, B.G.; Mathew, A. Bispecific antibody targeting of doxorubicin to carcinoembryonic antigen-expressing colon cancer cell lines *in vitro* and *in vivo*. *Int. J. Cancer* **2001**, *92*, 851–855.

237. Zhu, H.; Jain, R.K.; Baxter, L.T. Tumor pretargeting for radioimmunodetection and radioimmunotherapy. *J. Nucl. Med.* **1998**, *39*, 65–76.

238. Kipriyanov, S.M.; Le Gall, F. Recent advances in the generation of bispecific antibodies for tumor immunotherapy. *Curr. Opin. Drug Discov. Develop.* **2004**, *7*, 233–242.

239. Mack, M.; Riethmuller, G.; Kufer, P. A small bispecific antibody construct expressed as a functional single-chain molecule with high tumor cell cytotoxicity. *Proc. Natl. Acad. Sci. USA* **1995**, *92*, 7021–7025.

240. Mack, M.; Gruber, R.; Schmidt, S.; Riethmüller, G.; Kufer, P. Biologic properties of a bispecific single-chain antibody directed against 17-1A (EpCAM) and CD3: Tumor cell-dependent T cell stimulation and cytotoxic activity. *J. Immunol.* **1997**, *158*, 3965–39670.

241. Milstein, C.; Cuello, A.C. Hybrid hybridomas and their use in immunohistochemistry. *Nature* **1983**, *305*, 537–540.

242. Staerz, U.D.; Bevan, M.J. Hybrid hybridoma producing a bispecific monoclonal antibody that can focus effector T-cell activity. *Proc. Natl. Acad. Sci. USA* **1986**, *83*, 1453–1457.

243. Lindhofer, H.; Mocikat, R.; Steipe, B.; Thierfelder, S. Preferential species-restricted heavy/light chain pairing in rat/mouse quadromas. Implications for a single-step purification of bispecific antibodies. *J. Immunol.* **1995**, *155*, 219–225.

244. Brennan, M.; Davison, P.F.; Paulus, H. Preparation of bispecific antibodies by chemical recombination of monoclonal immunoglobulin G1 fragments. *Science* **1985**, *229*, 81–83.

245. Merchant, A.M.; Zhu, Z.; Yuan, J.Q.; Goddard, A.; Adams, C.W.; Presta, L.G.; Carter, P. An efficient route to human bispecific IgG. *Nat. Biotechnol.* **1998**, *16*, 677–681.

246. Ridgway, J.B.; Presta, L.G.; Carter, P. 'Knobs-into-holes' engineering of antibody CH3 domains for heavy chain heterodimerization. *Protein Eng.* **1996**, *9*, 617–621.

247. Davis, J.H.; Aperlo, C.; Li, Y.; Kurosawa, E.; Lan, Y.; Lo, K.-M.; Huston, J.S. SEEDbodies: Fusion proteins based on strand-exchange engineered domain (SEED) CH3 heterodimers in an Fc analogue platform for asymmetric binders or immunofusions and bispecific antibodies. *Protein Eng. Des. Sel.* **2010**, *23*, 195–202.

248. Holliger, P.; Prospero, T.; Winter, G. "Diabodies": Small bivalent and bispecific antibody fragments. *Proc. Natl. Acad. Sci. USA* **1993**, *90*, 6444–6448.

249. Kipriyanov, S.M.; Moldenhauer, G.; Schuhmacher, J.; Cochlovius, B.; Von der Lieth, C.-W.; Ronald Matys, E.; Little, M. Bispecific tandem diabody for tumor therapy with improved antigen binding and pharmacokinetics. *J. Mol. Biol.* **1999**,*293*, 41–56.

250. De Jonge, J.; Heirman, C.; de Veerman, M.; Van Meirvenne, S.; Moser, M.; Leo, O.; Thielemans, K. *In vivo* retargeting of T

cell effector function by recombinant bispecific single chain Fv (anti-CD3 x anti-idiotype) induces long-term survival in the murine BCL1 lymphoma model. *J. Immunol.* **1998**, *161*, 1454–1461.

251. Kufer, P.; Lutterbuse, R.; Baeuerle, P.A. A revival of bispecific antibodies. *Trends Biotechnol.* **2004**, *22*, 238–244.

252. Topp, M.S.; Kufer, P.; Gökbuget, N.; Goebeler, M.; Klinger, M.; Neumann, S.; Horst, H.-A.; Raff, T.; Viardot, A.; Schmid, M.; *et al.* Targeted therapy with the T-cell-engaging antibody blinatumomab of chemotherapy-refractory minimal residual disease in B-lineage acute lymphoblastic leukemia patients results in high response rate and prolonged leukemia-free survival. *J. Clin. Oncol.* **2011**, *29*, 2493–2498.

253. Baeuerle, P.A.; Reinhardt, C. Bispecific T-cell engaging antibodies for cancer therapy. *Cancer Res.* **2009**, *69*, 4941–4944.

254. Johnson, S.; Burke, S.; Huang, L.; Gorlatov, S.; Li, H.; Wang, W.; Zhang, W.; Tuaillon, N.; Rainey, J.; Barat, B.; *et al.* Effector cell recruitment with novel Fv-based dual-affinity re-targeting protein leads to potent tumor cytolysis and *in vivo* B-cell depletion. *J. Mol. Biol.* **2010**, *399*, 436–449.

255. Moore, P.A.; Zhang, W.; Jonah Rainey, G.; Burke, S.; Li, H.; Huang, L.; Gorlatov, S.; Veri, M.C.; Aggarwal, S.; Yang, Y.;*et al.* Application of dual affinity retargeting molecules to achieve optimal redirected T-cell killing of B-cell lymphoma. *Blood* **2011**, *117*, 4542–4551.

256. Wu, C.; Ying, H.; Grinnell, C.; Bryant, S.; Miller, R.; Clabbers, A.; Bose, S.; McCarthy, D.; Zhu, R.-R.; Santora, L.; *et al.* Simultaneous targeting of multiple disease mediators by a dual-variable-domain immunoglobulin. *Nat. Biotechnol.***2007**, *25*, 1290–1297.

257. F-star. Available online: www.f-star.com (accessed on 1 June 2013).

258. IMMUNOCORE. Available online: www.immunocore.com (accessed on 1 June 2013).

259. Hartmann, F.; Renner, C.; Jung, W.; da Costa, L.; Tembrink, S.; Held, G.; Sek, A.; König, J.; Bauer, S.; Kloft, M.; Pfreundschuh, M. Anti-CD16/CD30 bispecific antibody treatment for Hodgkin's disease: Role of infusion schedule and costimulation with cytokines. *Clin. Cancer Res.* **2001**, *7*, 1873–1881.

260. Schmitt, M.; Schmitt, A.; Reinhardt, P.; Thess, B.; Manfras, B.; Lindhofer, H.; Riechelmann, H.; Wiesneth, M.; Gronau, S. Opsonization with a trifunctional bispecific (alphaCD3 x alphaEpCAM) antibody results in efficient lysis *in vitro*and *in vivo* of EpCAM positive tumor cells by cytotoxic T lymphocytes. *Int. J. Oncol.* **2004**, *25*, 841–848.

261. Jager, M.; Schoberth, A.; Ruf, P.; Hess, J.; Hennig, M.; Schmalfeldt, B.; Wimberger, P.; Ströhlein, M.; Theissen, B.; Heiss, M.M.; *et al.* Immunomonitoring results of a phase II/III study of malignant ascites patients treated with the trifunctional antibody catumaxomab (anti-EpCAM x anti-CD3). *Cancer Res.* **2012**, *72*, 24–32.

262. Pluen, A.; Boucher, Y.; Ramanujan, S.; McKee, T.D.; Gohongi, T.; di Tomaso, E.; Brown, E.B.; Izumi, Y.; Campbell, R.B.; Berk, D.A.; *et al.* Role of tumor-host interactions in interstitial diffusion of macromolecules: Cranial *vs.* subcutaneous tumors. *Proc. Natl. Acad. Sci. USA* **2001**, *98*, 4628–4633.

263. Khawli, L.A.; Biela, B.; Hu, P.; Epstein, A.L. Comparison of recombinant derivatives of chimeric TNT-3 antibody for the radioimaging of solid tumors. *Hybrid. Hybridomics* **2003**, *22*, 1–9.

264. Tahtis, K.; Lee, F.-T.; Smyth, F.E.; Power, B.E.; Renner, C.; Brechbiel, M.W.; Old, L.J.; Hudson, P.J.; Scott, A.M. Biodistribution properties of (111)indium-labeled C-functionalized *trans*-cyclohexyl diethylenetriaminepentaacetic acid humanized 3S193 diabody and F(ab')(2) constructs in a breast carcinoma xenograft model. *Clin. Cancer Res.* **2001**,*7*, 1061–1072.

265. Thurber, G.M.; Wittrup, K.D. Quantitative spatiotemporal analysis of antibody fragment diffusion and endocytic

consumption in tumor spheroids. *Cancer Res.* **2008**, *68*, 3334–3341.

266. Ottiger, M.; Thiel, M.A.; Feige, U.; Lichtlen, P.; Urech, D.M. Efficient intraocular penetration of topical anti-TNF-alpha single-chain antibody (ESBA105) to anterior and posterior segment without penetration enhancer. *Invest. Ophthalmol. Vis. Sci.* **2009**, *50*, 779–786.

267. Cardoso, R.M.; Zwick, M.B.; Stanfield, R.L.; Kunert, R.; Binley, J.M.; Katinger, H.; Burton, D.R. Broadly neutralizing anti-HIV antibody 4E10 recognizes a helical conformation of a highly conserved fusion-associated motif in gp41.*Immunity* **2005**, *22*, 163–173.

268. Stijlemans, B.; Wyns, L.; Senter, P.; Revets, H.; De Baetselier, P.; Muyldermans, S.; Magez, S. Efficient targeting of conserved cryptic epitopes of infectious agents by single domain antibodies. African trypanosomes as paradigm. *J. Biol. Chem.* **2004**, *279*, 1256–1261.

269. Nuttall, S.D.; Humberstone, K.S.; Krishnan, U.V.; Carmichael, J.A.; Doughty, L.; Hattarki, M.; Coley, A.M.; Casey, J.L.; Anders, R.F.; Foley, M.; *et al.* Selection and affinity maturation of IgNAR variable domains targeting Plasmodium falciparum AMA1. *Proteins* **2004**, *55*, 187–197.

270. Streltsov, V.A.; Varghese, J.N.; Carmichael, J.A.; Irving, R.A.; Hudson, P.J.; Nuttall, S.D. Structural evidence for evolution of shark Ig new antigen receptor variable domain antibodies from a cell-surface receptor. *Proc. Natl. Acad. Sci. USA* **2004**, *101*, 12444–12449.

271. Choudhry, V.; Zhang, M.-Y.; Dimitrova, D.; Prabakaran, P.; Dimitrov, A.S.; Fouts, T.R.; Dimitrov, D.S. Antibody-based inhibitors of HIV infection. *Expert Opin. Biol. Ther.* **2006**, *6*, 523–531.

272. Chen, W.; Dimitrov, D.S. Human monoclonal antibodies and engineered antibody domains as HIV-1 entry inhibitors.*Curr. Opin. HIV AIDS* **2009**, *4*, 112–117.

273. Holliger, P.; Hudson, P.J. Engineered antibody fragments and the rise of single domains. *Nat. Biotechnol.* **2005**, *23*, 1126–1136.

274. Albrecht, H.; Burke, P.A.; Natarajan, A.; Xiong, C.-Y.; Kalicinsky, M.; DeNardo, G.L.; DeNardo, S.J. Production of soluble ScFvs with C-terminal-free thiol for site-specific conjugation or stable dimeric ScFvs on demand. *Bioconjug. Chem.* **2004**, *15*, 16–26.

275. Lu, D.; Jimenez, X.; Zhanga, H.; Atkins, A.; Brennanb, L.; Balderes, P.; Bohlend, P.; Witte, L.; Zhu, Z. Di-diabody: A novel tetravalent bispecific antibody molecule by design. *J. Immunol. Methods* **2003**, *279*, 219–232.

276. Robinson, M.K.; Doss, M.; Shaller, C.; Narayanan, D.; Marks, J.D.; Adler, L.P.; González Trotter, D.E.; Adams, G.P. Quantitative immuno-positron emission tomography imaging of HER2-positive tumor xenografts with an iodine-124 labeled anti-HER2 diabody. *Cancer Res.* **2005**, *65*, 1471–1478.

277. Olafsen, T.; Cheung, C.-W.; Yazaki, P.J.; Li, L.; Sundaresan, G.; Gambhir, S.S.; Sherman, M.A.; Williams, L.E.; Shively, J.E.; Raubitschek, A.A.; *et al.* Covalent disulfide-linked anti-CEA diabody allows site-specific conjugation and radiolabeling for tumor targeting applications. *Protein Eng. Des. Sel.* **2004**, *17*, 21–27.

278. Hu, S.; Shively, L.; Raubitschek, A.; Sherman, M.; Williams, L.E.; Wong, J.Y.C.; Shively, J.E.; Wu, A.M. Minibody: A novel engineered anti-carcinoembryonic antigen antibody fragment (single-chain Fv-CH3) which exhibits rapid, high-level targeting of xenografts. *Cancer Res.* **1996**, *56*, 3055–3061.

279. Nakamura, T.; Peng, K.-W.; Vongpunsawad, S.; Harvey, M.; Mizuguchi, H.; Hayakawa, T.; Cattaneo, R.; Russell, S.J. Antibody-targeted cell fusion. *Nat. Biotechnol.* **2004**, *22*, 331–336.

280. Brignole, C.; Pastorino, F.; Marimpietri, D.; Pagnan, G.; Pistorio, A.; Allen, T.M.; Pistoia, V.; Ponzoni, M. Immune cell-mediated antitumor activities of GD2-targeted liposomal c-myb antisense oligonucleotides containing CpG motifs. *J. Natl. Cancer Inst.* **2004**, *96*, 1171–1180.

281. van Broekhoven, C.L.; Parish, C.R.; Demange, C.; Britton, W.J.; Altin, J.G. Targeting dendritic cells with antigen-containing liposomes: A highly effective procedure for induction of antitumor immunity and for tumor immunotherapy. *Cancer Res.* **2004**, *64*, 4357–4365.

282. Sharma, S.K.; Barbara Pedley, R.; Bhatia, J.; Boxer, G.M.; El-Emir, E.; Qureshi, U.; Tolner, B.; Lowe, H.; Paul Michael, N.; Minton, N.; *et al.* Sustained tumor regression of human colorectal cancer xenografts using a multifunctional mannosylated fusion protein in antibody-directed enzyme prodrug therapy. *Clin. Cancer Res.* **2005**, *11*, 814–825.

283. Cortez-Retamozo, V.; Backmann, N.; Senter, P.D.; Wernery, U.; De Baetselier, P.; Muyldermans, S.; Revets, H. Efficient cancer therapy with a nanobody-based conjugate. *Cancer Res.* **2004**, *64*, 2853–2857.

284. Holt, L.J.; Herring, C.; Jespers, L.S.; Woolven, B.P.; Tomlinson, I.M. Domain antibodies: Proteins for therapy. *Trends Biotechnol.* **2003**, *21*, 484–490.

285. Ryckaert, S.; Pardon, E.; Steyaert, J.; Callewaert, N. Isolation of antigen-binding camelid heavy chain antibody fragments (nanobodies) from an immune library displayed on the surface of Pichia pastoris. *J. Biotechnol.* **2010**, *145*, 93–98.

286. Muyldermans, S.; Baral, T.N.; Cortez Retamozzo, V.; De Baetselier, P.; De Genst, E.; Kinnec, J.; Leonhardt, H.; Magez, S.; Nguyen, V.K.; Revets, H.; *et al.* Camelid immunoglobulins and nanobody technology. *Vet. Immunol. Immunopathol.***2009**, *128*, 178–183.

287. Vandenbroucke, K.; de Haard, H.; Beirnaert, E.; Dreier, T.; Lauwereys, M.; Huyck, L.; Van Huysse, J.; Demetter, P.; Steidler, L.; Remaut, E.; *et al.* Orally administered L. lactis secreting an anti-TNF Nanobody demonstrate efficacy in chronic colitis. *Mucosal. Immunol.* **2010**, *3*, 49–56.

288. Sanz, L.; Blanco, B.; Alvarez-Vallina, L. Antibodies and gene therapy: Teaching old 'magic bullets' new tricks. *Trends Immunol.* **2004**, *25*, 85–91.

289. Afanasieva, T.A.; Wittmer, M.; Vitaliti, A.; Ajmo, M.; Neri, D.; Klemenz, R. Single-chain antibody and its derivatives

directed against vascular endothelial growth factor: Application for antiangiogenic gene therapy. *Gene Ther.* **2003**, *10*, 1850–1859.

290. Blanco, B.; Holliger, P.; Vile, R.G.; Álvarez-Vallina, L. Induction of human T lymphocyte cytotoxicity and inhibition of tumor growth by tumor-specific diabody-based molecules secreted from gene-modified bystander cells. *J. Immunol.* **2003**, *171*, 1070–1077.

291. Jendreyko, N.; Popkov, M.; Beerli, R.R.; Chung, J.; McGavern, D.B.; Rader, C.; Barbas, C.F., III. Intradiabodies, bispecific, tetravalent antibodies for the simultaneous functional knockout of two cell surface receptors. *J. Biol. Chem.* **2003**, *278*, 47812–47819.

292. Grosse-Hovest, L.; Wick, W.; Minoia, R.; Weller, M.; Rammensee, H.-G.; Brem, G.; Jung, G. Supraagonistic, bispecific single-chain antibody purified from the serum of cloned, transgenic cows induces T-cell-mediated killing of glioblastoma cells *in vitro* and *in vivo*. *Int. J. Cancer* **2005**, *117*, 1060–1064.

293. Chambers, R.S. High-throughput antibody production. *Curr. Opin. Chem. Biol.* **2005**, *9*, 46–50.

294. McKeating, J.A.; Gow, J.; Goudsmit, J.; Pearl, L.H.; Mulder, C.; Weiss, R.A. Characterization of HIV-1 neutralization escape mutants. *AIDS* **1989**, *3*, 777–784.

295. Keck, Z.Y.; Li, S.H.; Xia, J.; von Hahn, T.; Balfe, P.; McKeating, J.A.; Witteveldt, J.; Patel, A.H.; Alter, H.; Rice, C.M.; *et al.* Mutations in hepatitis C virus E2 located outside the CD81 binding sites lead to escape from broadly neutralizing antibodies but compromise virus infectivity. *J. Virol.* **2009**, *83*, 6149–6160.

296. Zharikova, D.; Mozdzanowska, K.; Feng, J.; Zhang, M.; Gerhard, W. Influenza type A virus escape mutants emerge *in vivo* in the presence of antibodies to the ectodomain of matrix protein 2. *J. Virol.* **2005**, *79*, 6644–6654.

297. Prabakaran, M.; Prabhu, N.; He, F.; Qian, H.; Ho, H.-T.; Qiang, J.; Meng, T.; Goutama, M.; Kwang, J. Combination therapy

using chimeric monoclonal antibodies protects mice from lethal H5N1 infection and prevents formation of escape mutants. *PLoS One* **2009**, *4*, e5672.

298. Haurum, J.S. Recombinant human polyclonal antibodies: A new class of therapeutic antibodies against viral infections. *Curr. Pharm. Des.* **2006**, *12*, 2007–2015.

299. de Kruif, J.; Bakker, A.B.H.; Marissen, W.E.; Arjen Kramer, R.; Throsby, M.; Rupprecht, C.E.; Goudsmit, J. A human monoclonal antibody cocktail as a novel component of rabies postexposure prophylaxis. *Annu. Rev. Med.* **2007**, *58*, 359–368.

300. Elliott, E.V.; Pindar, A.; Stevenson, F.K.; Stevenson, G.T. Synergistic cytotoxic effects of antibodies directed against different cell surface determinants. *Immunology* **1978**, *34*, 405–409.

301. Hellstrom, I.; Brown, J.P.; Hellstrom, K.E. Monoclonal antibodies to two determinants of melanoma-antigen p97 act synergistically in complement-dependent cytotoxicity. *J. Immunol.* **1981**, *127*, 157–160.

302. Ziegler-Heitbrock, H.W.; Reiter, C.; Trenkmann, J.; Fütterer, A.; Riethmüller, G. Protection of mice against tetanus toxin by combination of two human monoclonal antibodies recognizing distinct epitopes on the toxin molecule.*Hybridoma (Larchmt)* **1986**, *5*, 21–31.

303. Bakker, A.B.; Python, C.; Kissling, C.J.; Pandyad, P.; Marissen, W.E.; Brinka, M.F.; Lagerwerf, F.; Worsta, S.; van Corven, E.; Kostense, S.; *et al.* First administration to humans of a monoclonal antibody cocktail against rabies virus: Safety, tolerability, and neutralizing activity. *Vaccine* **2008**, *26*, 5922–5927.

304. Mascola, J.R.; Louder, M.K.; VanCott, T.C.; Sapan, C.V.; Lambert, J.S.; Muenz, L.R.; Bunow, B.; Birx, D.L.; Robb, M.L. Potent and synergistic neutralization of human immunodeficiency virus (HIV) type 1 primary isolates by hyperimmune anti-HIV immunoglobulin combined with monoclonal antibodies 2F5 and 2G12. *J. Virol.* **1997**, *71*, 7198–7206.

305. Armbruster, C.; Stiegler, G.M.; Vcelar, B.A.; Jäger, W.; Köller, U.; Jilch, R.; Ammann, C.G.; Pruenster, M.; Stoiber, H.; Katinger, H.W.D. Passive immunization with the anti-HIV-1 human monoclonal antibody (hMAb) 4E10 and the hMAb combination 4E10/2F5/2G12. *J. Antimicrob. Chemother.* **2004**, *54*, 915–920.

306. Trkola, A.; Kuster, H.; Rusert, P.; Joos, B.; Fischer, M.; Leemann, C.; Manrique, A.; Huber, M.; Rehr, M.; Oxenius, A.; *et al.* Delay of HIV-1 rebound after cessation of antiretroviral therapy through passive transfer of human neutralizing antibodies. *Nat. Med.* **2005**, *11*, 615–622.

307. Spiridon, C.I.; Ghetie, M.-A.; Uhr, J.; Marches, R.; Li, J.-L.; Shen, G.-L.; Vitetta, E.S. Targeting multiple Her-2 epitopes with monoclonal antibodies results in improved antigrowth activity of a human breast cancer cell line *in vitro* and *in vivo*. *Clin. Cancer Res.* **2002**, *8*, 1720–1730.

308. Strauss, S.J.; Morschhauser, F.; Rech, J.; Repp, R.; Solal-Celigny, P.; Zinzani, P.L.; Engert, A.; Coiffier, B.; Hoelzer, D.F.; Wegener, W.A.; *et al.* Multicenter phase II trial of immunotherapy with the humanized anti-CD22 antibody, epratuzumab, in combination with rituximab, in refractory or recurrent non-Hodgkin's lymphoma. *J. Clin. Oncol.* **2006**, *24*, 3880–3886.

309. Nowakowski, A.; Wang, C.; Powers, D.B.; Amersdorfer, P.; Smith, T.J.; Montgomery, V.A.; Sheridan, R.; Blake, R.; Smith, L.A.; Marks, J.D. Potent neutralization of botulinum neurotoxin by recombinant oligoclonal antibody. *Proc. Natl. Acad. Sci. USA* **2002**, *99*, 11346–11350.

310. Jefferis, R. Glycosylation of recombinant antibody therapeutics. *Biotechnol. Prog.* **2005**, *21*, 11–16.

311. Burton, D.R.; Desrosiers, R.C.; Doms, R.W.; Koff, W.C.; Kwong, P.D.; Moore, J.P.; Nabel, G.J.; Sodronski, J.; Wilson, I.A.; Wyatt, R. HIV vaccine design and the neutralizing antibody problem. *Nat. Immunol.* **2004**, *5*, 233–236.

312. Marasco, W.A.; Sui, J. The growth and potential of human antiviral monoclonal antibody therapeutics. *Nat. Biotechnol.* **2007**, *25*, 1421–1434.

313. Brock, T.D., Ed.; *Milestones in Microbiology; 1556–1940*; ASM Press: Washington DC, USA, 1998.

314. Casadevall, A.; Scharff, M.D. Serum therapy revisited: Animal models of infection and development of passive antibody therapy. *Antimicrob. Agents Chemother.* **1994**, *38*, 1695–1702.

315. Logtenberg, T. Antibody cocktails: Next-generation biopharmaceuticals with improved potency. *Trends Biotechnol.***2007**, *25*, 390–394.

316. Glassy, M.C.; McKnight, M. The rate-limiting step in obtaining human monoclonal antibody drug pharmaceuticals.*Expert Opin. Investig. Drugs* **1995**, *4*, 225–228.

3
CHAPTER

Development of Microencapsulation Delivery System for Long-Term Preservation of Probiotics as Biotherapeutics Agent

Himanshu K. Solanki,[1,2] Dipak D. Pawar,[1] Dushyant A. Shah,[3] Vipul D. Prajapati,[1] Girish K. Jani,[1] Akil M. Mulla,[1] and Prachi M. Thakar[1]

[1]*Department of Pharmaceutics, S.S.R. College of Pharmacy, Sayli-Silvassa Road, Sayli, Silvassa, Dora and Nagar Haveli 396230, India*

[2]*Hemchandracharya North Gujarat University, Patan, Gujarat 384265, India*
[3]*APMC College of Pharmaceutical Education and Research, Motipura, Himmatnagar, Sabarkantha 383001, India*

ABSTRACT

The administration of probiotic bacteria for health benefit has rapidly expanded in recent years, with a global market worth $32.6 billion predicted by 2014. The oral administration of most of the probiotics results in the lack of ability to survive in a high proportion of the harsh conditions of acidity and bile concentration commonly encountered in the gastrointestinal tract of humans. Providing probiotic living cells with a physical barrier against adverse environmental conditions is therefore an approach currently receiving considerable interest. Probiotic encapsulation technology has the potential to protect microorganisms and to deliver them into the gut. However, there are still many challenges to overcome with respect to the microencapsulation process and the conditions prevailing in the gut. This review focuses mainly on the methodological approach of probiotic encapsulation including biomaterials selection and choice of appropriate technology in detailed manner.

1. INTRODUCTION

As described by the Food and Agriculture Association of the United Nations (FAO) and World Health Organization (WHO), probiotic are a group of live microorganisms that, when administered in adequate amounts, confer a health benefit on the host [1]. Probiotic is a term that means "for life" and defined as "live microorganisms that beneficially affect the host's health by improving its microbial balance" [2]. Lactobacillusand Bifidobacteria are the two most common types of microbes which are extensively used as probiotics [2, 3]. The use of probiotic bacterial culture stimulates the growth of preferred microorganisms, crowds out potentially harmful bacteria, and reinforces the body's natural defense mechanisms [4]. Some bacterial strains that have been widely discussed in the literature are outlined in Table 1 along with their therapeutic uses.

Lifestyle and eating habits play an important role in the overall health of individuals. Recently the use of probiotics for health benefits has increased, and hence it has created a huge market worldwide [5]. In the development of effective and safe encapsulated product, it is essential to maintain the adequate number of viable cells during the shelf life of the product as well as during the gastrointestinal (GI) tract transit after consumption [6–10].

Normally, any probiotic product must contain at least 10^6–10^7 cfu of viable probiotic bacteria per g of the product at the time of its consumption to exert beneficial effects on human health [1]. To overcome difficulty during development, microencapsulation technique is utilized to increase the viabilitys; of probiotic also several studies are carried out to investigate their role in different conditions in probiotic exposed [11–18].

Table 1: Clinical studies of appropriate probiotic strains which have convincingly demonstrated their therapeutic effect.

Most appropriate probiotic strain(s)	Therapeutic application	References
Lactobacillus plantarum 299v, *Bacillus coagulans* ATCC no. 31284, and *Lactobacillus acidophilus* L1	Hypercholesterolemia and cardiovascular disease	[33–36]
Lactobacillus rhamnosus GG	Prevention of atopy	[37, 38]
Lactobacillus rhamnosus GG, *Bifidobacterium lactis*, and *Lactobacillus paracasei*	Eczema	[39–44]
Lactobacillus rhamnosus GG, *Bifidobacterium lactis*, and *Lactobacillus paracasei*	Food allergies	[40–49]
Lactobacillus rhamnosus, *Bifidobacterium lactis*, *Lactobacillus johnsonii*, *Lactobacillus rhamnosus*, and; *Lactobacillus acidophilus*	Lowered immunity	[50–60]
Lactobacillus rhamnosus GG, *Saccharomyces cerevisiae*, *Lactobacillus acidophilus*, and *Lactobacillus plantarum* 299v	Antibiotic use (during and after)	[61–72]
Lactobacillus rhamnosus GG	Nonsteroidal anti-inflammatory Drug	[73]
Lactobacillus rhamnosus GG, *Saccharomyces cerevisiae*	Intestinal hyperpermeability	[41, 42, 74, 75]
Lactobacillus rhamnosus GG, *Lactobacillus reuteri* MM53, *Lactobacillus paracasei* CRL431, *Lactobacillus acidophilus* CRL730, *Lactobacillus johnsonii* La1, *Bifidobacterium lactis* Bb12, *Lactobacillus plantarum* 299v, and *Lactobacillus paracasei*	Gastroenteritis	[40, 41, 76–85]
Lactobacillus johnsonii La1[α], *Lactobacillus plantarum* 299v, and *Lactobacillus rhamnosus* GG	Giardia infection	[77, 86, 87]
Lactobacillus rhamnosus GG, *Lactobacillus johnsonii* La1, *Lactobacillus plantarum* 299v, *Lactobacillus paracasei*, and *propionibacterium freudenreichii* HA-101 and HA-102	Intestinal dysbiosis	[64, 65, 88–93]
Lactobacillus acidophilus, *Lactobacillus johnsonii* La1	Lactose intolerance	[94–98]

Lactobacillus johnsonii La1, *Lactobacillus acidophilus*, and *Lactobacillus rhamnosus* GG	Peptic ulcer disease Nonerosive gastritis	[50, 99–102]
Lactobacillus plantarum 299v, VSL no. 3^{β}	Irritable bowel syndrome	[103–105]
Lactobacillus acidophilus NCFB 1748, VSL no. 3^{α}	Radiation-induced diarrhoea	[106, 107]
Lactobacillus rhamnosus GG, *Bifidobacterium lactis* Bb12, *Lactobacillus acidophilus*, *Saccharomyces cerevisiae*, and *Lactobacillus plantarum* 299v	Traveller's diarrhoea	[77, 84, 108–110]
Lactobacillus rhamnosus GG, *Saccharomyces cerevisiae*	Crohn's disease	[111–114]
Escherichia coli Nissle 1917, VSL no. 3^{β}, *Lactobacillus plantarum* 299	Ulcerative colitis	[115–119]
Lactobacillus rhamnosus GG, *Lactobacillus acidophilus*, *Lactobacillus paracasei*, *Lactobacillus acidophilus*, and *Lactobacillus delbrueckii* ssp. *bulgaricus* strain LB-51	Prevention of colon cancer	[120–124]
Lactobacillus rhamnosus GR-1, *Lactobacillus fermentum* B-54, *Lactobacillus fermentum* RC-14, and *Lactobacillus acidophilus*	Urinary tract infection	[125–132]
Lactobacillus acidophilus, *Lactobacillus rhamnosus* GG, *Lactobacillus rhamnosus* GR-1, and *Lactobacillus fermentum* RC-14	Vaginal candidiasis (thrush)	[133–138]

1.1. Purpose of Microencapsulation

The purpose of microencapsulation of probiotic is to protects certain compound or biological cells against surrounding environment which destruct the core. It protects the bacteria from heat, oxygen, and moisture and also improves the flow properties during formulation development. It can be used for different drug delivery system and nowadays to apply for the encapsulation of probiotics in food product [19–21].

The core material is encapsulated in the food grade matrix type coating material. In the food industry, these materials form a barrier to protect the core material against the GI environment using different encapsulation systems as shown in Figure 1 [21].

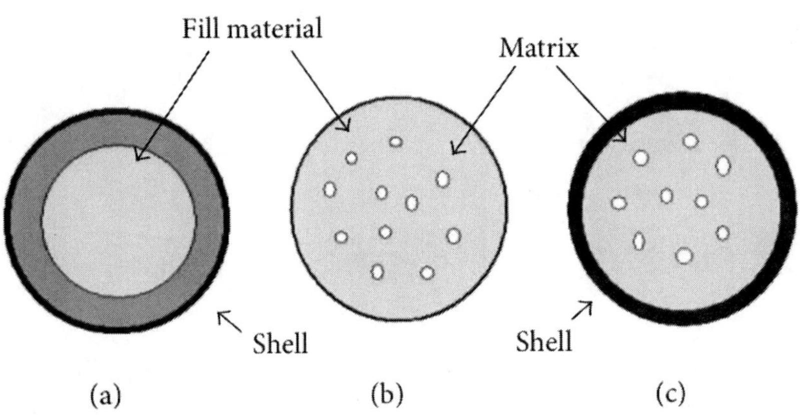

Figure 1: Schematic representation of encapsulation systems: (a) reservoir type, (b) matrix type, and (c) coated matrix type.

Finally, microencapsulation gives structure and innovative system to the core material for the probiotic food product. Physicochemical properties of coating material affect the viability of encapsulated probiotic cells. Type and concentration of coating material, particle size, initial cell number, and bacterial strains are important during formulation [22].

1.2. Structure of Microcapsule

Microcapsules, formed by using natural materials like sugar, gums, protein, lipid, and synthetic or modified polymers, can be formulated as gel beads or in dried powder form. The formed smooth or irregular microcapsules lack their encapsulation efficiency because of the presence of pores [23]. The coating material is classified on the basis of the matrix material such as with a single wall material like sodium alginate, or a mixture material such as xanthan, gellan gum, alginate, and Chitosan. Coating material also affects the structure of microcapsule. Generally sodium alginate produces microcapsules with smooth surface [24], while slow gelling property of milk results in formation of irregular shaped capsule [25, 26]. Different shapes of microspheres are shown in Figure 2.

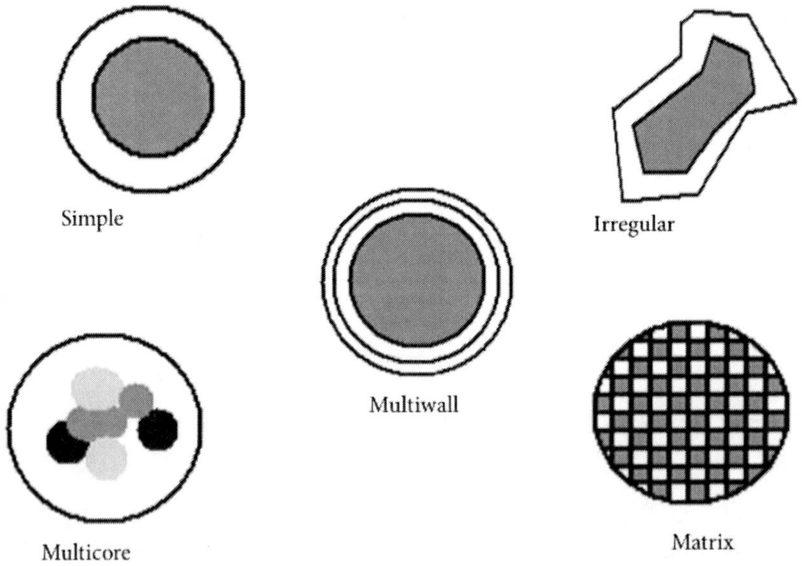

Figure 2: Various forms of microcapsule used in the food industry [19].

1.3. Advantages of Microencapsulated Probiotics

(i)It protects and enhances survival of bacteria in foods.(ii)It allows entrapped probiotic microorganisms to be incorporated into dairy products such as yogurt, cheese, and frozen milk product.(iii)About 40% of Lactobacilli survive in frozen ice cream when entrapped in calcium alginate sphere than free cells [27].(iv)The encapsulation of Bifidobacteria significantly improves survival, compared to free cells, throughout storage from 43%–44% to 50%–60% in frozen dairy product [28].(v)Microencapsulated form of B. pseudolongum exhibits improvement of survival in a simulated gastric environment when compared to free viable microorganisms [29, 30].

2. FACTOR AFFECTING MICROENCAPSULATION EFFECTIVENESS OF PROBIOTICS

For evaluation of effectiveness of probiotic encapsulation process different parameters are considered such as viability maintenance after encountering detrimental environmental conditions, cell release/recovery ability, and hardening time (time needed for capsule formation). Different factors affecting the microencapsulation are discussed below [23, 31].

2.1. Effect of Various Biomaterials on Viability of Probiotics

A wide variety of biomaterials have been used by researchers in order to check their effects on the process of microencapsulation as well as on the viability of probiotic bacteria. Supported report is shown in Table 2.

Table 2: Supported report provides evidence that encapsulation of probiotics results in increased viability.

Sr. no.	Supported report provides evidence that encapsulation of probiotics results in increased viability	References
1	It has been investigated that when yoghurt isolates of *L. acidophilus* and *Bifidobacterium* are encapsulated in 2% alginate solution, the viability was increased 15.9% and 16.6%, respectively, under acidic and bile salt condition	[139]
2	The use of calcium-induced alginate starch coating has also improved the survivability of encapsulated cells of *Lactobacillus acidophilus* and *Bifidobacterium lactis* (probiotic bacteria) up to 2 and 1 log cell numbers, respectively, in yoghurt	[140]
3	Whey protein-based microcapsules can improve the cell survival of probiotic bacteria under extreme conditions	[141]
4	A combination of gellan-alginate was used to encapsulate *Bifidobacterium bifidum*. The result showed that 2% sodium alginate and 1% gellan gum used as encapsulating materials have provided the highest thermotolerance in terms of *B. bifidum* count. The results of heat treatments also demonstrated that the addition of gellan gum in the walls of probiotic microcapsules provided improved protection for *B. bifidum*. The cell counts of *B. bifidum* remained at 10^5–10^6 CFU/g for the microcapsules stored for 2 months	[142]
5	Encapsulated cells also showed approximately 10^4 times increase in viability during exposure to acidic and bile salt conditions	[143]
6	It was found that cells microencapsulated in alginate, carrageenan, and xanthan gum survived better than free cells following 2 h incubation in acidic condition (pH 2)	[144]
7	It was found that cells encapsulated by extrusion using alginate and alginate with starch offered greater protection to cells in simulated gastric juice	[24]
8	Chitosan coating of microbeads resulted in a significant increase in survival time of *L. rhamnosus* from 40 to 120 min in acid condition, and the reduction in cell numbers was confined to 0.94 log over this time. Alginate macrobeads are more effective than microbeads in protecting *L. acidophilus* against high acid and bile	[145]

2.2. Capsule Characteristics with Respect to the Surrounding Environment

Selection of capsular material with respect to the surrounding environment is very important. When the microcapsule is formed using alginate and different combination, leaks the calcium ions from alginate capsule structure leading to its decomposition. Hence it should be avoided from the highly acidic environment. If probiotic cells are to be targeted in the small intestine, then selection of capsule material(s) should be such that their decomposition occurs after subjecting them to the small intestine pH or pancreatic enzymes. If the beads are to be retained in the large intestine, it is preferable to be tolerant against the pancreas and small intestine conditions. However, this is not always easily achievable due to the restrictions in the chemical characteristics of encapsulation materials. Generally, all the capsules must be resistant to the acidic conditions of gastric juices [32]. Sometimes it is necessary to use special types of hydrophobic components of encapsulation to make the beads tolerant against moisture.

2.3. Coating of the Capsule

Efficient coating of capsule improves its physicochemical property. For example, shell coating on the alginate capsules makes them resistant to the chelating agents of calcium ions and also increases their mechanical strength.

2.4. Concentration of Capsule Making Solution and Bead Diameter

Concentration of capsule making solution and final bead diameter are factors which affect encapsulation efficiency. As bead diameter increases, it causes inappropriate mouth feel and flavor. Furthermore, increasing capsule diameter decreases digestibility by pancreatic enzyme.

2.5. Environmental Conditions

Physiology of the GI tract is important during the probiotic encapsulation process (Table 3) [205].

Table 3: Relative pH and transit time at various locations within GIT.

Region	pH	Transit time
Oesophagus	~7.0	10–14 seconds
Stomach	1–2.5 (up to 5 fed)	Half emptying: ~80.5 mins
Proximal small intestine	6.15–7.35	3.2 ± 1.6 hrs (combined)
Distal small intestine	6.80–7.88	
Ascending colon	5.26–6.72	Highly variable, dependent on bowel evacuation
Descending colon	5.20–7.02	

Environmental factors are also found to reduce encapsulation effectiveness.

2.6. Modification of Capsule Materials

Chemical modification of capsular material improves encapsulation effectiveness. Structural modification of the capsule materials is by direct structural changes and/or addition of special additives.

2.7. Initial Concentration of Microbial Cells

As concentration of microbial cells in the encapsulation solution increases, the number of entrapped cells in each bead (cell load) increases and, as a result, quantitative efficiency of encapsulation increases. If cell load exceeds the limit, softening of capsule structure occurs.

2.8. Conditions of Processing Factors

Microencapsulation processes such as freeze drying, spray drying, micronization, and storage conditions are employed in order to avoid injuries to the beads and contained cells.

3. FORMULATION TECHNOLOGY FOR MICROENCAPSULATION OF PROBIOTICS

The presence of diverse condition in human digestive system makes designing of the probiotic release system difficult. Hence, highly tailored system like specific target location system is required [205].

Probiotic cell is commonly encapsulated by extrusion, emulsion, and spray drying. In these methods, probiotic bacteria are entrapped in the gel matrix using different gel forming mechanisms [206]. Whereas probiotic are living cells, the condition for implementation technology are designed to maintain cell viability, and solvents involved in the encapsulation technology must be nontoxic [207]. In Figure 3, it the different types of particles obtained (matrix or reservoir type) by each method can be seen Figure 3.

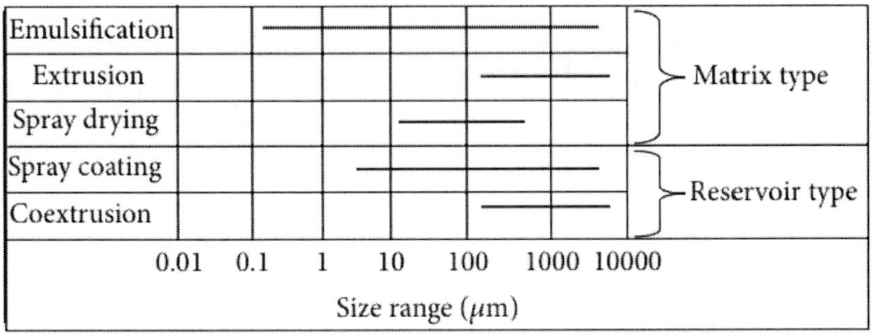

Figure 3: Probiotic encapsulation technologies: size range provided by each technique.

The ability of microorganisms to survive and multiply in the host strongly influences their probiotic benefits.

Microencapsulation techniques are divided into two parts:(i)encapsulation process,(ii)drying process.

3.1. Encapsulation Process

There are two basic techniques of microencapsulation that are used for encapsulation of probiotic bacteria. These encapsulated probiotics are then used for biomass production and also in various food products as functional food ingredients.

Depending on the method used, the two methods are extruded or droplet method and emulsion or two phase system method. From various studies it has been concluded that encapsulation by both of these methods has increased the viability of probiotic bacteria more than 80%.

3.1.1. Extrusion Technique for Microencapsulation

It is the oldest common technique for probiotic formulation [208]. Extrusion method in the case of alginate capsule consists of the following stages: preparation of hydrocolloid solution and the addition of probiotic cell in hydrocolloid solution to form cell suspension. These cells suspension is passed through the syringe needle to form droplets which are directly dripped into the hardening solution containimg cations like calcium. When the droplets come in contact with hardening solution, alginate polymers surround the core to form a three-dimensional lattice structure by cross-linking calcium ions as shown in Figure 4 [22, 29, 146, 209, 210].

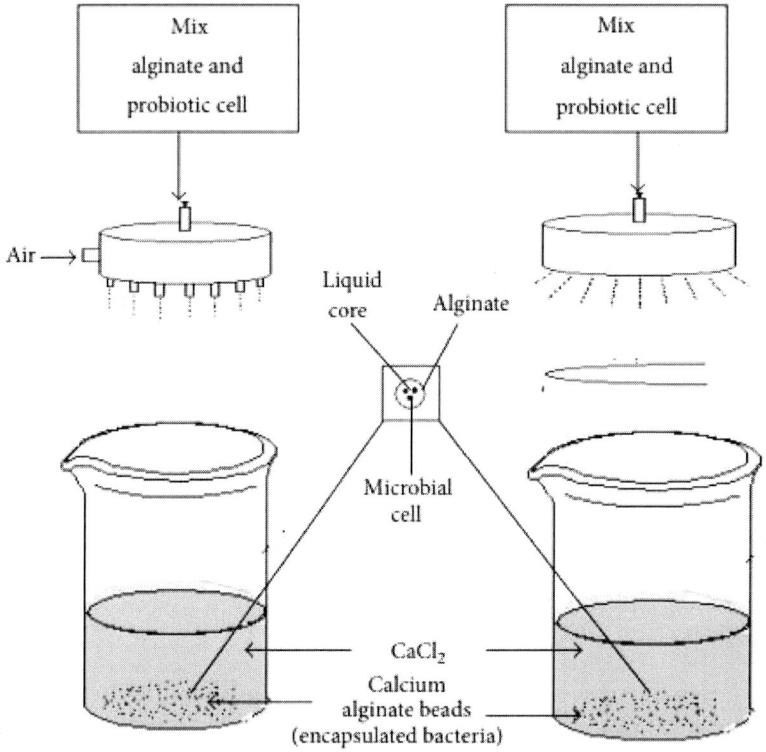

Figure 4: Extrusion technologies: simple needle droplet generator that usually is air driven (a) and pinning disk (b). The probiotic cells are added to the hydrocolloid solution and dripped through a syringe needle or a nozzle spray machine in the form of droplets which are allowed to free fall into a hardening solution such as calcium chloride.

Thereby entrapping the core material separated from liquid bath and is dried using a suitable technology. Formation of gel by alginate solution (0.6%) would be possible if calcium ion (0.3 M) is present [193]. Usually, alginate is used in the range of 1-2% and 0.005–1.5 M calcium chloride concentration. Generally, the diameter of forming beads in this method (2–5 mm) is larger than those formed in the emulsion method. Bead diameter is affected by concentration and viscosity of alginate solution and distance between the syringe and hardening solution, and diameter of extruder orifice affects the size of bead [156]. Bead diameter decreases along with increasing concentration and viscosity of the encapsulation solution. Using low glucuronic alginate, formation of beads with smaller diameter is possible [211]. For production of alginate capsule with Chitosan coat, alginate solution is dripped into the hardening batch containing calcium chloride and Chitosan [201, 212]. Soaking of alginate beads in the Chitosan solution (0.1%, pH 6.5) for 20 min forms beads with good properties [12].

Review work on this technique for probiotic microencapsulation is listed in Tables 4 and 5.

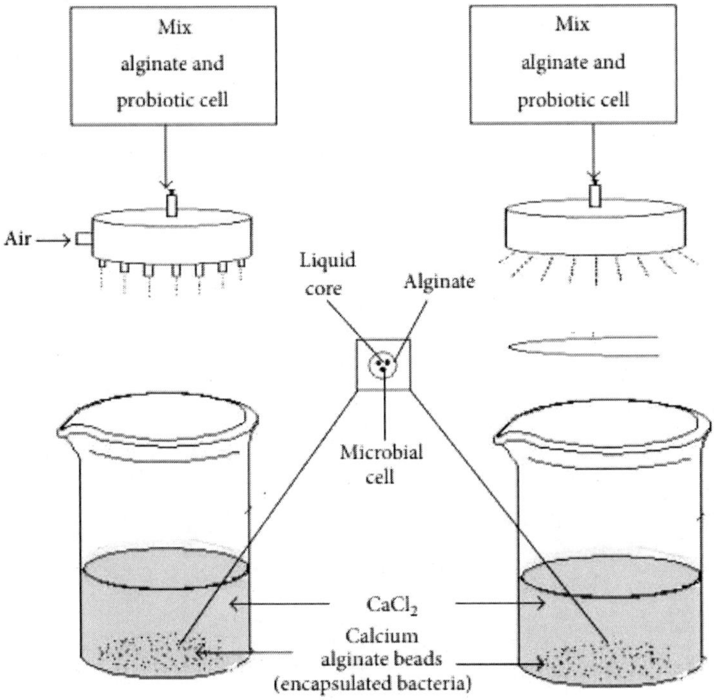

Table 4: Advantage and disadvantages of extrusion technique.

Advantages	Disadvantages
(i) Simple and cheap method that uses a gentle operation (ii) No damage to the probiotic cell (iii) Gives high probiotic viability [29] (iv) Does not involve deleterious solvent (v) Done under aerobic and anaerobic conditions	(i) Difficult to use for large scale production due to slow formation of microbeads (ii) Very poor payload of typically 8% (iii) Susceptibility of carbohydrate towards damage and structural defect, a larger size distribution (iv) Limited choice of wall material [146, 147].

Table 5: Different probiotic strain, biomaterial, and size of microcapsule encapsulated by extrusion technique.

Probiotic strain	Material	Size of capsule	Reference
Lactobacillus bulgaricus, *Streptococcus thermophilus*	1.875% alginate	2.5 mm	[148]
Streptococcus lactis ssp. *diacetylactis* *Streptococcus cremoris*	1.875% alginate	2.6 mm	[149]
Streptococcus cremoris	1% alginate	—	[150]
Lactococcus lactis ssp. *cremoris*	2% alginate + 0.4% chitosan	2 mm	[12, 147]
Lactobacillus plantarum	2% Alginate + 10% skim milk	2 mm	[151]
Lactococcus lactis ssp. *lactis* bv. *diacetylactis*	1.5% alginate	—	[152]
Lactococcus lactis ssp. *cremoris*	2% alginate	—	[153]
Streptococcus thermophilus *Lactobacillus delbrueckii* ssp. *bulgaricus*	2% alginate	—	[154]
Lactococcus lactis ssp. *lactis* bv. *diacetylactis*	1.8% alginate		[155]
Lactobacillus acidophilus	0.6% alginate + starch	5 mm	[156]
Bifidobacterium lactis	0.75% gellan gum + 1% xanthan gum	3 mm	[32, 157, 158]
Lactobacillus reuteri	1% xanthan gum + 0.5% gellan gum	—	[24]
Lactococcus lactis	1% alginate, poly-L-lysine	2 mm	[159]
Lactobacillus reuteri	1.5% alginate + 0.1% poly-L-lysine and 0.1% alginate	619 μm	[160]
Lactobacillus spp.	1.8% alginate	330–450 μm	[161]
Lactococcus lactis ssp. *cremoris*	2% alginate	1.62 mm	[12]
Lactococcus lactis ssp. *cremoris*	2% alginate + 0.17% alginate	1.89 mm	[12]
Saccharomyces boulardii	1.8% alginate + 0.4% chitosan	356 μm	[162]
Lactobacillus reuteri	2% alginate + 2% corn starch	—	[24]
Lactococcus lactis ssp. *cremoris*	2% alginate + 0.05% poly-L-lysine	1.89 mm	[12]
Bifidobacterium bifidum	2% alginate, 1% gellan, 0.86% peptides, 0.2% FOS	—	[163]
Lactobacillus acidophilus, *Lactobacillus casei*, *Bifidobacterium bifidum*, and *Bifidobacterium longum*	3% alginate, 1% peptides, 3% FOS	—	[164]
Bifidobacterium longum	2–4% alginate	1.03–2.62 mm	[165]
Lactobacillus reuteri, *Escherichia coli*	3% alginate	—	[24, 166, 167]
Lactobacillus reuteri	1.75% κ-carrageenan + 0.75% locust bean gum	—	[24]
Lactobacillus acidophilus, *Bifidobacterium lactis*	1.8% alginate + 1% Hi-Maize starch	—	[140, 168]
Bifidobacterium bifidum	3% κ-carrageenan	—	[169]

3.1.2. Emulsion Technique for Microencapsulation

It is successfully applied for the microencapsulation of lactic acid bacteria [170, 213]. In this method, small volume of cell/polymer slurry (dispersed phase) is added to the large volume of vegetable oil (as a continuous phase) such as soy oil, sunflower, corn, and light paraffin oil [174]. After the formation of emulsion, cross-linking is required to form gels. Gelification is done by different mechanisms like ionic, enzymatic, and interfacial polymerization as discussed next. Reported works on this technique are listed in Table 6.

Table 6: Different probiotic strain, biomaterial, and size of microcapsule encapsulated by emulsion technique.

Probiotic strain	Material	Size of microcapsule	Reference
Streptococcus thermophilus	3% κ-carrageenan and locust bean gum (2 : 1)	0.5–2 mm	[170]
Bifidobacterium pseudolongum	10% cellulose acetate phthalate	—	[171]
Lactobacillus delbrueckii ssp. *bulgaricus*	3% alginate	—	[172]
Lactobacillus casei ssp. *casei*	3% κ-carrageenan and locust bean gum (11 : 1)	1-2 mm	[173]
Lactococcus lactis ssp. *cremoris*	Chitosan (4%)	150 μm	[174]
Lactobacillus delbrueckii ssp. *bulgaricus*	3.6% alginate	30 μm	[175]
Lactobacillus delbrueckii ssp. *bulgaricus*	3% alginate	25–35 μm	[27]
Lactococcus lactis ssp. *cremoris*	24% gelatin	271–168 μm	[176]
Lactococcus lactis ssp. *cremoris*	2% alginate	50 μm–1 mm	[177]
Bifidobacterium bifidum, Bifidobacterium infantis	3% alginate	—	[28]
Lactobacillus casei NCDC-298	2–4% alginate	—	[178]
Lactobacillus bulgaricus KFRI 673	2% alginate, 5% glycerol, 0.26% xanthan gum + 0.8% chitosan	40–80 μm	[179]
Lactobacillus reuteri	2% alginate + 2% corn starch	—	[24]
Lactobacillus acidophilus, Bifidobacterium lactis	2% alginate + 2% Hi-Maize starch	0.5–1 mm	[140, 180, 181]
Lactobacillus reuteri	1.75% κ-carrageenan + 0.75% locust bean gum	—	[24]
Bifidobacterium breve	Milk fat + 10% whey protein isolate	3–80 μm	[141]
Lactobacillus reuteri	1% xanthan + 0.5% gellan		[24]
Bifidobacterium adolescentis 15703T	13% gelatin, 1.25 mM genipin + 1% alginate	49–53 μm	[182]

It can be easily scaled up, and the diameter of producing beads is considerably smaller (25 μm–2 mm). It is costly due to need of vegetable oil, surfactant, and emulsifier (Tween80 (0.2%)) for encapsulation in an emulsion [27, 175].

3.1.3. Emulsification Ionic Gelification

Emulsification is a chemical technique to encapsulate probiotic using alginate, carrageenan and pectin as an encapsulating material (Figure 5).

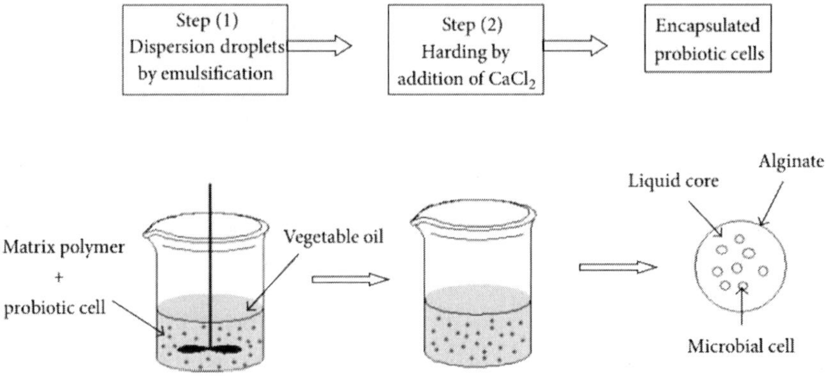

Figure 5: Schematic presentation of emulsification procedure: a small volume of the cell polymer suspension (i.e., the discontinuous phase) is added to a large volume of vegetable oil (i.e., the continuous phase). The mixture is then homogenized to form a water-in-oil emulsion. Once the water-in-oil emulsion is formed, the water-soluble polymer must be insolubilized to form tiny gel particles within the oil phase.

Once W/O emulsion is formed, water soluble polymer becomes insoluble after addition of ions of calcium chloride, by means of cross-linking forming gel particles in the oil phase. The smallest particle of the aqueous phase in W/O phase emulsion will lead to the formation of beads with smaller diameters. Agitation rate and type of emulsifier also affects the diameter of the beads [29, 214]. Microbeads produced by this technique are recovered by membrane filtration technology [29].

3.1.4. Emulsification and Enzymatic Gelification

In some countries, use of coating materials such as κ-carrageenan, gellan gum, or xanthan is not allowed in dairy product [141]. So milk protein is used to encapsulate probiotics by means of an enzyme-induced gelation [215, 216]. Milk proteins have excellent gelation properties and are a natural vehicle for probiotics [217]. This method gives water insoluble and spherical particles [215]. This method is an example of encapsulation by means of rennet gelation as shown in Figure 6, which is based on the principle of using dairy proteins which have been put in contact with rennet at low temperature.

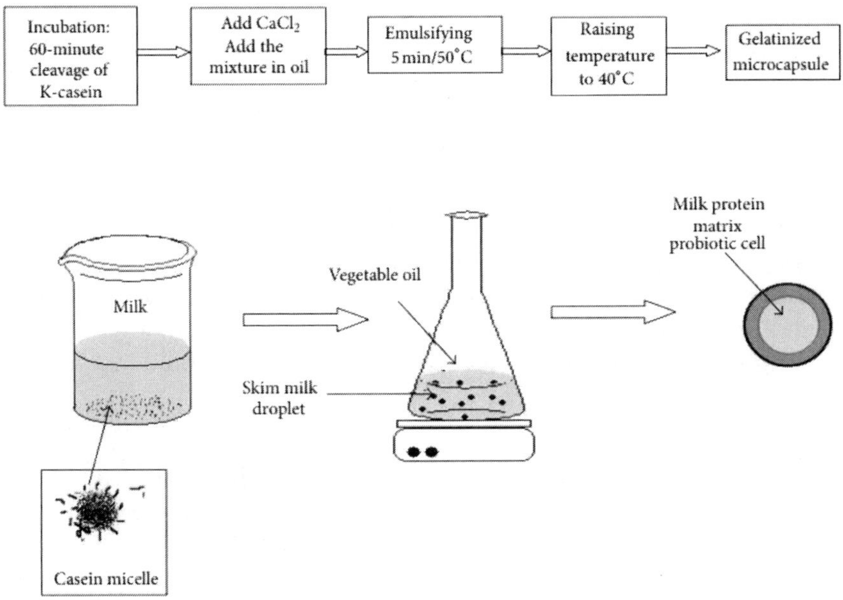

Figure 6: Schematic presentation of the microencapsulation of probiotic cells by means of rennet-gelation of milk proteins: The principle of the technique is based on using dairy proteins which have been put in contact with rennet at low temperature. This allows keeping a liquid system where κ-casein is cleaved by the enzyme. After that, dairy proteins have been emulsified in a cold oil to form water in oil emulsion. Thermal induction of enzymatic coagulation allows proteins flocculation and provides microparticles where probiotics are dispersed in coagulated dairy proteins.

This allows keeping a liquid system where κ-casein is cleaved by the enzyme. After that, dairy proteins are emulsified in a cold oil to form water in oil emulsion. Thermal induction of enzymatic coagulation allows protein flocculation and provides microparticles.

3.1.5. Emulsification and Interfacial Polymerization

This technique is a single step. It requires formation of an emulsion in which discontinuous phase contains an aqueous suspension of the cell and continuous phase contains organic solvent. To initiate the polymerization reaction, biocompatible agent which is soluble in the continuous phase is added. The drops of probiotic cell are coated to form thin and strong membrane [194]. Productivity of microorganisms is improved by interfacial polymerization in fermentation [218].

3.2. Drying Process for Microencapsulation

Drying improves stability of the encapsulated culture during prolonged storage. But the drying process causes some injuries to the microbeads, release of some cells, and reducing the viability of cells. Spray drying, freeze drying, and fluidized bed drying are common drying technology of probiotics used in industry and are summarized next [219].

3.2.1. Spray Drying

A solution containing probiotic living cells and the dissolved polymer matrix is prepared by using gum Arabic and starches because they tend to form a spherical microparticle during the drying process (Figure 7) [22, 209,210].

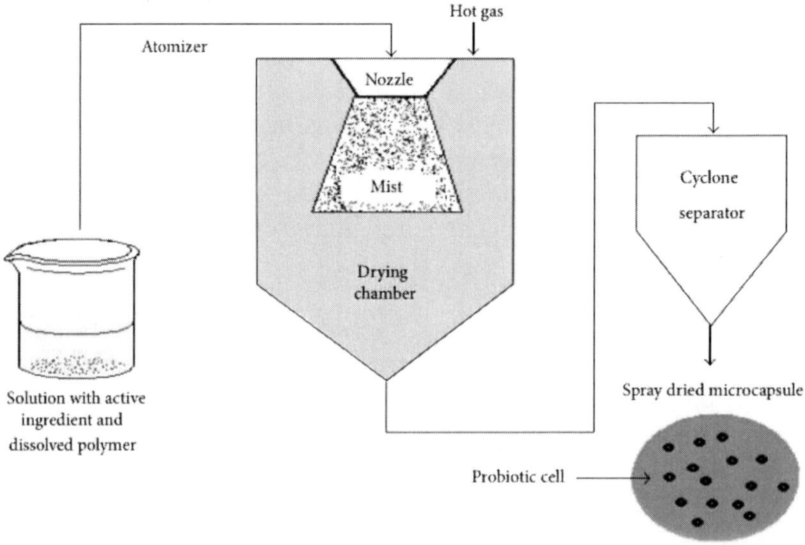

Figure 7: Schematic presentation of the spray-drying procedure: The solution is pressured and then atomized to form a "mist" into the drying chamber. The hot gas (air or nitrogen) is blown into the drying chamber too. This hot gas allows the evaporation of the solvent. The capsules are then transported to a cyclone separator for recovery.

In drying process, probiotic cell loses viability due to physical injury to microencapsule and heat generation (Table 8) [23]. So the loss of probiotic cell can be reduced by using proper cryoprotectant during freeze drying, optimizing the inlet and outlet temperature for spray drying [206] (Table 7).

Table 7: Different probiotic strain, biomaterial, inlet/outlet temperature, and size of microcapsule encapsulated by spray drying techniques.

Probiotic strain	Material	Inlet/outlet temperature	Size of capsule μm	Reference
Bifidobacterium infantis CCRC 14633, *Bifidobacterium infantis* CCRC 14661, *Bifidobacterium longum* ATCC 15708, *Bifidobacterium longum* CCRC 14634, and *Bifidobacterium longum* B6	10% gelatin, gum arabic, soluble starch, or skim milk	100°C/50°C	10–20	[183–185]
Lactobacillus paracasei NFBC 338	20% skim milk	175°C/68°C	—	[186]
Lactobacillus rhamnosus GG	20% skim milk + Raftilose or Polydextrose	—/80°C		[187]
Bifidobacterium breve R070 (BB R070), *Bifidobacterium longum* R023 (BL R023), and *Lactobacillus acidophilus* R335 (LA R335)	10% whey protein isolate	160°C/80°C	5–80	[188]
Bifidobacterium PL1	10% waxy maize starch	100°C/45°C	5	[189]
Lactobacillus acidophilus BCRC 14079, *Bifidobacterium longum* BCRC 14605	30% maltodextrin + 20% gum arabic	100°C/50°C	10	[190]
Lactobacillus acidophilus La-05 *Bifidobacterium lactis* Bb-12	Cellulose acetate phthalate	130°C/75°C	22	[191]
Lactobacillus paracasei NFBC 338	Gum acacia (gum arabic)	170°C/95–105°C	5–15	[192]

Table 8: Advantage and disadvantages of spray drying techniques.

Advantages	Disadvantages
The advantages of the spray drying process are ease of scaling up, low operational cost, continuous operation, and adaptability to most common industrial equipment	(i) However, spray drying may not be suitable particularly for probiotic bacteria due to requirement of high temperature drying [19, 193, 194] (ii) The loss of viability also depends upon the type of carrier used, for example, log reduction in soluble starch found to be higher compared to other carriers such as alginate, gum Arabic, and skim milk [183, 195]

Table 7 Presents the coating materials and temperatures used in this technique for probiotic microencapsulation.

3.2.2. Freeze Drying

In this technique, the solvent is frozen and removed via sublimation [220]. Freezing causes damage to the cell membrane due to ice crystal formation and also imparts stress condition by high osmolarity. It has been traditionally used to stabilize probiotic bacteria, but the combination of freeze-drying and encapsulation is relatively new concept. Recently, Lactobacillus F19 and Bifidobacterium Bb12 cells were first encapsulated into enzymatically gelled sodium caseinate, and gel particles were freeze-dried to study the storage stability [17]. They reported better postdrying survival and storage viability for encapsulated cell compared to free cell. In other recent work, gelatinized starch and lecithin were incorporated into the alginate microcapsule containing probiotic organisms in encapsulated form, and beads were freeze-dried to evaluate the storage stability at different temperature. It was shown that encapsulated bacteria had much better stability at 23°C for 12 weeks, and lecithin helped in obtaining higher efficiency and more stability [221].

3.3. The Other Drying Method Used for Microencapsulation

The other drying techniques are listed below.

3.3.1. Fluidized Bed Drying

In this process, cell suspension is sprayed and dried on inert carriers using a Wurster-based fluidized bed system (Table 9) [222].

Table 9: Advantage and disadvantages of fluidized bed drying.

Advantages	Disadvantages
The advantages of this process are total control over the temperature, lower comparable cost	Disadvantage being relatively longer duration (up to 2 hours) [195]. Before this drying, probiotic culture is encapsulated first in supporting material such as skimmed milk [196], potato starch [197], calcium alginate [198], or casein [199]

3.3.2. Vacuum Drying

Vacuum drying is suitable for heat sensitive probiotics because drying takes place at lower temperatures, and oxidation reaction can also be minimized, while disadvantage is batch operation and longer drying time which can be minimized by using a continuous vacuum dryer where cost is one-third of a freeze dryer, and the material can be dried at 1–4% moisture level at 40°C within 5–10 min [223].

3.4. Another Technique for Encapsulation

3.4.1. Spray Freeze Drying

In this technique, the probiotic cell solution is atomized into a cold vapor phase of a cryogenic liquid such as liquid nitrogen, which generates a dispersion of frozen droplets. These are dried in freeze dryer (Table 10) [200,209, 210, 224].

Table 10: Advantages and Disadvantages of spray freeze drying.

Advantages	Disadvantages
The advantages are controlled size, large specific surface area than spray dried capsule	(i) Disadvantages are required high energy, long time, expensive than spray drying [21] (ii) Additional coating is given to capsule for protection against adverse environmental conditions [200]

3.4.2. Encapsulation by Coating and Agglomeration

In this method, solid form of core material is kept in motion in a specially designed vessel (Figure 8) [206, 210].

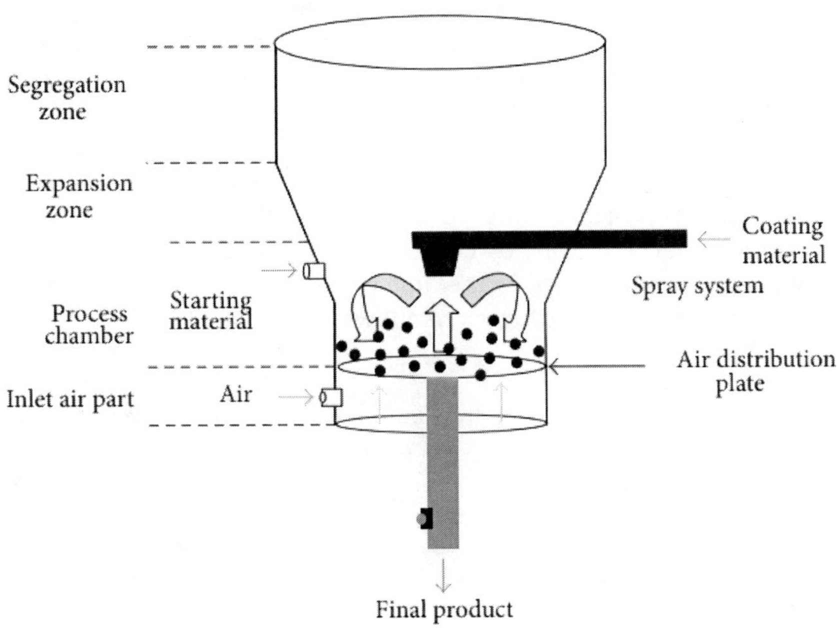

Figure 8: Schematic presentation of the spray coating technology.

It is easy to scale up hence used in the encapsulation of probiotics for nutraceutical. The Canadian private company developed and patented a microencapsulation technique known as Probiocap [225]. The process is based on coating freeze-dried Lactobacillus with fatty acids. This technology allows strains to resist the harsh effect of temperature, gastric acidity, and compression. Danish-Korean Company patented a duel coating technology for Lactobacillus, which is marketed under the brand name Duaolac. The first layer of coating is made of soy peptide, and the second layer is made of cellulose and gum.

3.4.3. Coacervation Technique for Encapsulation

In coacervation process, colloidal particle is separated from a solution and deposited around core material. It is used in encapsulating flavor oil but is also used in fish oil, vitamin, enzyme, nutrients, and preservatives (Table11). It is a three-step process comprising of phase separation, deposition, and solidification [26]. In the first step, coating material containing one or more polymer goes through a phase separation process and forms a coacervate. Suspended or emulsified form of core material remains, and as soon as wall material particles coalesce, it causes a decrease in surface area and total free interfacial energy of the system. In this process, coacervate nuclei adsorption to the surface of core material and form uniform layer around the core particles. Finally solidification of coating material is done by cross-linking using chemical, thermal, or enzymatic method. The formed microparticles are then collected by filtration or mild centrifugation followed by drying [26, 193].

Table 11: Advantages and disadvantages of coacervation technique.

Advantages	Disadvantages
(i) The advantages are high payload (99%) and controls the release of core material [146]	(i) The disadvantages are high cost of the particle isolation procedure and complexity of technique
(ii) The process can be carried out at room temperature making it particularly suitable for heat sensitive probiotic bacteria [26]	(ii) But it was suggested that the optimization of the last step and use of spray dryer instead of fluidized or freeze dryer can reduce the overall cost [146]

Glutaraldehyde, cross-linking agent, is not applied in the food industry due to toxicity issues; thus cross-linking enzyme transglutaminase is used [26, 226].

3.4.4. Cocrystallization

It is mainly used for the fruit juices, essential oils, flavor, and brown sugar [193]. In this method, core material is dispersed in supersaturated sucrose solution maintained at high temperature. The heat is gradually released allowing the solution to crystallize with the core material. Finally the product is dried and sieved as per the particle size requirement (Table 12) [227].

Table 12: Advantages and disadvantages of cocrystallization.

Advantages	Disadvantages
The advantages are economical with high payload (90%). It is utilized in the confectionery and pharmaceutical industries	Disadvantages are higher control rate of nucleation, crystallization, and thermal balance during operation [26]

3.4.5. Molecular Inclusion

This method involves entrapment of smaller molecule inside the hollow cavity of a larger molecule [193, 228]. Cyclodextrins are commonly used but restricted in the certain countries. In controlled release mechanism, core material is released when displaced by more favorable substrates. It is reported that β-cyclodextrin molecules containing core compound are highly heat stable, can tolerate up to 200°C, and are highly resistant to chemical degradation [146, 228].

Some of the major limitations of this molecular inclusion technology are low payload [146] and high cost of raw material [193].

3.4.6. Centrifugal Extrusion Technique

In this technique, core and coating materials are pumped through a separate tube to the surface of rotating cylinder. With the rotational motion of the cylinder, both materials are mixed and extruded as a fluid rod which is broken by the centrifugal force. The coating over the core material forms capsules caused by the difference in surface tension. Finally, formed capsules are placed on a moving bed of starch, which absorbs excess moisture and cushion the impact [26].

It is used in the food industry to encapsulate ingredients such as a flavor and seasoning [26], aspartame, vitamin, and methionine [19]. It produces smaller particles with a wide range of coating materials such as gelatin, alginate, carrageenan, starches, fatty acid, and waxes [19, 26].

The major advantage of this method is slower release properties of the capsule and higher throughput rate in comparison to the spray drying process [146].

4. BIOMATERIALS USED FOR MICROENCAPSULATION OF PROBIOTICS

This section aims to provide a short overview of commonly used bilateral to encapsulate probiotic cells.

Definition. "Any natural material or not, which is in contact with a living structure and is intended to act with biological system." It includes natural and synthetic polymerswhich are directly in contact with living cell so they should be biocompatible and biodegradable [229]. Encapsulation of probiotics in biodegradable polymer matrix has a number of advantages. Cryo- and osmoprotection agent can be incorporated into the matrix which enhances the survival of cell during storage and processing. Finally, microcapsules are dried; surface coating is altering the aesthetic and sensory properties of product and provides a high level of protection to the cells. It helps in the delayed release of cell by maintaining the dissolution properties of the coating layer. Microcapsule produced by using polymer is easy on a lab scale. But the scaling process is very difficult and processing cost is very high.

4.1. Use of Alginate System for Encapsulation of Probiotics

Alginate is a naturally derived polysaccharide extracted from various species of algae and composed of two monosaccharide units: -L-guluronic acid (G) and -D-mannuronic acid (M) linked from (1–4) glycosidic bond [230, 231]. M/G ratios determine the technological functionality of alginate. The gel strength depends upon high proportion block G. High temperature (60°C to 80°C) is needed to dissolve alginate in water. Alginate gels are insoluble in acidic media [6, 165, 232, 233]. Usually alginate is used in concentration range of 0.5–4% (Table 13) [27].

Table 13: Advantages and disadvantages of alginate system.

Advantages	Disadvantages
(i) The advantages are easy formation of gel matrices around bacterial cells, being nontoxic and cheap; mild process conditions are needed for their performance, easily prepared and performed and properly resolved in the intestine and release entrapped cell [85, 146, 201] (ii) Alginate gel matrix forms bacterial cell beads with a diameter of 1–3 μm, and the pore size does not exceed 7 NM [202]	(i) Disadvantages are susceptible to acidic environments, crackling and loss of mechanical stability in lactic acid [203, 204], difficulties in industrial scale applications due to their high expenses, and a weak ability of scaling up as well as the formation of crackled and porous bead surfaces, which leads to fast diffusion of moisture and fluids through capsules which reduces their barrier properties against unfavorable environment factor [146] (ii) This can be overcome by blending of alginate with another polymer like starch, coating other compound on its capsules [29, 30, 32, 181]

4.2. Use of Chitosan for Encapsulation of Probiotics

Chitosan is a linear polysaccharide with negative charge arising from its amine groups obtained by deacetylation of chitin. It can be isolated from crustacean shells, insect cuticles, and the membranes of fungi. It is a copolymer of two monomer residues anhydro-N-acetyl-D-glucosamine and anhydrous-D-glucosamine. It is soluble at pH < 6 and forms gel structure by ionotropic gelation. Chitosan can further polymerize by means of cross-linking formation in the presence of anions and polyanions [202]. It is used for coating of gelatin capsules, because its efficiency for the increasing viability of probiotic cells is not satisfactory; it is most often used as coat/shell but not capsule.

4.3. Use of Starch for Encapsulation of Probiotics

Starch consists of D-glucose unit joint together with glycosidic bonds. It has been used as a material for coating of alginate capsules. High-amylose corn starch (HACS) can be applied for enhancing functions of capsule or shell/coat formation [183]. Lyophilized corn starch (LCS) has been reported to be used as capsule-forming material; however, it decomposes after being subjected to pancreatic enzymes [234]. Resistant starch (RS) is not degraded by the pancreatic amylase. His specification apart from giving the microbeads good enteric delivery characteristic also gives them probiotic functionality as they can be used by the probiotic bacteria in the intestine [235]. The incorporation of Hi-Maize starch improved the encapsulation of viable bacteria compared with the bacteria encapsulated without starch [140, 236].

4.4. Use of Xanthan-Gellan Gum for Encapsulation of Probiotics

Gellan gum is an anionic polysaccharide derived from Sphingomonas elodea which is constituted of a repeating unit of four monomers that are glucose, glucuronic acid, glucose, and rhamnose [22]. Xanthan is an exopolysaccharide derived from Xanthomonas campestris. The optimum mixing proportion for xanthan-gellan gum is 1 : 0.75 [32]. In contrary with alginate, this mixture is resistant to acidic conditions [32, 181].

4.5. Use of κ-Carrageenan for Encapsulation of Probiotics

Carrageenan is polymer having linear structure consisting of D-galactose units alternatively linked by α-(1–3) and β (1–4) bonds. Types of carrageenan are kappa (κ), iota (ι), and lambda (λ) [237]. Monosulfated κ-carrageenan and bisulfated ι-carrageenan contain oxygen bridge between 3 and 6 of the D-galactose, which is responsible for the conformational transition and gelatin. The λ-carrageenan is trisulfated and does not have this bridge required for gel formation [238]. Carrageenan gelatin is induced by temperature changes. A rise in temperature (60–80°C) is required to dissolve it, and gelation occurs by cooling to room temperature [238,239], and then microparticles are stabilized by adding potassium ion [29]. It is commonly used as a food additive; its safety has been approved by several government agencies including FDA, Codex Alimentarius, and the joint FAO/WHO food additive [240]. It has good capacity to form gels that can entrap the cell. However, the cell slurry should be added to the heat sterilized suspension between 40–45°C; otherwise the gel hardens at room temperature [241]. Usually it is used in concentration such as 2–5% [242]. The encapsulation of probiotic cell in κ-carrageenan beads keeps the bacteria in a viable state [169], but the produced gels are brittle and do not withstand stresses [22].

4.6. Use of Various Proteins-Based Coating for Encapsulation of Probiotics

4.6.1. Gelatin

Gelatin is used as a thermally reversible gelling agent for encapsulation. Because of its amphoteric nature, it is an excellent candidate to incorporate with anionic-gel-forming polysaccharides, such as gellan gum.

It is frequently used in food and pharmaceutical industries [243]. It is a protein derived by partial hydrolysis of collagen of animal origin. It has versatile functional properties, and forms a solution of high viscosity in water which set to a gel on cooling.

4.6.2. Milk Protein

Milk proteins are natural vehicles for probiotic cells, and owing to their structural and physicochemical properties, they can be used as a delivery system [217]. The results of these studies are promising, and using milk proteins is an interesting way because of their biocompatibility [217].

4.6.3. Whey Protein

It easily heats denatured which affect aggregation and reduction in emulsion stability. Whey proteins are heat sensitive and show inferior surface activities. Whey protein appears as a potential candidate as coating agent as it is entirely biodegradable and frequently used in many types of food products.

The protein matrixes have different cell release properties than the other microencapsulation methods (polymer or fat based). Thus, applications are also extended to other foods for protection during processing as well as stability during storage but also in nutraceutical for protection and soil release in the GI tract [244].

4.7. Use of Cellulose Acetate Phthalate (CAP) for Encapsulation of Probiotics

Because of its safe nature, CAP is used for controlling drug release in the intestine [23]. It is not soluble at pH less than 5 but it is soluble at pH higher than 6 [236]. This property is essential for probiotic encapsulation because the bilateral must not dissolve in the stomach but only in the gut. The disadvantage of CAP is that it cannot form gel beads by ionotropic gelation so capsules have been developed by emulsification. CAP is widely used as a coating agent because it provides better protection for microorganisms in simulated GI conditions [191].

4.8. Criteria to Select a Proper Encapsulation Technology

When one chooses encapsulation as a technology to deliver the desired benefits, one should consider carefully the design of the encapsulation.(i)What are the physicochemical characteristics of the active?(ii)Which processing conditions are used during food production or processing?(iii)How will the encapsulates be stored prior to use?(iv)What will be the storage conditions of the food product containing the encapsulates prior to consumer use?(v)Which particle size and density are needed to have it incorporated properly in the food product?(vi)What are the trigger(s) and mechanism(s) of release?(vii)What are the cost constraints?

5. CONCLUSION AND FUTURE PERSPECTIVE

In the present article, principle, methods, and materials used in the encapsulation of probiotic cells are discussed. The advances in this field have been tremendous with nutraceutical and food ingredients. However, as to the microencapsulation of live probiotic bacterial cells, the technology seems to be not well developed. The delivery of viable microencapsulated probiotic bacteria will become important in near future. Any type of triggers can be used to prompt the release of encapsulated ingredients, such as pH changes, mechanical stress, temperature, enzymatic activity, time, and osmotic force. The challenges are to select the appropriate encapsulation technique and encapsulating materials. One important challenge for cell encapsulation is the largest size of microbial cells (typically 1–4 μm) or particles of freeze-dried culture (more than 100 mm). This characteristic limits cell loading for small capsules or, when large size capsules are produced, can negatively affect the textural and sensorial properties of food products in which they are added. In almost all cases, gel entrapment using natural polymers, such as calcium alginate, carrageenan, gellan gum, and Chitosan, is favored by researchers. However, despite promising on a laboratory scale, the developed technologies for producing gel beads still present serious difficulties for large-scale production of food grade microencapsulated microorganisms.

Another major challenge is to improve the viability of probiotics during the manufacturing processes, particularly heat processing. Consequently, there appears to be no commercial probiotic products available that are stable at high temperatures. Keeping in view the importance of producing thermoresistant probiotic microorganisms, as well as the interests of food and pharmaceutical companies, new approaches are needed in further research. There are at least two options: (1) discovering new strains of probiotic bacteria that are naturally heat stable or that have been genetically modified and (2) developing an encapsulation system that effectively acts like an "insulation material."

CONFLICT OF INTERESTS

The authors have no conflict of interests.

ACKNOWLEDGMENTS

The authors wish to thank the reviewers for making valuable comments on this paper. They also wish to thank the Dr. Girish K. Jani, Principal, S.S.R College of Pharmacy, Silvassa, for providing digital library for referencing.

REFERENCES

1. FAO/WHO, Guidelines for the Evaluation of Probiotics in Food, Food and Agriculture Organization of the United Nations/World Health Organization, London, UK, 2002.
2. R. Fuller, "Probiotics in man and animals," Journal of Applied Bacteriology, vol. 66, no. 5, pp. 365–378, 1989.

3. S. Rokka and P. Rantamäki, "Protecting probiotic bacteria by microencapsulation: challenges for industrial applications," European Food Research and Technology, vol. 231, no. 1, pp. 1–12, 2010.

4. C. Dunne, "Adaptation of bacteria to the intestinal niche: probiotics and gut disorder," Inflammatory Bowel Diseases, vol. 7, no. 2, pp. 136–145, 2001.

5. R. Agheyisi, "Ga-121 probiotics: ingredients, supplements, foods," Tech. Rep., Business Communication Company, Norwalk, Conn, USA, 2005.

6. S. K. Hood and E. A. Zottola, "Effect of low pH on the ability of Lactobacillus-acidophilus to survive and adhere to human intestinal cells," Journal of Food Science, vol. 53, no. 5, pp. 1514–1516, 1988.

7. F. A. M. Klaver, F. Kingma, and A. H. Weerkamp, "Growth and survival of bifidobacteria in milk,"Netherlands Milk and Dairy Journal, vol. 47, no. 3-4, pp. 151–164, 1993.

8. N. P. Shah and W. E. V. Lankaputhra, "Improving viability of Lactobacillus acidophilus and Bifidobacterium spp. in yogurt," International Dairy Journal, vol. 7, no. 5, pp. 349–356, 1997.

9. D. B. Hughes and D. G. Hoover, "Bifidobacteria: their potential for use in American dairy products,"Food Technology, vol. 45, no. 4, pp. 74–83, 1991.

10. C. Desmond, C. Stanton, G. F. Fitzgerald, K. Collins, and R. P. Ross, "Environmental adaptation of probiotic lactobacilli towards improvement of performance during spray drying," International Dairy Journal, vol. 12, no. 2-3, pp. 183–190, 2012.

11. A. K. Anal and H. Singh, "Recent advances in microencapsulation of probiotics for industrial applications and targeted delivery," Trends in Food Science and Technology, vol. 18, pp. 240–251, 2007.

12. W. Krasaekoopt, B. Bhandari, and H. Deeth, "The influence of coating materials on some properties of alginate beads and survivability of microencapsulated probiotic

bacteria," International Dairy Journal, vol. 14, no. 8, pp. 737–743, 2004.

13. P. Capela, T. K. C. Hay, and N. P. Shah, "Effect of cryoprotectants, prebiotics and microencapsulation on survival of probiotic organisms in yoghurt and freeze-dried yoghurt," Food Research International, vol. 39, no. 2, pp. 203–211, 2006.

14. K. N. Chen, M. J. Chen, and C. W. Lin, "Optimal combination of the encapsulating materials for probiotic microcapsules and its experimental verification (R1)," Journal of Food Engineering, vol. 79, pp. 313–320, 2006.

15. N. T. Annan, A. D. Borza, and L. T. Hansen, "Encapsulation in alginate-coated gelatin microspheres improves survival of the probiotic Bifidobacterium adolescentis 15703T during exposure to simulated gastro-intestinal conditions," Food Research International, vol. 41, no. 2, pp. 184–193, 2008.

16. G. K. Gbassi, T. Vandamme, S. Ennahar, and E. Marchioni, "Microencapsulation of Lactobacillus plantarum spp in an alginate matrix coated with whey proteins," International Journal of Food Microbiology, vol. 129, no. 1, pp. 103–105, 2009.

17. T. Heidebach, P. Först, and U. Kulozik, "Influence of casein-based microencapsulation on freeze-drying and storage of probiotic cells," Journal of Food Engineering, vol. 98, no. 3, pp. 309–316, 2010.

18. O. Sandoval-Castilla, C. Lobato-Calleros, H. S. García-Galindo, J. Alvarez-Ramírez, and E. J. Vernon-Carter, "Textural properties of alginate-pectin beads and survivability of entrapped Lb. casei in simulated gastrointestinal conditions and in yoghurt," Food Research International, vol. 43, no. 1, pp. 111–117, 2010.

19. B. F. Gibbs, S. Kermasha, I. Alli, and C. N. Mulligan, "Encapsulation in the food industry: a review,"International Journal of Food Sciences and Nutrition, vol. 50, no. 3, pp. 213–224, 1999.

20. C. P. Champagne and K. Kailasapathy, "Encapsulation of probiotics," in Delivery and Controlled Release of Bioactives

in Foods and Nutraceuticals, N. Garti, Ed., pp. 344–369, Woodhead, Cambridge, UK, 2008.

21. N. J. Zuidam and E. Shimoni, "Overview of microencapsulates for use in food products or processes and methods to take them," in Encapsulation Technologies for Active Food Ingredients and Food Processing, N. J. Zuidam and V. Nedovic, Eds., pp. 3–29, Springer, New York, NY, USA, 2009.

22. M. J. Chen and K. N. Chen, "Applications of probiotic encapsulation in dairy products," in Encapsulation and Controlled Release Technologies in Food Systems, J. M. Lakkis, Ed., pp. 83–107, Wiley-Blackwell, New York, NY, USA, 2007.

23. A. Mortazavian, S. H. Razavi, M. R. Ehsani, and S. Sohrabvandi, "Principle's and method of microencapsulation of probiotic microorganisms," Iranian Journal of Biotechnology, vol. 5, no. 1, pp. 1–18, 2007.

24. P. Muthukumarasamy, P. Allan-Wojtas, and R. A. Holley, "Stability of Lactobacillus reuteri in different types of microcapsules," Journal of Food Science, vol. 71, no. 1, pp. M20–M24, 2006.

25. A. Ainsley Reid, J. C. Vuillemard, M. Britten, Y. Arcand, E. Farnworth, and C. P. Champagne, "Microentrapment of probiotic bacteria in a Ca^{2+}-induced whey protein gel and effects on their viability in a dynamic gastro-intestinal model," Journal of Microencapsulation, vol. 22, no. 6, pp. 603–619, 2005.

26. K. G. H. Desai and H. J. Park, "Recent developments in microencapsulation of food ingredients," Drying Technology, vol. 23, no. 7, pp. 1361–1394, 2005.

27. T. Y. Sheu and R. T. Marshall, "Microencapsulation of lactobacilli in calcium alginate gels," Journal of Food Science, vol. 54, pp. 557–561, 1993.

28. K. M. K. Kebary, S. A. Hussein, and R. M. Badawi, "Improving viability of Bifidobacteria and their effect on frozen ice milk," Egyptian Journal of Dairy Science, vol. 23, pp. 319–337, 1998.

29. W. Krasaekoopt, B. Bhandari, and H. Deeth, "Evaluation of encapsulation techniques of probiotics for yoghurt," International Dairy Journal, vol. 13, no. 1, pp. 3–13, 2003.

30. H. L. Truelstrup, P. M. Allan-Wojtas, Y. L. Jin, and A. T. Paulson, "Survival of Ca-alginate microencapsulated Bifidobacterium spp. in milk and simulated gastrointestinal conditions," Food Microbiology, vol. 19, no. 1, pp. 35–45, 2002.

31. M. Borgogna, B. Bellich, L. Zorzin, R. Lapasin, and A. Cesàro, "Food microencapsulation of bioactive compounds: rheological and thermal characterisation of nonconventional gelling system," Food Chemistry, vol. 122, no. 2, pp. 416–423, 2010.

32. W. Sun and M. W. Griffiths, "Survival of bifidobacteria in yogurt and simulated gastric juice following immobilization in gellan-xanthan beads," International Journal of Food Microbiology, vol. 61, no. 1, pp. 17–25, 2000.

33. J. C. Mohan, R. Arora, and M. Khalilullah, "Short term hypolipidemic effects of oral Lactobacillus sporogenes therapy in patients with primary dyslipidemias," Indian Heart Journal, vol. 42, no. 5, pp. 361–364, 1990.

34. H. Bukowska, J. Pieczul-Mroz, M. Jastrzebska, K. Chelstowski, and M. Naruszewicz, "Decrease in fibrinogen and LDL-cholesterol levels upon supplementation of diet with Lactobacillus plantarum in subjects with moderately elevated cholesterol," Atherosclerosis, vol. 137, no. 2, pp. 437–438, 1998.

35. J. W. Anderson and S. E. Gilliland, "Effect of fermented milk (yogurt) containing Lactobacillus acidophilus L1 on serum cholesterol in hypercholesterolemic humans," Journal of the American College of Nutrition, vol. 18, no. 1, pp. 43–50, 1999.

36. M. Naruszewicz, M. Johansson, D. Zapolska-Downar, and H. Bukowska, "Effect of Lactobacillus plantarum 299v on cardiovascular disease risk factors in smokers," American

Journal of Clinical Nutrition, vol. 76, no. 6, pp. 1249–1255, 2002.

37. M. Kalliomäki, S. Salminen, H. Arvilommi, P. Kero, P. Koskinen, and E. Isolauri, "Probiotics in primary prevention of atopic disease: a randomised placebo-controlled trial," The Lancet, vol. 357, no. 9262, pp. 1076–1079, 2001.

38. S. Rautava, M. Kalliomäki, and E. Isolauri, "Probiotics during pregnancy and breast-feeding might confer immunomodulatory protection against atopic disease in the infant," Journal of Allergy and Clinical Immunology, vol. 109, no. 1, pp. 119–121, 2002.

39. T. Pessi, Y. Sütas, M. Hurme, and E. Isolauri, "Interleukin-10 generation in atopic children following oral lactobacillus rhamnosus GG," Clinical and Experimental Allergy, vol. 30, no. 12, pp. 1804–1808, 2000.

40. E. Isolauri, T. Arvola, Y. Sutas, E. Moilanen, and S. Salminen, "Probiotics in the management of atopic eczema," Clinical and Experimental Allergy, vol. 30, no. 11, pp. 1604–1610, 2000.

41. E. Isolauri, H. Majamaa, T. Arvola, I. Rantala, E. Virtanen, and H. Arvilommi, "Lactobacillus casei strain GG reverses increased intestinal permeability induced by cow milk in suckling rats," Gastroenterology, vol. 105, no. 6, pp. 1643–1650, 1993.

42. T. Pessi, Y. Sütas, A. Marttinen, and E. Isolauri, "Probiotics reinforce mucosal degradation of antigens in rats: implications for therapeutic use of probiotics," Journal of Nutrition, vol. 128, no. 12, pp. 2313–2318, 1998.

43. T. Matsuzaki, R. Yamazaki, S. Hashimoto, and T. Yokokura, "The effect of oral feeding of Lactobacillus casei strain Shirota on immunoglobulin E production in mice," Journal of Dairy Science, vol. 81, no. 1, pp. 48–53, 1998.

44. K. Shida, K. Makino, A. Morishita et al., "Lactobacillus casei inhibits antigen-induced IgE secretion through regulation of cytokine production in murine splenocyte cultures," International Archives of Allergy and Immunology, vol. 115, no. 4, pp. 278–287, 1998.

45. H. Majamaa and E. Isolauri, "Probiotics: a novel approach in the management of food allergy," Journal of Allergy and Clinical Immunology, vol. 99, no. 2, pp. 179–185, 1997.

46. L. Pelto, E. Isolauri, E.-M. Lillus, J. Nuutila, and S. Salminen, "Probiotic bacteria down-regulate the milk-induced inflammatory response in milk-hypersensitive subjects but have an immunostimulatory effect in healthy subjects," Clinical and Experimental Allergy, vol. 28, no. 12, pp. 1474–1479, 1998.

47. Y. Sütas, M. Hurme, and E. Isolauri, "Down-regulation of anti-CD3 antibody-induced IL-4 production by bovine caseins hydrolysed with Lactobacillus GG-derived enzymes," Scandinavian Journal of Immunology, vol. 43, no. 6, pp. 687–689, 1996.

48. Y. Sütas, E. Soppi, H. Korhonen et al., "Suppression of lymphocyte proliferation in vitro by bovine caseins hydrolyzed with Lactobacillus casei GG-derived enzymes," Journal of Allergy and Clinical Immunology, vol. 98, no. 1, pp. 216–224, 1996.

49. L. Pelto, S. Salminen, and E. Isolauri, "Lactobacillus GG modulates milkinduced immune inflammatory response in milk-hypersensitive adults," Nutrition Today, vol. 31, supplement 6, pp. 45S–47S, 1996.

50. K. Hatakka, E. Savilahti, A. Pönkä et al., "Effect of long term consumption of probiotic milk on infections in children attending day care centres: double blind, randomised trial," British Medical Journal, vol. 322, no. 7298, pp. 1327–1329, 2001.

51. E. J. Schiffrin, F. Rochat, H. Link-Amster, J. M. Aeschlimann, and A. Donnet-Hughes, "Immunomodulation of human blood cells following the ingestion of lactic acid bacteria," Journal of Dairy Science, vol. 78, no. 3, pp. 491–497, 1995.

52. E. J. Schiffrin, D. Brassart, A. L. Servin, F. Rochat, and A. Donnet-Hughes, "Immune modulation of blood leukocytes in humans by lactic acid bacteria: criteria for strain selection," American Journal of Clinical Nutrition, vol. 66, supplement 2, pp. 515S–520S, 1997.

53. G. Perdigon, M. E. N. de Macias, S. Alvarez, G. Oliver, and A. A. P. Holgado, "Enhancement of immune response in mice fed with Streptococcus thermophilus and Lactobacillus acidophilus," Journal of Dairy Science, vol. 70, no. 5, pp. 919–926, 1993.

54. M. V. Tejada-Simon, J. H. Lee, Z. Ustunol, and J. J. Pestka, "Ingestion of yogurt containing Lactobacillus acidophilus and Bifidobacterium to potentiate immunoglobulin A responses to cholera toxin in mice,"Journal of Dairy Science, vol. 82, no. 4, pp. 649–660, 1999.

55. G. E. Hatcher and R. S. Lambrecht, "Augmentation of macrophage phagocytic activity by cell-free extracts of selected lactic acid-producing bacteria," Journal of Dairy Science, vol. 76, no. 9, pp. 2485–2492, 1993.

56. P. Marteau, J. Vaerman, J. Dehennin et al., "Effects of intrajejunal perfusion and chronic ingestion of Lactobacillus johnsonii strain La1 on serum concentrations and jejunal secretions of immunoglobulins and serum proteins in healthy humans," Gastroenterologie Clinique et Biologique, vol. 21, no. 4, pp. 293–298, 1997.

57. K. Arunachalam, H. S. Gill, and R. K. Chandra, "Enhancement of natural immune function by dietary consumption of Bifidobacterium lactis (HN019)," European Journal of Clinical Nutrition, vol. 54, no. 3, pp. 263–267, 2000.

58. B. L. Chiang, Y. H. Sheih, L. H. Wang, C. K. Liao, and H. S. Gill, "Enhancing immunity by dietary consumption of a probiotic lactic acid bacterium (Bifidobacterium lactis HN019): optimization and definition of cellular immune responses," European Journal of Clinical Nutrition, vol. 54, no. 11, pp. 849–855, 2000.

59. Y.-H. Sheih, B.-L. Chiang, L.-H. Wang, C.-K. Liao, and H. S. Gill, "Systemic immunity-enhancing effects in healthy subjects following dietary consumption of the lactic acid bacterium Lactobacillus rhamnosus HN001," Journal of the American College of Nutrition, vol. 20, no. 2, pp. 149–156, 2001.

60. H. S. Gill, K. J. Rutherfurd, J. Prasad, and P. K. Gopal, "Enhancement of natural and acquired immunity by

Lactobacillus rhamnosus (HN001), Lactobacillus acidophilus (HN017) and Bifidobacterium lactis (HN019)," British Journal of Nutrition, vol. 83, no. 2, pp. 167–176, 2000.

61. A. Armuzzi, F. Cremonini, F. Bartolozzi et al., "The effect of oral administration of Lactobacillus GG on antibiotic-associated gastrointestinal side-effects during Helicobacter pylori eradication therapy,"Alimentary Pharmacology and Therapeutics, vol. 15, no. 2, pp. 163–169, 2001.

62. J. A. Vanderhoof, D. B. Whitney, D. L. Antonson, T. L. Hanner, J. V. Lupo, and R. J. Young, "Lactobacillus GG in the prevention of antibiotic-associated diarrhea in children," Journal of Pediatrics, vol. 135, no. 5, pp. 564–568, 1999.

63. S. Siitonen, H. Vapaatalo, S. Salminen et al., "Effect of Lactobacillus GG yoghurt in prevention of antibiotic associated diarrhoea," Annals of Medicine, vol. 22, no. 1, pp. 57–59, 1990.

64. J. A. Biller, A. J. Katz, A. F. Flores, T. M. Buie, and S. L. Gorbach, "Treatment of recurrent Clostridium difficile colitis with Lactobacillus GG," Journal of Pediatric Gastroenterology and Nutrition, vol. 21, no. 2, pp. 224–226, 1995.

65. R. G. Bennett, S. L. Gorbach, B. R. Goldin, et al., "Treatment of relapsing Clostridium difficile diarrhea with Lactobacillus GG," Nutrition Today, vol. 31, pp. 35S–39S, 1996.

66. F. Black, K. Einarsson, A. Lidbeck, K. Orrhage, and C. E. Nord, "Effect of lactic acid producing bacteria on the human intestinal microflora during ampicillin treatment," Scandinavian Journal of Infectious Diseases, vol. 23, no. 2, pp. 247–254, 1991.

67. M. Hickson, A. L. D'Souza, N. Muthu et al., "Use of probiotic Lactobacillus preparation to prevent diarrhoea associated with antibiotics: randomised double blind placebo controlled trial," British Medical Journal, vol. 335, article 80, 2007.

68. C. M. Surawicz, G. W. Elmer, P. Speelman, L. V. McFarland, J. Chinn, and G. van Belle, "Prevention of antibiotic-associated diarrhea by Saccharomyces boulardii: a prospective study," Gastroenterology, vol. 96, no. 4, pp. 981–988, 1989.

69. L. V. McFarland, C. M. Surawicz, R. N. Greenberg et al., "Prevention of β-lactam-associated diarrhea by Saccharomyces boulardii compared with placebo," American Journal of Gastroenterology, vol. 90, no. 3, pp. 439–448, 1995.

70. F. Cremonini, S. Di Caro, M. Covino et al., "Effect of different probiotic preparations on anti-Helicobacter pylori therapy-related side effects: a parallel group, triple blind, placebo-controlled study,"American Journal of Gastroenterology, vol. 97, no. 11, pp. 2744–2749, 2002.

71. T. Arvola, K. Laiho, S. Torkkeli et al., "Prophylactic Lactobacillus GG reduces antibiotic-associated diarrhea in children with respiratory infections: a randomized study," Pediatrics, vol. 104, no. 5, pp. 1–4, 1999.

72. J. Levy, "Experience with live Lactobacillus plantarum 299V: a promising adjunct in the management of recurrent Clostridium difficile infection," Gastroenterology, vol. 112, article A379, 1997.

73. M. Gotteland, S. Cruchet, and S. Verbeke, "Effect of lactobacillus ingestion on the gastrointestinal mucosal barrier alterations induced by indometacin in humans," Alimentary Pharmacology and Therapeutics, vol. 15, no. 1, pp. 11–17, 2001.

74. H. Jahn, R. Ullrich, T. Schneider et al., "Immunological and trophical effects of Saccharomyces boulardii on the small intestine in healthy human volunteers," Digestion, vol. 57, no. 2, pp. 95–104, 1996.

75. J.-P. Buts, N. de Keyser, and L. de Raedemaeker, "Saccharomyces boulardii enhances rat intestinal enzyme expression by endoluminal release of polyamines," Pediatric Research, vol. 36, no. 4, pp. 522–527, 1994.

76. A. Shornikova, I. A. Casas, H. Mykkänen, E. Salo, and T. Vesikari, "Bacteriotherapy with Lactobacillus reuteri in rotavirus gastroenteritis," Pediatric Infectious Disease Journal, vol. 16, no. 12, pp. 1103–1107, 1997.

77. D. R. Mack, S. Michail, S. Wei, L. McDougall, and M. A. Hollingsworth, "Probiotics inhibit enteropathogenic E.

coli adherence in vitro by inducing intestinal mucin gene expression," American Journal of Physiology, vol. 276, no. 4, pp. G941–G950, 1999.

78. A.-V. Shornikova, E. Isolauri, L. Burkanova, S. Lukovnikova, and T. Vesikari, "A trial in the Karelian Republic of oral rehydration and Lactobacillus GG for treatment of acute diarrhoea," Acta Paediatrica, International Journal of Paediatrics, vol. 86, no. 5, pp. 460–465, 1997.

79. M. Kaila, E. Isolauri, E. Soppi, E. Virtanen, S. Laine, and H. Arvilommi, "Enhancement of the circulating antibody secreting cell response in human diarrhea by a human Lactobacillus strain," Pediatric Research, vol. 32, no. 2, pp. 141–144, 1992.

80. J. M. Saavedra, N. A. Bauman, I. Oung, J. A. Perman, and R. H. Yolken, "Feeding of Bifidobacterium bifidum and Streptococcus thermophilus to infants in hospital for prevention of diarrhoea and shedding of rotavirus," The Lancet, vol. 344, no. 8929, pp. 1046–1049, 1994.

81. S. Gonzalez, G. Albarracin, M. L. Pesce, M. Appela, A. P. Holgado, and G. Oliver, "Prevention of infantile diarrhoea by fermented milk," Microbiologie, Aliments, Nutrition, vol. 8, pp. 349–354, 1990.

82. S. N. Gonzalez, R. Cardozo, M. C. Apella, and G. Oliver, "Biotherapeutic role of fermented milk,"Biotherapy, vol. 8, no. 2, pp. 129–134, 1994.

83. T. Sugita and M. Togowa, "Efficacy of Lactobacillus preparation Biolactis powder in children with rotavirus enteritis," Japan Journal of Pediatrics, vol. 47, pp. 213–220, 1994.

84. S. Michail and F. Abernathy, "Lactobacillus plantarum reduces the in vitro secretory response of intestinal epithelial cells to enteropathogenic Escherichia coli infection," Journal of Pediatric Gastroenterology and Nutrition, vol. 35, no. 3, pp. 350–355, 2002.

85. M. Ogawa, K. Shimizu, K. Nomoto et al., "Protective effect of Lactobacillus casei strain Shirota on Shiga toxin-producing Escherichia coli O157:H7 infection in infant

rabbits," Infection and Immunity, vol. 69, no. 2, pp. 1101–1108, 2001.

86. P. F. Pérez, J. Minnaard, M. Rouvet et al., "Inhibition of Giardia intestinalis by extracellular factors from lactobacilli: an in vitro study," Applied and Environmental Microbiology, vol. 67, no. 3–12, pp. 5037–5042, 2001.

87. I. Adlerberth, S. Ahrné, M. Johansson, G. Molin, L. A. Hanson, and A. E. Wold, "A mannose-specific adherence mechanism in Lactobacillus plantarum conferring binding to the human colonic cell line HT-29," Applied and Environmental Microbiology, vol. 62, no. 7, pp. 2244–2251, 1996.

88. M. Silva, N. V. Jacobus, C. Deneke, and S. L. Gorbach, "Antimicrobial substance from a human Lactobacillus strain," Antimicrobial Agents and Chemotherapy, vol. 31, no. 8, pp. 1231–1233, 1987.

89. D. Bouglé, N. Roland, F. Lebeurrier, and P. Arhan, "Effect of propionibacteria supplementation on fecal bifidobacteria and segmental colonic transit time in healthy human subjects," Scandinavian Journal of Gastroenterology, vol. 34, no. 2, pp. 144–148, 1999.

90. S. Spanhaak, R. Havenaar, and G. Schaafsma, "The effect of consumption of milk fermented by Lactobacillus casei strain Shirota on the intestinal microflora and immune parameters in humans,"European Journal of Clinical Nutrition, vol. 52, no. 12, pp. 899–907, 1998.

91. M. F. Bernet, D. Brassart, J. R. Neeser, and A. L. Servin, "Lactobacillus acidophilus LA 1 binds to cultured human intestinal cell lines and inhibits cell attachment and cell invasion by enterovirulent bacteria," Gut, vol. 35, no. 4, pp. 483–489, 1994.

92. M.-L. Johansson, G. Molin, B. Jeppsson, S. Nobaek, S. Ahrne, and S. Bengmark, "Administration of different Lactobacillus strains in fermented oatmeal soup: in vivo colonization of human intestinal mucosa and effect on the indigenous flora," Applied and Environmental Microbiology, vol. 59, no. 1, pp. 15–20, 1993.

93. C. N. Jacobsen, V. R. Nielsen, A. E. Hayford et al., "Screening of probiotic activities of forty-seven strains of Lactobacillus spp. by in vitro techniques and evaluation of the colonization ability of five selected strains in humans," Applied and Environmental Microbiology, vol. 65, no. 11, pp. 4949–4956, 1999.

94. R. G. Montes, T. M. Bayless, J. M. Saavedra, and J. A. Perman, "Effect of milks inoculated with Lactobacillus acidophilus or a yogurt starter culture in lactose-maldigesting children," Journal of Dairy Science, vol. 78, no. 8, pp. 1657–1664, 1995.

95. D. O. Noh and S. E. Gilliland, "Influence of bile on cellular integrity and beta-galactosidase activity of Lactobacillus acidophilus," Journal of Dairy Science, vol. 76, no. 5, pp. 1253–1259, 1993.

96. M. Y. Lin, D. Savaiano, and S. Harlander, "Influence of nonfermented dairy products containing bacterial starter cultures on lactose maldigestion in humans," Journal of Dairy Science, vol. 74, no. 1, pp. 87–95, 1991.

97. T. Jiang and D. A. Savaiano, "In vitro lactose fermentation by human colonic bacteria is modified by Lactobacillus acidophilus supplementation," Journal of Nutrition, vol. 127, no. 8, pp. 1489–1495, 1997.

98. H. S. Kim and S. E. Gilliland, "Lactobacillus acidophilus as a dietary adjunct for milk to aid lactose digestion in humans," Journal of Dairy Science, vol. 66, no. 5, pp. 959–966, 1983.

99. J. Rasic, I. Klem, D. Jovanovic, and M. Ac, "Antimicrobial effect of Lactobacillus acidophilus and Lactobacillus delbrueckii subsp. bulgaricus against Heelicobacter pylori in vitro," Archives of Gastroenterohepatology, vol. 14, no. 4, pp. 158–160, 1995.

100. P. Michetti, G. Dorta, P. H. Wiesel et al., "Effect of whey-based culture supernatant of Lactobacillus acidophilus (johnsonii) La1 on Helicobacter pylori infection in humans," Digestion, vol. 60, no. 3, pp. 203–209, 1999.

101. C. P. Felley, I. Corthésy-Theulaz, J.-L. Rivero et al., "Favourable effect of an acidified milk (LC-1) on Helicobacter pylori gastritis in man," European Journal of Gastroenterology and Hepatology, vol. 13, no. 1, pp. 25–29, 1999.

102. M. Coconnier, V. Lievin, E. Hemery, and A. L. Servin, "Antagonistic activity against Helicobacter infection in vitro and in vivo by the human Lactobacillus acidophilus strain LB," Applied and Environmental Microbiology, vol. 64, no. 11, pp. 4573–4580, 1998.

103. K. Niedzielin, H. Kordecki, and B. Birkenfeld, "A controlled, double-blind, randomized study on the efficacy of Lactobacillus plantarum 299V in patients with irritable bowel syndrome," European Journal of Gastroenterology and Hepatology, vol. 13, no. 10, pp. 1143–1147, 2001.

104. S. Nobaek, M. Johansson, G. Molin, S. Ahrné, and B. Jeppsson, "Alteration of intestinal microflora is associated with reduction in abdominal bloating and pain in patients with irritable bowel syndrome,"American Journal of Gastroenterology, vol. 95, no. 5, pp. 1231–1238, 2000.

105. G. . Bazzocchi, M. Campieri, P. Gionchetti, et al., "Change in colonic function and fecal microbiological and enzymatic activities induced by a new probiotic preparation," Gastroenterology International, vol. 11, supplement 1, article 111, 1998.

106. E. Salminen, I. Elomaa, J. Minkkinen, H. Vapaatalo, and S. Salminen, "Preservation of intestinal integrity during radiotherapy using live Lactobacillus acidophilus cultures," Clinical Radiology, vol. 39, no. 4, pp. 435–437, 1988.

107. P. Delia, G. Sansotta, V. Donato et al., "Prevention of radiation-induced diarrhea with the use of VSL#3, a new high-potency probiotic preparation," American Journal of Gastroenterology, vol. 97, no. 8, pp. 2150–2152, 2002.

108. P. J. Oksanen, S. Salminen, M. Saxelin et al., "Prevention of travellers' diarrhoea by Lactobacillus GG,"Annals of Medicine, vol. 22, no. 1, pp. 53–56, 1990.

109. A. C. Ouwehand, P. V. Kirjavainen, C. Shortt, and S. Salminen, "Probiotics: mechanisms and established effects," International Dairy Journal, vol. 9, no. 1, pp. 43–52, 1999.

110. G. W. Elmer, C. M. Surawicz, and L. V. McFarland, "Biotherapeutic agents: a neglected modality for the treatment and prevention of selected intestinal and vaginal infections," Journal of the American Medical Association, vol. 275, no. 11, pp. 870–876, 1996.

111. M. Malin, H. Suomalainen, M. Saxelin, and E. Isolauri, "Promotion of IgA immune response in patients with Crohn's disease by oral bacteriotherapy with Lactobacillus GG," Annals of Nutrition and Metabolism, vol. 40, no. 3, pp. 137–145, 1996.

112. P. Gupta, H. Andrew, B. S. Kirschner, and S. Guandalini, "Is Lactobacillus GG helpful in children with Crohn's disease? Results of a preliminary, open-label study," Journal of Pediatric Gastroenterology and Nutrition, vol. 31, no. 4, pp. 453–457, 2000.

113. M. Guslandi, G. Mezzi, M. Sorghi, and P. A. Testoni, "Saccharomyces boulardii in maintenance treatment of Crohn's disease," Digestive Diseases and Sciences, vol. 45, no. 7, pp. 1462–1464, 2000.

114. K. Plein and J. Hotz, "Therapeutic effects of Saccharomyces boulardii on mild residual symptoms in a stable phase of Crohn's disease with special respect to chronic diarrhea—a pilot study," Zeitschrift fur Gastroenterologie, vol. 31, no. 2, pp. 129–134, 1993.

115. A. Venturi, P. Gionchetti, F. Rizzello et al., "Impact on the composition of the faecal flora by a new probiotic preparation: preliminary data on maintenance treatment of patients with ulcerative colitis,"Alimentary Pharmacology and Therapeutics, vol. 13, no. 8, pp. 1103–1108, 1999.

116. W. Kruis, E. Schutz, P. Fric, B. Fixa, G. Judmaier, and M. Stolte, "Double-blind comparison of an oralEscherichia coli prepration and mesalazine in maintaining remission of

ulcerative colitis," Alimentary Pharmacology and Therapeutics, vol. 11, no. 5, pp. 853–858, 1997.

117. B. J. Rembacken, A. M. Snelling, P. M. Hawkey, D. M. Chalmers, and A. T. R. Axon, "Non-pathogenicEscherichia coli versus mesalazine for the treatment of ulcerative colitis: a randomised trial," The Lancet, vol. 354, no. 9179, pp. 635–639, 1999.

118. P. Gionchetti, F. Rizzello, A. Venturi et al., "Oral bacteriotherapy as maintenance treatment in patients with chronic pouchitis: a double-blind, placebo-controlled trial," Gastroenterology, vol. 119, no. 2, pp. 584–587, 2000.

119. R. J. Kennedy, S. J. Kirk, and K. R. Gardiner, "Probiotics in IBD," Gut, vol. 49, no. 6, p. 873, 2001.

120. W. H. L. Ling, R. Korpela, H. Mykkanen, S. Salminen, and O. Hanninen, "Lactobacillus strain GG supplementation decreases colonic hydrolytic and reductive enzyme activities in healthy female adults,"Journal of Nutrition, vol. 124, no. 1, pp. 18–23, 1994.

121. P. Bailey and K. Shahani, "Inhibitory effect of acidophilus cultured colostrum and milk upon the proliferation of ascites tumor," in Proceedings of the 71st Annual Meeting of the American Dairy Science Association, 1979.

122. G. H. McIntosh, P. J. Royle, and M. J. Playne, "A probiotic strain of L. Acidophilus reduces DMH-induced large intestinal tumors in male sprague-dawley rats," Nutrition and Cancer, vol. 35, no. 2, pp. 153–159, 1999.

123. B. R. Goldin and S. L. Gorbach, "The effect of milk and lactobacillus feeding on human intestinal bacterial enzyme activity," American Journal of Clinical Nutrition, vol. 39, no. 5, pp. 756–761, 1984.

124. I. G. Bogdanov, P. G. Dalev, and A. I. Gurevich, "Antitumour glycopeptides from Lactobacillus bulgaricus cell wall," FEBS Letters, vol. 57, pp. 3–8, 1975.

125. G. Reid, A. W. Bruce, and M. Taylor, "Influence of three-day antimicrobial therapy and lactobacillus vaginal suppositories

on recurrence or urinary tract infections," Clinical Therapeutics, vol. 14, no. 1, pp. 11–16, 1992.

126. A. W. Bruce, G. Reid, J. A. McGroarty, M. Taylor, and C. Preston, "Preliminary study on the prevention of recurrent urinary tract infection in adult women using intravaginal Lactobacilli," International Urogynecology Journal, vol. 3, no. 1, pp. 22–25, 1992.

127. G. Reid, A. W. Bruce, N. Fraser, C. Heinemann, J. Owen, and B. Henning, "Oral probiotics can resolve urogenital infections," FEMS Immunology and Medical Microbiology, vol. 30, no. 1, pp. 49–52, 2001.

128. G. Reid, "Probiotic therapy and functional foods for the prevention of urinary tract infections: state of the art and science," Current Infectious Disease Reports, vol. 2, pp. 518–522, 2000.

129. G. Reid and A. W. Bruce, "Selection of Lactobacillus strains for urogenital probiotic applications," Journal of Infectious Diseases, vol. 183, supplement 1, pp. S77–S80, 2001.

130. G. Reid, A. W. Bruce, R. L. Cook, and M. Llano, "Effect of urogenital flora of antibiotic therapy for urinary tract infection," Scandinavian Journal of Infectious Diseases, vol. 22, no. 1, pp. 43–47, 1990.

131. G. Reid, A. W. Bruce, and M. Taylor, "Instillation of Lactobacillus and stimulation of indigenous organisms to prevent recurrence of urinary tract infections," Microecology and Therapy, vol. 23, pp. 32–45, 1995.

132. G. Reid, "In vitro testing of Lactobacillus acidophilus NCFM(TM) as a possible probiotic for the urogenital tract," International Dairy Journal, vol. 10, no. 5-6, pp. 415–419, 2000.

133. A. B. Williams, C. Yu, K. Tashima, J. Burgess, and K. Danvers, "Evaluation of two self-care treatments for prevention of vaginal candidiasis in women with HIV," The Journal of the Association of Nurses in AIDS Care, vol. 12, no. 4, pp. 51–57, 2001.

134. E. Hilton, H. D. Isenberg, P. Alperstein, K. France, and M. T. Borenstein, "Ingestion of yogurt containing Lactobacillus acidophilus as prophylaxis for candidal vaginitis," Annals of Internal Medicine, vol. 116, no. 5, pp. 353–357, 1992.

135. R. D. Wagner, C. Pierson, T. Warner et al., "Biotherapeutic effects of probiotic bacteria on candidiasis in immunodeficient mice," Infection and Immunity, vol. 65, no. 10, pp. 4165–4172, 1997.

136. M. Plockova, J. Chumchalova, and J. Tomanova, "Antifungal activity of Lactobacillus acidophilus, CH5 metabolites," Potravinarske Vedy, vol. 15, no. 1, pp. 39–48, 1997.

137. E. Hilton, P. Rindos, and H. D. Isenberg, "Lactobacillus GG vaginal suppositories and vaginitis," Journal of Clinical Microbiology, vol. 33, no. 5, p. 1433, 1995.

138. P. Cadieux, J. Burton, G. Gardiner et al., "Lactobacillus strains and vaginal ecology," Journal of the American Medical Association, vol. 287, no. 15, pp. 1940–1941, 2002.

139. R. Sridar, M. Nguyen, and K. Kailasapathy, "Studies on the effect of encapsulation on the survival of probiotic microorganisms under high acid and bile conditions," Journal of Food Science and Technology, vol. 40, no. 5, pp. 458–460, 2003.

140. K. Kailasapathy and L. Masondole, "Survival of free and microencapsulated Lactobacillus acidophilus and Bifidobacterium lactis and their effect on texture of feta cheese," Australian Journal of Dairy Technology, vol. 60, no. 3, pp. 252–258, 2005.

141. A. Picot and C. Lacroix, "Encapsulation of bifidobacteria in whey protein-based microcapsules and survival in simulated gastrointestinal conditions and in yoghurt," International Dairy Journal, vol. 14, no. 6, pp. 505–515, 2004.

142. E. S. Chan and Z. Zhang, "Bioencapsulation by compression coating of probiotic bacteria for their protection in an acidic medium," Process Biochemistry, vol. 40, no. 10, pp. 3346–3351, 2005.

143. R. C. W. Hou, M. Y. Lin, M. M. C. Wang, and J. T. C. Tzen, "Increase of viability of entrapped cells of Lactobacillus delbrueckii ssp. bulgaricus in artificial sesame oil emulsions," Journal of Dairy Science, vol. 86, no. 2, pp. 424–428, 2003.

144. W. K. Ding and N. P. Shah, "Effect of various encapsulating materials on the stability of probiotic bacteria," Journal of Food Science, vol. 74, no. 2, pp. M100–M107, 2009.

145. A. Sohail, M. S. Turner, A. Coombes, T. Bostrom, and B. Bhandari, "Survivability of probiotics encapsulated in alginate gel microbeads using a novel impinging aerosols method," International Journal of Food Microbiology, vol. 145, no. 1, pp. 162–168, 2011.

146. S. Gouin, "Microencapsulation: industrial appraisal of existing technologies and trends," Trends in Food Science and Technology, vol. 15, no. 7-8, pp. 330–347, 2004.

147. Y. Zhou, E. Martins, A. Groboillot, C. P. Champagne, and R. J. Neufeld, "Spectrophotometric quantification of lactic bacteria in alginate and control of cell release with chitosan coating," Journal of Applied Microbiology, vol. 84, no. 3, pp. 342–348, 1998.

148. H. Prevost, C. Divies, and E. Rousseau, "Continuous yoghurt production with Lactobacillus bulgaricus and Streptococcus thermophilus entrapped in Ca-alginate," Biotechnology Letters, vol. 7, no. 4, pp. 247–252, 1985.

149. H. Prevost and C. Divies, "Fresh fermented cheese production with continuous pre-fermented milk by a mixed culture of mesophilic lactic streptococci entrapped in Ca-Al ginate," Biotechnology Letters, vol. 9, no. 11, pp. 789–794, 1987.

150. L. R. Steenson, T. R. Klaenhammer, and H. E. Swaisgood, "Calcium alginate-immobilized cultures of lactic Streptococci are protected from bacteriophages," Journal of Dairy Science, vol. 70, no. 6, pp. 1121–1127, 1987.

151. L. Kearney, M. Upton, and A. McLoughlin, "Enhancing the viability of Lactobacillus plantarum inoculum by immobilizing the cells in calcium-alginate beads

incorporating cryoprotectants," Applied and Environmental Microbiology, vol. 56, no. 10, pp. 3112–3116, 1990.

152. H. Prevost and C. Divies, "Cream fermentation by a mixed culture of Lactococci entrapped in two-layer calcium alginate gel beads," Biotechnology Letters, vol. 14, no. 7, pp. 583–588, 1992.

153. N. Morin, M. Bernier-Cardou, and C. P. Champagne, "Production of Lactococcus lactis biomass by immobilized cell technology," Journal of Industrial Microbiology, vol. 9, no. 2, pp. 131–135, 1992.

154. C. P. Champagne, F. Girard, and N. Rodrigue, "Production of concentrated suspensions of thermophilic lactic acid bacteria in calcium-alginate beads," International Dairy Journal, vol. 3, no. 3, pp. 257–275, 1993.

155. R. Cachon and C. Divies, "Localization of Lactococcus lactis ssp lactis bv diacetylactis in alginate gel beads affects biomass density and synthesis of several enzymes involved in lactose and citrate metabolism," Biotechnology Techniques, vol. 7, no. 6, pp. 453–456, 1993.

156. T. Jankowski, M. Zielinska, and A. Wysakowska, "Encapsulation of lactic acid bacteria with alginate/starch capsules," Biotechnology Techniques, vol. 11, no. 1, pp. 31–34, 1997.

157. L. D. McMaster, S. A. Kokott, and P. Slatter, "Micro-encapsulation of Bifidobacterium lactis for incorporation into soft foods," World Journal of Microbiology and Biotechnology, vol. 21, no. 5, pp. 723–728, 2005.

158. L. D. McMaster, S. A. Kokott, S. J. Reid, and V. R. Abratt, "Use of traditional African fermented beverages as delivery vehicles for Bifidobacterium lactis DSM 10140," International Journal of Food Microbiology, vol. 102, no. 2, pp. 231–237, 2005.

159. C. P. Champagne, C. Gaudy, D. Poncelet, and R. J. Neufeld, "Lactococcus lactis release from calcium alginate beads," Applied and Environmental Microbiology, vol. 58, no. 5, pp. 1429–1434, 1992.

160. C. Martoni, J. Bhathena, A. M. Urbanska, and S. Prakash, "Microencapsulated bile salt hydrolase producing Lactobacillus reuteri for oral targeted delivery in the gastrointestinal tract," Applied Microbiology and Biotechnology, vol. 81, no. 2, pp. 225–233, 2008.

161. V. Chandramouli, K. Kailasapathy, P. Peiris, and M. Jones, "An improved method of microencapsulation and its evaluation to protect Lactobacillus spp. in simulated gastric conditions," Journal of Microbiological Methods, vol. 56, no. 1, pp. 27–35, 2004.

162. S. Graff, J. Chaumeil, P. Boy, R. Lai-Kuen, and C. Charrueau, "Formulations for protecting the probiotic Saccharomyces boulardii from degradation in acidic condition," Biological and Pharmaceutical Bulletin, vol. 31, no. 2, pp. 266–272, 2008.

163. M. Chen, K. Chen, and Y. Kuo, "Optimal thermotolerance of Bifidobacterium bifidum in gellan-alginate microparticles," Biotechnology and Bioengineering, vol. 98, no. 2, pp. 411–419, 2007.

164. K. Chen, M. Chen, and C. Lin, "Optimal combination of the encapsulating materials for probiotic microcapsules and its experimental verification (R1)," Journal of Food Engineering, vol. 76, no. 3, pp. 313–320, 2006.

165. K. Lee and T. Heo, "Survival of Bifidobacterium longum immobilized in calcium alginate beads in simulated gastric juices and bile salt solution," Applied and Environmental Microbiology, vol. 66, no. 2, pp. 869–873, 2000.

166. P. Muthukumarasamy and R. A. Holley, "Survival of Escherichia coli O157:H7 in dry fermented sausages containing micro-encapsulated probiotic lactic acid bacteria," Food Microbiology, vol. 24, no. 1, pp. 82–88, 2007.

167. P. Muthukumarasamy and R. A. Holley, "Microbiological and sensory quality of dry fermented sausages containing alginate-microencapsulated Lactobacillus reuteri," International Journal of Food Microbiology, vol. 111, no. 2, pp. 164–169, 2006.

168. K. Kailasapathy, "Survival of free and encapsulated probiotic bacteria and their effect on the sensory properties of yoghurt," Lebensmittel-Wissenschaft und Technologie, vol. 39, no. 10, pp. 1221–1227, 2006.

169. P. Dinakar and V. V. Mistry, "Growth and viability of Bifidobacterium bifidum in cheddar cheese,"Journal of Dairy Science, vol. 77, no. 10, pp. 2854–2864, 1994.

170. P. Audet, C. Paquin, and C. Lacroix, "Immobilized growing lactic acid bacteria with κ-carrageenan—locust bean gum gel," Applied Microbiology and Biotechnology, vol. 29, no. 1, pp. 11–18, 1988.

171. A. V. Rao, N. Shiwnarain, and I. Maharaj, "Survival of microencapsulated Bifidobacterium pseudolongum in simulated gastric and intestinal juices," Canadian Institute of Food Science and Technology Journal, vol. 22, no. 4, pp. 345–349, 1989.

172. T. Y. Sheu and R. T. Marshall, "Improving culture viability in frozen dairy desserts by microencapsulation," Journal of Dairy Science, vol. 74, supplement 1, article 107, 1991.

173. J.-P. Arnaud, C. Lacroix, and L. Choplin, "Effect of agitation rate on cell release rate and metabolism during continuous fermentation with entrapped growing—Lactobacillus casei subsp. casei,"Biotechnology Techniques, vol. 6, no. 3, pp. 265–270, 1992.

174. A. F. Groboillot, C. P. Champagne, G. D. Darling, D. Poncelet, and R. J. Neufeld, "Membrane formation by interfacial cross-linking of chitosan for microencapsulation of Lactococcus lactis," Biotechnology and Bioengineering, vol. 42, no. 10, pp. 1157–1163, 1993.

175. T. Y. Sheu, R. T. Marshall, and H. Heymann, "Improving survival of culture bacteria in frozen desserts by microentrapment," Journal of Dairy Science, vol. 76, no. 7, pp. 1902–1907, 1993.

176. C. L. Hyndman, A. F. Groboillot, D. Poncelet, C. P. Champagne, and R. J. Neufeld, "Microencapsulation of Lactococcus lactis within cross-linked gelatin membranes," Journal of Chemical

Technology and Biotechnology, vol. 56, no. 3, pp. 259–263, 1993.

177. B. C. Larisch, D. Poncelet, C. P. Champagne, and R. J. Neufeld, "Microencapsulation of Lactococcus lactis subsp. cremoris," Journal of Microencapsulation, vol. 11, no. 2, pp. 189–195, 1994.

178. S. Mandal, A. K. Puniya, and K. Singh, "Effect of alginate concentrations on survival of microencapsulated Lactobacillus casei NCDC-298," International Dairy Journal, vol. 16, no. 10, pp. 1190–1195, 2006.

179. J. S. Lee, D. S. Cha, and H. J. Park, "Survival of freeze-dried Lactobacillus bulgaricus KFRI 673 in chitosan-coated calcium alginate microparticles," Journal of Agricultural and Food Chemistry, vol. 52, no. 24, pp. 7300–7305, 2004.

180. A. Homayouni, A. Azizi, M. R. Ehsani, M. S. Yarmand, and S. H. Razavi, "Effect of microencapsulation and resistant starch on the probiotic survival and sensory properties of synbiotic ice cream," Food Chemistry, vol. 111, no. 1, pp. 50–55, 2008.

181. K. Sultana, G. Godward, N. Reynolds, R. Arumugaswamy, P. Peiris, and K. Kailasapathy, "Encapsulation of probiotic bacteria with alginate-starch and evaluation of survival in simulated gastrointestinal conditions and in yoghurt," International Journal of Food Microbiology, vol. 62, no. 1-2, pp. 47–55, 2000.

182. N. T. Annan, A. D. Borza, and L. T. Hansen, "Encapsulation in alginate-coated gelatin microspheres improves survival of the probiotic Bifidobacterium adolescentis 15703T during exposure to simulated gastro-intestinal conditions," Food Research International, vol. 41, no. 2, pp. 184–193, 2008.

183. W. Lian, H. Hsiao, and C. Chou, "Survival of bifidobacteria after spray-drying," International Journal of Food Microbiology, vol. 74, no. 1-2, pp. 79–86, 2002.

184. W. Lian, H. Hsiao, and C. Chou, "Viability of microencapsulated bifidobacteria in simulated gastric juice and bile solution," International Journal of Food Microbiology, vol. 86, no. 3, pp. 293–301, 2003.

185. H. Hsiao, W. Lian, and C. Chou, "Effect of packaging conditions and temperature on viability of microencapsulated bifidobacteria during storage," Journal of the Science of Food and Agriculture, vol. 84, no. 2, pp. 134–139, 2004.

186. G. E. Gardiner, P. Bouchier, E. O'Sullivan et al., "A spray-dried culture for probiotic Cheddar cheese manufacture," International Dairy Journal, vol. 12, no. 9, pp. 749–756, 2002.

187. E. Ananta, M. Volkert, and D. Knorr, "Cellular injuries and storage stability of spray-dried Lactobacillus rhamnosus GG," International Dairy Journal, vol. 15, no. 4, pp. 399–409, 2005.

188. A. Picot and C. Lacroix, "Effects of micronization on viability and thermotolerance of probiotic freeze-dried cultures," International Dairy Journal, vol. 13, no. 6, pp. 455–462, 2003.

189. K. O'Riordan, D. Andrews, K. Buckle, and P. Conway, "Evaluation of microencapsulation of a Bifidobacterium strain with starch as an approach to prolonging viability during storage," Journal of Applied Microbiology, vol. 91, no. 6, pp. 1059–1066, 2001.

190. L. Su, C. Lin, and M. Chen, "Development of an Oriental-style dairy product coagulated by microcapsules containing probiotics and filtrates from fermented rice," International Journal of Dairy Technology, vol. 60, no. 1, pp. 49–54, 2007.

191. C. S. Fávaro-Trindade and C. R. F. Grosso, "Microencapsulation of L. acidophilus (La-05) and B. lactis (Bb-12) and evaluation of their survival at the pH values of the stomach and in bile," Journal of Microencapsulation, vol. 19, no. 4, pp. 485–494, 2002.

192. C. Desmond, R. P. Ross, E. O'Callaghan, G. Fitzgerald, and C. Stanton, "Improved survival of Lactobacillus paracasei NFBC 338 in spray-dried powders containing gum acacia," Journal of Applied Microbiology, vol. 93, no. 6, pp. 1003–1011, 2002.

193. A. Madene, M. Jacquot, J. Scher, and S. Desobry, "Flavour encapsulation and controlled release—a

review," International Journal of Food Science and Technology, vol. 41, no. 1, pp. 1–21, 2006.

194. K. Kailasapathy, "Microencapsulation of probiotic bacteria: technology and potential applications,"Current Issues in Intestinal Microbiology, vol. 3, no. 2, pp. 39–48, 2002.

195. C. Santivarangkna, U. Kulozik, and P. Foerst, "Alternative drying processes for the industrial preservation of lactic acid starter cultures," Biotechnology Progress, vol. 23, no. 2, pp. 302–315, 2007.

196. E. Roelans and D. Taeymans, "Effect of drying condition on survival and enzyme activity of microorganisms," in Engineering and Food Volume 3, W. E. L. Spiess and H. Schubert, Eds., Advanced Process, pp. 559–569, Elsevier Applied Science, London, UK, 1990.

197. L. J. M. Linders, W. F. Wolkers, F. A. Hoekstra, and K. van't Riet, "Effect of added carbohydrate on membrane phase behaviour and survival of dried Lactobacillus plantarum," Cryobiology, vol. 35, no. 1, pp. 31–40, 1997.

198. E. Selmer-Olsen, T. Sørhaug, S.-E. Birkeland, and R. Pohrson, "Survival of Lactobacillus helveticus entrapped in Ca-alginate in relation to water content, storage and rehydration," Journal of Industrial Microbiology and Biotechnology, vol. 23, no. 2, pp. 79–85, 1999.

199. Y. Mille, J. Obert, L. Beney, and P. Gervais, "New drying process for lactic bacteria based on their dehydration behavior in liquid medium," Biotechnology and Bioengineering, vol. 88, no. 1, pp. 71–76, 2004.

200. D. Semyonov, O. Ramon, Z. Kaplun, L. Levin-Brener, N. Gurevich, and E. Shimoni, "Microencapsulation of Lactobacillus paracasei by spray freeze drying," Food Research International, vol. 43, no. 1, pp. 193–202, 2010.

201. A. Martinsen, G. Skjak-Braek, and O. Smidsrod, "Alginate as immobilization material: i. Correlation between chemical and physical properties of alginate gel beads," Biotechnology and Bioengineering, vol. 33, no. 1, pp. 79–89, 1989.

202. J. Klein, J. Stock, and K.-D. Vorlop, "Pore size and properties of spherical Ca-alginate biocatalysts,"European Journal of Applied Microbiology and Biotechnology, vol. 18, no. 2, pp. 86–91, 1983.

203. H. Eikmeier and H. J. Rehm, "Stability of calcium-alginate during citric acid production of immobilized Aspergillus niger," Applied Microbiology and Biotechnology, vol. 26, no. 2, pp. 105–111, 1987.

204. J. C. Ellenton, Encapsulation bifidobacteria [M.S. thesis], University of Guelph, Guelph, Canada, 1998.

205. M. T. Cook, G. Tzortzis, D. Charalampopoulos, and V. V. Khutoryanskiy, "Microencapsulation of probiotics for gastrointestinal delivery," Journal of Controlled Release, vol. 162, pp. 56–57, 2012.

206. C. P. Champagene and P. Fustier, "Microencapsulation for delivery of probiotics and other ingredients in functional dairy products," Functional Dairy Products, vol. 2, pp. 404–426, 2007.

207. G. K. Gbassi and T. Vandamme, "Probiotic encapsulation technology: from microencapsulation to release into the gut," Pharmaceutics, vol. 4, no. 1, pp. 149–163, 2012.

208. A. H. King, "Encapsulation of food ingredients: a review of available technology, focussing on hydrocolloid," in Encapsulation and Controlled Release of Food Ingredients, J. R. Sara and A. R. Gary, Eds., vol. 590 of ACS Symposium Series, pp. 26–39, American Chemical Society, Washington, DC, USA.

209. K. Kailasapathy, "Encapsulation technologies for functional foods and nutraceutical product development," CAB Reviews, vol. 4, no. 6, pp. 1–19, 2009.

210. P. de Vos, M. M. Faas, M. Spasojevic, and J. Sikkema, "Encapsulation for preservation of functionality and targeted delivery of bioactive food components," International Dairy Journal, vol. 20, no. 4, pp. 292–302, 2010.

211. O. Smidsrod and G. Skjak-Braek, "Alginate as immobilization matrix for cells," Trends in Biotechnology, vol. 8, no. 3, pp. 71–75, 1990.

212. S. Overgaard, J. M. Scharer, M. Moo-Young, and N. C. Bols, "Immobilization of hybridoma cells in chitosan alginate beads," Canadian Journal of Chemical Engineering, vol. 69, no. 2, pp. 439–443, 1991.

213. C. Lacroix, C. Paquin, and J.-P. Arnaud, "Batch fermentation with entrapped growing cells of Lactobacillus casei. Optimization of the rheological properties of the entrapment gel matrix," Applied Microbiology and Biotechnology, vol. 32, no. 4, pp. 403–408, 1990.

214. A. W. Adamson, Physical Chemistry of Surfaces, Wiley, New York, NY, USA, 1982.

215. T. Heidebach, P. Först, and U. Kulozik, "Microencapsulation of probiotic cells by means of rennet-gelation of milk proteins," Food Hydrocolloids, vol. 23, no. 7, pp. 1670–1677, 2009.

216. T. Heidebach, P. Först, and U. Kulozik, "Transglutaminase-induced caseinate gelation for the microencapsulation of probiotic cells," International Dairy Journal, vol. 19, no. 2, pp. 77–84, 2009.

217. Y. D. Livney, "Milk proteins as vehicles for bioactives," Current Opinion in Colloid and Interface Science, vol. 15, no. 1-2, pp. 73–83, 2010.

218. J. Yáñez-Fernández, E. G. Ramos-Ramírez, and J. A. Salazar-Montoya, "Rheological characterization of dispersions and emulsions used in the preparation of microcapsules obtained by interfacial polymerization containing Lactobacillus sp," European Food Research and Technology, vol. 226, no. 5, pp. 957–966, 2008.

219. A. Dimantov, M. Greenberg, E. Kesselman, and E. Shimoni, "Study of high amylose corn starch as food grade enteric coating in a microcapsule model system," Innovative Food Science and Emerging Technologies, vol. 5, no. 1, pp. 93–100, 2003.

220. M. J. Pikal, "Freeze-drying of protein, part-I: process design," PharmTech International, vol. 1, pp. 37–43, 1991.

221. A. R. Donthidi, R. F. Tester, and K. E. Aidoo, "Effect of lecithin and starch on alginate-encapsulated probiotic bacteria," Journal of Microencapsulation, vol. 27, no. 1, pp. 67–77, 2010.

222. N. Huyghebaert, A. Vermeire, P. Rottiers, E. Remaut, and J. P. Remon, "Development of an enteric-coated, layered multi-particulate formulation for ileal delivery of viable recombinant Lactococcus lactis,"European Journal of Pharmaceutics and Biopharmaceutics, vol. 61, no. 3, pp. 134–141, 2005.

223. H. Hayashi, E. Kumazawa, Y. Saeki, and Y. Ishioka, "Continuous vaccum dryer for energy saving," Drying Technology, vol. 1, no. 2, pp. 275–284, 1983.

224. Z. L. Wang, W. H. Finlay, M. S. Peppler, and L. G. Sweeney, "Powder formation by atmospheric spray-freeze-drying," Powder Technology, vol. 170, no. 1, pp. 45–52, 2006.

225. H. Durand and J. Panes, "Particles containing coated living micro-organisms, and method for producing same," US patent and Trademark Office, N20030109025.

226. V. Truong, D. A. Clare, G. L. Catignani, and H. E. Swaisgood, "Cross-linking and rheological changes of whey protein treated with microbial transglutaminase," Journal of Agricultural and Food Chemistry, vol. 52, no. 5, pp. 1170–1176, 2004.

227. B. R. Bhandari, N. Datta, B. R. D'Arcy, and G. B. Rintoul, "Co-crystallization of honey with sucrose,"Food Science and Technology, vol. 31, no. 2, pp. 138–142, 1998.

228. A. Hedges and C. McBride, "Utilization of β-cyclodextrin in food," Cereal Foods World, vol. 44, no. 10, pp. 700–704, 1999.

229. F. T. Gentile, E. J. Doherty, D. H. Rein, M. S. Shoichet, and S. R. Winn, "Polymer science for macroencapsulation of cells for central nervous system transplantation," Reactive Polymers, vol. 25, no. 2-3, pp. 207–227, 1995.

230. Z. Dong, Q. Wang, and Y. Du, "Alginate/gelatin blend films and their properties for drug controlled release," Journal of Membrane Science, vol. 280, no. 1-2, pp. 37–44, 2006.

231. K. I. Draget, K. Steinsvåg, E. Onsøyen, and O. Smidsrød, "Na^+ and K^+alginate; effect on Ca^{2+}-gelation,"Carbohydrate Polymers, vol. 35, no. 1-2, pp. 1–6, 1998.

232. T. Harnsilawat, R. Pongsawatmanit, and D. J. McClements, "Characterization of β-lactoglobulin-sodium alginate interactions in aqueous solutions: a calorimetry, light scattering, electrophoretic mobility and solubility study," Food Hydrocolloids, vol. 20, no. 5, pp. 577–585, 2006.

233. L. T. Hansen, P. M. Allan-Wojtas, Y.-L. Jin, and A. T. Paulson, "Survival of Ca-alginate microencapsulated Bifidobacterium spp. in milk and simulated gastrointestinal conditions," Food Microbiology, vol. 19, no. 1, pp. 35–45, 2002.

234. G. F. Fanta, C. A. Knutson, K. S. Eskins, and F. C. Felker, "Starch microcapsules for delivery of active agents," US patent. 2001, 6, 238, 677.

235. S. G. Haralampu, "Resistant starch—a review of the physical properties and biological impact of RS3,"Carbohydrate Polymers, vol. 41, no. 3, pp. 285–292, 2000.

236. C. J. Malm, J. Emerson, and G. D. Hiatt, "Cellulose acetate phthalate as an enteric coating material,"Journal of the American Pharmaceutical Association, vol. 40, no. 10, pp. 520–525, 1951.

237. S. Gaaloul, S. L. Turgeon, and M. Corredig, "Influence of shearing on the physical characteristics and rheological behaviour of an aqueous whey protein isolate-κappa-carrageenan mixture," Food Hydrocolloids, vol. 23, no. 5, pp. 1243–1252, 2009.

238. Y. Yuguchi, T. T. T. Thuy, H. Urakawa, and K. Kajiwara, "Structural characteristics of carrageenan gels: temperature and concentration dependence," Food Hydrocolloids, vol. 16, no. 6, pp. 515–522, 2002.

239. M. R. Mangione, D. Giacomazza, D. Bulone, V. Martorana, and P. L. san Biagio, "Thermoreversible gelation of κ-

Carrageenan: relation between conformational transition and aggregation," Biophysical Chemistry, vol. 104, no. 1, pp. 95–105, 2003.

240. H. P. Sarett, "Safety of carrageenan used in foods," The Lancet, vol. 1, no. 8212, pp. 151–152, 1981.

241. Y. Doleyres, I. Fliss, and C. Lacroix, "Continuous production of mixed lactic starters containing probiotic using immobilised cell technology," Biotechnology Progress, vol. 20, no. 1, pp. 145–150, 2004.

242. J. Klien and D. K. Vorlop, "Immobilisation technique cells," in Comprehensive Biotechnology, M. Moo-Yong, C. L. Cooney, and A. E. Humphery, Eds., pp. 542–550, Pergamon Press, Oxford, UK, 1985.

243. S. Rokka and P. Rantamäki, "Protecting probiotic bacteria by microencapsulation: challenges for industrial applications," European Food Research and Technology, vol. 231, no. 1, pp. 1–12, 2010.

244. A. A. Reid, C. P. Champagne, N. Gardner, P. Fustier, and J. C. Vuillemard, "Survival in food systems of Lactobacillus rhamnosus R011 microentrapped in whey protein gel particles," Journal of Food Science, vol. 72, no. 1, pp. M31–M37, 2006.

4

CHAPTER

Immunogenicity of Biotherapeutics: Causes and Association with Posttranslational Modifications

Anshu Kuriakose, Narendra Chirmule, and Pradip Nair

Biocon Research Limited, Research & Development, Bangalore, Karnataka 560099, India

ABSTRACT

Today, potential immunogenicity can be better evaluated during the drug development process, and we have rational approaches to manage the clinical consequences of immunogenicity. The focus of the scientific community should be on developing sensitive diagnostics that can predict immunogenicity-mediated adverse events in the small fraction of subjects that develop clinically relevant anti-drug antibodies. Here, we discuss the causes of immunogenicity which could be product-related (inherent property of the product or might be picked up during the manufacturing process), patient-related (genetic profile or eating habits), or linked to the route of administration. We describe various posttranslational modifications (PTMs) and how they may influence immunogenicity. Over the last three decades, we have significantly improved our understanding about the types of PTMs of biotherapeutic proteins and their association with immunogenicity. It is also now clear that all PTMs do not lead to clinical immunogenicity. We also discuss the mechanisms of immunogenicity (which include T cell-dependent and T cell-independent responses) and immunological tolerance. We further elaborate on the management of immunogenicity in preclinical and clinical setting and the unique challenges raised by biosimilars, which may have different immunogenic potential from their parent biotherapeutics.

1. INTRODUCTION

Posttranslational modifications (PTMs) refer to enzymatic modifications that occur after translation, and which result in mature protein products. PTMs increase the functional diversity of the proteome, by the covalent addition of functional groups, proteolytic cleavage of regulatory subunits, or selective degradation of entire proteins. These modifications include glycosylation, acetylation, acylation, ADP-ribosylation, amidation, γ-carboxylation, β-hydroxylation, disulfide bond formation, phosphorylation, proteolytic processing, and sulfation and influence almost all aspects of normal cell biology and pathogenesis. Therefore, all living cells are tuned to use PTMs to regulate cellular activity. In addition, these PTMs have a major impact on evolution; multisite PTMs lead to a combinatorial explosion in the number of potential molecular states. Such complexity may provide the foundation for sophisticated forms of cellular information processing that are essential for the emergence of complex organisms [1].

In comparison with small molecule drugs, protein pharmaceuticals are complex entities; and since they are usually expressed in cellular systems, they are exposed to factors which could influence PTMs. The PTM profile is dependent on several factors including the type and differentiation status of the host cell, upstream and downstream manufacturing process, formulation, and storage conditions and microheterogeneities formed during fermentation and downstream processing. Naturally occurring PTMs have been associated with unwanted immunogenicity and autoimmune diseases. Recent studies have identified anticitrullinated protein antibodies, along with other antibodies to specific posttranslational modified proteins, as biomarkers in rheumatoid arthritis, psoriatic arthritis, periodontitis, and osteoarthritis [2]. It is hypothesized that such PTMs induce neoepitopes that can generate novel antibody specificities probably triggering autoimmunity. Given the multiplicity of possible PTMs, any variation in a recombinant protein's PTM profile relative to the natural product might be of concern and should be evaluated. Adverse immune reactions can lead to clinical consequences, such as anaphylaxis, reduced drug half-life, and neutralization of the therapeutic protein as well as its endogenous human homologue [3, 4]. However, it should be noted that, of the very large number of patients treated with biotherapeutic proteins over the years, only a few are affected by undesirable immune responses [5, 6]. For example, a ~2% incidence of adverse reactions (attributable to anti-drug antibodies, ADAs) for insulin and an even rarer but more clinically serious effect for erythropoietin has been reported [7,8]. These studies clearly indicate that some patients are more susceptible to immune responses than others.

In this review, we will identify some of the causes of immunogenicity in therapeutic proteins and will discuss the association of immunogenicity with PTMs, with other critical quality attributes of protein therapeutics, and with patient characteristics.

2. IMMUNOGENICITY AND ITS CAUSES

Immunogenic response to therapeutic molecules can generate anti-drug antibodies (ADAs), which can be either neutralizing or nonneutralizing. Neutralizing antibodies (NAbs) bind to sites in therapeutic proteins in such a way that they directly impair or abrogate the biological functions of therapeutic proteins [6, 9]. NAb responses have the potential to cause negative clinical consequences by neutralizing the therapeutic product and therefore reducing efficacy, as has been seen with factor VIII or streptokinase [10, 11]. This reduced efficacy would, in some cases, require the need to dose patients more frequently to get the desired clinical effect. The situation can further be aggravated if the NAbs neutralize not only therapeutic proteins but also the endogenous counterpart of the therapeutic agent, resulting in severe adverse consequences. Examples of drugs inducing ADAs which also inactivate autologous proteins include recombinant human thrombopoietin [12,13], erythropoietin [5, 14, 15], GM-CSF [16], and many interferons [17–19]. The problem is most often seen with non-mAb therapeutic proteins with significant similarity to host proteins (except for a few amino acid changes or glycosylation differences) [13]. However, some non-mAb proteins such as insulin, factor XIII, and αinterferons (IFNs) primarily induce nonneutralizing ADAs and the effect is not physiologically debilitating. In these cases, clinicians often continue treatment in the presence of ADAs. This may indicate that it is not always possible to break self-tolerance even when the self-protein is exogenously chronically administered. Overall, only a small percentage of treated patients develop adverse immunogenic reactions attributed to the formation of NAbs [6].

Most patients who develop ADA response to therapeutic proteins generate nonneutralizing antibodies (NNAbs). These antibodies bind to antigenic sites in the therapeutic proteins in ways that do not affect the therapeutic effects of these drugs. Examples are NNAbs generated against tumor necrosis factor receptor and recombinant human growth hormone [20]. In some cases NNAbs can accelerate the clearance of therapeutic proteins resulting in reduced drug efficacy [13]. Product- and process-related factors can affect immunogenicity by minor alterations in the tertiary structure of the molecule such as altered protein folding. Additionally, patient characteristics, dose, and route of administration of the biotherapeutics can also lead to an increased risk of immunogenicity [21]. This will be described in more detail in later sections.

2.1. Product- and Process-Related Causes of Immunogenicity

The first therapeutic insulin products in the 1920s were of bovine or porcine origin and were therefore immunogenic in humans. In some cases, fatal anaphylactic reactions were reported [22]. The molecular structure of proteins purified from animal sources is different from that of their human counterparts. Thus it is expected that these proteins will be seen as "foreign" by the human immune system. Interestingly, removal of proinsulin, C-peptide, glucagon, and somatostatin from porcine insulin preparations led to a remarkable decrease in immunogenicity [22]. These results suggested that the anti-insulin antibodies generated may have been against noninsulin proteins or adjuvant-like contaminants [23]. This observation indicated that deviation from the structure of the human homologue is not the only determinant of immunogenicity.

Impurities have been held responsible for the immunogenicity of several therapeutic proteins. Human growth hormone (hGH) derived from the pituitary glands of cadavers and from patients undergoing hypophysectomy had been used in hypopituitary children to stimulate their growth [43]. Fifty percent of treated children developed immune reaction to the first clinical grade hGH; and this was attributed to the presence of 40% to 70% aggregated hGH in the product [44]. Improvement of the purification process decreased the aggregates to less than 5%, which resulted in slower onset of antibody production. Resulting antibodies had high affinities but were significantly less persistent [4].

Humanization of monoclonal antibodies has significantly decreased immunogenicity, especially the intense immunogenicity (allergic reactions culminating in anaphylactic shock) observed with early murine antibodies, which generated a human anti-mouse antibody (HAMA) response. However, some humanized and even fully human sequence-derived antibody molecules still carry immunological risk. Often the cause for immunogenicity with these fully human molecules is associated with unique (nonhuman) sequences in the cluster of differentiation regions (CDRs) of these antibodies [24] and modifying certain amino acids in these regions could reduce immunogenicity risk. For example, despite being humanized, alemtuzumab induced binding antibodies and NAbs in 30% to 70% of patients. It was shown that pretreatment with an altered version of alemtuzumab, which no longer binds to its target, induced immunogenic tolerance to alemtuzumab itself [28]. Other fully human antibodies such as canakinumab, ofatumumab, and pembrolizumab induced ADAs at very low incidence (<0.5%) [30, 35, 39, 45]. Details of immunogenicity and NAbs reported for mAbs are shown in Table 1.

Table 1: Immunogenicity of FDA-approved biologics.

SI number	Biologic	Type/target	Indications	Immunogenicity (% patients)		Reference
				Binding antibodies	Neutralizing antibodies	
(1)	Adalimumab	Human IgG1 antibody specific for TNF alpha	Rheumatoid arthritis, psoriasis	5%–89%	5%–89%	[24–27]
(2)	Alemtuzumab	Humanized monoclonal antibody which binds to CD52 on leukocytes	B cell chronic lymphocytic leukaemia	30%–70%	30%–70%	[28]
(3)	Belimumab	Human monoclonal antibody that inhibits the biologic activity of the soluble form of the essential B cell survival factor B-lymphocyte stimulator	Systemic lupus erythematosus	4.8%	3/11	[29] European Medicines Agency Assessment Report (http://www.ema.europa.eu/docs/en_GB/document_library/EPAR_-_Public_assessment_report/human/002015/WC500110152.pdf)
(4)	Canakinumab	Human monoclonal antibody anti-IL-1β	Inflammatory diseases related to cryopyrin-associated periodic syndromes (familial cold autoinflammatory syndrome and Muckle-Wells syndrome)	0%	0%	[24, 30]
(5)	Cetuximab	Human/mouse chimeric monoclonal antibody that binds specifically to the extracellular domain of the human epidermal growth factor receptor	Colorectal cancer, squamous cell carcinoma of the head and neck	5%	Data not available	Drug label (http://pi.lilly.com/us/erbitux-uspi.pdf)

SI number	Biologic	Type/target	Indications	Immunogenicity (% patients)		Reference
				Binding antibodies	Neutralizing antibodies	
(6)	Denosumab	Human monoclonal antibody RANK ligand inhibitor	Treatment of postmenopausal women with osteoporosis at high risk for fracture To increase bone mass in men at high risk for fracture receiving androgen deprivation therapy for nonmetastatic prostate cancer To increase bone mass in women at high risk for fracture receiving adjuvant aromatase inhibitor therapy for breast cancer	<1%	0%	Drug label (http://www.accessdata.fda.gov/drugsatfda_docs/label/2011/125320s5s6lbl.pdf)
(7)	Golimumab	Human monoclonal antibody anti-TNF-alpha	Rheumatoid arthritis, psoriatic arthritis, and ankylosing spondylitis	4%	Data not available	[31–33]
(8)	Infliximab	Chimeric monoclonal antibody TNF blocker	Crohn's disease, ulcerative colitis, rheumatoid arthritis, ankylosing spondylitis, and psoriasis	Crohn's Disease: 10%, psoriatic arthritis: 15% psoriasis: 36–51%	Data not available	Drug label (http://www.accessdata.fda.gov/drugsatfda_docs/label/2013/103772s5359lbl.pdf)
(9)	Ipilimumab	Human monoclonal antibody that binds to cytotoxic T-lymphocyte-associated antigen 4 (CTLA-4)	Melanoma	1.1% of 1024 evaluable patients tested positive for binding antibodies and 6.9% of 58 evaluable patients, who were treated with 0.3 mg/kg (dose cohort with the lowest trough levels) dose, tested positive for binding antibodies.	0%	Drug label (http://www.accessdata.fda.gov/drugsatfda_docs/label/2013/103772s5359lbl.pdf)

SI number	Biologic	Type/target	Indications	Immunogenicity (% patients)		Reference
				Binding antibodies	Neutralizing antibodies	
(10)	Natalizumab	Human monoclonal antibody, which works against the cell adhesion molecule α4-integrin	Multiple sclerosis and Crohn's disease	9%	9%	Drug label (http://www.accessdata.fda.gov/drugsatfda_docs/label/2008/125104s033lbl.pdf)
(11)	Nivolumab	Human monoclonal antibody IgG4 PD-1 immune checkpoint inhibitor	Squamous non-small cell lung cancer, unresectable or metastatic melanoma, and disease progression following ipilimumab and, if BRAF V600 mutation positive, a BRAF inhibitor	8.5%	0.7%	[34] Drug label (http://www.accessdata.fda.gov/drugsatfda_docs/label/2014/125554lbl.pdf)
(12)	Ofatumumab	Human monoclonal antibody anti-CD20	Rheumatoid arthritis, chronic lymphocytic leukaemia	0%	0%	[24, 35]
(13)	Panitumumab	Human monoclonal antibody against the epidermal growth factor receptor	Colorectal carcinoma	1–4.6%	0.8–1.6%	[24, 36–38] Drug label (http://www.accessdata.fda.gov/drugsatfda_docs/label/2009/125147s080lbl.pdf)
(14)	Pembrolizumab	Human monoclonal antibody PD-1 blocking	Unresectable or metastatic melanoma and disease progression following ipilimumab and, if BRAF V600 mutation positive, a BRAF inhibitor, metastatic NSCLC whose tumors express PD-L1	0.3%	0.3%	[39] Drug label (http://www.accessdata.fda.gov/drugsatfda_docs/label/2015/125514s004s006lbl.pdf)

SI number	Biologic	Type/target	Indications	Immunogenicity (% patients)		Reference
				Binding antibodies	Neutralizing antibodies	
(15)	Ramucirumab	Human monoclonal antibody vascular endothelial growth factor receptor 2 antagonist	Gastric cancer	6%	1%	Drug label (http://www.accessdata.fda.gov/drugsatfda_docs/label/2014/125477s002lbl.pdf)
(16)	Rituximab	Chimeric monoclonal antibody that targets the CD20 molecule expressed on the surface of B cells	Non-Hodgkin's lymphoma, rheumatoid arthritis	11%	Data not available	[40]
(17)	Secukinumab	Human monoclonal antibody against IL-17A	Plaque psoriasis	0.4%	3/10	[41] Drug information (http://www.fda.gov/downloads/AdvisoryCommittees/CommitteesMeetingMaterials/Drugs/DermatologicandOphthalmicDrugsAdvisoryCommittee/UCM419023.pdf)
(18)	Siltuximab	Chimeric monoclonal antibody anti-IL-6	Multicentric Castleman's disease (a rare lymphoproliferative disorder) being human immunodeficiency virus-negative and human herpes virus-8-negative	0.2%	0%	Drug label (http://www.accessdata.fda.gov/drugsatfda_docs/label/2014/125496s000lbl.pdf)
(19)	Ustekinumab	Human monoclonal antibody that binds to the p40 protein subunit used by both the IL-12 and IL-23 cytokines.	Psoriasis	6.6%	Data not available	[42]
(20)	Vedolizumab	Humanised IgG1 monoclonal antibody that binds to the human $\alpha4\beta7$ integrin	Ulcerative colitis and Crohn's disease	4%	33/56	Drug label (http://www.accessdata.fda.gov/drugsatfda_docs/label/2014/125476s000lbl.pdf)

IgG: immunoglobulin G; IL: interleukin; TNF: tumour necrosis factor; CD: cluster of differentiation; RANK: receptor activator of nuclear factor kappa-B; PD-1: programmed cell death protein-1; PDL-1: programmed death ligand-1; NSCLC: non-small cell lung cancer.

Intrinsic factors influence the immunogenicity of antibodies; for example, antibodies directed at cell surface markers are deemed to have a higher risk of immunogenicity than those against soluble factors [24]. The reasons for this are not completely understood but may include antigen internalization and subsequent processing and presentation by target cells [24, 46]. A similar intrinsic factor is the presence of carbohydrate side-chains attached to the antibody via glycosylation sites, conferred by the amino acid sequence of the light chain constant region, the heavy chain constant region, or the V region itself [47, 48]. The presence of a galactose-alpha-1,3-galactose sugar within a carbohydrate structure on the Fab fragment of cetuximab was found to be associated with severe anaphylactic reactions to the antibody. Most patients were found to have preexisting immunoglobulin E (IgE) antibodies specific for the galactose-alpha-1,3-galactose sugars [49]. Notably, when cetuximab was manufactured in a cell line that could not add galactose-alpha-1,3-galactose to the antibody carbohydrate (a Chinese hamster ovary- [CHO-] derived manufacturing cell line), the product was much less immunogenic [49].

Other PTMs, such as glycation, deamidation, and oxidation of amino acid side-chains, may confer immunogenicity as well [24, 50]. Introducing additional N-linked glycosylation sites to create an erythropoietin (EPO) product with improved efficacy and catabolic half-life [51] did not result in increased immunogenicity [52]. However, it was noted that the subcutaneous administration of EPO was associated with pure red cell aplasia (PRCA) in some cases, because of NAbs generated to endogenous EPO. Although the cause of this reaction is still uncertain [53], extractables and leachates from the container are thought to have been responsible [54]. An increased concentration of anti-ESA IgG4 antibody is associated with the development of antibody mediated PRCA (amPRCA) [55].

2.2. Patient-Related Causes of Immunogenicity and Influence of Route of Administration

Generally, patients with impaired immune systems (e.g., cancer patients receiving chemotherapy) may be less likely to develop antibodies to therapeutic proteins than immunocompetent individuals [56, 57].

Exposure of patients to replacement therapeutic proteins that the patients cannot synthesize frequently leads to the generation of NAbs [58]. For example, NAbs frequently develop in severe congenital factor (F) XI-, FIX-, and FVIII-deficient patients treated with the missing therapeutic proteins [10, 59–61]. The inherent polymorphism of human proteins may be another contributing factor toward immunogenicity. This is especially applicable in hemophilia, where patients are predominantly categorized into two major groups. One group has large deletions, nonsense mutations, and intron 22 inversions leading to nondetection of FVIII protein in the plasma. This group, who have never been exposed to FVIII, generate anti-FVIII in more than 30% of treated patients. The second group of patients have small deletions, insertions, and point mutations and therefore might be innately tolerant to therapeutic FVIII administration. In this latter group, anti-FVIII antibody prevalence is less than 10% [62]. When mutation types are further subdivided based on their risk of antibody formation, patients with large deletions have highest risk (~75%), followed by patients with nonsense mutations and those with inversions of intron 22 [63–65]. Since small deletion/insertion mutations cause a frameshift, resulting in subsequent stop codon and truncated protein, a risk similar to that of a major deletion might be expected. Surprisingly, these patients had a relatively low risk (7.5%) [60]. This was attributed to polymerase errors which lead to restoration of reading frames for small deletion/insertion mutations. The small amount of endogenous FVIII produced was apparently sufficient to generate tolerance [63, 66]. However, mutations in the FVIII gene do not completely explain immunogenicity to therapeutic FVIII. Only one-third of the patients with intron 22 inversion develop anti-FVIII antibodies. Speculations explaining this include presentation of maternal FVIII to the fetal immune system to induce immunogenic tolerance and polymorphism in the immune systems of patients, which either hinders or synergizes anti-FVIII antibody formation [64, 67].

A meta-analysis conducted by Scharrer et al. indicated influence of race on the risk of antibody formation [68]. The incidence of antibody formation in African-Americans was double that in Caucasians (51.9%, 14 of 27, versus 25.8%, 51 of 191). This again indicates that genetic polymorphism has a role in immunogenicity. The incidence of antibody formation in siblings (50%) is significantly higher than in extended hemophilia A relatives (9%), suggesting that sibling risk is correlated [69]. However, nongenetic factors could also influence immune response as variations in response in monozygotic twins have been described [70]. Since the genetic defects in FVIII are assumed to be similar in siblings and extended relatives, polymorphisms in immune response genes may influence the risk of anti-FVIII antibody formation. An analysis of MHC class I and II alleles identified A3, B7, C7, DQA0102, DQB0602, and DR15 as risk alleles (relative risk: 1.9–4.0). MHC class I/II alleles C2, DQA0103, DQB0603, and DR13 were identified as protective alleles (relative risk 0.1–0.2) since they occurred more often in patients who did not develop antibodies than in those who did. However, sample sizes were generally too small for statistical confirmation of differences.

Immunogenicity is associated with the route of administration of a therapeutic molecule. The skin and the mucosal membranes make up the primary surface barriers to pathogens, and just beneath these lies the primary machinery to protect the body when these barriers are breached, abundant professional antigen-presenting cells (APCs). Routes of administration that involve the skin or mucosa thus may carry the greatest potential for an immunological response. Interestingly, exposure via gut mucosa is generally tolerogenic; however the challenge is the effective oral delivery with bioavailability of the biotherapeutic [71]. The probability of immune response is highest after subcutaneous injection, followed by intramuscular, intranasal, and intravenous routes. Subcutaneous administration generally localizes and prolongs the exposure of the protein to a small area within close proximity of lymph nodes, where B and T cells are present [72]. Lymphatic uptake can enhance exposure to APCs. Dendritic cells may potentially be activated if an adjuvant-like factor (e.g., impurities, host cell proteins, or endotoxin) or a danger signal is present. Peng et al. showed that changing the route administration reduces the frequency of ADAs [73, 74]. Extensive clinical experience with pulmonary delivery of biotherapeutic insulin showed that patients with type 1 and type 2 diabetes switching from subcutaneous dosing resulted in larger ADA responses [75, 76]. The antibodies were of the immunoglobulin G (IgG) class, were not neutralizing, and had no impact on clinical efficacy and safety. The importance of route of administration is not accepted by all; Schellekens argues that the immune reaction is not predicated by route of administration but rather is inherent in a therapeutic molecule itself [77].

Generally, short-term therapy is less likely to be immunogenic than long-term therapy, although intermittent treatment is more likely to elicit a response than continuous therapy [78, 79]. Also, lower doses are generally more immunogenic than higher doses, as typically seen with mAbs where the phenotype is more tolerogenic. This may be because of the evolution of the immune system to be generally less tolerant of low-abundance proteins. This was observed in a primate study of adalimumab where 16/16 monkeys developed PAHA response at low dose while only 2/16 animals developed PAHA response at high dose [72]. Therefore in clinical practice, high-dose regimens are used as a mode of therapy to induce tolerance (e.g., for factor VIII) [80].

3. MECHANISMS OF IMMUNOGENICITY OF BIOTHERAPEUTICS

The immune system can generate antibodies to therapeutic proteins by two general mechanisms: one relies on T cell costimulation of B cells while the other is independent of T cell [58].

3.1. T Cell-Dependent Immune Response

Analysis of antibodies from clinical studies suggests that serious side effects are mainly driven by high levels of IgG antibodies, suggesting a T cell-dependent pathway. In fact, IgG antibodies make up the majority of the ADA responses [81]. Naïve B cells require two signals for their proliferation and differentiation into antibody secreting plasma cells. The first signal is generated by the direct binding of the antigenic protein to B cell receptors on naïve B cell surfaces. This protein is then internalized, processed, and returned to the surface as peptides bound to the MHC class II molecules. The second signal is delivered by the armed T helper (Th) cells, which recognize the same antigen (or a peptide within the antigen, a concept known as linked recognition), via the binding of the T cell receptors (TCRs) to the peptide: MHC class II complex on the surface of naïve B cells. Another interaction is governed by the binding of B7 on B cells to

CD28 on T cells. B-T cell contact leads to the overexpression of the B cell costimulatory molecule CD154 (CD40L) on the Th cell surface and secretion of B cell stimulatory cytokines (IL-4, IL-5, and IL-6) by the Th cells. This in turn activates the B cells and leads to their differentiation into antibody-secreting (short- and long-lived) plasma B cells. Some of these activated B cells also become memory cells, which maintain the pool of long-lived plasma cells and react rapidly to rechallenge by producing short-lived plasma cells. This T cell dependent immune response is thus usually long-lasting and of high titer, particularly for foreign or exogenous proteins [81].

3.2. T Cell-Independent Immune Response

In the T cell-independent antibody response, the ability to bypass Th cell costimulation leads to a more rapid antibody response. This type of response is typically evoked by particulate antigens and sequences of microbial and viral origin [6] (repetitive epitopes termed pathogen associated molecular patterns). Antigens that are expressed on the surface of pathogens in an organized, highly repetitive form can activate specific B cells by cross-linking of antigen receptors in a multivalent fashion [82]. This activation is dependent on the formation of a small number of antigen receptor clusters, each of which contains approximately 10 to 20 antigen-bound membrane Ig (mIg) molecules [82]. These clusters induce local membrane association of multiple activated Btk (Bruton's tyrosine kinase) molecules, which results in long-term mobilization of intracellular ionized calcium. Such persistent calcium fluxes efficiently recruit transcription factors, and thereby induce T-cell-independent B cell activation and proliferation. While this first signal of multivalent mIg cross-linking can induce B cell proliferation, a second signal in the form of engagement of members of the Toll-like receptor (TLR) family could selectively induce Ig secretion in B cells that were activated by multivalent, but not by bivalent, antigen receptor engagement. Due to the lack of affinity maturation, this pathway typically results in an IgM-type response, which is transient, of low titer, and of poor specificity [72]. Changes to the structure of a therapeutic protein may alter its miscibility in ways that enhance aggregation or cause it to resemble a pathogen, thereby greatly increasing antigenicity.

Typically, an immune reaction can be triggered by most therapeutic proteins inducing antibody responses. Based on the trigger, the immune reaction can vary from low-titer, low-affinity, transient IgM antibody responses to high-titer, high-affinity responses, followed by class switching and IgG responses. Consequences of this transition can range from minimal to severe and life-threatening [72].

4. POSTTRANSLATIONAL MODIFICATIONS AND THEIR CORRELATION WITH IMMUNOGENICITY

Most therapeutic proteins are synthesized in the endoplasmic reticulum (ER) and are eventually secreted. While some modifications occur before the proteins are secreted, others happen afterwards, during in vitroprocessing, including purification, formulation, and storage, and during administration into patients [83].

Modifications of proteins that occur in the ER, golgi, and exocellular spaces have been reviewed in detail by Fineberg et al. [75]. These modifications are disulphide bond formation, gamma carboxylation of glutamate residues, and beta hydroxylation of aspartate and asparagine residues in the ER; tyrosine sulfation, propeptide processing, O-linked glycosylation, phosphorylation, and amidation in the golgi; and deamidation, glycation, N-terminal pyroglutamate formation, oxidation, and proteolytic processing in the exocellular spaces. Here, we will discuss protein structure, glycosylation, and chemical modifications.

Posttranslational modifications can have direct or indirect effects on immunogenicity. The modified part of the biotherapeutic itself could induce an immune response, or its presence can affect the tertiary structure of the protein subtly causing the biotherapeutic to become immunogenic [4].

4.1. Protein Structure

Primary amino acid sequence can affect protein structure, and hence immunogenicity, as is observed with animal-derived insulins [22]. For similar reasons, immunogenicity was higher for the first murine therapeutic antibodies, as compared to later chimeric, humanized, or fully human antibodies [84]. It is very interesting to note that while there are only 20 standard amino acids (19 amino acids and 1 imino acid), there are about 200 different functional amino acids after hydrolysis. The role of PTMs is thus significant [83]. Over the years, a significant number of modifications have been identified and several of them characterized [3, 85]. New epitopes in protein structure may be created due to the chemical modification of the protein, whereby new covalent crosslinks between amino acid residues are formed. These new protein structures could lead to the formation of aggregates, which may contain danger signals that greatly enhance immunogenicity.

4.2. Glycosylation

Glycosylation is the covalent addition of carbohydrate molecules (glycans) to the protein surface. It is the most common, complex, and heterogeneous PTM that can occur in both endogenous and therapeutic proteins [3,86]. Almost half of the therapeutic proteins that are approved or in clinical trials are glycosylated [87]. The considerable heterogeneity in glycosylation profile of products can arise from the differences in the glycan itself (type, structure) or from the attachment pattern (site, extent of occupancy of possible sites). These variabilities may depend on the production and purification process [88]. Since glycans can influence the physicochemical (e.g., solubility, electrical charge, mass, size, folding, and stability) as well as the biological (e.g., activity, half-life, and cell surface receptor function) properties of proteins [89], any change with respect to the production or purification process, even in cell line, can alter glycosylation, thereby potentially altering physiological effects [4]. Glycosylation can have a direct or indirect impact on the immunogenicity of therapeutic proteins as well. The glycan structure itself can induce an immune response, or its presence can affect protein structure in such a way that the protein becomes immunogenic. Recent advances in analytical abilities, including matrix-assisted laser desorption ionization (MALDI), electrospray ionisation mass spectrometry (ESI-MS), and novel fluorescent tags for high performance liquid chromatography

(HPLC), can help in effectively characterizing and picking up potential changes in glycan profile of therapeutics [90].

Over the past decade, at least four nonhuman carbohydrate structures that are able to induce an immune response in humans have been identified. They are galactose-α1,3-galactose (α-Gal epitope), N-glycolylneuraminic acid (Neu5Gc epitope), β1,2-xylose (core-xylose epitope), and α1,3-fucose (core-α1,3-fucose epitope) [4], of which the first two are well studied and are described here. The first observations of immune reactions against α-Gal and Neu5Gc were described in the context of xenotransplantation of pig organs in humans [91] and the targeting of vaccines to APCs in cancer immunotherapy. Autologous tumor cell membranes from solid tumors are processed to express α-Gal epitopes by incubation with neuraminidase, recombinant alpha1,3GT, and uridine diphosphate galactose [92].

Recently, the presence of α-Gal and/or Neu5Gc was demonstrated in several therapeutic mAbs [4], including cetuximab, a chimeric mouse-human IgG1 monoclonal antibody approved for use in colorectal cancer and squamous-cell carcinoma of the head and neck [4]. About 3% of patients develop severe hypersensitivity reactions within minutes after the first exposure to cetuximab, and a higher prevalence (up to 33%) may be seen in certain geographical regions. Most patients with hypersensitivity possess IgE antibodies against cetuximab before the start of therapy. These antibodies were found to be specific for the α-Gal epitope and related to IgE antibodies involved in anaphylactic reactions to red meat [4, 93]. All humans have IgA, IgM, and IgG antibodies against α-Gal, representing approximately 1% of circulating immunoglobulin. To our knowledge, the presence of IgA, IgM, and IgG antibodies against α-Gal did not correlate with accelerated clearance of cetuximab. Life-threatening hypersensitivity reaction with cetuximab was associated with preexisting IgE anti-α-Gal antibodies [94]. Qian et al. [95] demonstrated that the α-Gal epitopes are located in the Fab regions of the cetuximab antibody. The intravenous injection method and the presence of α-Gal on both Fab regions, which enables efficient cross-linking of IgE on mast cells, may explain the prompt immune reaction to cetuximab in a certain patient subset. The murine cell line SP2/0 used to produce cetuximab expresses the gene encoding for α1,3-galactosyltransferase, the enzyme responsible for the synthesis of the α-Gal epitope. Prevention of incorporation of the terminal α-Gal motif in therapeutic mAbs during production could help combat the problem of immunogenicity to an extent. Measures could include knocking out the gene for α1,3-galactosyltransferase in murine cells or using another expression system such as the CHO cells which may not produce the α-Gal epitope glycoform [96]. Other biotherapeutics like infliximab also have α-Gal epitopes located on Fc linked glycans but these were not found to be recognized by IgE anti-α-Gal antibodies. The relative low abundance of α-Gal epitopes and their location within the Fc region might be possible reasons for this lack of recognition. So far, IgE anti-α-Gal antibodies seem to have a significant importance to patients treated with cetuximab [94].

Humans synthesize the sialic acid N-acetylneuraminic acid (Neu5Ac) but are not able to synthesize Neu5Gc [4]. Consumption of Neu5Gc-rich foods, for example, red meat and milk products, allows for the accumulation of Neu5Gc on the surface of epithelial and endothelial cells [93]. As a result, the human immune system recognizes Neu5Gc as foreign and shows high levels of IgA, IgM, and IgG antibodies against Neu5Gc (0.1%–0.2% of circulating immunoglobulin) [93]. Injecting products that contain Neu5Gc in individuals with preexisting antibodies can cause the formation of immune complexes that potentially activate complement or affect half-life of the drug. Ghaderi et al. [97] showed that the clearance of cetuximab increases significantly in mice when anti-Neu5Gc antibodies are preinjected. Maeda et al. [98] detected the presence of the Neu5Gc epitope in three commercial mAb pharmaceuticals produced in murine cell lines (cetuximab, gemtuzumab, and infliximab), whereas it was absent in other mAbs produced in CHO cell lines (tocilizumab, bevacizumab, and adalimumab). CHO cells are reported to be negative for α-Gal and Neu5Gc epitopes. However, these cells are capable of taking up these glycoforms from the cell culture media and metabolically incorporating them into the expressed protein [4]. Therefore, in addition to using these cell lines, media and other components should be void of components such as Neu5Gc [97].

Analysis of biotherapeutic mAbs purified from serum of subjects demonstrates that the PTM profile of the protein changes in vivo. Examples include deamidation at Asn-33 and oxidation at Trp-105 in the light chain and heavy chains, respectively, of two therapeutic mAbs [99]. Furthermore, a recent study shows that different levels of mannosylation of mAbs can have significant impact on pharmacokinetic parameters, including clearance and area under the curve (AUC) [100]; however, the increase in mannose did not impact immunogenicity rates [101]. Mannose receptors, expressed at high levels on DCs, mediate the capture, processing, and presenting of antigens (mannose-expressing glycoproteins) for an immune response. This response, depending on several factors, could either be immunogenic or tolerogenic [100, 102].

Glycans may also indirectly impact the immunogenicity of biotherapeutics through changes in the folding, solubility, or stability of the proteins. For example, recombinant human IFN β produced in E. coli is not glycosylated and is prone to aggregation leading to increased immunogenicity, as compared to the recombinant IFN β from CHO cells, where glycosylation reduces immunogenicity [4, 103].

4.3. Chemical Composition

Compared to glycosylation, other PTMs are less well understood [104, 105]. A biopharmaceutical may be chemically modified through accidental degradation in one of the many bioprocessing steps: fermentation, virus inactivation, purification, polishing, formulation, filtration, filling, storage, transport, and administration. Chemical modifications during bioprocessing may include deamidation, oxidation, isomerization, hydrolysis, glycation, and C/N terminal heterogeneity of the protein [106]. The susceptibility of an individual amino acid residue to chemical modification is dependent on neighboring residues; tertiary structure of the protein; and solution conditions such as temperature, pH, and ionic strength. Chemical modification may give rise to a less favorable charge, thus leading to structural changes or even the formation of new covalent crosslinks [107]. Covalent crosslinking could enhance immunogenicity by causing aggregation [108–110]. Multiple studies have indicated a strong correlation between aggregates and immunogenicity [89, 111–113]. Deamidation, isomerization, and oxidation have also been associated with potential immunogenicity [4].

Deamidation of proteins accelerates at high temperature and high pH and can occur during bioprocessing and storage. Deamidation of

Asn and Gln contributes to charge heterogeneity of therapeutic proteins, determines the irreversible thermal denaturation of proteins at acidic and neutral pH, regulates the rate of protein breakdown, and could shorten in vivo half-life. Deamidation followed by isomerization of asparagine to isoaspartate (isoAsp) has been shown to alter protein structure, thereby potentially making the protein immunogenic [114]. Deamidation can be accompanied by some degree of oxidation, conformational changes, and fragmentation and aggregation, again posing a serious risk of enhanced immunogenicity [4].

Oxidative chemical modification of amino acid residues alters secondary and tertiary protein structures. This favors interaction between protein surfaces and subsequently leads to noncovalent aggregation [115]. Studies using metal-catalyzed oxidation (MCO) have shown that therapeutic proteins can aggregate and can also be immunogenic [4, 115]. Chemical stresses during manufacturing and storage can be caused by exposure to light or elevated temperatures and by the presence of oxygen, metal ions, or peroxide impurities from excipients. Trace amounts of iron, chromium, and nickel were found to leach into the formulation buffer via contact with the stainless steel surfaces typically used during bioprocessing [116]. Tungsten oxide-mediated oxidation caused precipitation of monoclonal antibodies and was pH-dependent [117]. Similarly in EPO, aggregation due to tungsten leachates from the container was associated with immunogenicity [54].

Despite limited information on the association of actual chemical modifications during biopharmaceutical manufacturing and immunogenicity, it is always prudent to be prepared for an untoward possibility. Preventative measures should include careful evaluation of buffers, surface materials, and conditions during manufacturing, transport, and storage. Extensive characterization of molecules using techniques like size exclusion chromatography, supported by orthogonal techniques like analytical ultracentrifugation (identifying aggregation) [118], circular dichroism (CD), and intrinsic fluorescence spectroscopy, can indicate deviations from secondary and tertiary structures. These steps incorporated into the process development will help in mitigating risks of immunogenicity.

5. MANAGING IMMUNOGENICITY

5.1. Managing Immunogenicity in a Preclinical Setting

The 2011 ICH S6 Guideline (preclinical safety evaluation of biotechnology-derived pharmaceuticals) describes the need for detection and characterization of antibodies in repeat-dose studies using animal models. However, relevant species must be used for in vivo studies, that is, one in which the target epitope is expressed. Immune responses are species-specific; therefore, induction is not entirely predictive of antibody formation in humans [119, 120]. Animal models are constrained by lack of genetic diversity which is a primary factor for diverse immune response frequently observed in human beings [121]. Rodent models for immunogenicity testing are, therefore, less useful than animals that show a higher degree of homology with humans and more genetic diversity than inbred mouse strains, such as nonhuman primates; however, these are not widely used due to ethical constraints. Conventional nontransgenic animal models can be useful for highly conserved proteins, but a lack of immune tolerance to human proteins limits their use for immunogenicity testing. These animal models can be useful for comparing the immunogenicity of two similar products, that is, the immunogenicity of an originator and biosimilar product; this may not reflect the human situation but may provide a warning against advancement of a biosimilar if the immunogenicity profile observed differs from that of the originator.

Despite the limitations associated with the use of animals to predict immunogenicity, several transgenic animal models have been generated for this purpose. Transgenic mice are often the preferred in vivo model to predict immunogenicity as they are tolerant to the administered human protein [122, 123] and can be used to study the immunogenicity of biotherapeutic aggregates. In a study by van Beers et al., the IFNb-1a aggregate percentage and extent of denaturation were shown to influence the ability of aggregates to break tolerance in transgenic mice. In these experiments, immune tolerant mice were immunized with IFNb-1a formulations and antibody responses measured. Only noncovalently bound aggregates that retained some native epitopes were able to break tolerance resulting in a transient immune response; removal of aggregates prevented this breakdown of tolerance [123]. Additionally, mice expressing human MHC molecules can be used to compare antibody and T cell responses to vaccines and protein therapeutics [124]. High ADA titers were observed after injection of a metal catalyzed, oxidized, and aggregated IgG1 sample in nontransgenic and transgenic mice [4]. Therapeutic interferons oxidized and aggregated via the same metal-catalysis method were able to overcome the immune tolerance of transgenic mice that were immune tolerant for the administered human proteins [125, 126]. The transgenic mice also developed antibodies against oxidized and aggregated rhIFNβ-1a treated with H_2O_2 [126], but not against oxidized rhIFNα-2b treated with H_2O_2 [89], probably due to the absence of aggregation. Use of animal models in immunogenicity testing is discussed more extensively in the review by Brinks et al. [121].

In vitro techniques can also be used to assess the immunogenic potential of therapeutic proteins. These could be used to predict the risk of immunogenicity in preclinical setting. The expression of APC-surface molecules differs following activation; for example, the expression of MHC (class I and II), costimulatory molecules, and cytokine receptors is enhanced. Flow cytometry is an in vitro technique that can be used to determine differences in cell surface molecule expression, indicative of APC maturation that may initiate T cell responses [127, 128]. T cell proliferation assays are also useful tools to study the activation and proliferation of T cells in the presence of antigen [129]. Additionally, the release of immunomodulatory cytokines can be characterized by enzyme-linked immunosorbent assay. This approach can be used to assess the quality of an induced immune response, as specific cytokines can be markers of Th1 (IL-12 and IFNγ) or Th2 immunity (IL-4 and IL-10). T cells that respond to a particular epitope in vitro can be labeled with MHC class II oligomers and sorted by flow cytometry; the phenotype of responsive T cells can then be determined using intracellular cytokine staining [124, 130]. Human peripheral blood mononucleated cells, when stimulated with aggregated monoclonal antibody, induce an adaptive T cell response characterized by CD4 T cell proliferation and release of cytokines like interleukin- (IL-) 1β, IL-6 and TNFα. These cytokines can be used as potential biomarkers for aggregate immunogenicity [129]. It should be noted that these in vitro techniques may indicate the probability of an immune response for a biotherapeutic but cannot predict its clinical consequences. Correlative studies with marketed biotherapeutics in these assays may refine these methods further, to enable prediction of relevant immunogenicity [4, 127].

In addition to the assays described above, in silico techniques have been developed for the prediction of antigenicity by identification of potential T cell epitopes [131]. In silico methods have been shown to successfully identify MHC class II-restricted epitopes within biotherapeutics [132]. Knowledge of aggregation-prone regions may also help in the design and selection of biotherapeutic candidates and reduce aggregation concerns [133]. For example, aggregation motifs that lack charge have been found in the light chain regions of mAbs, including Erbitux and Raptiva. This computational approach could, therefore, be useful to screen biotherapeutic candidates early in drug development [128].

Overall, preclinical methods have been focused on identifying potential immunogenicity associated with formation of aggregates often considered the "bête noire" for immunogenicity [134]. However, the challenge remains in identifying potential immunogenicity with low levels of aggregation induced naturally by PTMs (as described previously) especially in contexts of process change, shipping, and clinical use. The preclinical techniques to predict immunogenic potential described here are still exploratory. Developing more robust methods to predict possible immunogenicity attributable to PTMs should be the way forward to reduce clinical risk.

5.2. Managing Immunogenicity in the Clinic

Prior to treatment, patients should be screened for established biomarkers to check for potential immunogenicity. A retrospective analysis of cetuximab evaluated whether the presence of pretreatment IgE antibodies against cetuximab is associated with severe infusion reactions (SIRs) during the initial cetuximab infusion. This analysis used 545 banked serum or plasma samples from cancer patients participating in clinical trials. Patients with a positive test indicating the presence of pretreatment antibodies had a higher risk of experiencing an SIR. Although this test had low positive predictive value, it clearly indicated an association between the presences of preexisting IgE antibodies against cetuximab with SIRs, supporting prior association studies [135].

Infantile Pompe disease resulting from a deficiency of lysosomal acid α-glucosidase (GAA) requires enzyme replacement therapy (ERT) with recombinant human GAA (rhGAA); immunogenicity can be managed with a combination of rituximab with methotrexate ± intravenous gamma globulins (IVIG). This is an option for tolerance induction of CRIM negative Pompe to ERT when instituted in the naïve setting or following antibody development [136].

With adalimumab, dosing over the NAb response is probably effective in recapturing symptomatic response. In patients with Crohn's disease, adalimumab dose escalation is effective for recapturing symptomatic response after secondary loss of response, but more than half of the patients eventually experience a tertiary loss of response [137]. An additional risk with dosing over the prescribed dose could involve adverse events such as serum sickness and hypersensitivity reactions [138]. Another strategy commonly adopted with anti-TNF therapeutics is to switch the biologic when a patient becomes refractive to a particular anti-TNF. In some cases, suppressing the immune response (formation of ADAs) with mild doses of methotrexate was seen to be beneficial [139]. Figure 1 gives a schematic representation of managing immunogenicity.

5.3. Managing Immunogenicity against Biosimilars

In recent years, follow-on biologics (or biosimilars) and generic protein therapeutics have become more prevalent as the patents associated with the original drugs expire. The first biosimilar reached the market almost a decade ago [140]; and biosimilar use has been steadily rising. Managing immunogenicity arising due to biosimilars is another challenge.

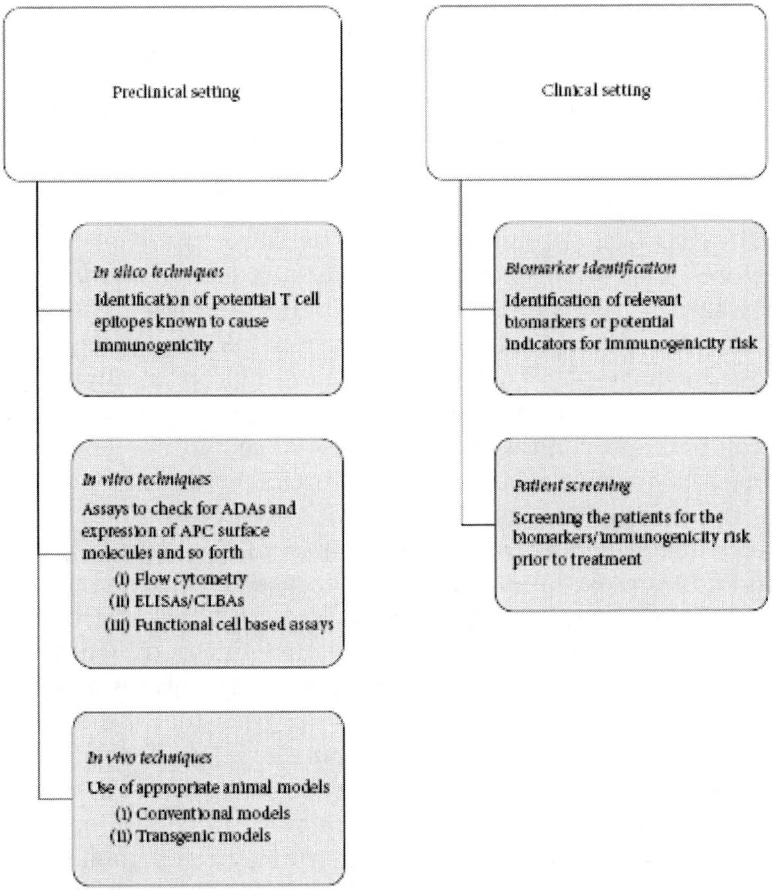

Figure 1: Management of immunogenicity in preclinical and clinical settings. ADAs: anti-drug antibodies; APC: antigen presenting cell; ELISA: enzyme-linked immunosorbent assay; CLBA: competitive ligand binding assay.

For small molecules approved in the EU, the generic paradigm applies; a product is pharmaceutically equivalent to a competitor molecule when it has the same qualitative and quantitative composition. If the products are shown through pharmacokinetic studies to have the same bioavailability, they are deemed bioequivalent. Generally, this is demonstrated in a limited number of studies in healthy volunteers [141]. Once products are deemed bioequivalent, they are assumed to be therapeutically equivalent and essentially similar in terms of benefits and risks in vivo.

However, such paradigm is not applicable for biopharmaceuticals. Biopharmaceuticals are large and intricate molecules and frequently subjected to extensive PTMs that are sensitive to differences in manufacturing conditions [142]. Pharmaceutical equivalence for biopharmaceutical products cannot be directly demonstrated. Therefore, the biosimilar pathway was established. In this pathway, "biosimilarity" to an approved reference product must be demonstrated through an extensive comparability exercise. This exercise includes physicochemical studies, appropriate nonclinical studies, limited pharmacokinetic and pharmacodynamics studies, and comparative clinical studies to establish efficacy and safety (European Medicines agency, London 2006). The United States (US) Food and Drug Administration (FDA) has proposed a stepwise approach for providing totality of evidence of similarity between a proposed biosimilar product and a US-licensed (reference) product. This stepwise approach starts with the assessment of critical quality attributes that are relevant to clinical outcomes in structural and functional characterization in manufacturing process of the proposed biosimilar product. The FDA suggests that these critical quality attributes be identified first and then classified into three tiers depending upon their criticality: most (Tier 1), mild to moderate (Tier 2), and least (Tier 3) relevant to clinical outcomes [143]. However, even after demonstrating comparability, the products might not be similar in terms of risk of immunogenicity. Therefore, a detailed immunogenicity assessment is still warranted.

6. CONCLUSION

Recent years have seen an expansion in the development and manufacturing of protein therapeutic drugs, both in terms of number of molecules and in terms of global production capacity. In this review, we discussed the causes of immunogenicity which could be product-related (inherent property of the product or might be picked up during the manufacturing process), patient-related, or linked to the route of administration. We also discussed the impact of PTMs of therapeutic proteins on immunogenicity; and it is clear that some PTMs lead to increased immunogenicity. Managing immunogenicity in both preclinical and clinical settings is very important. With the advent of novel analytical technologies, there has been a dramatic enhancement of the capability to analyze and characterize therapeutics. Also, analysis of these proteins in vivo is critical to understand biological effects of PTMs. Relevant human immune system-specific animal models are now being established to study these biological effects. Future studies should focus on the development of sensitive diagnostics that can predict immunogenicity-mediated adverse events in small fraction of subjects that develop clinically relevant ADAs and hence mitigate the risk due to unwarranted immunogenicity.

COMPETING INTERESTS

Anshu Kuriakose, Narendra Chirmule, and Pradip Nair are full time employees of Biocon Ltd.

ACKNOWLEDGMENTS

The authors would like to acknowledge Dr. Anand Jacob and Parag Pipalava from Medical Writing, Biocon Research Limited, for editorial assistance. They also acknowledge Dr. Ramakrishnan Melarkode for reviewing the paper.

REFERENCES

1. O. N. Jensen, "Modification-specific proteomics: characterization of post-translational modifications by mass spectrometry," Current Opinion in Chemical Biology, vol. 8, no. 1, pp. 33–41, 2004.
2. A. N. Burska, L. Hunt, M. Boissinot et al., "Autoantibodies to posttranslational modifications in rheumatoid arthritis," Mediators of Inflammation, vol. 2014, Article ID 492873, 19 pages, 2014.

3. N. Jenkins, "Modifications of therapeutic proteins: challenges and prospects," Cytotechnology, vol. 53, no. 1–3, pp. 121–125, 2007.

4. M. M. C. van Beers and M. Bardor, "Minimizing immunogenicity of biopharmaceuticals by controlling critical quality attributes of proteins," Biotechnology Journal, vol. 7, no. 12, pp. 1473–1484, 2012.

5. N. Casadevall, "Antibodies against rHuEPO: native and recombinant," Nephrology Dialysis Transplantation, vol. 17, supplement 5, pp. 42–47, 2002.

6. I. Mukovozov, T. Sabljic, G. Hortelano, and F. A. Ofosu, "Factors that contribute to the immmunogenicity of therapeutic recombinant human proteins," Thrombosis and Haemostasis, vol. 99, no. 5, pp. 874–882, 2008.

7. M. K. Ghazavi and G. A. Johnston, "Insulin allergy," Clinics in Dermatology, vol. 29, no. 3, pp. 300–305, 2011.

8. I. C. MacDougall, S. D. Roger, A. De Francisco et al., "Antibody-mediated pure red cell aplasia in chronic kidney disease patients receiving erythropoiesis-stimulating agents: new insights," Kidney International, vol. 81, no. 8, pp. 727–732, 2012.

9. P. Jolicoeur and R. L. Tacey, "Development and validation of cell-based assays for the detection of neutralizing antibodies to drug products: a practical approach," Bioanalysis, vol. 4, no. 24, pp. 2959–2970, 2012.

10. M. G. Jacquemin and J.-M. R. Saint-Remy, "Factor VIII immunogenicity," Haemophilia, vol. 4, no. 4, pp. 552–557, 1998.

11. U. Rosenschein, R. Lenz, J. Radnay, T. Ben Tovim, and L. A. Rozenszajn, "Streptokinase immunogenicity in thrombolytic therapy for acute myocardial infarction," Israel Journal of Medical Sciences, vol. 27, no. 10, pp. 541–545, 1991.

12. J. Li, C. Yang, Y. Xia et al., "Thrombocytopenia caused by the development of antibodies to thrombopoietin," Blood, vol. 98, no. 12, pp. 3241–3248, 2001.

13. G. Shankar, C. Pendley, and K. E. Stein, "A risk-based bioanalytical strategy for the assessment of antibody immune responses against biological drugs," Nature Biotechnology, vol. 25, no. 5, pp. 555–561, 2007.

14. L.-C. Lim, "Acquired red cell aplasia in association with the use of recombinant erythropoietin in chronic renal failure," Hematology, vol. 10, no. 3, pp. 255–259, 2005.

15. N. Casadevall, J. Nataf, B. Viron et al., "Pure red-cell aplasia and antierythropoietin antibodies in patients treated with recombinant erythropoietin," The New England Journal of Medicine, vol. 346, no. 7, pp. 469–475, 2002.

16. P. Ragnhammar and M. Wadhwa, "Neutralising antibodies to granulocyte-macrophage colony stimulating factor (GM-CSF) in carcinoma patients following GM-CSF combination therapy," Medical Oncology, vol. 13, no. 3, pp. 161–166, 1996.

17. Y. C. Q. Zang, D. Yang, J. Hong, M. V. Tejada-Simon, V. M. Rivera, and J. Z. Zhang, "Immunoregulation and blocking antibodies induced by interferon beta treatment in MS," Neurology, vol. 55, no. 3, pp. 397–404, 2000.

18. V. R. Dharnidharka, C. Takemoto, B. M. Ewenstein, S. Rosen, and H. W. Harris, "Membranous glomerulonephritis and nephrosis post factor IX infusions in hemophilia B," Pediatric Nephrology, vol. 12, no. 8, pp. 654–657, 1998.

19. H.-P. Hartung, F. Munschauer III, and H. Schellekens, "Significance of neutralizing antibodies to interferon beta during treatment of multiple sclerosis: expert opinions based on the Proceedings of an International Consensus Conference," European Journal of Neurology, vol. 12, no. 8, pp. 588–601, 2005.

20. E. Koren, L. A. Zuckerman, and A. R. Mire-Sluis, "Immune responses to therapeutic proteins in humans—clinical significance, assessment and prediction," Current Pharmaceutical Biotechnology, vol. 3, no. 4, pp. 349–360, 2002.

21. M. G. Tovey and C. Lallemand, "Immunogenicity and other problems associated with the use of

biopharmaceuticals," Therapeutic Advances in Drug Safety, vol. 2, no. 3, pp. 113–128, 2011.

22. G. Schernthaner, "Immunogenicity and allergenic potential of animal and human insulins," Diabetes Care, vol. 16, supplement 3, pp. 155–165, 1993.

23. S. E. Fineberg, T. T. Kawabata, D. Finco-Kent, R. J. Fountaine, G. L. Finch, and A. S. Krasner, "Immunological responses to exogenous insulin," Endocrine Reviews, vol. 28, no. 6, pp. 625–652, 2007.

24. F. A. Harding, M. M. Stickler, J. Razo, and R. B. DuBridge, "The immunogenicity of humanized and fully human antibodies: residual immunogenicity resides in the CDR regions," mAbs, vol. 2, no. 3, pp. 256–265, 2010.

25. N. K. Bender, C. E. Heilig, B. Dröll, J. Wohlgemuth, F.-P. Armbruster, and B. Heilig, "Immunogenicity, efficacy and adverse events of adalimumab in RA patients," Rheumatology International, vol. 27, no. 3, pp. 269–274, 2007.

26. T. R. D. J. Radstake, M. Svenson, A. M. Eijsbouts et al., "Formation of antibodies against infliximab and adalimumab strongly correlates with functional drug levels and clinical responses in rheumatoid arthritis," Annals of the Rheumatic Diseases, vol. 68, no. 11, pp. 1739–1745, 2009.

27. R. L. West, Z. Zelinkova, G. J. Wolbink, E. J. Kuipers, P. C. F. Stokkers, and C. J. van der Woude, "Immunogenicity negatively influences the outcome of adalimumab treatment in Crohn's disease,"Alimentary Pharmacology and Therapeutics, vol. 28, no. 9, pp. 1122–1126, 2008.

28. A. J. Coles, "Alemtuzumab therapy for multiple sclerosis," Neurotherapeutics, vol. 10, no. 1, pp. 29–33, 2013.

29. R. Furie, W. Stohl, E. M. Ginzler et al., "Biologic activity and safety of belimumab, a neutralizing anti-B-lymphocyte stimulator (BLyS) monoclonal antibody: a phase I trial in patients with systemic lupus erythematosus," Arthritis Research and Therapy, vol. 10, no. 5, article R109, 2008.

30. E. Dhimolea, "Canakinumab," mAbs, vol. 2, no. 1, pp. 3–13, 2010.

31. D.-Y. Chen, Y.-M. Chen, W.-T. Hung et al., "Immunogenicity, drug trough levels and therapeutic response in patients with rheumatoid arthritis or ankylosing spondylitis after 24-week golimumab treatment," Annals of the Rheumatic Diseases, vol. 74, no. 12, pp. 2261–2264, 2015.

32. A. Chovel-Sella, R. Karplus, T. Sella, and H. Amital, "Clinical efficacy and adverse effects of golimumab in the treatment of rheumatoid arthritis," Israel Medical Association Journal, vol. 14, no. 6, pp. 390–394, 2012.

33. I. Zidi, A. Bouaziz, W. Mnif, A. Bartegi, F. A. Al-Hizab, and N. B. Amor, "Golimumab therapy of rheumatoid arthritis: an overview," Scandinavian Journal of Immunology, vol. 72, no. 2, pp. 75–85, 2010.

34. N. A. Rizvi, J. Mazières, D. Planchard et al., "Activity and safety of nivolumab, an anti-PD-1 immune checkpoint inhibitor, for patients with advanced, refractory squamous non-small-cell lung cancer (CheckMate 063): a phase 2, single-arm trial," The Lancet Oncology, vol. 16, no. 3, pp. 257–265, 2015.

35. P. C. Taylor, E. Quattrocchi, S. Mallett, R. Kurrasch, J. Petersen, and D. J. Chang, "Ofatumumab, a fully human anti-CD20 monoclonal antibody, in biological-naive, rheumatoid arthritis patients with an inadequate response to methotrexate: a randomised, double-blind, placebo-controlled clinical trial,"Annals of the Rheumatic Diseases, vol. 70, no. 12, pp. 2119–2125, 2011.

36. A. Jakobovits, R. G. Amado, X. Yang, L. Roskos, and G. Schwab, "From XenoMouse technology to panitumumab, the first fully human antibody product from transgenic mice," Nature Biotechnology, vol. 25, no. 10, pp. 1134–1143, 2007.

37. J. A. Lofgren, S. Dhandapani, J. J. Pennucci et al., "Comparing ELISA and surface plasmon resonance for assessing clinical immunogenicity of panitumumab," The Journal of Immunology, vol. 178, no. 11, pp. 7467–7472, 2007.

38. D. Weeraratne, A. Chen, J. J. Pennucci et al., "Immunogenicity of panitumumab in combination chemotherapy clinical trials," BMC Clinical Pharmacology, vol. 11, article 17, 2011.

39. L. Khoja, M. O. Butler, S. P. Kang, S. Ebbinghaus, and A. M. Joshua, "Pembrolizumab," Journal for ImmunoTherapy of Cancer, vol. 3, article 36, 2015.

40. C. C. Mok, "Rituximab for the treatment of rheumatoid arthritis: an update," Drug Design, Development and Therapy, vol. 8, pp. 87–100, 2013.

41. A. Karle, S. Spindeldreher, and F. Kolbinger, "Secukinumab, a novel anti–IL-17A antibody, shows low immunogenicity potential in human in vitro assays comparable to other marketed biotherapeutics with low clinical immunogenicity," mAbs, vol. 8, no. 3, pp. 536–550, 2016.

42. H.-Y. Chiu, T. W. Chu, Y.-P. Cheng, and T.-F. Tsai, "The association between clinical response to ustekinumab and immunogenicity to ustekinumab and prior adalimumab," PLoS ONE, vol. 10, no. 11, Article ID e0142930, 2015.

43. M. S. Raben, "Treatment of a pituitary dwarf with human growth hormone," The Journal of Clinical Endocrinology and Metabolism, vol. 18, no. 8, pp. 901–903, 1958.

44. W. V. Moore and P. Leppert, "Role of aggregated human growth hormone (hGH) in development of antibodies to hGH," Journal of Clinical Endocrinology and Metabolism, vol. 51, no. 9, pp. 691–697, 1980.

45. E. Van Cutsem, S. Siena, Y. Humblet et al., "An open-label, single-arm study assessing safety and efficacy of panitumumab in patients with metastatic colorectal cancer refractory to standard chemotherapy,"Annals of Oncology, vol. 19, no. 1, pp. 92–98, 2008.

46. P. Gogolák, B. Réthi, G. Hajas, and É. Rajnavölgyi, "Targeting dendritic cells for priming cellular immune responses," Journal of Molecular Recognition, vol. 16, no. 5, pp. 299–317, 2003.

47. J. N. Arnold, M. R. Wormald, R. B. Sim, P. M. Rudd, and R. A. Dwek, "The impact of glycosylation on the biological function and structure of human immunoglobulins," Annual Review of Immunology, vol. 25, pp. 21–50, 2007.

48. D. M. Sheeley, B. M. Merrill, and L. C. E. Taylor, "Characterization of monoclonal antibody glycosylation: comparison of expression systems and identification of terminal α-linked galactose," Analytical Biochemistry, vol. 247, no. 1, pp. 102–110, 1997.

49. C. H. Chung, B. Mirakhur, E. Chan et al., "Cetuximab-induced anaphylaxis and IgE specific for galactose-α-1,3-galactose," The New England Journal of Medicine, vol. 358, no. 11, pp. 1109–1117, 2008.

50. P. Eggleton, R. Haigh, and P. G. Winyard, "Consequence of neo-antigenicity of the 'altered self',"Rheumatology, vol. 47, no. 5, pp. 567–571, 2008.

51. J. C. Egrie and J. K. Browne, "Development and characterization of novel erythropoiesis stimulating protein (NESP)," British Journal of Cancer, vol. 84, supplement 1, pp. 3–10, 2001.

52. D. T. Mytych, T. E. Barger, C. King et al., "Development and characterization of a human antibody reference panel against erythropoietin suitable for the standardization of ESA immunogenicity testing,"Journal of Immunological Methods, vol. 382, no. 1-2, pp. 129–141, 2012.

53. J. Rossert, N. Casadevall, and K.-U. Eckardt, "Anti-erythropoietin antibodies and pure red cell aplasia,"Journal of the American Society of Nephrology, vol. 15, no. 2, pp. 398–406, 2004.

54. A. Seidl, O. Hainzl, M. Richter et al., "Tungsten-induced denaturation and aggregation of epoetin alfa during primary packaging as a cause of immunogenicity," Pharmaceutical Research, vol. 29, no. 6, pp. 1454–1467, 2012.

55. D. K. Weeraratne, A. J. Kuck, N. Chirmule, and D. T. Mytych, "Measurement of anti-erythropoiesis-stimulating agent IgG4 antibody as an indicator of antibody-mediated pure red cell

aplasia," Clinical and Vaccine Immunology, vol. 20, no. 1, pp. 46–51, 2013.

56. G. Antonelli and F. Dianzani, "Development of antibodies to interferon beta in patients: technical and biological aspects," European Cytokine Network, vol. 10, no. 3, pp. 413–422, 1999.

57. C. L. Wagner, A. Schantz, E. Barnathan et al., "Consequences of immunogenicity to the therapeutic monoclonal antibodies ReoPro and Remicade," Developments in biologicals, vol. 112, pp. 37–53, 2003.

58. V. Jawa, L. P. Cousens, M. Awwad, E. Wakshull, H. Kropshofer, and A. S. De Groot, "T-cell dependent immunogenicity of protein therapeutics: preclinical assessment and mitigation," Clinical Immunology, vol. 149, pp. 534–555, 2013.

59. M. G. Jacquemin, B. G. Desqueper, A. Benhida et al., "Mechanism and kinetics of factor VIII inactivation: study with an IgG4 monoclonal antibody derived from a hemophilia A patient with inhibitor," Blood, vol. 92, no. 2, pp. 496–506, 1998.

60. J. Oldenburg, J. Schröder, C. Schmitt, H. H. Brackmann, and R. Schwaab, "Small deletion/insertion mutations within poly-A runs of the factor VIII gene mitigate the severe haemophilia A phenotype,"Thrombosis and Haemostasis, vol. 79, no. 2, pp. 452–453, 1998.

61. M. Franchini and P. M. Mannucci, "Inhibitors of propagation of coagulation (factors VIII, IX and XI): a review of current therapeutic practice," British Journal of Clinical Pharmacology, vol. 72, no. 4, pp. 553–562, 2011.

62. R. Schwaab, H.-H. Brackmann, C. Meyer et al., "Haemophilia A: mutation type determines risk of inhibitor formation," Thrombosis and Haemostasis, vol. 74, no. 6, pp. 1402–1406, 1995.

63. G. Kemball-Cook, E. G. D. Tuddenham, and A. I. Wacey, "The factor VIII structure and mutation resource site: HAMSTeRS version 4," Nucleic Acids Research, vol. 26, no. 1, pp. 216–219, 1998.

64. J. Oldenburg, O. El-Maarri, and R. Schwaab, "Inhibitor development in correlation to factor VIII genotypes," Haemophilia, vol. 8, supplement 2, pp. 23–29, 2002.

65. G. S. Pandey, C. Yanover, L. M. Miller-Jenkins et al., "Endogenous factor VIII synthesis from the intron 22-inverted F8 locus may modulate the immunogenicity of replacement therapy for hemophilia A,"Nature Medicine, vol. 19, no. 10, pp. 1318–1324, 2013.

66. M. Young, H. Inaba, L. W. Hoyer, M. Higuchi, H. H. Kazazian Jr., and S. E. Antonarakis, "Partial correction of a severe molecular defect in hemophilia A, because of errors during expression of the factor VIII gene," American Journal of Human Genetics, vol. 60, no. 3, pp. 565–573, 1997.

67. J. Oldenburg, J. K. Picard, R. Schwaab, H. H. Brackmann, E. G. D. Tuddenham, and E. Simpson, "HLA genotype of patients with severe haemophilia a due to intron 22 inversion with and without inhibitors of factor VIII," Thrombosis and Haemostasis, vol. 77, no. 2, pp. 238–242, 1997.

68. I. Scharrer, G. L. Bray, and O. Neutzling, "Incidence of inhibitors in haemophilia A patients—a review of recent studies of recombinant and plasma-derived factor VIII concentrates," Haemophilia, vol. 5, no. 3, pp. 145–154, 1999.

69. J. Astermark, "Basic aspects of inhibitors to factors VIII and IX and the influence of non-genetic risk factors," Haemophilia, vol. 12, supplement 6, pp. 8–14, 2006.

70. J. Astermark, E. Berntorp, G. C. White et al., "The Malmö International Brother Study (MIBS): further support for genetic predisposition to inhibitor development," Haemophilia, vol. 7, no. 3, pp. 267–272, 2001.

71. R. Singh, S. Singh, and J. W. Lillard, "Past, present, and future technologies for oral delivery of therapeutic proteins," Journal of Pharmaceutical Sciences, vol. 97, no. 7, pp. 2497–2523, 2008.

72. S. K. Singh, "Impact of product-related factors on immunogenicity of biotherapeutics," Journal of Pharmaceutical Sciences, vol. 100, no. 2, pp. 354–387, 2011.

73. A. Peng, P. Gaitonde, M. P. Kosloski, R. D. Miclea, P. Varma, and S. V. Balu-Iyer, "Effect of route of administration of human recombinant factor VIII on its immunogenicity in hemophilia A mice," Journal of Pharmaceutical Sciences, vol. 98, no. 12, pp. 4480–4484, 2009.

74. P. Perini, A. Facchinetti, P. Bulian et al., "Interferon-β (INF-β) antibodies in interferon-β1a- and interferon-β1b-treated multiple sclerosis patients. Prevalence, kinetics, cross-reactivity, and factors enhancing interferon-beta immunogenicity in vivo," European Cytokine Network, vol. 12, no. 1, pp. 56–61, 2001.

75. S. E. Fineberg, T. Kawabata, D. Finco-Kent, C. Liu, and A. Krasner, "Antibody response to inhaled insulin in patients with type 1 or type 2 diabetes. An analysis of initial phase II and III inhaled insulin (Exubera) trials and a two-year extension trial," Journal of Clinical Endocrinology and Metabolism, vol. 90, no. 6, pp. 3287–3294, 2005.

76. K. Hermansen, T. Rönnemaa, A. H. Petersen, S. Bellaire, and U. Adamson, "Intensive Therapy with Inhaled Insulin via the AERx Insulin Diabetes Management System: a 12-week proof-of-concept trial in patients with type 2 diabetes," Diabetes Care, vol. 27, no. 1, pp. 162–167, 2004.

77. H. Schellekens, "Factors influencing the immunogenicity of therapeutic proteins," Nephrology Dialysis Transplantation, vol. 20, supplement 6, pp. vi3–vi9, 2005.

78. E.-M. Jahn and C. K. Schneider, "How to systematically evaluate immunogenicity of therapeutic proteins—regulatory considerations," New Biotechnology, vol. 25, no. 5, pp. 280–286, 2009.

79. A. S. Rosenberg and A. S. Worobec, "A risk-based approach to immunogenicity concerns of therapeutic protein products, part 2: considering host-specific and product-specific factors impacting immunogenicity," BioPharm International, vol. 17, no. 12, pp. 34–42, 2004.

80. I. Hwang and S. Park, "Computational design of protein therapeutics," Drug Discovery Today: Technologies, vol. 5, no. 2-3, pp. e43–e48, 2009.

81. M. P. Baker and T. D. Jones, "Identification and removal of immunogenicity in therapeutic proteins,"Current Opinion in Drug Discovery and Development, vol. 10, no. 2, pp. 219–227, 2007.

82. Q. Vos, A. Lees, Z.-Q. Wu, C. M. Snapper, and J. J. Mond, "B-cell activation by T-cell-independent type 2 antigens as an integral part of the humoral immune response to pathogenic microorganisms,"Immunological Reviews, vol. 176, pp. 154–170, 2000.

83. X. Zhong and J. F. Wright, "Biological insights into therapeutic protein modifications throughout trafficking and their biopharmaceutical applications," International Journal of Cell Biology, vol. 2013, Article ID 273086, 19 pages, 2013.

84. R. Jefferis and M.-P. Lefranc, "Human immunoglobulin allotypes: possible implications for immunogenicity," mAbs, vol. 1, no. 4, pp. 332–338, 2009.

85. J. Seo and K.-J. Lee, "Post-translational modifications and their biological functions: proteomic analysis and systematic approaches," Journal of Biochemistry and Molecular Biology, vol. 37, no. 1, pp. 35–44, 2004.

86. R. J. Solá and K. Griebenow, "Glycosylation of therapeutic proteins: an effective strategy to optimize efficacy," BioDrugs, vol. 24, no. 1, pp. 9–21, 2010.

87. G. Walsh, "Biopharmaceutical benchmarks 2010," Nature Biotechnology, vol. 28, no. 9, pp. 917–924, 2010.

88. Y. Vugmeyster, X. Xu, F. P. Theil, L. A. Khawli, and M. W. Leach, "Pharmacokinetics and toxicology of therapeutic proteins: advances and challenges," World Journal of Biological Chemistry, vol. 3, no. 4, pp. 73–92, 2012.

89. S. Hermeling, D. J. A. Crommelin, H. Schellekens, and W. Jiskoot, "Structure-immunogenicity relationships of therapeutic proteins," Pharmaceutical Research, vol. 21, no. 6, pp. 897–903, 2004.

90. C. Sheridan, "Commercial interest grows in glycan analysis," Nature Biotechnology, vol. 25, no. 2, pp. 145–146, 2007.

91. J.-Y. Park, M.-R. Park, D.-N. Kwon et al., "Alpha 1,3-galactosyltransferase deficiency in pigs increases sialyltransferase activities that potentially raise non-gal xenoantigenicity," Journal of Biomedicine and Biotechnology, vol. 2011, Article ID 560850, 8 pages, 2011.

92. U. Galili, "The α-gal epitope and the anti-Gal antibody in xenotransplantation and in cancer immunotherapy," Immunology and Cell Biology, vol. 83, no. 6, pp. 674–686, 2005.

93. V. Padler-Karavani and A. Varki, "Potential impact of the non-human sialic acid N-glycolylneuraminic acid on transplant rejection risk," Xenotransplantation, vol. 18, no. 1, pp. 1–5, 2011.

94. K. A. van Schie, G.-J. Wolbink, and T. Rispens, "Cross-reactive and pre-existing antibodies to therapeutic antibodies—effects on treatment and immunogenicity," mAbs, vol. 7, no. 4, pp. 662–671, 2015.

95. J. Qian, T. Liu, L. Yang, A. Daus, R. Crowley, and Q. Zhou, "Structural characterization of N-linked oligosaccharides on monoclonal antibody cetuximab by the combination of orthogonal matrix-assisted laser desorption/ionization hybrid quadrupole-quadrupole time-of-flight tandem mass spectrometry and sequential enzymatic digestion," Analytical Biochemistry, vol. 364, no. 1, pp. 8–18, 2007.

96. X. Xu, H. Nagarajan, N. E. Lewis et al., "The genomic sequence of the Chinese hamster ovary (CHO)-K1 cell line," Nature Biotechnology, vol. 29, no. 8, pp. 735–741, 2011.

97. D. Ghaderi, R. E. Taylor, V. Padler-Karavani, S. Diaz, and A. Varki, "Implications of the presence of N-glycolylneuraminic acid in recombinant therapeutic glycoproteins," Nature Biotechnology, vol. 28, no. 8, pp. 863–867, 2010.

98. E. Maeda, S. Kita, M. Kinoshita, K. Urakami, T. Hayakawa, and K. Kakehi, "Analysis of nonhuman N-glycans as the minor constituents in recombinant monoclonal antibody pharmaceuticals," Analytical Chemistry, vol. 84, no. 5, pp. 2373–2379, 2012.

99. A. M. Goetze, M. R. Schenauer, and G. C. Flynn, "Assessing monoclonal antibody product quality attribute criticality through clinical studies," mAbs, vol. 2, no. 5, pp. 500–507, 2010.

100. A. M. Goetze, Y. D. Liu, Z. Zhang et al., "High-mannose glycans on the Fc region of therapeutic IgG antibodies increase serum clearance in humans," Glycobiology, vol. 21, no. 7, pp. 949–959, 2011.

101. D. Reusch and M. L. Tejada, "Fc glycans of therapeutic antibodies as critical quality attributes,"Glycobiology, vol. 25, no. 12, pp. 1325–1334, 2015.

102. F. Sallusto, M. Cella, C. Danieli, and A. Lanzavecchia, "Dendritic cells use macropinocytosis and the mannose receptor to concentrate macromolecules in the major histocompatibility complex class II compartment: downregulation by cytokines and bacterial products," Journal of Experimental Medicine, vol. 182, no. 2, pp. 389–400, 1995.

103. L. Runkel, W. Meier, R. B. Pepinsky et al., "Structural and functional differences between glycosylated and non-glycosylated forms of human interferon-β (IFN-β)," Pharmaceutical Research, vol. 15, no. 4, pp. 641–649, 1998.

104. A. J. Chirino and A. Mire-Sluis, "Characteristics biological products and assessing comparability following manufacturing changes," Nature Biotechnology, vol. 22, no. 11, pp. 1383–1391, 2004.

105. R. J. Harris, "Heterogeneity of recombinant antibodies: linking structure to function," Developments in Biologicals, vol. 122, pp. 117–127, 2005.

106. M. C. Manning, D. K. Chou, B. M. Murphy, R. W. Payne, and D. S. Katayama, "Stability of protein pharmaceuticals: an update," Pharmaceutical Research, vol. 27, no. 4, pp. 544–575, 2010.

107. R. Torosantucci, O. Mozziconacci, V. Sharov, C. Schöneich, and W. Jiskoot, "Chemical modifications in aggregates of recombinant human insulin induced by metal-catalyzed oxidation: covalent cross-linking via michael addition to

tyrosine oxidation products," Pharmaceutical Research, vol. 29, no. 8, pp. 2276–2293, 2012.

108. W. Chen, N. J. Ede, D. C. Jackson, J. McCluskey, and A. W. Purcell, "CTL recognition of an altered peptide associated with asparagine bond rearrangement. Implications for immunity and vaccine design,"The Journal of Immunology, vol. 157, no. 3, pp. 1000–1005, 1996.

109. J. L. Cleland, M. F. Powell, and S. J. Shire, "The development of stable protein formulations: a close look at protein aggregation, deamidation, and oxidation," Critical Reviews in Therapeutic Drug Carrier Systems, vol. 10, no. 4, pp. 307–377, 1993.

110. H. A. Doyle, J. Zhou, M. J. Wolff et al., "Isoaspartyl post-translational modification triggers anti-tumor T and B lymphocyte immunity," Journal of Biological Chemistry, vol. 281, no. 43, pp. 32676–32683, 2006.

111. A. S. Rosenberg, "Effects of protein aggregates: an immunologic perspective," AAPS Journal, vol. 8, no. 3, pp. E501–E507, 2006.

112. H. Schellekens, "Biosimilar therapeutics—what do we need to consider?" NDT Plus, vol. 2, supplement 1, pp. i27–i36, 2009.

113. M. Sauerborn, V. Brinks, W. Jiskoot, and H. Schellekens, "Immunological mechanism underlying the immune response to recombinant human protein therapeutics," Trends in Pharmacological Sciences, vol. 31, no. 2, pp. 53–59, 2010.

114. S. Noguchi, "Structural changes induced by the deamidation and isomerization of asparagine revealed by the crystal structure of Ustilago sphaerogena ribonuclease U2B," Biopolymers, vol. 93, no. 11, pp. 1003–1010, 2010.

115. R. Torosantucci, V. S. Sharov, M. van Beers, V. Brinks, C. Schöneich, and W. Jiskoot, "Identification of oxidation sites and covalent cross-links in metal catalyzed oxidized interferon Beta-1a: potential implications for protein aggregation and immunogenicity," Molecular Pharmaceutics, vol. 10, no. 6, pp. 2311–2322, 2013.

116. A. Basu, K. Yang, M. Wang et al., "Structure-function engineering of interferon-β-1b for improving stability, solubility, potency, immunogenicity, and pharmacokinetic properties by site-selective mono-PEGylation," Bioconjugate Chemistry, vol. 17, no. 3, pp. 618–630, 2006.

117. J. S. Bee, S. A. Nelson, E. Freund, J. F. Carpenter, and T. W. Randolph, "Precipitation of a monoclonal antibody by soluble tungsten," Journal of Pharmaceutical Sciences, vol. 98, no. 9, pp. 3290–3301, 2009.

118. P. Hong, S. Koza, and E. S. P. Bouvier, "A review size-exclusion chromatography for the analysis of protein biotherapeutics and their aggregates," Journal of Liquid Chromatography and Related Technologies, vol. 35, no. 20, pp. 2923–2950, 2012.

119. G. Shankar, E. Shores, C. Wagner, and A. Mire-Sluis, "Scientific and regulatory considerations on the immunogenicity of biologics," Trends in Biotechnology, vol. 24, no. 6, pp. 274–280, 2006.

120. J. Wang, J. Lozier, G. Johnson et al., "Neutralizing antibodies to therapeutic enzymes: considerations for testing, prevention and treatment," Nature Biotechnology, vol. 26, no. 8, pp. 901–908, 2008.

121. V. Brinks, W. Jiskoot, and H. Schellekens, "Immunogenicity of therapeutic proteins: the use of animal models," Pharmaceutical Research, vol. 28, no. 10, pp. 2379–2385, 2011.

122. S. Hermeling, H. Schellekens, D. J. A. Crommelin, and W. Jiskoot, "Micelle-associated protein in epoetin formulations: a risk factor for immunogenicity?" Pharmaceutical Research, vol. 20, no. 12, pp. 1903–1907, 2003.

123. M. M. C. van Beers, M. Sauerborn, F. Gilli, V. Brinks, H. Schellekens, and W. Jiskoot, "Aggregated recombinant human interferon beta induces antibodies but no memory in immune-tolerant transgenic mice," Pharmaceutical Research, vol. 27, no. 9, pp. 1812–1824, 2010.

124. A. S. De Groot and W. Martin, "Reducing risk, improving outcomes: bioengineering less immunogenic protein

therapeutics," Clinical Immunology, vol. 131, no. 2, pp. 189–201, 2009.

125. S. Hermeling, L. Aranha, J. M. A. Damen et al., "Structural characterization and immunogenicity in wild-type and immune tolerant mice of degraded recombinant human interferon alpha2b,"Pharmaceutical Research, vol. 22, no. 12, pp. 1997–2006, 2005.

126. M. M. C. van Beers, M. Sauerborn, F. Gilli, V. Brinks, H. Schellekens, and W. Jiskoot, "Oxidized and aggregated recombinant human interferon beta is immunogenic in human interferon beta transgenic mice," Pharmaceutical Research, vol. 28, no. 10, pp. 2393–2402, 2011.

127. P. Gaitonde and S. V. Balu-Iyer, "In vitro immunogenicity risk assessment of therapeutic proteins in preclinical setting," in Drug Design and Discovery, vol. 716 of Methods in Molecular Biology, pp. 267–280, Springer, Berlin, Germany, 2011.

128. K. D. Ratanji, J. P. Derrick, R. J. Dearman, and I. Kimber, "Immunogenicity of therapeutic proteins: influence of aggregation," Journal of Immunotoxicology, vol. 11, no. 2, pp. 99–109, 2014.

129. M. K. Joubert, M. Hokom, C. Eakin et al., "Highly aggregated antibody therapeutics can enhance the in vitro innate and late-stage T-cell immune responses," The Journal of Biological Chemistry, vol. 287, no. 30, pp. 25266–25279, 2012.

130. T. W. Tobery, S. A. Dubey, K. Anderson et al., "A comparison of standard immunogenicity assays for monitoring HIV type 1 gag-specific T cell responses in Ad5 HIV type 1 gag vaccinated human subjects,"AIDS Research and Human Retroviruses, vol. 22, no. 11, pp. 1081–1090, 2006.

131. M. G. Tovey, J. Legrand, and C. Lallemand, "Overcoming immunogenicity associated with the use of biopharmaceuticals," Expert Review of Clinical Pharmacology, vol. 4, no. 5, pp. 623–631, 2011.

132. E. Koren, A. S. De Groot, V. Jawa et al., "Clinical validation of the 'in silico' prediction of immunogenicity of a human

recombinant therapeutic protein," Clinical Immunology, vol. 124, no. 1, pp. 26–32, 2007.

133. X. Wang, T. K. Das, S. K. Singh, and S. Kumar, "Potential aggregation prone regions in biotherapeutics: a survey of commercial monoclonal antibodies," mAbs, vol. 1, no. 3, pp. 254–267, 2009.

134. R. Jefferis, "Aggregation, immune complexes and immunogenicity," mAbs, vol. 3, no. 6, pp. 503–504, 2011.

135. S. Maier, C. H. Chung, M. Morse et al., "A retrospective analysis of cross-reacting cetuximab IgE antibody and its association with severe infusion reactions," Cancer Medicine, vol. 4, no. 1, pp. 36–42, 2015.

136. Y. H. Messinger, N. J. Mendelsohn, W. Rhead et al., "Successful immune tolerance induction to enzyme replacement therapy in CRIM-negative infantile Pompe disease," Genetics in Medicine, vol. 14, no. 1, pp. 135–142, 2012.

137. C. Ma, V. Huang, D. K. Fedorak et al., "Adalimumab dose escalation is effective for managing secondary loss of response in Crohn's disease," Alimentary Pharmacology and Therapeutics, vol. 40, no. 9, pp. 1044–1055, 2014.

138. S.-L. Wang, S. Hauenstein, L. Ohrmund et al., "Monitoring of adalimumab and antibodies-to-adalimumab levels in patient serum by the homogeneous mobility shift assay," Journal of Pharmaceutical and Biomedical Analysis, vol. 78-79, pp. 39–44, 2013.

139. R. Jefferis, "Posttranslational modifications and the immunogenicity of biotherapeutics," Journal of Immunology Research, vol. 2016, Article ID 5358272, 15 pages, 2016.

140. H. C. Ebbers, S. A. Crow, A. G. Vulto, and H. Schellekens, "Interchangeability, immunogenicity and biosimilars," Nature Biotechnology, vol. 30, no. 12, pp. 1186–1190, 2012.

141. G. M. Peterson, "Generic substitution: a need for clarification," British Journal of Clinical Pharmacology, vol. 71, no. 6, pp. 966–968, 2011.

142. G. Walsh, "Post-translational modifications of protein biopharmaceuticals," Drug Discovery Today, vol. 15, no. 17-18, pp. 773–780, 2010.

143. A. Colbert, A. Umble-Romero, S. Prokop et al., "Bioanalytical strategy used in development of pharmacokinetic (PK) methods that support biosimilar programs," mAbs, vol. 6, no. 5, pp. 1178–1189, 2014.

5

CHAPTER

Investigation of Genipin Cross-Linked Microcapsule for Oral Delivery of Live Bacterial Cells and Other Biotherapeutics: Preparation and In Vitro Analysis in Simulated Human Gastrointestinal Model

Hongmei Chen, Wei Ouyang, Christopher Martoni, Fatemeh Afkhami, Bisi Lawuyi, Trisna Lim, and Satya Prakash

Department of Biomedical Engineering and Physiology, Biomedical Technology and Cell Therapy Research Laboratory, Artificial Cells and Organs Research Centre, Faculty of Medicine, McGill University, Montreal, Qc, Canada H3A 2B4

ABSTRACT

Oral therapy utilizing engineered microorganisms has shown promise in the treatment of many diseases. By microencapsulation, viable cells can overcome the harsh gastrointestinal (GI) environment and secrete needed therapeutics into the gut. These engineered cells should be encased without escaping into the GI tract for safety concerns, thus robust microcapsule membrane is requisite. This paper examined the GI performance of a novel microcapsule membrane using a dynamic simulated human GI model. Results showed that the genipin cross-linked alginate-chitosan (GCAC) microcapsules possessed strong resistance to structural disintegration in the simulated GI environment. Leakage of encapsulated high molecular weight dextran, a model material to be protected during the simulated GI transit, was negligible over 72 h of exposure, in contrast to considerable leakage of dextran from the non-cross-linked counterparts. These microcapsules did not alter the microflora and enzymatic activities in the simulated human colonic media. This study suggested the potential of the GCAC microcapsules for oral delivery of live microorganisms and other biotherapeutics.

1. INTRODUCTION

Advances in molecular biology research have introduced a wide range of genetically engineered (GE) microorganisms with a superior capacity to produce disease-modifying substrates, such as cytokines, enzymes, vaccines, hormones, antibodies, growth factors, and other therapeutic products [1, 2]. The use of these microorganisms opens up new hopes of treating a wide array of human diseases. Because the secreted biologics are generally fragile and easily degraded or denatured [3], encapsulation technology may offer significant advantages over the conventional biotechnological production methods. Being protected against external stresses, encapsulated bacteria remain viable and functional. They can be delivered proximally to the target sitein vivo and continuously secrete therapeutic products to the host at a more effective concentration [4]. Recent research on the microencapsulation of GE cells has demonstrated great potential in the treatment of kidney failure, cancers, hypercholesteraemia, and many other diseases [5–13].

Oral ingestion is usually a preferred route of administration for therapy; however, microcapsules containing bacterial cells and other biotherapeutic molecules can be disrupted in the harsh gastrointestinal (GI) system by a number of means such as low pH, antimicrobial substances and mechanical stress [14]. Furthermore, the eruption of microcapsules and the subsequent release of engineered bacteria could induce many adverse effects on the body [2]. It was previously shown that oral administration of repeated doses of bacteria may stimulate a host immune response [15, 16]. Propagation of foreign bacteria in the GI tract may cause uncontrolled and persistent production of harmful substances, and may detrimentally disrupt and/or replace the natural microflora [2, 17]. There are also risks of immunomodulation and gene transfer associated with the use of novel microorganisms [18]. Therefore, it is essential that GE bacteria be encased in the microcapsules, perform the therapeutic functions during the GI transit, and be excreted along with the intact microcapsules in feces without being retained in the body, even though these GE cells are classified as nonpathogenic [7]. To fulfill these requirements, it is important to maintain the structural integrity of microcapsules and thus prevent cell leakage during the GI transit. Current literature reports on oral delivery systems mainly focus on the controlled release of encapsulated contents, for example, probiotics and drugs [4, 19–23]. Scanty research is available on microcapsules intended to retain cells throughout the GI transit.

Alginate and chitosan are biomaterials widely studied for cell encapsulation because of their excellent biocompatibility, status as FDA approved food additives, and mild process conditions [24–28]. It was reported that the ionically linked alginate-chitosan (AC) membrane improved gastric survival of probiotics, but some limitations such as inadequate stability, susceptibility to degradation and cell leakage persist [29–33]. Genipin and its derivatives, extracted from gardenia fruits [34], have traditionally been used as a herbal medicine and a natural colorant in the food industry [35]. Previous research has demonstrated its low cytotoxicity and potential in protein and live cell delivery [36–38]. We have previously developed a novel covalently cross-linked microcapsule system composed of a calcium alginate core with a genipin cross-linked chitosan membrane [36,39]. Our recent data showed that this microcapsule membrane possessed strong membrane stability and resistance to enzymatic degradation [40]. The purpose of this study is to further evaluate the potential of this genipin cross-linked alginate-chitosan (GCAC) microcapsule system for GI applications by using a dynamic human GI model. For comparison, the frequently used AC microcapsules were also tested.

2. MATERIALS AND METHODS

2.1. Chemicals

Sodium alginate (low viscosity), and fluorescein isothiocyanate (FITC) labeled dextran (2,000 KD) were supplied by Sigma-Aldrich, USA. Chitosan (low viscosity,, degree of deacetylation or DDA = 73.5%) and genipin were purchased from Wako BioProducts, USA. 4-nitrophenyl--D galactopyranoside, 4-nitrophenyl--D glucopyranoside, and 4-nitrophenyl--D galactopyranoside were obtained from Acros Organics, USA. 4-nitrophenol, 4-nitrophenyl--D glucopyranoside, and 4-nitrophenyl--D glucuronide were purchased from Sigma-Aldrich, USA. All other reagents and solvents were of reagent grade and used as received without further purification.

2.2. Preparation of Microcapsules

The AC and GCAC microcapsules were prepared as per previously reported protocol [39]. Unless otherwise specified, the cross-linking reaction was performed by suspending the AC microcapsules in a genipin solution (2.5 mg/mL) at room temperature (RT). Sterile microcapsules were prepared similarly except that the entire encapsulation procedure was carried out in a biological containment hood and all solutions used were either 0.22 m filtered or autoclaved to ensure sterility. Microcapsules containing high molecular weight FITC-labeled dextran were prepared by mixing FITC-dextran with an alginate solution, making the final concentrations of alginate and FITC-dextran at 15 mg/mL and 2 mg/mL, respectively. The subsequent processes, including the formation of alginate beads, coating and cross-linking were performed using the aforementioned procedures.

2.3. Simulation of the Human Gastrointestinal (GI) Environment

The human GI conditions used in this study were simulated in vitro by means of five sequential bioreactors (Figure 1). Each compartment simulates a different part of the human GI tract: the stomach, the small intestine, the ascending colon, the transverse colon, and the descending colon [41, 44]. Human fecal slurries containing normal human GI bacterial cells were inoculated into the simulated colon (the last three vessels). Food content of human western diet suspension, composed of (per liter) 1 g arabinogalactan, 2 g pectin, 1 g xylan, 3 g potato starch, 0.4 g glucose, 3 g yeast extract, 1 g peptone, 4 g mucin, and 0.5 g cystein, was fed to the first vessel three times a day. After feeding, acidification of the stomach (pH 2) occurred, followed by neutralization (pH6.8) in the second vessel and addition of simulated pancreatic juice (0.9 g pancreatin, 6 g bile salts, and 12 g NaHC per liter) to the simulated small intestine. Afterwards, the suspension was transferred to the simulated ascending colon, the transverse colon, and the descending colon, and finally excreted as effluent. The first two reactors were of the fill-and-draw principle with programmed periods of residence and stirring, and the last three were continuously agitated (approximately 250 rpm). The whole system was maintained under anaerobic conditions by flushing the headspace of each vessel with N2 for 15 minutes every day and the temperature of each vessel was kept constant at by a thermostat. The pH conditions, fluid volume, retention time at each stage, as well as the entire transit were simulated under computer control. This in vitro human GI model was validated against in vivo data by earlier studies [41].

2.4. Resistance of Microcapsules to the Simulated Human GI Transit

To study the microcapsule resistance to the simulated human GI transit, microcapsules (0.80 g) were exposed to the simulated human GI fluids for the estimated maximum period of time for the human GI transit (Table 1) [42]. Microcapsule samples were withdrawn at varied stages for morphological examination under an inverted microscope (LOMO, PC), and microphotographs taken as records using a digital camera (Canon Power shot G2, Japan). Percent defective microcapsules were estimated in three randomly picked observation fields.

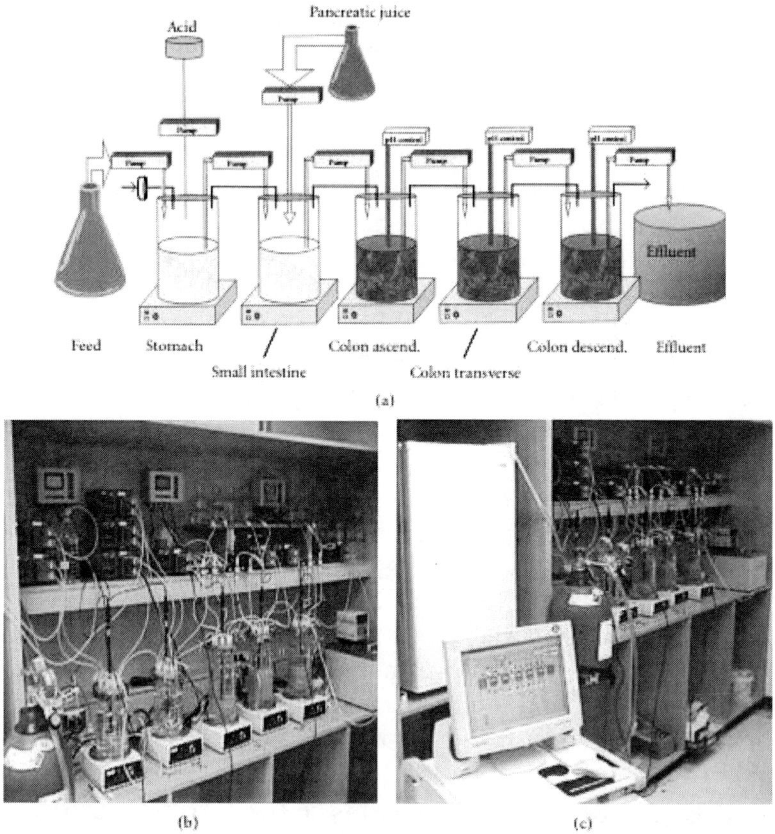

Figure 1: Computer controlled dynamic in vitro human GI model. (a) schematic; (b) 5-bioreactors set-up; and (c) online computer control.

Table 1: Exposure of microcapsules to the simulated human GI transit (72 h in total) and the corresponding morphological changes.

Compartment in GI model	Stomach (V1[a])	Small intestine (V2[a])	Ascend. Colon (V3[a])	Transverse colon (V4[a])	Descend. Colon (V5[a])
pH	≤2	7.2–7.4	5.6–5.8	6.2–6.4	6.6–6.8
Exposure time (h)	2	4	18	24	24
Microcapsule morphology[b]	Intact	Swelled, ~15% deformed	Collapsed	Collapsed or dissolved	Adhesive, ~30% ruptured
Microcapsule morphology[c]	Intact	Slightly swelled, <1% burst	Spherical, <2% broken	Spherical intact	Spherical intact

[a]Vessel (V) of bioreactors in the GI model representing the human GI tract.
[b]Microcapsules cross-linked by genipin at 4°C.
[c]Microcapsules cross-linked by genipin at RT.

To assess the recovery of microcapsules after the simulated human GI transit, microcapsules of known weight were placed in a sealed teabag-like container and exposed to the simulated GI media according to the timetable described in Table 1. At the final stage, the retrieved microcapsules were washed, dried using filter paper for approximately 10 min and weighed. Percent recovery was defined as: % recovery = (−W)/*100, where and W are the weights of the microcapsules before and after being exposed to the simulated GI transit, respectively.

2.5. Retention of Encapsulated Macromolecules against Leaching to the Simulated Human GI Fluids

To evaluate the capacity of the GCAC microcapsules to retain enclosed large-sized materials, high molecular weight FITC-dextran was encapsulated as a model macromolecule. These FITC-dextran-containing microcapsules (g) were exposed to 2 mL of the simulated human gastric fluid taken from the GI model and incubated in an Environ shaker at , 100 rpm for 1 hour, followed by a 72 hours incubation in 2 mL of the simulated human intestinal fluid from the GI model (, 100 rpm). Samples of the incubation media were withdrawn periodically and leaking of the encapsulated FITC-dextran was assessed spectrofluorometrically using a Microplate Fluorescence Reader (FLx800, Bio-Tek Instruments, Inc.) at absorption and emission wavelengths of 485 nm and 528 nm, respectively. Volume of the incubation medium was kept constant by adding fresh simulated fluid after sampling. Data are presented as . from triplicate experiments.

2.6. Effect of Microcapsules on the Simulated Gut Microflora

To investigate the influence of oral administered microcapsules on gut microflora, sterile microcapsules (1.0 g) were mixed with the suspension of the simulated transverse colon (10 mL). After 0, 6, 12, and 24 hours of anaerobic incubation at , samples of the incubation medium were aseptically withdrawn and serially diluted with physiological saline. Bacterial enumeration for specific fecal marker microorganisms, Escherichia coli, Staphylococcus sp., Lactobacillus sp. as well as total aerobes and total anaerobes, was performed using an agar-plate-count assay. The plating media and incubation conditions used in the experiments are listed in Table2. The simulated colonic suspension without microcapsules was used as control.

Table 2: Media and incubation conditions used for enumeration of representative microbes in the simulated human colon.

Microbial group	Medium	Incubation conditions and time	Colonies formed
Total aerobes	Brain heart infusion agar	Aerobic, 37°C, 24 hours	White
Total anaerobes	Brain heart infusion agar	Anaerobic, 37°C, 72 hours	White
Escherichia coli	Mc Conkey agar	Aerobic, 43°C, 24 hours	Red-purple
Staphylococcus sp.	Mannitol Salt agar	Aerobic, 37°C, 48 hours	White with yellow/purple zone
Lactobacillus sp.	Rogosa agar	Anaerobic, 37°C, 72 hours	White

2.7. Effect of Microcapsules on the Microbial Enzyme Activities in the Simulated Colonic Media

To assess the effect of oral administered microcapsules on the GI microbial enzyme activities, the suspension from the simulated transverse colon (20 mL) was incubated anaerobically at in the presence of sterile microcapsules (2.0 g) for up to 24 hours. At different time points of 0, 12, and 24 hours, the enzymatic activities of -galactosidase, -glucosidase, -glucuronidase, -galactosidase, and -glucosidase in the incubation medium were analyzed spectrometrically using the method described earlier [43, 44]. The absorbance at 405 nm was recorded by a Quant multiplate reader (Bio-Tek Instruments). The simulated colonic fluid free of microcapsules was used as control. Results are expressed as percentage of enzymatic activities relative to the control at each time point. Data of the control samples at each time point were normalized to 100%.

Numerical values are shown as mean ± standard deviation. Statistical analyses used the two-tailed Student's t-test with considered significantly different.

3. RESULTS

3.1. Resistance of Microcapsule to the Simulated Human GI Transit

To assess the resistance to the GI environment, the GCAC microcapsules were exposed to the simulated GI media representing different phases of digestion for a length of time based on the estimated maximum retention in the human GI tract (Table 1). Figure 2 depicts the photomicrographs of the microcapsules after exposure to the simulated human GI fluids. The tested microcapsules remained morphologically stable during the simulated gastric incubation (2 hours,) (Figures 2(a), 2(d)), but behaved differently in the subsequent simulated intestinal transit depending on the extent of cross-linking. The GCAC microcapsules cross-linked at swelled appreciably in the simulated small intestine (pH 7.2–7.4) (Figure 2(b)). They became fragile and adhesive in the simulated descending colon where shriveled or partially dissolved beads were observed. When leaving the simulated descending colon, 30–40% of the microcapsules lost their structural integrity (Figure 2(c)). In contrast, the majority of the GCAC microcapsules cross-linked at higher temperature (RT) maintained their physical stability during the entire simulated human GI transit (Figures 2(e)and 2(f)), with more than 80% recovery after 72 hours exposure (Figure 3). In comparison, the recovery of the GCAC microcapsules with less cross-link (cross-linked at) was lower (61.4%) (Figure 3).

3.2. Retention of Encapsulated HMW Dextran during the Simulated GI Transit

To examine the capacity of the GCAC microcapsules to encase large-sized materials in the GI environment, encapsulated high molecular weight FITC-labeled dextran was exposed to the simulated human GI media. Being a large polymer of 2,000 KD, this fluorescent probe was indefinitely withheld inside the intact microcapsules and could not leak out unless the microcapsule membranes became defective or damaged [45]. During the first hour of exposure to the simulated gastric fluid, no FITC-dextran was detected in the incubation medium (data not shown). In the subsequent exposure to the simulated intestinal medium, the leakage of the encapsulated FITC-dextran from the non-cross-linked AC microcapsules increased gradually with the incubation time, attaining the fluorescence intensity of 70, 100 and 115 at 24, 48 and 72 hours, respectively. In contrast, negligible amounts of FITC-dextran escaped from the GCAC microcapsules, with very low fluorescence intensity of the medium detected (not exceeding 50) throughout the experiment (Figure 4), which significantly outran those of the AC microcapsules.

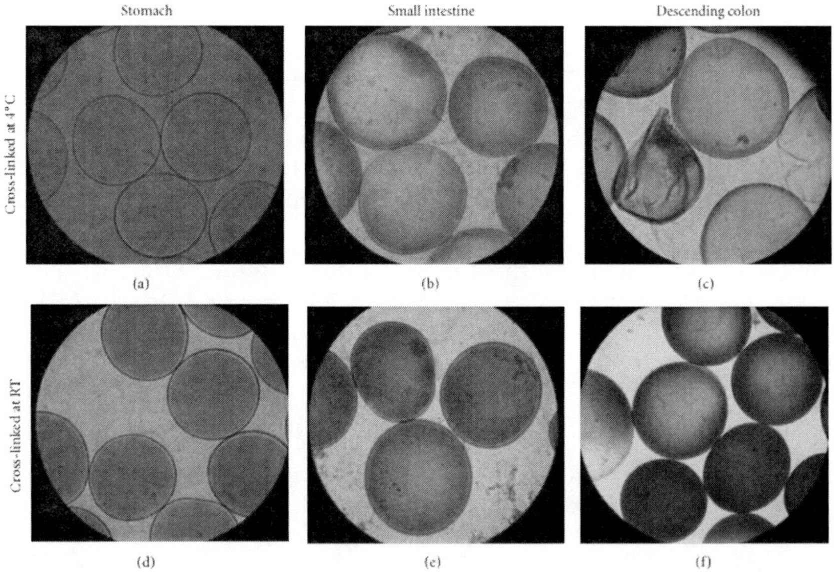

Figure 2: Microphotographs of the GCAC microcapsules cross-linked at (a)–(c) and RT (d)–(f) during the simulated human GI transit in the simulated stomach, small intestine, and descending colons. Original magnification at 90x.

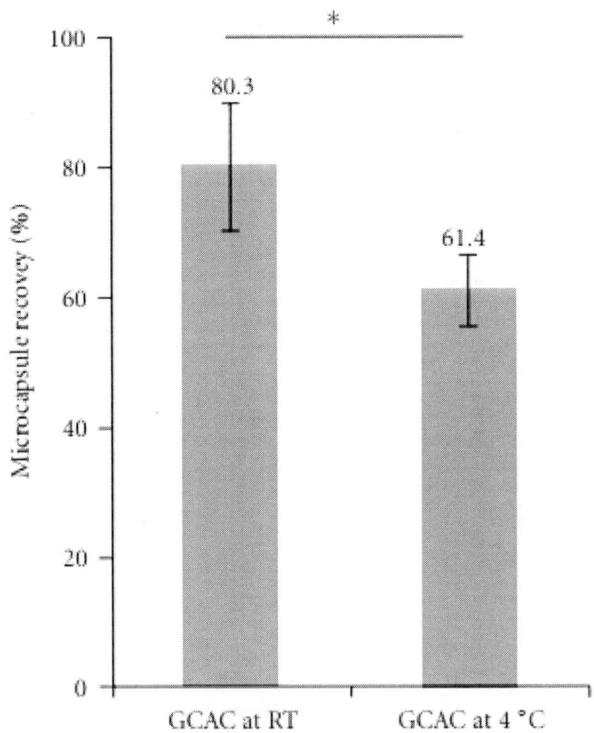

Figure 3: Recovery of microcapsules after 72 hours of the simulated human GI transit. indicates significant difference at

3.3. Oral Administration of Microcapsules on Gut Microflora and Enzymatic Activities

The effect of microcapsules on human GI microflora was assessed by investigating the population of fecal marker microorganisms and the activity of 5 representative GI microbial enzymes in the simulated colonic media containing sterile microcapsules. Since the simulated GI model is a dynamic system, static experiments were performed in this study to maximize the effects. We found no marked differences in the tested microbial population including total aerobes, total anaerobes, Escherichia coli, Staphylococcus sp., and Lactobacillus sp. in the stimulated colonic media containing tested microcapsules of either AC or GCAC formulation when compared to the control media in the absence of tested microcapsules (Table 3, all).

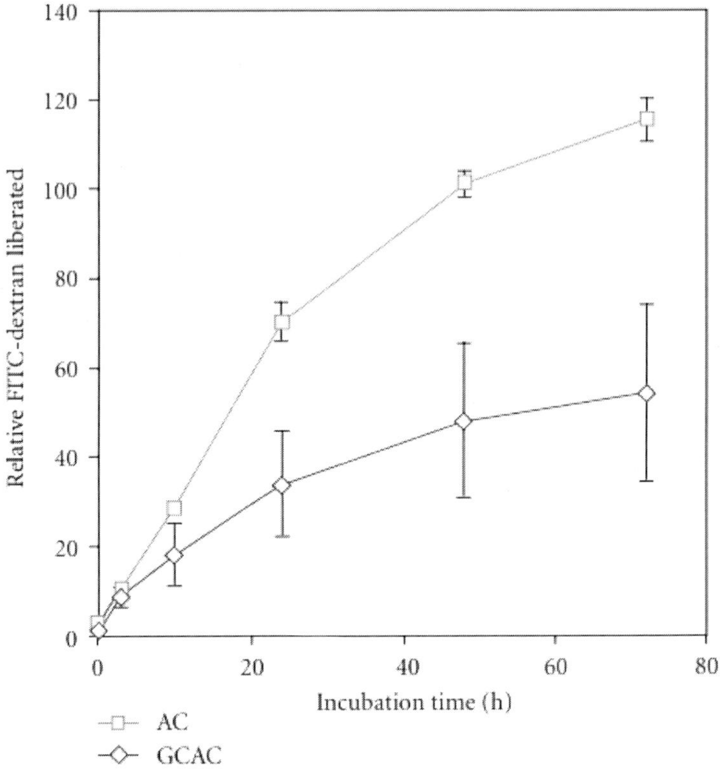

Figure 4: Leaching of the encapsulated FITC-dextran into the simulated intestinal medium following 1 hour simulated gastric exposure. Error bars indicate standard deviation of the mean ().

Figure 5 shows the effect of the microcapsules on the activities of microbial enzymes in the simulated transverse colon suspension. As time elapsed, a slight decline in the tested enzymatic activities was found in the simulated colonic fluids in the presence of microcapsules. As an exception, a decrease of more than 20% in the activity of -glucuronidase was detected after 12 hours of contact with microcapsules, yet the loss remained at a similar level with extended incubation for up to 24 hours (Figure 5(c)). No significant differences in the alteration of enzymatic activities were found when the GCAC microcapsules were compared with the AC microcapsules ().

Table 3: Effects of microcapsules on fecal marker microbes in the simulated transverse colon.

Microbes	Incubation time (h)	Log CFU/mL medium[a]		
		GCAC[b]	AC[b]	Control[c]
Total aerobes	0	8.41	8.41	8.41
	6	8.37	8.32	8.36
	12	8.36	8.37	8.39
	24	8.22	8.17	8.04
Total anaerobes	0	8.44	8.44	8.44
	6	8.37	8.33	8.41
	12	8.37	8.43	8.40
	24	8.41	8.30	8.03
Escherichia coli	0	8.31	8.31	8.31
	6	8.18	7.97	8.18
	12	8.20	8.02	8.41
	24	8.10	8.03	8.68
Staphylococcus sp.	0	6.96	6.96	6.96
	6	6.52	6.60	6.81
	12	6.61	6.72	6.77
	24	6.57	6.62	6.54
Lactobacillus sp.	0	5.48	5.48	5.48
	6	5.45	5.52	5.51
	12	5.35	5.40	5.32
	24	5.50	5.46	5.37

[a] $n = 3$, standard deviation <0.20.
[b] Colonic suspension in the presence of microcapsules.
[c] Colonic suspension in the absence of microcapsules.

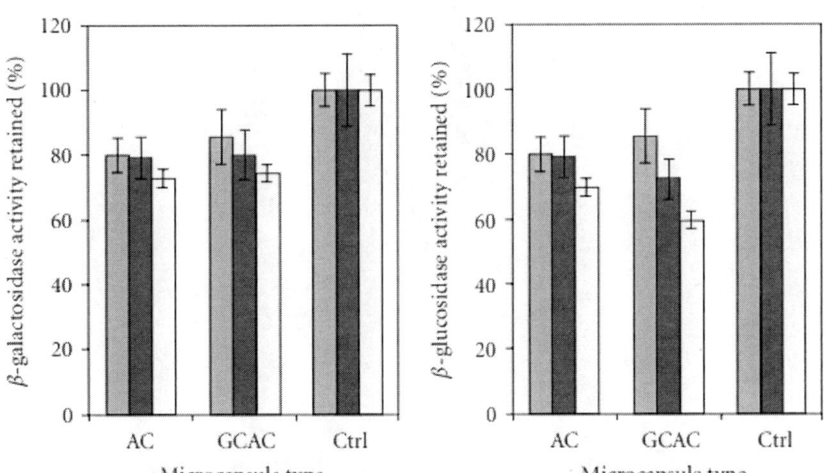

(a) (b)

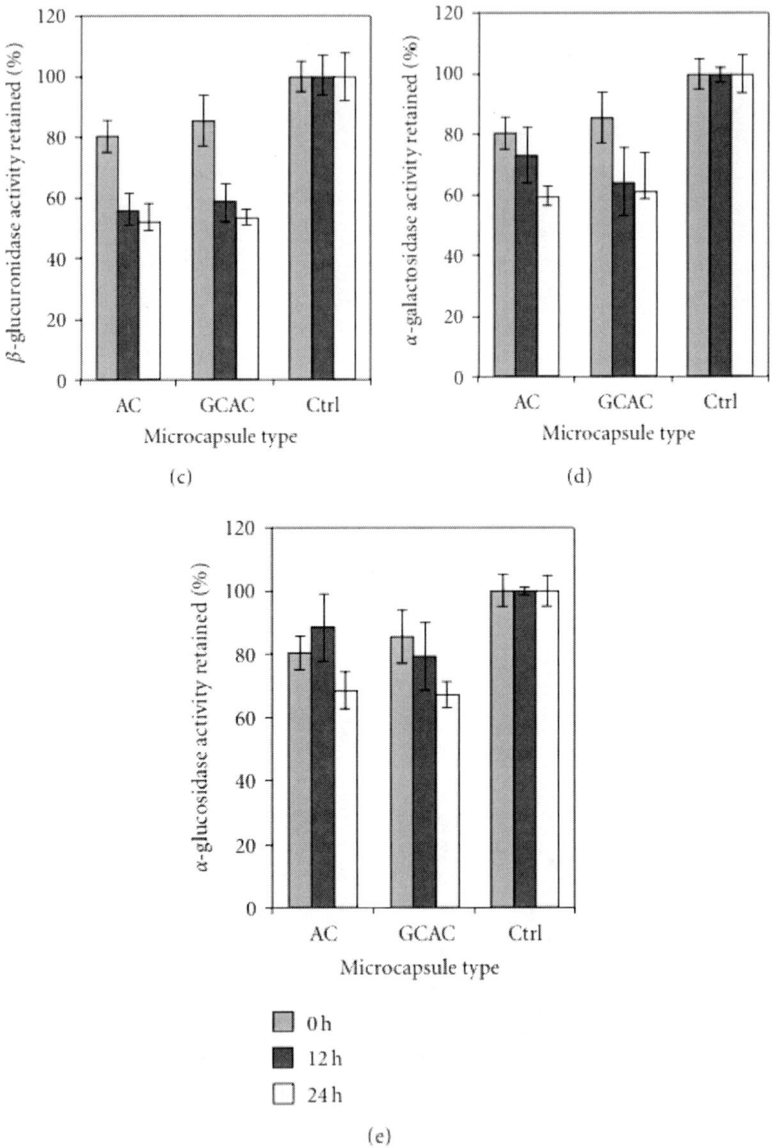

Figure 5: Percent microbial enzyme activities retained in the suspension of the simulated human transverse colon in the presence of microcapsules relative to that in the absence of microcapsules (control). Values for the controls at each time point were normalized to 100 % and were used to calculate the percent enzyme activities retained in the microcapsule-containing media at corresponding time points. (a) -galactosidase; (b) -glucosidase; (c) -glucuronidase; (d) -galactosidase; and (e) -glucosidase.

4. DISCUSSION

For successful exploitation of microcapsules as an oral delivery device, understanding of their performance under physiologically pertinent conditions that represent the human GI tract is essential. Although in vivoresearch using specific techniques such as histological sectioning [46], radiography [47] and gamma scintigraphy [48, 49] can progressively track the microcapsules in the GI tract, it remains difficult to follow the orally administered microcapsule at every stage of digestion on either animals or humans due to tedious processing, small size of the microcapsules, limited detection resolution and ethical constraints. In vitrosimulation offers a number of advantages, for example, well-controlled experimental conditions and easy sampling, especially preferable for screening and examining a variety of samples. Buffered solutions, for example, with pH at 1-2 or 6.5-7.5, are frequently reported in literature as the simulated GI fluids [31, 50, 51]; however they only represent the pH in the stomach and in the intestine, and do not mimic the complex human GI microbial ecosystem. While other ex vivo and in vitro simulated models including USP apparatus were also reported [52], most of them were static systems, where fluids cannot be continuously transferred into the sequential GI compartments. Our present study used a dynamic computer-controlled human simulated GI model, which mimics the gradual transit of ingested materials through the simulated GI tract from feeding to discharge. It also maintains the microbial community actually presented in the human intestinal system, which allows for assessing the behavior of the microcapsules under more physiologically pertinent conditions.

As has been noted earlier, it is imperative that microcapsules maintain physical integrity during the GI transit to prevent the leaking of genetically engineered cells, which is strongly dependent on the microcapsule's robustness and stability. So far few studies were reported to address this matter [44]. The present study investigated the behaviour of the GCAC microcapsules in the simulated human GI environment. When exposed to the simulated GI media, the microcapsules experienced the simulated transit through the GI tract including pH fluctuation, enzymatic degradation, microorganism actions, mechanical stresses, as well as other related chemical and physiological constraints. The exposure time was chosen according to the maximum period retention in the human GI tract that represents the most challenging case for the tested microcapsules. The better-preserved morphology and higher retrieval rate associated with the GCAC microcapsules cross-linked at RT (Figures 2 and 3) indicated improved membrane stability by higher degree of cross-linking. Moreover, negligible amounts of encapsulated fluorescent probe were released into the incubation GI media from the GCAC microcapsules (Figure 4), suggesting that the integrity of the microcapsule membrane was withheld. In contrast, the non-cross-linked AC microcapsules were found vulnerable to structural disruption in the harsh GI condition, likely due to the relatively weak polyelectrolyte complexation of membrane materials that are prone to gastric and proteolytic degradation. These findings corroborated the results reported previously [44, 53–55]. The present study demonstrated that covalent cross-linking of microcapsule membranes by genipin substantially improved the resistance to membrane degradation in the simulated human GI environment.

Another important prerequisite of oral therapy utilizing microencapsulation is that the administration of microcapsules should not disturb the natural colonic flora, particularly when prolonged and repeated oral intake of a rather large quantity of microcapsules is required for therapy. Microcapsules are made of various materials and chemicals through complexation and cross-linking reactions, all of which may have an effect on the biocompatibility of the final microcapsules. In particular, the well-balanced gut microbiota are important in maintaining human health [56, 57] and should not be altered by the intake of microcapsules. When taken into account the static nature and a rather large dosage (1.0 g of microcapsules in 10 mL of intestinal fluid) of the experiments in this in vitro study, our results suggested that the materials used to construct the microcapsules did not evoke appreciable adverse effects on the human intestinal flora and that genipin cross-linked chitosan membranes did not compromise the biocompatibility of the microcapsules when compared to the non-cross-linked subjects. Decrease in the activities of the tested microbial enzymes in the simulated colonic media containing microcapsules was detected. It could possibly be attributed to the binding effect or diffusion of the enzymes to the microcapsules, though further research may continue to elucidate the consequence.

5. CONCLUSIONS

This study examined the performance of the genipin cross-linked alginate-chitosan microcapsules under physiologically pertinent GI conditions using a dynamic simulated human GI model. Results showed that these GCAC microcapsules possessed superior resistance against disintegration in the simulated GI environment and did not appreciably alter the normal gut flora. This novel microcapsule formulation is promising for oral delivery of genetically engineered bacteria; however, further studies on encapsulated cell viability in the gut lumen are needed before its full potential can be realized.

ACKNOWLEDGMENTS

This paper was supported by the Canadian Institutes of Health Research (CIHR) MOP 64308. Postgraduate fellowships from the Natural Sciences and Engineering Research Council of Canada (to H. Chen and C. Martoni) and Fonds Québécois de la Recherche sur la Nature et les Technologies (to H. Chen and W. Ouyang) are greatly acknowledged. The authors also thank M. L. Jones for his help with the GI model set-up, T. Haque, M. Shafiei, and H. Wightman for assistance in the experiments.

REFERENCES

1. S. Prakash and J. Bhathena, "Live bacterial cells as orally delivered therapeutics," Expert Opinion on Biological Therapy, vol. 5, no. 10, pp. 1281–1301, 2005.
2. L. Steidler, "Genetically engineered probiotics," Bailliere's Best Practice and Research in Clinical Gastroenterology, vol. 17, no. 5, pp. 861–876, 2003.

3. M. Goldberg and I. Gomez-Orellana, "Challenges for the oral delivery of macromolecules," Nature Reviews Drug Discovery, vol. 2, no. 4, pp. 289–295, 2003.

4. G. Orive, R. M. Hernández, A. Rodríguez Gascón et al., "History, challenges and perspectives of cell microencapsulation," Trends in Biotechnology, vol. 22, no. 2, pp. 87–92, 2004.

5. G. Bergers and D. Hanahan, "Cell factories for fighting cancer," Nature Biotechnology, vol. 19, no. 1, pp. 20–21, 2001.

6. J. Bloch, A. C. Bachoud-Lévi, N. Déglon et al., "Neuroprotective gene therapy for Huntington's disease, using polymer-encapsulated cells engineered to secrete human ciliary neurotrophic factor: results of a phase I study," Human Gene Therapy, vol. 15, no. 10, pp. 968–975, 2004.

7. T. M. S. Chang, "Therapeutic applications of polymeric artificial cells," Nature Reviews Drug Discovery, vol. 4, no. 3, pp. 221–235, 2005.

8. M. L. Jones, H. Chen, W. Ouyang, T. Metz, and S. Prakash, "Microencapsulated genetically engineeredLactobacillus plantarum 80 (pCBH1) for bile acid deconjugation and its implication in lowering cholesterol," Journal of Biomedicine and Biotechnology, vol. 2004, no. 1, pp. 61–69, 2004.

9. S. Prakash and T. M. S. Chang, "Microencapsulated genetically engineered live E. coli DH5 cells administered orally to maintain normal plasma urea level in uremic rats," Nature Medicine, vol. 2, no. 8, pp. 883–887, 1996.

10. T.-A. Read, D. R. Sorensen, R. Mahesparan et al., "Local endostatin treatment of gliomas administered by microencapsulated producer cells," Nature Biotechnology, vol. 19, no. 1, pp. 29–34, 2001.

11. C. J. D. Ross, L. Bastedo, S. A. Maier, M. S. Sands, and P. L. Chang, "Treatment of a lysosomal storage disease, mucopolysaccharidosis VII, with microencapsulated recombinant cells," Human Gene Therapy, vol. 11, no. 15, pp. 2117–2127, 2000.

12. A. D. Tagalakis, I. A. Diakonov, I. R. Graham et al., "Apolipoprotein E delivery by peritoneal implantation of encapsulated recombinant cells improves the hyperlipidaemic profile in apoE-deficient mice," Biochimica et Biophysica Acta, vol. 1686, no. 3, pp. 190–199, 2005.

13. J. M. Van Raamsdonk, C. J. D. Ross, M. A. Potter et al., "Treatment of hemophilia B in mice with nonautologous somatic gene therapeutics," Journal of Laboratory and Clinical Medicine, vol. 139, no. 1, pp. 35–42, 2002.

14. L. R. Johnson, Physiology of the Gastrointestinal Tract, Elsevier Academic Press, Burlington, Mass, USA, 2006.

15. J. Chin, B. Turner, I. Barchia, and A. Mullbacher, "Immune response to orally consumed antigens and probiotic bacteria," Immunology and Cell Biology, vol. 78, no. 1, pp. 55–66, 2000.

16. N. Ishibashi and S. Yamazaki, "Probiotics and safety," American Journal of Clinical Nutrition, vol. 73, no. 2, pp. 465S–470S, 2001.

17. C. P. Champagne, N. J. Gardner, and D. Roy, "Challenges in the addition of probiotic cultures to foods,"Critical Reviews in Food Science and Nutrition, vol. 45, no. 1, pp. 61–84, 2005.

18. S. Salminen, A. von Wright, L. Morelli et al., "Demonstration of safety of probiotics—a review,"International Journal of Food Microbiology, vol. 44, no. 1-2, pp. 93–106, 1998.

19. S. Freiberg and X. X. Zhu, "Polymer microspheres for controlled drug release," International Journal of Pharmaceutics, vol. 282, no. 1-2, pp. 1–18, 2004.

20. L. R. Moses, K. J. Dileep, and C. P. Sharma, "Beta cyclodextrin-insulin-encapsulated chitosan/alginate matrix: oral delivery system," Journal of Applied Polymer Science, vol. 75, no. 9, pp. 1089–1096, 2000.

21. E. Nechaeva, "Development of oral microencapsulated forms for delivering viral vaccines," Expert Review of Vaccines, vol. 1, no. 3, pp. 385–397, 2002.

22. G. Orive, A. R. Gascón, R. M. Hernández, A. Domínguez-Gil, and J. L. Pedraz, "Techniques: new approaches to the delivery

of biopharmaceuticals," Trends in Pharmacological Sciences, vol. 25, no. 7, pp. 382–387, 2004.

23. V. R. Sinha and A. Trehan, "Biodegradable microspheres for protein delivery," Journal of Controlled Release, vol. 90, no. 3, pp. 261–280, 2003.

24. A. Bartkowiak, "Optimal conditions of transplantable binary polyelectrolyte microcapsules," Annals of the New York Academy of Sciences, vol. 944, pp. 120–134, 2001.

25. D. W. Green, I. Leveque, D. Walsh et al., "Biomineralized polysaccharide capsules for encapsulation, organization, and delivery of human cell types and growth factors," Advanced Functional Materials, vol. 15, no. 6, pp. 917–923, 2005.

26. T. Haque, H. Chen, W. Ouyang et al., "In vitro study of alginate-chitosan microcapsules: an alternative to liver cell transplants for the treatment of liver failure," Biotechnology Letters, vol. 27, no. 5, pp. 317–322, 2005.

27. D. Maysinger, O. Berezovskaya, and S. Fedoroff, "The hematopoietic cytokine colony stimulating factor 1 is also a growth factor in the CNS.2. Microencapsulated CSF-1 and LM-10 cells as delivery systems,"Experimental Neurology, vol. 141, no. 1, pp. 47–56, 1996.

28. D. Maysinger, K. Krieglstein, J. Filipovic-Grcic, M. Sendtner, K. Unsicker, and P. Richardson, "Microencapsulated ciliary neurotrophic factor: physical properties and biological activities,"Experimental Neurology, vol. 138, no. 2, pp. 177–188, 1996.

29. T. Chandy, D. L. Mooradian, and G. H. R. Rao, "Evaluation of modified alginate-chitosan-polyethylene glycol microcapsules for cell encapsulation," Artificial Organs, vol. 23, no. 10, pp. 894–903, 1999.

30. G. Klinkenberg, K. Q. Lystad, D. W. Levine, and N. Dyrset, "Cell release from alginate immobilized Lactococcus lactis ssp. lactis in chitosan and alginate coated beads," Journal of Dairy Science, vol. 84, no. 5, pp. 1118–1127, 2001.

31. W. Krasaekoopt, B. Bhandari, and H. Deeth, "The influence of coating materials on some properties of alginate beads and

survivability of microencapsulated probiotic bacteria," International Dairy Journal, vol. 14, no. 8, pp. 737–743, 2004.

32. G. Orive, A. Bartkowiak, S. Lisiecki et al., "Biocompatible oligochitosans as cationic modifiers of alginate/Ca microcapsules," Journal of Biomedical Materials Research—Part B, vol. 74, no. 1, pp. 429–439, 2005.

33. A. Zanina, A. Vilesov, and T. Budtova, "Shear-induced solvent release from gel particles: application to drug-delivery systems," International Journal of Pharmaceutics, vol. 242, no. 1-2, pp. 137–146, 2002.

34. C. Djerassi, J. D. Gray, and F. A. Kincl, "Naturally occurring oxygen heterocyclics. 9. Isolation and characterization of genipin," Journal of Organic Chemistry, vol. 25, no. 12, pp. 2174–2177, 1960.

35. J.-E. Park, J.-Y. Lee, H.-G. Kim, T.-R. Hahn, and Y.-S. Paik, "Isolation and characterization of water-soluble intermediates of blue pigments transformed from geniposide of Gardenia jasminoides," Journal of Agricultural and Food Chemistry, vol. 50, no. 22, pp. 6511–6514, 2002.

36. H. Chen, W. Ouyang, M. Jones et al., "Preparation and characterization of novel polymeric microcapsules for live cell encapsulation and therapy," Cell Biochemistry and Biophysics, vol. 47, no. 1, pp. 159–167, 2007.

37. J. Jin, M. Song, and D. J. Hourston, "Novel chitosan-based films cross-linked by genipin with improved physical properties," Biomacromolecules, vol. 5, no. 1, pp. 162–168, 2004.

38. F.-L. Mi, Y.-C. Tan, H.-F. Liang, and H.-W. Sung, "In vivo biocompatibility and degradability of a novel injectable-chitosan-based implant," Biomaterials, vol. 23, no. 1, pp. 181–191, 2002.

39. H. Chen, W. Ouyang, B. Lawuyi, and S. Prakash, "Genipin cross-linked alginate-chitosan microcapsules: membrane characterization and optimization of cross-linking reaction," Biomacromolecules, vol. 7, no. 7, pp. 2091–2098, 2006.

40. H. Chen, W. Ouyang, C. Martoni, and S. Prakash, "Genipin cross-linked polymeric alginate-chitosan microcapsules for oral delivery: in-vitro analysis," International Journal of Polymer Science, vol. 2009, Article ID 617184, 16 pages, 2009.

41. K. Molly, M. V. Woestyne, and W. Verstraete, "Development of a 5-step multi-chamber reactor as a simulation of the human intestinal microbial ecosystem," Applied Microbiology and Biotechnology, vol. 39, no. 2, pp. 254–258, 1993.

42. N. Berrada, J. F. Lemeland, G. Laroche, P. Thouvenot, and M. Piaia, "Bifidobacterium from fermented milks: survival during gastric transit," Journal of Dairy Science, vol. 74, no. 2, pp. 409–413, 1991.

43. J. O. Berg, C. E. Nord, and T. Wadstrom, "Formation of glycosidases in batch and continuous culture of Bacteroides fragilis," Applied and Environmental Microbiology, vol. 35, no. 2, pp. 269–273, 1978.

44. H. Chen, W. Ouyang, M. Jones, T. Haque, B. Lawuyi, and S. Prakash, "In-vitro analysis of APA microcapsules for oral delivery of live bacterial cells," Journal of Microencapsulation, vol. 22, no. 5, pp. 539–547, 2005.

45. F. A. Leblond, J. Tessier, and J.-P. Hallé, "Quantitative method for the evaluation of biomicrocapsule resistance to mechanical stress," Biomaterials, vol. 17, no. 21, pp. 2097–2102, 1996.

46. J. Kovacs-Nolan and Y. Mine, "Microencapsulation for the gastric passage and controlled intestinal release of immunoglobulin Y," Journal of Immunological Methods, vol. 296, no. 1-2, pp. 199–209, 2005.

47. R. Narayani and K. P. Rao, "Polymer-coated gelatin capsules as oral delivery devices and their gastrointestinal tract behaviour in humans," Journal of Biomaterials Science. Polymer Edition, vol. 7, no. 1, pp. 39–48, 1995.

48. Y. Sato, Y. Kawashima, H. Takeuchi, H. Yamamoto, and Y. Fujibayashi, "Pharmacoscintigraphic evaluation of riboflavin-containing microballoons for a floating controlled drug

delivery system in healthy humans," Journal of Controlled Release, vol. 98, no. 1, pp. 75–85, 2004.

49. I. R. Wilding, D. Clark, H. Wray, J. Alderman, N. Muirhead, and C. R. Sikes, "In vivo disintegration profile of encapsulated and nonencapsulated sumatriptan: gamma scintigraphy in healthy volunteers,"Journal of Clinical Pharmacology, vol. 45, no. 1, pp. 101–105, 2005.

50. A. Lamprecht, H. Yamamoto, H. Takeuchi, and Y. Kawashima, "Design of pH-sensitive microspheres for the colonic delivery of the immunosuppressive drug tacrolimus," European Journal of Pharmaceutics and Biopharmaceutics, vol. 58, no. 1, pp. 37–43, 2004.

51. T. Reddy and S. Tammishetti, "Gastric resistant microbeads of metal ion cross-linked carboxymethyl guar gum for oral drug delivery," Journal of Microencapsulation, vol. 19, no. 3, pp. 311–318, 2002.

52. F. Delie, "Evaluation of nano- and microparticle uptake by the gastrointestinal tract," Advanced Drug Delivery Reviews, vol. 34, no. 2-3, pp. 221–233, 1998.

53. S. R. Bhatia, S. F. Khattak, and S. C. Roberts, "Polyelectrolytes for cell encapsulation," Current Opinion in Colloid and Interface Science, vol. 10, no. 1-2, pp. 45–51, 2005.

54. B. R. S. Hsu, S. H. Fu, J. S. Tsai, Y. Y. Huang, H. S. Huang, and K. S. S. Chang, "The plasminogen-plasmin fibrinolytic system accelerates degradation of alginate-poly-L-lysine-alginate microcapsules in vitro,"Transplantation Proceedings, vol. 29, no. 3, pp. 1877–1880, 1997.

55. H. Zimmermann, D. Zimmermann, R. Reuss et al., "Towards a medically approved technology for alginate-based microcapsules allowing long-term immunoisolated transplantation," Journal of Materials Science, vol. 16, no. 6, pp. 491–501, 2005.

56. K. Hirayama and J. Rafter, "The role of lactic acid bacteria in colon cancer prevention: mechanistic considerations," Antonie Van Leeuwenhoek, International Journal of General and Molecular Microbiology, vol. 76, no. 1–4, pp. 391–394, 1999.

57. G. L. Simon and S. L. Gorbach, "Intestinal flora in health and disease," Gastroenterology, vol. 86, no. 1, pp. 174–193, 1984.

6

CHAPTER

Use of In Vitro Assays to Assess Immunogenicity Risk of Antibody-Based Biotherapeutics

Marisa K. Joubert ,Meghana Deshpande, Jane Yang, Helen Reynolds, Christine Bryson, Mark Fogg, Matthew P. Baker, Jonathan Herskovitz, Theresa J. Goletz, Lei Zhou, Michael Moxness, Gregory C. Flynn, Linda O. Narhi, Vibha Jawa

Department of Clinical Immunology, Amgen Inc., Thousand Oaks, California, United States of America

ABSTRACT

An *In Vitro* Comparative Immunogenicity Assessment (IVCIA) assay was evaluated as a tool for predicting the potential relative immunogenicity of biotherapeutic attributes. Peripheral blood mononuclear cells from up to 50 healthy naïve human donors were monitored up to 8 days for T-cell proliferation, the number of IL-2 or IFN-γ secreting cells, and the concentration of a panel of secreted cytokines. The response in the assay to 10 monoclonal antibodies was found to be in agreement with the clinical immunogenicity, suggesting that the assay might be applied to immunogenicity risk assessment of antibody biotherapeutic attributes. However, the response in the assay is a measure of T-cell functional activity and the alignment with clinical immunogenicity depends on several other factors. The assay was sensitive to sequence variants and could differentiate single point mutations of the same biotherapeutic. Nine mAbs that were highly aggregated by stirring induced a higher response in the assay than the original mAbs before stirring stress, in a manner that did not match the relative T-cell response of the original mAbs. In contrast, mAbs that were glycated by different sugars (galactose, glucose, and mannose) showed little to no increase in response in the assay above the response to the original mAbs before glycation treatment. The assay was also used successfully to assess similarity between multiple lots of the same mAb, both from the same manufacturer and from different manufacturers (biosimilars). A strategy for using the IVCIA assay for immunogenicity risk assessment during the entire lifespan development of biopharmaceuticals is proposed.

INTRODUCTION

Immunogenicity to protein based biotherapeutics is a complex process that involves numerous patient and product specific factors [1,2]. Monoclonal antibodies (mAbs) are a major class of protein biotherapeutics that have many product specific factors that are critical for the quality of the drug product. These critical quality attributes may include: variations in the primary sequence, host-cell specific post-translational modifications, the presence of host cell proteins, formulation changes, aggregation, chemical modifications (oxidation, deamidation, or glycation), and changes in protein structure. Some critical quality attributes of mAb drug products have been suggested to affect patient safety through enhancing the sequence based risk of immunogenicity, although the exact contribution of specific types of attributes is not known.

T-cell dependent responses are the primary drivers of the long-term affinity matured immune response to biologics in the clinic [3,4]. Several formats of cell-based assay platforms have been explored to assess the risk of immunogenicity. These include assay systems using: whole blood, peripheral blood mononuclear cells (PBMC), $CD8^{+}$-depleted PBMC, immortalized cell lines, dendritic cells/monocytes/macrophages co-cultured with autologous $CD4^{+}$ T-cells, and artificial lymph node systems, to name a few [5–12]. These assays aim to replicate the response of typical cells associated with propagation of an immune response via monocytes, dendritic cells, T- and B-cells. Various biological outcomes can be measured at different stages of immune cell activation in these *in vitro* assays including: cytokine secretion, expression of cell surface markers of activation, identification of HLA-DR bound peptides, signal transduction events, phagocytosis by antigen presenting cells (APC), and proliferation.

Historically, *in vitro* immune cell-based assays have been used for testing rejection during transplantation [13]. These assays have also been used during pre-clinical development of immune modulatory therapeutics to understand human responses using the appropriate assay with immune cells as components [12,14,15]. More recently, PBMC-based assays have been used to describe the potential immunogenicity of protein molecules and unwanted product quality attributes for both early and late phase responses [8,16–21]. In one study, highly aggregated antibodies used therapeutically were shown to enhance the cytokine secretion and T-cell proliferation responses of a population of PBMC from healthy human donors [8].

Many different critical quality attributes are assessed as part of the product profile evaluation during early development. These attributes and changes in formulations that warrant risk assessments could be evaluated by adapting and applying *in vitro* human PBMC assays [22]. A kinetic analysis of responses following stimulation with the protein antigens of interest could be useful for detecting both low and high frequency antigen-specific effector cells. T-cell responses after stimulation *in vitro* can be assessed by enzyme-linked immunosorbent assay (ELISA), multiplex cytokine analysis, enzyme-linked immunospot spot (Elispot), proliferation, and flow cytometry analysis of cellular activation markers. With this strategy, the risk of immunogenicity could potentially be predicted much earlier than the clinical outcome [5–8,23].

In this work, we assessed one type of cell-based IVCIA assay as a potentially valuable method for predictive immunogenicity risk assessment. We evaluated the response in the assay to mAbs with different sequences and known observed clinical immunogenicity rates, examined the response to several mAb attributes, and compared the response to different drug product lots. Multiple readouts from this individual assay were evaluated to determine the best readout or combination of readouts to obtain the most effective relative risk ranking. Overall, these results indicate that this type of IVCIA assay might be readily employed for relative immunogenicity risk assessment of sequence and other manufacturing associated attributes during the drug product development lifecycle.

MATERIALS AND METHODS

Materials

Human IgG_1 monoclonal antibodies (Herceptin, Campath, Xolair, Erbitux, Avastin, Rituxan, Remicade, and Humira) are currently (or were previously) commercially available as highly purified solutions used therapeutically. Purified human IgG_2 monoclonal antibodies (mAb1 and mAb2), IgG_1 monoclonal antibodies (mAb3, ABP 501, and ABP 980), a fusion protein of an enzyme linked to the Fc domain of a monoclonal antibody (FP1), three mutants of FP1 (mutant-1 (XXLL**D**VLXX), mutant-2 (XXL**W**NVLXX) and mutant-3 (XXL**FD**VLXX)), and the fusion protein alone (FP1 (no Fc)) were supplied by Amgen as high concentration solutions. The form of the protein before stress treatment is called "original" throughout the manuscript.

Modified Sample Preparation

Generation of Aggregates.
Stirring induced aggregates were generated to resemble those that are created during the manufacturing, shipping and administration of biotherapeutics, as described previously [8]. Herceptin, Campath, Xolair, Erbitux, Avastin, Rituxan, mAb1, Remicade, mAb2, and Humira were diluted to 1 mg/mL in 10 mM Acetate pH 5.0 (A5 buffer). The protein sample (2 mL) was then stirred with a 6 X 6 mm Teflon stirrer bar at ~ 700 rpm, creating a vortex, in a 5 mL glass vial capped and placed vertically on a magnetic stirrer plate for 20 h (labeled as stir-20h). The purity of the samples was assessed by denaturing SDS-PAGE and silver staining (SilverXpress, Invitrogen, Paisley, UK), and indicated no significant degradation or detectable contaminating species (data not shown).

Generation of Glycated mAbs.
Avastin, mAb1, and Humira were diluted to 2.5 mg/mL with a volume of phosphate buffer saline stock sugar solution, galactose,

glucose, or mannose (0.5–1.6 M), to reach a targeted forced glycation level of 40% (0.4 mole sugar/mole mAb) over the initial content for each mAb before treatment, as previously described [24]. The mAbs were also diluted and incubated similarly with 1.0 M sorbitol to prepare a control sample that was treated with sugar, but without an increase in the level of glycation. Samples were incubated at 37°C for 8 hr (Avastin and Humira) or 21 hr (mAb1). After incubation, the forced glycation samples were dialyzed into A5 buffer. The protein concentration of each sample was determined by absorbance at 280 nm. The integrity of the samples was verified by size exclusion chromatography and the level of forced glycation was determined by reverse phased liquid chromatography/mass spectrometry (data not shown), as previously described [24].

The samples before aggregation or glycation treatment were used to monitor the response to the original form of the mAb (labeled as original in the text and Figs).

Endotoxin Testing

All protein samples and buffers were assessed for endotoxin levels by a LAL (Limulus amebocyte lysate) test with the Charles River Endosafe-PTS (Charles River, Wilmington, MA) system prior to being used in the biological assay. The analysis was performed according to the manufacturer's instructions. All samples were found to have endotoxin levels that were within the limit acceptable for these cell based assays (< 1.00 EU/mL).

In Vitro Comparative Immunogenicity Assessment (IVCIA) Assays

An IVCIA assay was performed to assess $CD4^+$ T-cell responses by Antitope (Antitope Ltd., Babraham Institute, Cambridge, UK) to monitor the response in a 50 donor population, as described previously [5,6,8]. Briefly, PBMC were isolated from blood drawn within 24 h from healthy donors from the UK National Blood Transfusion Service (Addenbrooke's Hospital, Cambridge, UK) according to approval granted by Addenbrooke's Hospital Local Research Ethics Committee, using Lymphoprep (Axis-shield, Dundee, UK) density centrifugation. $CD8^+$T-cells were depleted using

CD8⁺ RosetteSep (StemCell Technologies Inc, London, UK). Donors were characterized by identifying HLA-DR haplotypes using an HLA SSP-PCR based tissue typing kit (Biotest, Solihull, UK) or the HISTO Spot SSO HLA typing method. PBMC were frozen and stored in liquid nitrogen until required. A population of 50 human donors was selected to best represent the number and frequency of HLA-DR allotypes expressed in the world population and to include all major HLA-DR allotypes (individual allotypes with a frequency >5% expressed in the world population) (S1 Fig). Several experiments were performed at different times, so not all mAbs were tested in the same set of 50 donors. PBMC were resuspended in AIM-V medium (Life Technologies, Carlsbad, CA) at a concentration of 4–6 X 10^6 cells/mL. PBMC were added to the 24-well proliferation plates (2 mL final volume) and 48-well cytokine secretion plates (1 mL final volume) at a final concentration of 2–4 X 10^6cells/mL, and then challenged with a final concentration of 40 μg/mL of each sample. This concentration was optimized during previous experiments based on what the cells can tolerate and their response to a protein with associated attributes, and was not intended to simulate dosing conditions in the clinic. For each donor, responses to a negative control, consisting of medium-treated cells (referred to as the background response), and several reproducibility controls, including keyhole limpet hemocyanin (KLH, Pierce, Cramlington, UK), phytohemagglutinin (PHA, Sigma, Poole, UK), and a benchmark clinical control (the humanized A33 antibody produced at Antitope), were also included. T-cell proliferative responses were monitored on days 5, 6, 7, and 8 for all experiments except the biosimilars comparison (day 7 only). The viability of PBMC from 10 representative donors for each sample was assessed by trypan blue dye exclusion on day 7 after challenge, and found to be greater than 90% for all samples.

To evaluate the ability of an IVCIA assay to potentially be applied in a manufacturing setting in a smaller group of donors (n≤12), a slightly modified IVCIA assay was also performed at Amgen in a similar fashion (with a few modifications that are described below). This format was used for the glycation experiment, lot-to-lot comparison, and biosimilars comparison. Whole blood from healthy naïve human donors was supplied by Amgen's Environmental Health and Safety department (EH&S) according to local ethical practices. Written consent was obtained from each donor. PBMC from up to 12 donors per experiment (see individual experiment for exact number) were isolated, cryopreserved in freezing medium, thawed and plated on the day of the study, and stimulated as previously described [8]. In brief, PBMC were plated at 2.5 X 10^6 cells/mL in a total volume of 200 µL of RPMI growth media at 37°C containing: 89% RPMI Medium 1640, 10% heat-inactivated fetal bovine serum, and 1% penicillin/streptomycin/L-glutamine (Life Technologies, Carlsbad, CA) in 96-well culture plates. An overnight acclimatization step was performed for the glycation experiment only so that PBMC and adherent monocytes could be challenged together. Cells were then challenged with a final concentration of 40 µg/ml (glycation and lot-to-lot comparison) or 100 µg/mL (biosimilars comparison) of the different mAb samples. The sorbitol control was added at an equivalent volume to the glycated mAb samples. The glycated and sorbitol samples were centrifuged at 13,000 rpm for 2 min before challenge. All donors had greater than 81% viability before plating (except 2 donors that were 71–77%). Plates were placed in a 5% CO_2 incubator at 37°C for 20 h (early phase) or 7 days (late phase). A negative control, consisting of medium-treated cells, and positive controls, including lipopolysaccharide (LPS) and PHA, were also tested.

Adherent Monocyte Evaluation

For the glycation experiment only, a duplicate plate of PBMC from the same donors was isolated, plated and acclimatized as described above. After the overnight acclimatization step, non-adherent cells were removed from the culture by removing all standing liquid. Adherent monocytes in the bottom of each well were washed two times with 200 µl of RPMI growth media. 200 µl of fresh RPMI growth media was then added to each well. Adherent monocytes were challenged with the original and glycated mAbs at 40 µg/ml, as described in the PBMC simulation section.

All cell derived supernatants were frozen at appropriate time points and stored at -70°C for multiplex cytokine analysis.

T-cell Proliferation

Culture plates for T-cell proliferation assays were incubated in a 5% CO_2 incubator at 37°C for up to 8 days. On days 5, 6, 7 and 8, the cells in each well of the plate were gently resuspended and transferred to a round bottom 96-well plate. The cultures were then pulsed with 0.75 μCi [^{3}H]-thymidine (Perkin Elmer, Beaconsfield, UK) in AIM-V culture media, and incubated for 18 h. Cultures were harvested onto filter mats (Perkin Elmer, Beaconsfield, UK) using a TomTec Mach III cell harvester (Hamden). Counts per minute (cpm) for each well were determined by scintillation counting using a 1450 Microbeta Wallac Trilux Liquid Scintillation Counter (Perkin Elmer, Beaconsfield, UK) in paralux, low background counting. For data analysis, the stimulation index (SI) was calculated by dividing the proliferative response of the test well (cpm) by the proliferative response of the medium-only treated well (cpm) for each donor. A response was considered positive if the SI was greater than 2.0 (SI≥2.0) and statistically significant (p<0.05) as compared to medium-only treated wells using an unpaired two sample student's t-test. The percentage of donors that responded (% donors responding) was calculated by taking the number of donors that had a positive response (SI≥2.0, p<0.05) over the entire time course (5–8 days) as a percentage of the total number of donors that were tested. Positive thresholds in all assays were previously established based on statistically derived cut points. Extensive assay development and previous studies have shown that this is the minimum signal to noise threshold allowing maximum sensitivity without detecting large numbers of false positive responses or omitting subtle immunogenic events.

IL-2 and IFN-γ Elispot

For the IL-2 Elispot readout, anti-human IL-2 Elispot plates (Millipore, Watford, UK) that were pre-wetted and coated overnight with IL-2 capture antibody (R&D Systems, Abingdon, UK) were used. PBMC were added to the IL-2 Elispot plates at a final concentration of 2–4 X 10^6cells/mL, and then challenged with 40 μg/mL of each sample. IL-2 Elispot Plates were incubated 8 days before developing according to the manufacturer's instructions (R&D Systems). Dried plates were scanned on an Immunoscan Analyzer (Cellular

Technology Limited, Shaker Heights, Ohio) and the number of spot forming cells (SFC) per well were determined using Immunoscan Version 4 software. The SI was calculated by dividing the number of IL-2 secreting cells in the test well (SFC) by the number of IL-2 secreting cells in the medium-only treated well (SFC) for each donor. A response was considered positive if the $SI \geq 2.0$ and used to calculate the percentage of donors that responded similar to the T-cell proliferation section.

For the IFN-γ Elispot readout, Elispot was performed using a kit according to the manufacturer's instructions (Mabtech, Stockholm, Sweden). Briefly, PBMC from 6 donors were added at a concentration of 1.5×10^6 cells/ml to a 96-well Elispot plate and then challenged with 40 μg/mL of the original or glycated samples. The IFN-γ Elispot plates were incubated for 7 days and then developed according to the manufacturer's instructions. Negative controls testing medium only or no cells as well as a PHA positive control were also included. The dried plates were scanned on an AID Elispot Reader version 7.0 (AID GmbH, Strassberg, Germany), and SFC were determined using AID EliSpot Software v5.0. For data analysis, to highlight the potential differential response of glycated mAbs, the SI was calculated as the SFC for donors treated with glycated mAbs divided by the SFC for donors treated with the original mAbs before glycation treatment. An $SI \geq 2.0$ was considered positive.

Multiplex Cytokine Analysis

Multiplex cytokine analysis was performed on culture supernatants by Luminex technology using Milliplex human panel kits (EMD Millipore, Billerica, MA) and a Luminex FlexMAP 3D instrument with the XPonent version 4.0 software, as described by Joubert et al. [8]. Cell culture supernatants were thawed and then centrifuged at 1200 rpm for 5 min before testing. For analysis of the PBMC supernatants at the early phase (after 20h incubation), the following cytokines were monitored: IL-1α, IL-1β, IL-1ra, IL-6, IL-8, IL-10, MCP-1, MIP-1α, MIP-1β, TNF-α, and TNF-β. For analysis of the PBMC supernatants at the late phase (after 7 days of incubation), the following cytokines were monitored: IFN-γ, IL-2, IL-4, IL-5, IL-6, IL-7, IL-8, IL-10, IL-12p40, IL-12p70, IL-13, and TNF-α. For data analysis, the SI was calculated by dividing the amount of cytokine detected (pg/mL) in the treated sample by the relevant control sample. The relevant control sample for the cytokine analysis was either the medium-only treated wells or the original mAb (see Fig legends for the type of baseline used for each experiment). A response was considered positive if the SI was greater than 2.0 at the early phase in PBMC (SI≥2.0), greater than 3.0 at the early phase in monocytes (SI ≥3.0), or greater than 1.9 at the late phase (SI≥1.9). Assay cut points were based on statistical analysis and/or the differential response observed to the media alone in the different assay systems used. The percentage of donors that responded (% donors responding) was calculated by taking the number of donors that had a positive SI as a percentage of the total number of donors that were tested. In all cases, the negative controls such as medium-treated cells showed a minimal response and positive controls such as LPS, PHA and/or KLH showed a very high response (SI>>3.0; only select data shown). In all cases, the percentage of donors that responded to the mAb samples was much lower than that induced by the positive controls, KLH (72–86%) and PHA (98%).

Statistical Analysis

Statistical analysis of the proliferative responses and concentration of cytokines determined by multiplex cytokine analysis was performed using a mixed effect analysis of variance model as previously described [8]. Briefly, the model assumed correlated responses from the same donor and independent responses from difference donors. When evaluating the response to the original mAb relative to background, the model included compound (mAb), condition (original and background), and the two-way interaction between compound and condition as fixed effects, calculated for the proliferative response or each cytokine. The response to each original mAb was compared with the background response, and a one-sided p value was reported. When evaluating the response to aggregated mAbs relative to the response to the original form, the model included compound (mAb), condition (stir-20h, original and background), and the two-way interaction between compound and condition as fixed effects, calculated for the proliferative response or each cytokine. *p* values less than 0.05 were considered as statistically significant.

Aggregate Analysis

Aggregated solutions were characterized for particle count, size distribution and morphology as described in our previous report [25]. Aggregated samples made at 1 mg/mL were diluted in A5 buffer (20-100X), degassed, and then analyzed by the appropriate instrument. Particle counting and size distribution in the micron size range was performed on a HIAC/Royco Liquid Particle Counter model 9703 with an HRLD-150 sensor and the software PharmSpec (HACH Ultra Analytics, Grants Pass, OR). Particle imaging in the micron and visible size range (≥ 125 μm) was achieved by a liquid-borne particle Micro-Flow Imaging (MFI) System DPA4100 (Protein Simple, Santa Clara, CA). All final particle numbers were adjusted for the initial dilution factor.

RESULTS

The IVCIA Assay Correlates with the Rate of Clinical Immunogenicity

In order to appraise the IVCIA assay as an effective *in vitro* tool for assessing the relative risk of immunogenicity in the clinic, ten IgG1 and IgG2 biotherapeutic monoclonal antibodies, with known rates of clinical immunogenicity (Table 1) [26,27], were tested in the IVCIA assay for their ability to elicit an immune response in PBMC. An additional mAb (mAb1), which has not been tested in the clinic, was also tested and is predicted to have a rate of clinical immunogenicity that is intermediate among the selected mAbs based on *in silico* methods. It is important to note that the immunogenicity rates shown are based on the anti-drug antibody (ADA) responses associated with diverse disease indications and assay testing platforms with variable sensitivity. The responses of PBMC from 50 healthy naïve human donors were monitored 5 to 8 days for T-cell proliferation, the number of IL-2 secreting cells (Elispot), and the concentration of secreted cytokines (multiplex cytokine secretion).

Table 1. Biotherapeutic mAb rates of clinical immunogenicity.

mAb	*Generic*	*Subtype*	*Rate of Clinical Immunogenicity* [a]
Herceptin	trastuzumab	IgG1	0.1% * [b]
Campath	alemtuzumab	IgG1	1.9% **
Xolair	omalizumab	IgG1	0.1%
Erbitux	cetuximab	IgG1	5% *
Avastin	bevacizumab	IgG1	0–8% *, [c]
Rituxan	rituximab	IgG1	1–23% * [c,d]
mAb1	NA	IgG2	NT
Remicade	Infliximab	IgG1	13–27% * [c,e]
mAb2	NA	IgG2	12–16% [f]
mAb3	NA	IgG1	14–50% [f]
Humira	adalimumab	IgG1	1–87% * [c,e]

[a] All rates were taken from the product label except in a few cases as specified below. Rates are based on the anti-drug antibody response associated with diverse disease indications and assay testing platforms with variable sensitivity. The highest observed incidence reported for each mAb (except Rituxan, see below) was used to show association in all subsequent figures.

[b] Definition of symbols: *- rate based on immunogenicity in immune compromised patients; **—rate was impacted by the immunomodulatory nature of the molecule; NA—not applicable; NT—not tested in the clinic.

[c] Some mAbs have a wide range of immunogenicity rates reported. In some cases, the lower incidence of the range shown has been attributed to technical limitations of the immunogenicity assays used to support the analysis and the influence of standard of care immune suppressive medications administered to the subjects. In the case of Avastin, 0% immunogenicity was observed due to these limitations (according to the label), so the incidence for Lucentis (8%) is also shown.

[d] The results of several clinical studies are reported on the label for Rituxan. The majority of patients (85%) were tested in one of these clinical studies that resulted in 11% incidence of immunogenicity. This value is used to show association in all subsequent figures.

[e] The highest incidences shown for Remicade and Humira were taken from references 26 and 27, respectively.

[f] The rates for mAb2 and mAb3 are based on testing in early clinical trials

Fig 1 shows that the relative response of PBMC to biotherapeutic mAbs agrees with the observed rate of clinical immunogenicity for most mAbs. Individual readouts were found to correlate with the rate of immunogenicity, including the T-cell proliferative response (Fig 1A) and the number of IL-2 secreting cells (Fig 1B). The concentrations of 11 cytokines were tested on Day 7, and the cytokine IL-2, a major driver of T-cell proliferation, was found to be the most statistically significant ($p<0.05$) cytokine induced by the mAb samples above the background. The remaining cytokines were found not to correlate with the rate of clinical immunogenicity for most mAbs (data not shown). To evaluate if the correlation with the rate of clinical immunogenicity could be further improved, the number of donors that responded by more than one readout of the assay was also determined. In Fig 1C, donors that responded by either an increase in T-cell proliferation or IL-2 concentration were counted as responders. Including the donors that responded by IL-2 concentration improved the readout for mAb3, which has a high rate of clinical immunogenicity (up to 50%), but seemed, on first glance, to over predict the rate of immunogenicity for other molecules (mAb1) (compare Fig 1A with 1C). It is important to note that mAb1 is a unique case in that this molecule had severe aggregation and instability issues during early development and thus was not pursued as a therapeutic candidate. Therefore, the high response observed to mAb1 in Fig 1C may correctly reflect the increased risk of immunogenicity of this molecule. Similarly, donors that responded by both T-cell proliferation and an increase in the number of IL-2 secreting cells were tabulated (Fig 1D). This decreased the readout for Xolair from 8% to 2% responding donors, which agrees with the low rate of clinical immunogenicity for this molecule (0.1%) (compare Fig 1B with 1D).

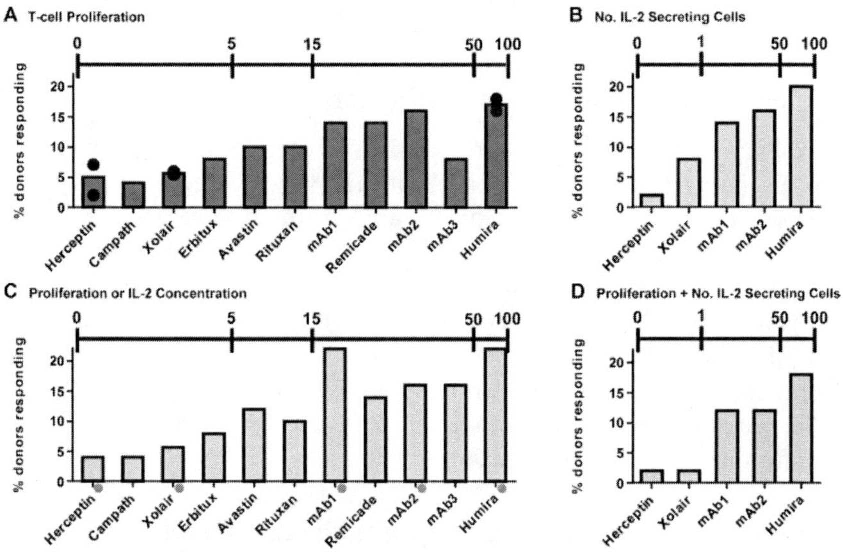

Fig 1. The response of CD4+ T-cells in the IVCIA assay agrees with the rate of clinical immunogenicity for biotherapeutic mAbs.

10 mAbs, with known rates of clinical immunogenicity, were evaluated in the IVCIA assay in a population of 50 healthy human donors over 5–8 days. mAb1 has not been tested in the clinic. Donors that responded by multiple readouts were evaluated for the most effective relative risk ranking. The percentage of donors that showed A) a positive T-cell proliferative response ([^{3}H]-thymidine uptake) or B) an increase in the number (No.) of IL-2 secreting cells (Elispot) over the course of the entire study are displayed. Results were also combined to illustrate the percentage of donors that showed C) either a positive T-cell proliferation response or an increase in the

concentration of IL-2 secreted (multiplex cytokine analysis) or D) a positive T-cell proliferation response and an increase in the number of IL-2 secreting cells are shown. Not all donors were tested for IL-2 for some samples (*grey circles*). A response was considered positive if the SI ≥ 2.0 ($p<0.05$) for proliferation or number of IL-2 secreting cells or the SI ≥ 1.9 for IL-2 concentration (above the background response). mAbs are ordered approximately within each graph from the lowest to the highest response in the IVCIA assay. The scale bars at the top of each graph show the highest incidence of immunogenicity reported for each mAb in Table 1. All rates are associated with diverse disease indications and assay testing platforms with variable sensitivity. *Black circles* represent duplicate experiments in different sets of 50 donors.

To judge the reproducibility of the results, three representative mAbs (Herceptin, Xolair, and Humira), were tested in a duplicate experiment, on different days, and with different sets of 50 donors. Fig 1A (*black circles*) shows that the T-cell proliferative results were highly reproducible. For each mAb, the standard deviation between the percentages of donors that responded in each duplicate experiment was less than 4%. The correlation of the assay with the rate of clinical immunogenicity and the reproducibility of the results suggests that this assay is a reasonable approach for immunogenicity risk evaluation.

Differences in Amino Acid Sequence can be Detected

To determine whether the IVCIA assay can be utilized to differentiate and rank order different biotherapeutic candidates during early drug product development, the response of the assay to different sequence variants of the same biotherapeutic was tested. FP1 is a biotherapeutic fusion protein of an enzyme homodimer fused to the Fc domain of a monoclonal antibody. Several sequence variants, including proteins containing either one (mutant-1 and mutant-2) or two (mutant-3) mutations in amino acid residues, or a construct lacking the Fc domain (FP1 (no Fc)) were evaluated. All of the FP1 mutants had similar secondary and tertiary structures, and similar profiles of chemically modified amino acids. However, under accelerated stress conditions, some differences in the stability and aggregation profiles were observed (data not shown), indicating that the change in amino acid sequence may have caused differences in other attributes. FP1 has not been tested in the clinic so the rate of clinical immunogenicity for this molecule is not known. However, *in silico* immunogenicity risk assessment analysis (which evaluated the primary protein sequences for the presence of peptides with the potential to bind to human leukocyte antigen (HLA) class II alleles) showed that the non-tolerant aggretope content of FP1 and the three mutants is absent or very low (data not shown). This suggests that the risk of immunogenicity (based on the method of *in silico* analysis used) for FP1 and the three mutants is low and relatively similar. To evaluate the risk of immunogenicity of the FP1 variants in the IVCIA assay, the responses of PBMC from 50 healthy human drug naïve donors were monitored up to 8 days for T-cell proliferation, and the number of IL-2 secreting cells. Fig 2 shows that the different FP1 variants evaluated induced different levels of T-cell proliferation and number of IL-2 secreting cells in the IVCIA assay, and that the trends agreed for both readouts. The assay was found to be highly sensitive to sequence differences as little as one amino acid. For example, FP1 mutant-1 and mutant-3 differ by one amino acid yet mutant-1 gave the highest response (20% responding donors) and mutant-3 gave the lowest response (6% responding donors) of all variants. This result demonstrates the ability of the IVCIA assay to differentiate biotherapeutic proteins with minor differences in sequence during early candidate selection that might not be differentiated by *in silico* analysis alone.

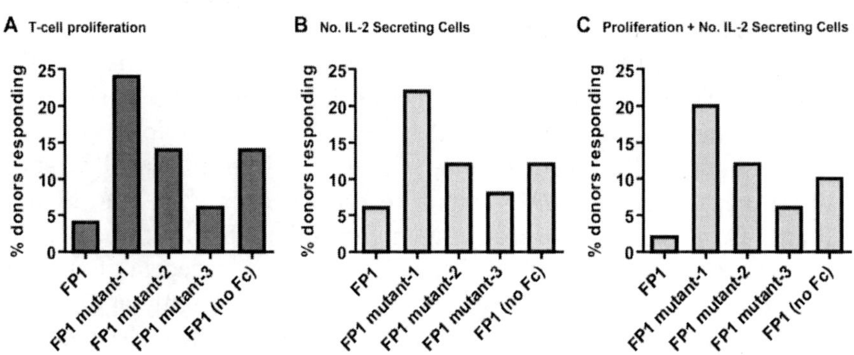

Fig 2. Biotherapeutics with minor differences in sequence can be distinguished by the IVCIA assay.

Several sequence variants of FP1 varying by one (mutant-1 and mutant-2) or two (mutant-3) amino acids, as well as FP1 lacking the Fc domain (FP1 (no Fc)) were tested in the in the IVCIA assay using 50 healthy human donors over 5–8 days. FP1 is a biotherapeutic fusion protein of an enzyme fused to the Fc domain of a monoclonal antibody. The percentage of donors with either A) a positive T-cell proliferative response ([3H]-thymidine uptake) or B) an increase in the number (No.) of IL-2 secreting cells (Elispot), or C) both positive T-cell proliferative responses and an increase in the number of IL-2 secreting cells are shown. A response was considered positive if the SI≥2.0 ($p<0.05$) above the background response.

Evaluation of Aggregated Biotherapeutics in the IVCIA Assay

Our group previously demonstrated that high numbers of stirring induced aggregates of mAb1 (previously referred to as mAb2 [8]) can enhance the early and late stage responses of PBMC in the IVCIA assay above the response to the original mAb1 (before stress treatment) [8,9]; in agreement with the response seen by other groups to aggregated samples *in vitro*[10,16,21,28]. To investigate if the assay can be used for evaluating aggregates across a wider range of mAbs, stirring induced aggregates of 10 mAbs were generated and characterized. Fig 3 shows the particle counts, size distribution, and morphology of the stirring induced aggregates that were generated. All protein solutions treated by stirring stress contained a high number of aggregates in the subvisible size range (Fig 3A), that were heterogeneous, amorphous, and irregular in morphology (Fig 3B). Although trends were similar between different mAbs, some differences between mAbs could be observed as well. The highest numbers of particles were seen in the Xolair, Erbitux, mAb1, and Remicade stirred samples, followed by the Herceptin, Campath, mAb2, and Humira stirred samples. Although still highly aggregated, the least number of particles, which were mostly in the 2–10 μm size range, were seen in the Avastin and Rituxan samples. As expected, the original mAb samples contained only a few small-sized aggregates. Fig 3B shows images of the largest aggregates that were detected in the original samples, which were very few in number.

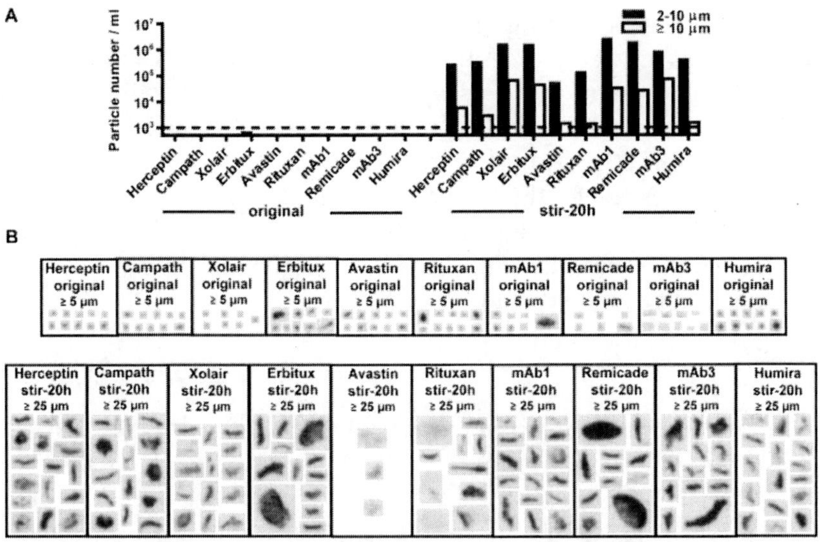

Fig 3. Particle counts, size distribution, and morphology of stirring induced aggregates of a broad array of antibodies.

10 mAbs (with known or predicted rates of clinical immunogenicity) were aggregated by stirring stress and then examined for their subvisible and visible aggregate content. A) Aggregates were quantitated by HIAC to determine the number and size range of particles present. Bar height represents the differential particle counts per ml in each size range (average of 3 runs). B) Aggregates images were captured on a Micro-flow Imaging System to evaluate the morphology of particles present. Representative images of the largest particles detected are shown. The size threshold indicates the lower size limit of the particles that were used for comparison. The aggregate content of the original mAbs (before stirring stress) is also shown and highlights that only a few small sized aggregates were detected.

The 10 highly aggregated mAb samples were then tested in the IVCIA assay in PBMC taken from 50 healthy human donors for their ability to elicit an immune response. Fig 4 shows that stirring induced aggregates of 9 of the 10 Abs were able to enhance the response of PBMC above the original mAb for T-cell proliferation (Fig 4A), number of IL-2 secreting cells (Fig 4B), and concentration of IL-2 (Fig 4C). Aggregated Herceptin, Xolair, Erbitux, and Avastin induced the highest response in the assay, in contrast to aggregated Campath which did not induce a response. Aggregated Rituxan, mAb1, Remicade, mAb3, and Humira induced a response that was intermediate between the high and low groups. Different aggregated preparations of the same mAb tested in a different set of 50 donors yielded similar results (Fig 4A, black circles), demonstrating the reproducibility of the results.

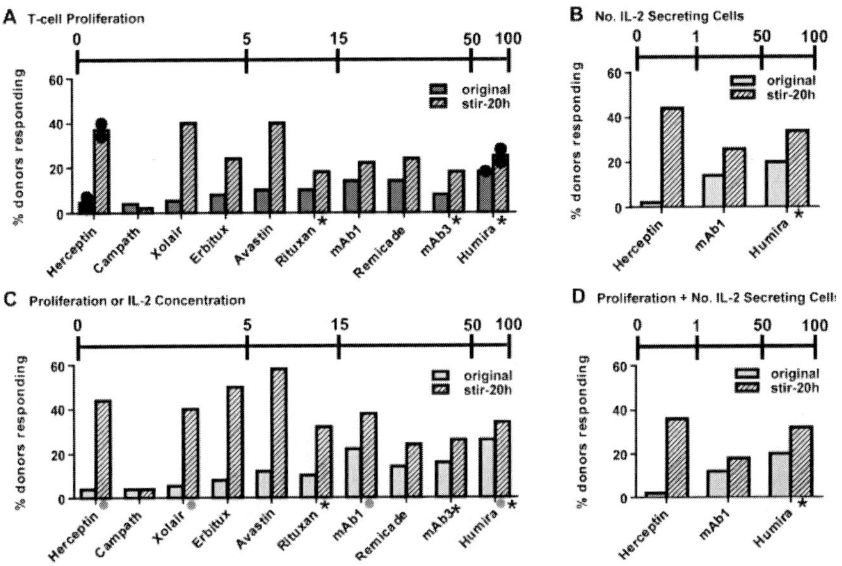

Fig 4. High numbers of aggregates of a wide array of antibodies can be detected by the IVCIA assay.

10 mAbs (with known or predicted rates of clinical immunogenicity) were aggregated by stirring stress and then evaluated in the IVCIA assay in a population of 50 heathy human donors. The percentage of donors that responded to the original mAb (*solid bars*) and the aggregated mAb (*striped bars*) by A) positive T-cell proliferative responses ([^{3}H]-thymidine uptake) or B) an increase in the number (No.) of IL-2 secreting cells (Elispot) over the course of the entire study (5–8 days) are displayed. The percentage of donors that showed C) either a positive T-cell proliferation response or an

increase in the concentration of IL-2 secreted (multiplex cytokine analysis) or D) a positive T-cell proliferation response and an increase in the number of IL-2 secreting cells are depicted. The y-axes of graphs in Figs 1 and 4 are on different scales. Not all donors were tested for IL-2 concentration for some samples (*grey circles*). A response was considered positive if the SI ≥ 2.0 (p<0.05) for proliferation or number of IL-2 secreting cells, or the SI ≥ 1.9 for IL-2 concentration (above the background response). Borderline responses were also included in some cases (SI≥1.9, p<0.05), and are shown with one asterisk. mAbs are in the same order as Fig 1. The scale bars at the top of each graph show the highest incidence of immunogenicity reported for each mAb in Table 1. All rates are associated with diverse disease indications and assay testing platforms with variable sensitivity. *Black circles* show the responses in duplicate experiments in different sets of 50 donors.

The secretion of signature cytokines was also tested at the early and late phases and found to be enhanced in the presence of all 10 mAbs that were treated by stirring stress (Fig 4D, S2 Fig), in agreement with previous results [8]. Overall the trends in cytokine secretion were aligned with T-cell proliferation results, where stirring induced aggregates of Erbitux and Avastin induced the highest response and mAb3 induced the lowest response (above the monomer) at both the early and late phases. Some donors that showed positive T-cell proliferative responses to aggregated samples also showed enhanced secretion of the immunosuppressive cytokine, IL-10, indicating the possible involvement of regulatory T-cells or monocytes which may lead to immunological tolerance (S3 Fig). In contrast, the original mAbs induced little to no IL-10 above the background response.

The Potential Immunological Risk from Chemical Modification

Glycation of amino acids is a potential chemical modification that can occur during the manufacture of biotherapeutics or upon administration to patients and may pose an increased risk of immunogenicity. The IVCIA assay was used to evaluate biotherapeutics that had been glycated by different types of sugars to determine the potential risk of immunogenicity of this type of modification. Three representative mAbs (Avastin, mAb1, and

Humira) with low, medium and high rates of clinical (or predicted) immunogenicity, respectively, were used. mAbs were treated by galactose, glucose, mannose, and a non-glycating sugar, sorbitol, as a negative control, and then analyzed by mass spectrometry for total glycation analysis as previously described [24]. Results of the analysis showed that all samples had an increased level of glycation of approximately 40% above the original sample before glycation treatment (data not shown). This means that for the forced glycated samples, 40% of the antibodies in each sample had a single sugar attached (0.4 mole attached sugar/mole protein) above what is typically found in these specific antibody drug products, 4–10% (0.04–0.1 mole attached glucose/mole protein).

Glycated mAbs were then evaluated in the IVCIA assay in 11 healthy human donors for their ability to stimulate an immune response in PBMC. For this experiment only, both PBMC and adherent monocytes (from the same donors) were tested to determine the potential response of a specialized cell type to glycated mAbs. Only the secretion of signature cytokines was further monitored for evaluating attribute related changes, as this readout was found to be sufficient for sensing the response to aggregates, which could be detected by cells of the innate immune system as soon as the early phase (Fig 4D and S2 Fig) [8]. Fig 5 is a heatmap representation of the percentage of donors that responded to the glycated mAbs above the original mAbs (mAbs before glycation treatment). The heatmap shows that the glycated mAbs induced little to no increase in cytokine secretion or number of IFN-γ secreting cells in both adherent monocytes and PBMC. For the few donors that did show a response, the magnitude of the response was very low (SI<9%, except for the adherent monocytes from two donors which were slightly higher) in all cases (data not shown). This was in contrast to the strong signal induced by the LPS and PHA positive controls, which induced a response in all donors (100%) and a SI of 200–7000+ above background for at least one cytokine per donor. In addition, the response of adherent monocytes to LPS at the early phase was higher than the response of PBMC in terms of percentage of responding donors (Fig 5) and magnitude of the response (data not shown), indicating that adherent monocytes may provide a more sensitive readout than PBMC. Overall, these *in vitro* results suggest that the increased levels of glycation tested do not pose an increased potential risk of immunogenicity. These results are limited, however, by the sensitivity of this assay, which is currently being investigated.

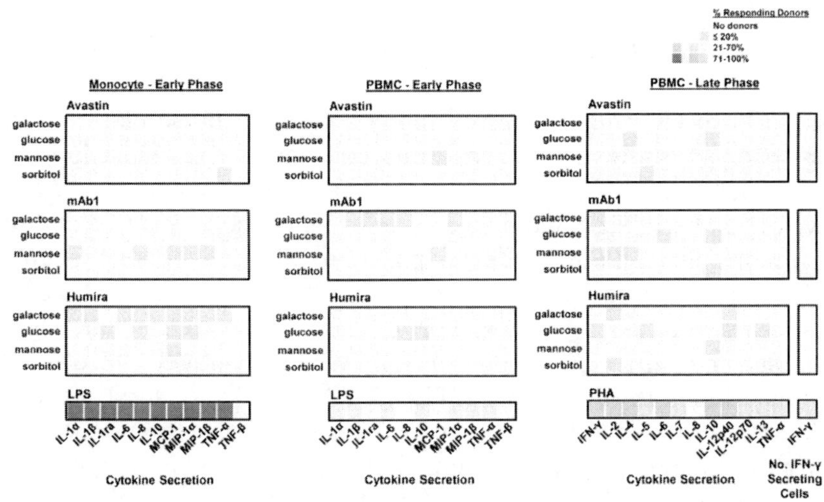

Fig 5. Chemical Modification by glycation does not enhance the response of PBMC in the IVCIA assay.

Three representative mAbs (Avastin, mAb1, and Humira), that were treated by glycation with different sugars (galactose, glucose and mannose, and a non-glycating sugar, sorbitol), were tested in the IVCIA assay at the early (20 h) (n = 11 donors for most samples) and late (7 day) phases (n = 6 donors). Avastin, mAb1, and Humira have low, medium, and high rates of clinical or predicted immunogenicity, respectively. Heatmaps depict the percentage of donors that responded to the glycated mAbs above the original forms of each molecule (mAb before glycation treatment) and were at least two fold above the background, to highlight the differential response that might be due to glycated mAbs. The percentage of donors with increased secretion of signature cytokines in adherent monocytes at the early phase (red), and in PBMC at the early (yellow) and late (green) phases is highlighted. The percentage of donors with an increase in the number of IFN-γ secreting cells is shown on the far right (blue). The grey boxes show low level responses that were observed in less than or equal to 20% of donors, in contrast to colored boxes (red, yellow, green and blue) that show responses in a greater number of donors (40–100%).

The IVCIA Assay can be used for Lot-to-lot and Biosimilar Comparability

To test if the IVCIA assay is suitable for comparability assessments, the response to several lots of the same mAb, from both the same manufacturer and different manufacturers (biosimilars), were tested. Fig 6 shows several case studies where the response in PBMC to a variety of different samples, at both the early and late phases, was compared. Fig 6Acompares the levels of the secreted signature cytokines from PBMC when exposed to different lots of 3 mAbs (Erbitux, Remicade, and Humira), from the same manufacturer, at the early phase (n = 12 donors). These lots induced an overall similar cytokine secretion profile when averaged across the population at the early phase (Fig 6A, *white and grey bars*), although donor to donor differences could be observed (Fig 6A, *colored circles*). Some donors showed slight differences in response to different lots of the same mAb (compare the response of the same colored dots in Fig 6A), which might be due to differences in attributes since there are no differences in sequence between lots being compared. The consistency of the average cytokine secretion profile across the population demonstrates the reproducibility of the response at the early phase.

A) Several different lots of Erbitux (2 lots), Remicade (2 lots) and Humira (5 lots) were tested in the IVCIA assay for a response at the early (20 h) phase (n = 12 donors), at 40 μg/mL. The concentration (pg/mL) of signature cytokines that were secreted 20 hours after stimulation is shown. B) Biosimilars, Humira and ABP 501, from two different manufacturers were compared in the IVCIA assay for the secretion of signature cytokines at the early (20 h) and late (7 day) phases (n = 4 donors), at 100 μg/mL. C) Multiple lots of another set of biosimilars, Herceptin and ABP 980, from two different manufacturers (which are both associated with a low rate of clinical immunogenicity), were assessed in the IVCIA assay at 40 μg/mL for T-cell proliferative responses on Day 7 only. No statistically different responses in the assay were observed between different lots of Herceptin and mAb5-B (p = 0.12). In all assays, the average response across the population tested was similar, although slightly different responses in specific donors could be observed. In all panels, *bars in shades of white and grey* show the average level of cytokine secretion at the early and late phases, and *purple bars* depict the average level of T-cell proliferation, across the population. *Colored and black circles*represent the response of individual donors and show the variability of the population tested.

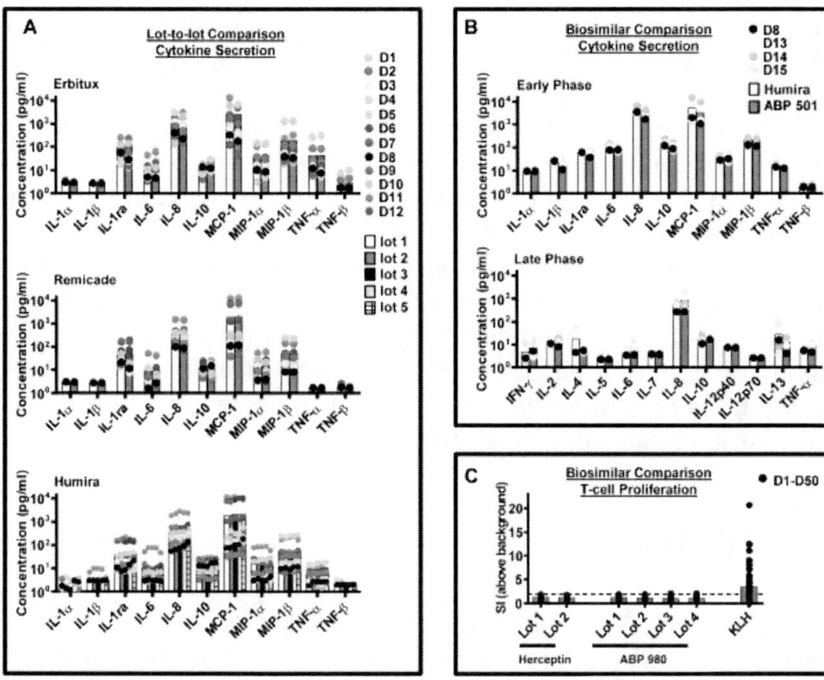

Fig 6. The IVCIA assay can be used to compare mAb lots from both the same manufacturer and from different manufacturers (biosimilars).

The response of the IVCIA assay to biosimilar mAbs was also tested and found to give similar responses across the population. Fig 6B shows that biosimilars Humira and ABP 501 (produced by different manufacturers), induced comparable levels of cytokine secretion (n = 4). Furthermore, no statistical differences between these biosimilars ($p \geq 0.05$) were observed for most of the 23 cytokines that were tested at both the early (IL-1β, IL-1ra, IL-6, MIP-1α, MIP-1β, TNF-α, and TNF-β) and late (IL-10, IL-13, IL-2, IL-4, IL-5,

IL-6, IL-7, IL-8, and TNF-α) phases. Three cytokines (IL-1α, IL-12p40, and IL-12p70) were at a comparably low concentration in both biosimilar samples, however they could not be statistically analyzed as the cytokine concentration was at the limit of quantitation. Statistical differences ($p<0.05$) were observed for a few remaining cytokines at the early (IL-8, IL-10, and MCP-1) and late (IFN-γ) phases, however the stimulation index between the two products was well below the cutoff used to determine a positive response in the assay ($SI \geq 1.9–2.0$) for all cytokines, indicating that were indeed comparable. Overall, although differences in donor specific responses could be observed (Fig 6B), the differences were similar to those observed for unique lots of the same mAb from one manufacturer (Fig 6A). Another pair of biosimilars from two different manufacturers, Herceptin and ABP 980 (which have low rates of clinical immunogenicity), were tested in a single time point assay (Day 7 only) for T-cell proliferation in a 50 donor population. All lots of Herceptin and ABP 980 that were tested showed a comparably low response in the assay (Fig 6C), and were not found to be statistically different ($p = 0.12$), which agrees with the low rate of clinical immunogenicity for this molecule.

DISCUSSION

The responses observed in the IVCIA assay were aligned with the relative clinical responses of the 10 mAbs tested. The assay may help rank order and select therapeutic mAb candidates that would be expected to have the least potential to be immune activating in the clinic based on their ability to drive a T-cell functional response *in vitro*. For example, mAb therapeutics such as Xolair and Herceptin, with low T-cell responses (≤10% of donors responded), would be ranked low on the scale for potential immunogenicity risk. Similarly, Remicade and Humira, that showed higher T-cell responses (≥10% of donors responded), will be ranked toward the right side of the scale with a higher risk for potential immunogenicity (>10% of donors responded) (Table 1). This threshold between biotherapeutics with lower and higher risk of immunogenicity is in agreement with other published results, where molecules with a low rate of clinical immunogenicity induced less than 10% of donors to respond in the assay [5,6,8]. The primary readout of the IVCIA assay is T-cell proliferation; however this includes the responses of both T-effector and T-regulatory cells. As T-regulatory cells do not secrete IL-2 [29], two orthogonal readouts, number of IL-2 secreting cells and concentration of IL-2 secreted, were also used. This helped to confirm that the T-cell profiles observed were associated with an inflammatory output that could eventually drive an antibody response. Therefore, for mAb rank ordering and therapeutic selection, the use of the IVCIA assay with at least two orthogonal readouts (T-cell proliferation and either number of IL-2 secreting cells or concentration of IL-2 secreted) is suggested.

There are multiple operational benefits to these types of cell-based assays including the ability to: screen the same donor with a large number of samples, test a variety of different sample types (i.e. highly stressed) that may not be safe to test in the clinic, achieve a production level that is not possible with *in vivo* experiments, retrospectively assess manufacturing changes, and potentially operationalize in a manufacturing setting. Additional advantages include that these assays can: incorporate the HLA diversity of the human population, be evaluated in human donors with a known medical history, simulate potential immune cell activation, and contain a relevant mixture of immune cells without the confounding influence of other components of tissues and blood [22,23].

Although the IVCIA assay is useful for relative risk ranking and candidate selection, the utility of this assay is limited by several factors. It is notable that these assays lack many of the components that may contribute to an immune response *in vivo*, including: the route of administration and disposition of the biologic, processing of the biologic by the relevant professional antigen presenting cells, buffering of the response by the presence of other relevant cell types in physiologically relevant ratios, and the interaction with surrounding tissues and lymph nodes [22,23]. Even though the assay was effective at identifying the likelihood of mAbs to be potentially immunogenic in the clinic, the assay cannot be used for predicting the rate of immunogenicity in the clinic. Furthermore, actual immunogenic potential may only be measured via a multi-dose clinical assessment. It is important to note that the assay does not account for the disease state and underlying immune status as well as standard care of treatment of patients that can modulate such responses. Additionally, the anti-drug antibody assays used to measure clinical immunogenicity are not harmonized across industry and face technical limitations of low sensitivity, specificity, and interference due to circulating mAbs or other soluble factors [23]. Therefore, using the observed immunogenicity incidence numbers from the label of the marketed products as well as from published clinical studies should be interpreted with caution. Another exception to this analysis is the observed or clinical immunogenicity rates of biotherapeutics with an immunomodulatory target (i.e. Campath, Rituxan, or therapeutics with cytokine/chemokine targets [30]). For these types of molecules, the level of T-cell response detected *in vitro* may not be consistent with immunogenicity observed in the clinic [31].

The application of the IVCIA assay to the development of biopharmaceuticals can range from candidate selection at the early development phase to the late stage evaluation of specific attributes that may impact the risk of immunogenicity. Fig 7 shows a proposed schematic for immunogenicity risk assessment of biotherapeutics during the drug product development lifecycle. During candidate selection, there are often multiple variants of a biotherapeutic. For a therapeutic protein with an endogenous counterpart, a comparison between the native protein and the biotherapeutic itself is performed to make sure that the biotherapeutic is as close to the self-protein as possible. Here, a comparison of FP1 to FP1 (no Fc) in the IVCIA assay showed a minor decrease in the T-cell response when the FP1 molecule was fused to an antibody Fc domain. However the assay was the most meaningful in distinguishing the immunogenic potential of the mutations associated with the FP1 molecule itself. An *in silico*evaluation could not identify and rank order the variants as they are all predicted to have a similar risk of immunogenicity. A rank ordering of the FP1 candidates from highest to lowest risk (with FP1 mutant 1 > FP1 mutant 2 > FP1 mutant 3) was achieved by the IVCIA assay, confirming that minor mutations in the sequence, that were not differentiated by *in silico*analysis alone, could be detected by the T-cell functional assay. Although the different FP1 mutants did show differences in a few additional attributes (including the aggregation profile) which might impact the response in the IVCIA assay, the assay is capable of detecting both differences in sequence and differences in attributes that result from changes in the sequence. The sensitivity of T-cells *in vitro* to minor changes in sequence in viral antigens has been shown by others [32].

However, the ability of the assay to detect differences in sequence in other protein molecules may depend on the exact location and nature of the variation in sequence.

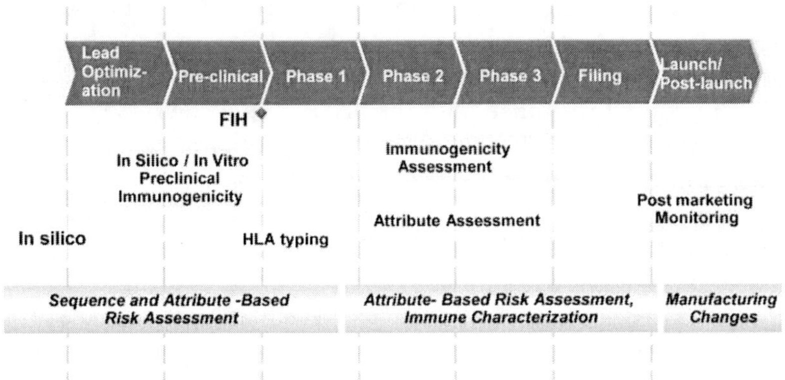

Fig 7. Stages of biotherapeutic development where the IVCIA assay can be used for risk assessment related to attributes.

In silico or algorithm based assessments rank order and identify lead candidates based on the least sequence based risk. *In vitro* assessments identify non-sequence attributes and any immune mediated target based risk at preclinical stage prior to first in human (FIH). Pharmacogenomic assessments for HLA can be introduced in long-term clinical studies (Phase 1b/2) to evaluate associations of HLA with clinical immunogenicity. Immunogenicity assessments measured in serum as ADA span the breadth of clinical trials and disease indications (FIH to Launch/post launch). *In vitro*assays also provide attribute related risk assessment of manufactured lots, lot-to-lot comparability, and risk post packaging due to attributes related to storage, shipping, handling, and device-related leachates.

During later stage development, the potential risk of immunogenicity due to attributes that can vary due to the manufacturing process (such as protein aggregation and chemical modification) [8,33–37] becomes more evident. Protein aggregates in the sub-visible size range is one attribute that has been suspected of posing an increased risk of immunogenicity [4,22,38–41]. The original and highly aggregated forms of 10 diverse mAbs were tested in the IVCIA assay for changes in immune functional response at the early and late phases. The question posed was whether the aggregated forms of these mAbs would all be able to activate the immune cells in the assay. Although each mAb tested had an individual sequence-associated or target-related immunogenic potential, when aggregated, all but one mAb showed a similar trend of being higher in their functional response than the original mAb. This is consistent with published results that show that high numbers of aggregates in the 2–10 μm size range (far above that found in marketed products) have the potential to activate immune cells *in vitro* and induce weak and transient responses *in vivo* [8–10,16,21,22,42]. This enhanced response due to aggregation was detected by measuring a panel of signature cytokines and could be observed as soon as the early phase, indicating that a single readout at the early phase may be sufficient for detecting the potential risk of immunogenicity due to attributes. Therefore, a risk of immunogenicity scoring system could be devised by calculating the percentage of donors that responded by one or more readouts in the assay.

Herceptin, Xolair, Erbitux, and Avastin samples containing high levels of aggregates induced the highest response in the assay, although the mAbs before aggregation were not strong elicitors of a T-cell functional response. Furthermore, mAbs that caused a higher T-cell functional response, such as Remicade, mAb3 and Humira, were only slightly more immunogenic when stress treated. The lower response could be attributed to the more immunogenic nature of these molecules as observed by their higher T-cell functional responses before stress treatment (>10% donors responded). The response to aggregates could be detected as early as 20 hours post-stimulation as shown by increased levels of monocyte-specific cytokines (S2 Fig), indicating the involvement of monocytes, macrophages and immature dendritic cells. The same aggregates were also able to elicit a T-cell functional response at a later stage (7–8 days). In most cases, donors that responded significantly at the late stage (SI≥5) had also induced a response at the early phase. Our previously published results in the transgenic Xeno-het mouse model showed that the response to high numbers of aggregates is transient and weak and not associated with long-term memory [42]. Hence, the initial innate phase activation could lead to engagement of antigen presenters that could potentially drive a weak T-cell response at the late phase.

Overall, this indicates that the relative response to aggregates in the assay does not correlate with the rate of clinical immunogenicity of the unstressed molecule. Aggregates may possess unique structural features or 3-dimensional epitopes that can lead to B-cell or T-cell activation (perhaps through enhanced uptake and subsequent activation of antigen presenting cells) in a manner that is not dependent on the T-cell epitope content of the linear amino acid sequence. In addition, two of the aggregated samples that induced the highest response (Herceptin and Avastin) did not have the highest number of particles present (Avastin was one of the lowest) suggesting that additional aggregate attributes (besides aggregate number) are contributing to the immune response observed. The assay also demonstrated the target mediated effect of Campath on T-cells. Campath, both before and after aggregation, showed no response in the assay, suggesting that the monomeric (or monomer fraction of the stirred sample that was not aggregated upon stress treatment) and/or aggregated Campath retained its ability to bind to the target in the assay. It is important to note that all of these aggregated samples are heavily aggregated and have particle numbers that are orders of magnitude above what would be in a marketed product. Future experiments that evaluate the threshold of aggregate activation in the IVCIA assay will be key to establishing the sensitivity of the assay. Further correlation between the threshold of activation in the IVCIA assay to the threshold of response in humans will be necessary for setting biologically relevant specifications during product manufacturing.

Glycation is the non-enzymatic addition of sugars to proteins and occurs on lysine side chains and the N-terminal amine. Glucose is traditionally used as a carbon source during mammalian cell culture expression, although other sugars could be used. Glycation levels of antibody biotherapeutics are product quality attributes that can vary during the expression and manufacturing of the drug product, or after administration to patients *in vivo* [24,43]. Although there is a theoretical risk of activation of antigen presenters, such as monocytes or dendritic cells through mannose receptors [44–46], the immunological impact of protein biotherapeutics modified by glycation with different sugars is unknown. The IVCIA assay was used to explore the impact of mAbs with elevated levels of glycation by different sugars (galactose, glucose, and mannose), to approximately 40% above the original mAbs, on the potential risk of immunogenicity. At both the early and late phases, glycation of mAbs showed a very low or negligible response. Some donors were associated with a low level response that could be attributed to the inherent biological state of the donor as compared to other healthy subjects. Overall, antibody glycation from galactose, glucose, and mannose at the levels tested does not appear to trigger activation of a potential immune reaction, as judged by cytokine release assays of certain immune cells *in vitro*.

The suitability of the IVCIA assay for comparing various lots of the same mAb, from both the same manufacturer and from different manufacturers (biosimilars), was demonstrated. The different lots that were compared had the same sequence but contained varying levels of certain product quality attributes. For example, Humira lots varied in several characteristics including: some N-linked glycan species (high mannose, non-fucosylated complex glycans, degree of galactosylation of complex glycans, and degree of sialylation of complex glycans) and number of sub-visible particles in the 2–10 μm and greater than 10 μm size ranges (data not shown). It is important to note that Humira is administered in a pre-filled syringe so particle numbers showed high variability between lots and are mostly silicone oil droplets (>98%). As another example, Erbitux lots also showed variability in some N-linked glycan species (high mannose, non-fucosylated complex glycans, and degree of sialylation of complex glycans) and % high molecular weight by size exclusion chromatography (data not shown). The IVCIA assay showed a similar average profile across the population to different lots of the same mAb, although individual donor to donor differences could be observed. The IVCIA assay may therefore be an important comparability technique for showing both high-level similarity and detecting minor attribute-related differences.

In conclusion, the IVCIA assay is an informative cell-based system for relative immunogenicity risk assessment, and has multiple applications from early development through the lifespan of the drug product.

ACKNOWLEDGMENTS

The authors wish to thank Edward Cloake, Alyson Rust, Gary Bembridge, and Tim Jones from Antitope Ltd for data generation and/or analysis. Thanks to Dan Mytych and Michael Hall for technical advice and reviewing the manuscript. Thanks to Tamer Eris, Kate Hutterer, Jennifer Liu, Richard Marcus, Linda Lai, Theresa Born, Victor Fung, Primal Kaur, Mark Kroenke, Monica Ramchandani-Toddywala, and Margaret Karow for providing material and/or useful discussions. Thanks to Rex Pai for characterizing the mAbs.

AUTHOR CONTRIBUTIONS

1. **Conceived and designed the experiments:** MJ JY JH TG MM GF LN VJ.
2. **Performed the experiments:** MJ MD JY HR CB JH.
3. **Analyzed the data:** MJ MD JY HR CB MF MB JH TG LZ LN VJ.
4. **Wrote the paper:** MJ MD MB TG LZ GF LN VJ.

REFERENCES

1. U. S. Food and Drug Administration/Center for Drug Evaluation and Research (2014). Guidance for Industry: Immunogenicity Assessment for Therapeutic Protein Products. Forms based on FDA Drugs guidance (FDA Maryland).
2. European Medicines Agency/Committee for Medicinal Products for Human Use (2007). Guideline on Immunogenicity Assessment of Biotechnology-derived Therapeutic Proteins (EMEA/CHMP London, UK).
3. Barbosa MD, Vielmetter J, Chu S, Smith DD, Jacinto J (2006) Clinical link between MHC class II haplotype and interferon-beta (IFN-beta) immunogenicity. Clin Immunol 118: 42–50.

4. Koren E, Zuckerman LA, Mire-Sluis AR (2002) Immune responses to therapeutic proteins in humans—clinical significance, assessment and prediction. Curr Pharm Biotechnol 3: 349–360.

5. Baker MP, Jones TD (2007) Identification and removal of immunogenicity in therapeutic proteins. Curr Opin Drug Discov Devel 10: 219–227.

6. Jaber A, Baker M (2007) Assessment of the immunogenicity of different interferon beta-1a formulations using ex vivo T-cell assays. J Pharm Biomed Anal 43: 1256–1261.

7. Jaber A, Driebergen R, Giovannoni G, Schellekens H, Simsarian J, et al. (2007) The Rebif new formulation story: it's not trials and error. Drugs R D 8: 335–348.

8. Joubert MK, Hokom M, Eakin C, Zhou L, Deshpande M, et al. (2012) Highly aggregated antibody therapeutics can enhance the in vitro innate and late-stage T-cell immune responses. J Biol Chem 287: 25266–25279.

9. Telikepalli S, Shinogle HE, Thapa PS, Kim JH, Deshpande M, et al. (2015) Physical characterization and in vitro biological impact of highly aggregated antibodies separated into size-enriched populations by fluorescence-activated cell sorting. J Pharm Sci 104: 1575–1591. doi: 10.1002/jps.24379.

10. Rombach-Riegraf V, Karle AC, Wolf B, Sorde L, Koepke S, et al. (2014) Aggregation of human recombinant monoclonal antibodies influences the capacity of dendritic cells to stimulate adaptive T-cell responses in vitro. PLoS One 9: e86322. doi: 10.1371/journal.pone.0086322.

11. Zaitseva M, Romantseva T, Blinova K, Beren J, Sirota L, et al. (2012) Use of human MonoMac6 cells for development of in vitro assay predictive of adjuvant safety in vivo. Vaccine 30: 4859–4865. doi: 10.1016/j.vaccine.2012.05.002.

12. Haile LA, Puig M, Kelley-Baker L, Verthelyi D (2015) Detection of innate immune response modulating impurities in therapeutic proteins. PLoS One 10: e0125078. doi: 10.1371/journal.pone.0125078.

13. Kendal AR, Chen Y, Regateiro FS, Ma J, Adams E, et al. (2011) Sustained suppression by Foxp3+ regulatory T cells is vital for infectious transplantation tolerance. J Exp Med 208: 2043–2053. doi: 10.1084/jem.20110767.

14. Brinks V, Jiskoot W, Schellekens H (2011) Immunogenicity of therapeutic proteins: the use of animal models. Pharm Res 28: 2379–2385. doi: 10.1007/s11095-011-0523-5.

15. Mosmann TR, Fong TA (1989) Specific assays for cytokine production by T cells. J Immunol Methods 116: 151–158. pmid:2642947 doi: 10.1016/0022-1759(89)90198-1

16. CJ, Cloake EA, Welch K, Filipe V, et al. (2015) Small amounts of sub-visible aggregates enhance the immunogenic potential of monoclonal antibody therapeutics. Pharm Res 32: 1383–1394.

17. Shankar G, Devanarayan V, Amaravadi L, Barrett YC, Bowsher R, et al. (2008) Recommendations for the validation of immunoassays used for detection of host antibodies against biotechnology products. J Pharm Biomed Anal 48: 1267–1281.

18. Wang P, Sidney J, Dow C, Mothe B, Sette A, et al. (2008) A systematic assessment of MHC class II peptide binding predictions and evaluation of a consensus approach. PLoS Comput Biol 4: e1000048.

19. Welsh RM, Che JW, Brehm MA, Selin LK (2010) Heterologous immunity between viruses. Immunol Rev 235: 244–266.

20. L, Bramhall E, Kuck A, Goletz TJ, et al. (2010) Considerations for optimization and validation of an in vitro PBMC derived T cell assay for immunogenicity prediction of biotherapeutics. Clin Immunol 137: 5–14.

21. Pardeshi N, Ahmadi M, Fogg M, Baker M, Carpenter J (2015) Investigating the immunogenic potential of particles in intravenous solutions of infliximab. Poster presentation at the IABS 2nd Progress and Challenges in Protein Particles and Immunogenicity of Biotherapeutics 2015: Filling in the Gaps in Risk Evaluation and Mitigation Conference, Rockville, MD.

22. Moussa EM, Panchal JP, Moorthy BS, Blum JS, Joubert MK, et al. (2016) Immunogenicity of therapeutic protein aggregates. Journal of Pharmaceutical Sciences 105: 417–430.

23. Jawa V, Cousens LP, Awwad M, Wakshull E, Kropshofer H, et al. (2013) T-cell dependent immunogenicity of protein therapeutics: Preclinical assessment and mitigation. Clin Immunol 149: 534–555.

24. Yang J, Primack R, Frohn M, Wang W, Luan P, et al. (2015) Impact of glycation on antibody clearance. AAPS J 17: 237–244.

25. Joubert MK, Luo Q, Nashed-Samuel Y, Wypych J, Narhi LO (2011) Classification and characterization of therapeutic antibody aggregates. J Biol Chem 286: 25118–25133.

26. Bender NK, Heilig CE, Dröll B, Wohlgemuth J, Armbruster FP, et al. (2007) Immunogenicity, efficacy and adverse events of adalimumab in RA patients. Rheumatol Int 27: 269–274.

27. Gottlieb AB, Evans R, Li S, Dooley LT, Guzzo CA, et al. (2004) Infliximab induction therapy for patients with severe plaque-type psoriasis: a randomized, double-blind, placebo-controlled trial. J Am Acad Dermatol 51: 534–542.

28. Ling ZD, Ziltener HJ, Webb BT, Matheson DS (1990) Aggregated immunoglobulin and Fc fragment of IgG induce IL-6 release from human monocytes. Cell Immunol 129: 95–103.

29. de la Rosa M, Rutz S, Dorninger H, Scheffold A (2004) Interleukin-2 is essential for CD4+CD25+ regulatory T cell function. Eur J Immunol 34: 2480–2488.

30. Zhou L, Hoofring SA, Wu Y, Vu T, Ma P, et al. (2013) Stratification of antibody-positive subjects by antibody level reveals an impact of immunogenicity on pharmacokinetics. AAPS J 15: 30–40.

31. Xue L, Hickling T, Song R, Nowak J, Rup B (2016) Contribution of enhanced engagement of antigen presentation machinery to the clinical immunogenicity of a human interleukin (IL)-21 receptor-blocking therapeutic antibody. Clin Exp Immunol 183: 102–113.

32. Collen T, Douglas AJ, Paton DJ, Zhang G, Morrison WI (2000) Single amino acid differences are sufficient for CD4(+) T-cell recognition of a heterologous virus by cattle persistently infected with bovine viral diarrhea virus. Virology 276: 70–82.

33. **33.**Bessa J, Boeckle S, Beck H, Buckel T, Schlicht S, et al. (2015) The immunogenicity of antibody aggregates in a novel transgenic mouse model. Pharm Res 32: 2344–2359.

34. Bukofzer S, Ayres J, Chavez A, Devera M, Miller J, et al. (2015) Industry perspective on the medical risk of visible particles in injectable drug products. PDA J Pharm Sci Technol 69: 123–139.

35. Luo Q, Joubert MK, Stevenson R, Ketchem RR, Narhi LO, et al. (2011) Chemical Modifications in Therapeutic Protein Aggregates Generated under Different Stress Conditions. J Biol Chem 286: 25134–25144.

36. Barnard JG, Babcock K, Carpenter JF (2013) Characterization and quantitation of aggregates and particles in interferon-beta products: potential links between product quality attributes and immunogenicity. J Pharm Sci 102: 915–928.

37. Van Beers MM, Gilli F, Schellekens H, Randolph TW, Jiskoot W (2012) Immunogenicity of recombinant human interferon beta interacting with particles of glass, metal, and polystyrene. J Pharm Sci 101: 187–199.

38. Carpenter JF, Randolph TW, Jiskoot W, Crommelin DJ, Middaugh CR, et al. (2009) Overlooking subvisible particles in therapeutic protein products: gaps that may compromise product quality. J Pharm Sci 98: 1201–1205.

39. den Engelsman J, Garidel P, Smulders R, Koll H, Smith B, et al. (2011) Strategies for the assessment of protein aggregates in pharmaceutical biotech product development. Pharm Res 28: 920–933.

40. Rosenberg AS (2006) Effects of protein aggregates: an immunologic perspective. Aaps J 8: E501–507.

41. Singh SK (2011) Impact of product-related factors on immunogenicity of biotherapeutics. J Pharm Sci 100: 354–387.

42. Bi V, Jawa V, Joubert MK, Kaliyaperumal A, Eakin C, et al. (2013) Development of a human antibody tolerant mouse model to assess the immunogenicity risk due to aggregated biotherapeutics. J Pharm Sci 102: 3545–3555.

43. Goetze AM, Liu YD, Arroll T, Chu L, Flynn GC (2012) Rates and impact of human antibody glycation in vivo. Glycobiology 22: 221–234.

44. Banchereau J, Steinman RM (1998) Dendritic cells and the control of immunity. Nature 392: 245–252.

45. Kzhyshkowska J, Gordon S (2009) Vesicular trafficking in immune cells. Immunobiology 214: 493–494.

46. Varin A, Gordon S (2009) Alternative activation of macrophages: immune function and cellular biology. Immunobiology 214: 630–641.

7

CHAPTER

Converting Monoclonal Antibody-based Immunotherapies from Passive to Active: Bringing Immune Complexes into Play OPEN

Jennifer Lambour[1], Mar Naranjo-Gomez[1], Marc Piechaczyk[1] and Mireia Pelegrin[1]

[1]'Equipe Labellisée par la Ligue Contre le Cancer' - Institut de Génétique Moléculaire de Montpellier, UMR 5535, CNRS, 34293 Montpellier Cedex 5, France; Université de Montpellier, 34090 Montpellier, France

ABSTRACT

Monoclonal antibodies (mAbs), which currently constitute the main class of biotherapeutics, are now recognized as major medical tools that are increasingly being considered to fight severe viral infections. Indeed, the number of antiviral mAbs developed in recent years has grown exponentially. Although their direct effects on viral blunting have been studied in detail, their potential immunomodulatory actions have been overlooked until recently. The ability of antiviral mAbs to modulate antiviral immune responses in infected organisms has recently been revealed. More specifically, upon recognition of their cognate antigens, mAbs form immune complexes (ICs) that can be recognized by the Fc receptors expressed on different immune cells of infected individuals. This binding may be followed by the modulation of the host immune responses. Harnessing this immunomodulatory property may facilitate improvements in the therapeutic potential of antiviral mAbs. This review focuses on the role of ICs formed with different viral determinants and mAbs in the induction of antiviral immune responses in the context of both passive immunotherapies and vaccination strategies. Potential deleterious effects of ICs on the host immune response are also discussed.

Keywords

Antiviral therapy; DC; Fc receptors; immunotherapy; immune complexes; monoclonal antibodies; vaccine-like effects; vaccine strategies

POTENTIAL OF ANTIVIRAL MONOCLONAL ANTIBODIES

Monoclonal antibodies (mAbs) have gained an important place in the therapeutic arsenal against severe human diseases. More than 50 mAbs have been approved or are under review for human use, and several hundred are currently being tested in the clinic,[1, 2] most of them to treat patients suffering from a variety of cancers or inflammatory diseases.

Concerning antiviral mAbs, only one, directed against respiratory syncytial virus (RSV), has been approved for the prophylactic treatment of pediatric infections. However, employing mAbs as antiviral drugs is under consideration for the treatment of several chronic and acute severe viral infections, especially to address the public health emergencies such as the recent Ebola virus and Middle East respiratory syndrome coronavirus outbreaks.[3, 4, 5, 6, 7] Illustrating this trend, the number of antiviral mAbs developed and tested in preclinical and clinical trials has grown exponentially in the past 10 years and includes mAbs directed against life-threatening agents, such as human immunodeficiency virus (HIV), hepatitis B virus (HBV), hepatitis C virus (HCV), influenza virus, dengue virus, Ebola virus and severe acute respiratory syndrome virus coronavirus, among others.[8, 9, 10, 11, 12, 13, 14, 15, 16, 17, 18, 19, 20, 21, 22] Importantly, recent clinical data have also demonstrated the efficacy of anti-HIV mAbs in controlling viremia, when administered to HIV-infected patients, lending strong support to the idea that mAbs could broaden the therapeutic arsenal against severe viral infections.[23,24] Their use as antiviral agents is all the more likely to be considered given that multiple biological activities may account for their therapeutic effects.

Although a few mAbs have been developed to inhibit the recognition of viral receptors or co-receptors on the surface of target cells, most antiviral mAbs have been selected for their ability to neutralize virions through the binding of their antigen-binding (Fab) fragment to viral surface antigens essential for entry into host cells. However, the biological activity of antibodies is also mediated by the fragment crystallizable region (Fc) moiety. Thus, it is interesting to note that most antiviral mAbs in use are immunoglobulin (Ig)-Gs displaying a variety of effector functions, including binding to both complement and Fcγ receptors (FcγRs). Different types of FcγRs are expressed in a regulated manner by many cells of the immune system, including B cells, natural killer cells, dendritic cells (DCs), monocytes/macrophages, granulocytes and mast cells, and their engagement by the Fc antibody moiety is essential for regulating the antibody effector functions.[25,26] Upon recognition of their target antigens, antiviral mAbs can facilitate virus elimination via two types of complement-mediated mechanisms: (i) inactivation of viral particles and/or phagocytosis of opsonized virus mediated by cells of the innate immune system (Figure 1) and (ii) opsonization and subsequent lysis of infected cells, when viral antigens are also expressed on the cell surface (for example, envelope (Env) glycoprotein of lentiviruses such as HIV) via complement-dependent cytotoxicity. In addition to complement-mediated actions, recognition of FcγRs can entail antibody-dependent cellular phagocytosis and antibody-dependent cell-mediated cytotoxicity (Figure 1).[20,27,28,29,30] Finally, antiviral mAbs also have a role in viral blunting by inhibiting cell-to-cell viral transmission.[31]

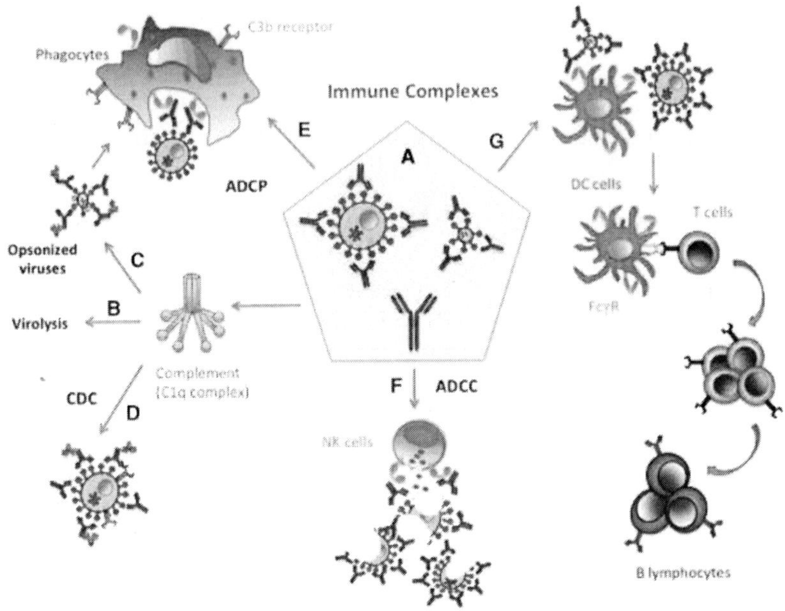

Figure 1. Multiple Fc-mediated activities of antiviral mAbs (monoclonal antibodies). Antiviral mAbs can opsonize viruses, as well as infected cells in situations when viral antigens are also expressed on their surface (A). This can lead to viral clearance through various immune-mediated mechanisms. The Fc domain allows the binding of complement to free virions, inducing direct virolysis (B). Fcγ- and complement receptors can recognize opsonized virions, leading to their phagocytosis by cells of the innate immune system (C). Infected cells can also be eliminated by complement-dependent cytotoxicity (CDC), antibody-dependent cellular phagocytosis (ADCP) and/or antibody-dependent cell-mediated cytotoxicity (ADCC) mediated by innate immunity effector cells expressing FcγRs (D–F). Immune complexes (ICs) made with mAbs and different viral determinants (virions or infected cells) can be recognized by FcγRs expressed on antigen-presenting cells such as dendritic cells (DCs) (G). IC recognition by DCs subsequently leads to enhanced antigen uptake and presentation, allowing the induction of stronger antiviral immune responses.

In addition to controlling the viral propagation by these mechanisms, the opsonization of viral particles and/or infected cells by therapeutic antiviral mAbs of the IgG type leads to the formation of immune complexes (ICs) recognizable by the FcγRs expressed on antigen-presenting cells (APCs) such as DCs. This can potentially affect the endogenous antiviral adaptive immune response of passive immunotherapy-treated individuals. Despite the fact that the immunoregulatory functions of antibodies (as well as ICs) have been known for a long time, and have been reported in different experimental settings and physiopathological situations,[25, 32, 33, 34, 35, 36, 37, 38] the immunomodulatory role of mAbs with clinical potential as antiviral drugs has only recently been considered.

This review mainly focuses on the induction of antiviral immune responses by ICs in both passive immunotherapies and vaccination strategies. The potential deleterious effects of antiviral antibodies on the host immune dysfunction and/or viral propagation are also discussed.

Topof page

ANTIVIRAL MABS CAN ENHANCE THE HOST ANTIVIRAL IMMUNE RESPONSE IN AN FC-DEPENDENT MANNER

Only recently have studies addressed whether and how passive immunotherapies utilizing antiviral mAbs are able to enhance the antiviral immunity in infected individuals. This is largely due to the limited availability of suitable immunocompetent animal models of viral infection that allow in-depth investigations of the endogenous immune response. The concept that passive immunotherapies utilizing antiviral mAbs can induce long-term protective immunity has recently been established using an immunocompetent mouse model, consisting of short immunotherapies given to young animals infected with the FrCasE murine leukemia virus. The induction of such 'vaccine-like' effects by antiviral mAbs, as well as some of the mechanisms involved, are reviewed in detail elsewhere.[39] In brief, the inoculation of mouse pups with FrCasE is fatal because the antiviral immune response is too weak to control the viral propagation. In contrast, treatment with a neutralizing mAb for several days shortly after infection blunts viral propagation and induces a lifelong protective antiviral immunity composed of both a highly neutralizing humoral response and a cytotoxic CD8+ T-cell response.[40, 41, 42, 43, 44, 45] This induction of protective immunity strictly depends on the Fc fragment of the neutralizing mAbs.[43, 44]Moreover, the formation of ICs composed of the administered mAbs and infected cells rather than virions is crucial for the enhanced antiviral immune response.[43]Such ICs are recognized by the FcγRs expressed by DCs, which facilitate ICs internalization and lead to stronger activation and more efficient antigen presentation by DCs, eventually leading to stronger cytotoxic T-lymphocyte (CTL) responses. An Fc-mediated effect that occurs concurrently is the inhibition of regulatory T-cell (Treg) expansion. This depends on the mAb effector functions[45]and occurs rapidly. Moreover, it is necessary for the development of the protective humoral and cellular responses, as Treg-mediated immunosuppression is observed in all cases of chronic viral infections, where it dampens antiviral immune responses, thereby permitting the establishment of chronicity. Finally, breastfeeding and placental transfer of maternal anti-FrCasE Igs induced by mAb immunotherapy not only led to the viral propagation blunting in infected pups, but also to the induction of long-lasting protective humoral immunity in these animals.[42] This is a particularly interesting observation when one considers that the FrCasE model is reminiscent of perinatal infection by HIV, including breastfeeding-mediated mother-to-child virus transmission.

Other evidence for the induction of 'vaccine-like' effects by antiviral mAbs comes from studies in several preclinical models of human viral infections and from HIV-infected patients.

In a mouse model of RSV infection, the administration of a neutralizing mAb directed against the virus attachment protein G induced a shift in the adaptive immune response from Th2- to Th1-type, leading to sustained and enhanced humoral and CD8+ T-cell responses.[46] However, this effect was not Fc-dependent, but rather due to the ability of the therapeutic mAb to counteract the intrinsic immunosuppressive activity of the RSV G protein.

mAb-driven enhancement of the humoral response has also been reported in two preclinical models of henipavirus infection in African green monkeys.[47, 48]Recovery from both Hendra and Nipah virus-induced disease correlated with the development of host antibody responses consequent to the administration of the highly neutralizing 102.4 mAb. This Hendra and Nipah virus cross-reactive mAb is currently being considered for human use.

Finally, anti-HIV antibodies can modulate immune responses in infected organisms. Such effects were initially reported in several non-human primate models of HIV infection and then observed in infected humans. Macaques were infected with different strains of simian immunodeficiency virus (SIV) or simian HIV (SHIV, a chimeric virus in which HIV Env substitutes for that of SIV and allows for the assessment of the antiviral effects of anti-HIV antibodies) following different protocols. These experiments showed that the administration of highly neutralizing antibodies (either mAbs or polyclonal Igs) enhanced both the humoral and cellular antiviral immune responses of treated animals.[8, 49, 50,51] Interestingly, recent clinical data describe the elicitation of host humoral responses in viremic subjects upon single injection of the potent 3BNC117 anti-HIV mAb.[52] However, the mechanisms leading to the stimulation of antiviral immune responses in these preclinical models of HIV infection or in infected patients remain uncharacterized. Moreover, it is unknown whether these antiviral responses have genuine protective vaccine-like effects. In any case, these important observations open new avenues for the improvement of mAb-based antiviral HIV therapies. Moreover, as the *in vivo* activity of anti-HIV-1 bNAbs, including viral load control, was recently shown to crucially depend on Fc effector functions,[53, 54] an important issue is identifying that Fc–FcγRs interactions are involved in the induction of vaccine-like effects by antiviral mAbs.

ICS ENHANCE DC ACTIVATION AND INDUCE STRONGER ANTIVIRAL T-CELL RESPONSES: EVIDENCE FROM *IN VITRO*STUDIES

To understand the mechanisms underlying the enhancement of antiviral responses by ICs, several *in vitro* studies have addressed whether antibody-mediated viral uptake by DCs could lead to stronger activation of these cells and the development of stronger virus-specific CD4+ and CD8+ T-cell responses in an Fc-dependent manner. Such an increase in the cellular immune response has been reported in different infectious settings using ICs made with different types of antigens, including recombinant viral proteins and whole virions, as well as infected cells (Table 1).

Table 1 - In vitro studies of T-cell responses modulation by IC-activated DC.

Type of viral determinant	Antigen	Antibody	Immune outcome	Reference
Viral proteins	Recombinant HBsAg	Polyclonal Anti-HBSAg (patients sera)	Increased uptake of IC Augmented *in vitro* proliferation of T cells Augmented production of IFN-γ by T cells	55
	HBsAg (purified from patients)	Polyclonal anti-HBV (patients sera)	Enhanced IL-2 and IFN-γ production by co-cultured T cells	56
	Recombinant SIV Gag-p55	Polyclonal anti-p55 (monkeys sera)	Enhanced cross-presentation Induction of anti-Gag-specific CD8+ T-cell responses	57
Virions	SIV virions	Highly neutralizing SIVIG (monkeys sera)	Enhanced virus-specific CD4+ T-cell responses	58
	HIV-1	Polyclonal anti-HIV (patients sera)	Weak stimulating capacity of HIV-specific CTL response	59
Infected cells	FrCasE-infected cells	Anti-gp70 mAb	Enhanced proliferation of Gag-specific CD8+ T cells	43

Abbreviations: cytotoxic T lymphocyte, CTL; immune complex, IC; interferon, IFN; interleukin, IL; hepatitis B surface antigen, HBsAg; HBV, hepatitis B virus; human immunodeficiency virus, HIV; polyclonal immune globulin prepared from hyperimmune SIV infecetd animals, SIVIG.

Concerning ICs made with viral proteins, several reports have shown that ICs made up of anti-HBV mAbs and the hepatitis B surface antigen (HBsAg) can affect DC function and enhance T-cell responses. HBsAg/anti-HBV ICs significantly increased the uptake of the immunocomplexed HBsAg antigen, and augmented the *in vitro* proliferation of virus-specific T cells and their production of interferon (IFN)-γ.[55] Moreover, DCs from HBV-infected patients incubated with HBsAg/anti-HBV ICs showed higher expression of major histocompatibility complex (MHC)-II molecules and higher production of interleukin (IL)-12. IC-loaded DCs also enhanced production of IL-2 and IFN-γ by co-cultured T cells.[56] Interestingly, the therapeutic efficacy of HBsAg/anti-HBV ICs has been tested in clinical trials (see below) in HBV-infected patients with encouraging results.[60, 61, 62] More recently, in experiments aimed at visualizing immunopotentialization by HBsAg/anti-HBV ICs (see below), live-cell imaging revealed that ICs were internalized via the FcγRs of APCs and were subsequently transported through early and late endosomes into lysosomes, where they co-localized with MHC-I and MHC-II molecules.[63] Consistent with the latter observation, the administration of DCs loaded with HBsAg/anti-HBV ICs to mice increased the number of IFN-γ- and tumor necrosis factor-α-producing $CD8^+$ and $CD4^+$ T cells. Similarly, in an SIV infection setting, the incubation of APCs with ICs made with a recombinant full-length Gag p55 protein and an anti-p55 IgG increased SIV capsid cross-presentation. Capsid cross-presentation was dependent on FcγR-mediated uptake of the immunocomplexed SIV capsid protein, and required its proteasomal and endosomal degradation to generate stronger Gag-specific $CD8^+$ T-cell responses.[57] From a mechanistic standpoint, these studies indicate that antiviral antibodies might enhance the priming and expansion of virus-specific $CD4^+$ and $CD8^+$ T cells by both promoting the secretion of key cytokines and facilitating the uptake and cross-presentation of viral Ags by FcγR-expressing DCs.

Immune-complexed whole virions have also been shown to affect the functional activation of DCs. The stimulation of DCs with ICs composed of SIV virions and highly neutralizing SIV-hyperimmune sera (SVIG) led to the increased virus-specific $CD4^+$ T-cell responses in an Fc-dependent manner.[58] In contrast, DCs stimulated with ICs made of HIV-1 and a polyclonal IgG pool from HIV-infected subjects showed only weak HIV-specific CTL-stimulating activity. This suggested that opsonization of HIV-1 by IgGs might be associated with decreased CTL-stimulatory DC activity.[59] However, not all IgG isotypes display equivalent effector functions. Therefore, the undefined nature of the antibodies (both in terms of predominant isotypes and neutralization potential) used to form the HIV-ICs in these experiments might explain these observations. Whether HIV-ICs made with highly neutralizing anti-HIV mAbs of a specific IgG isotype might induce stronger $CD8^+$ T-cell responses is an important issue deserving further investigation (Figure 2). Moreover, the nature of the viral determinant present in ICs might also be crucial in the stimulation of antiviral responses. Interestingly, as mentioned above, in the mouse FrCasE infection model, ICs made up of a neutralizing mAb and infected cells, but not those made with virions, efficiently induce strong Gag-specific $CD8^{+}$ T-cell responses with high cytotoxic activity.[43]This observation shows that the viral and cellular ICs can trigger different immunologic outcomes. In the case of FrCasE, this is explained by the fact the FrCasE-GagL CTL immunodominant epitope is, at best, poorly incorporated into virions. Taken together, these data indicate that the uptake of cellular ICs might allow the presentation of a broader viral antigenic repertoire, leading to stronger effects on immunity (Figure 2).

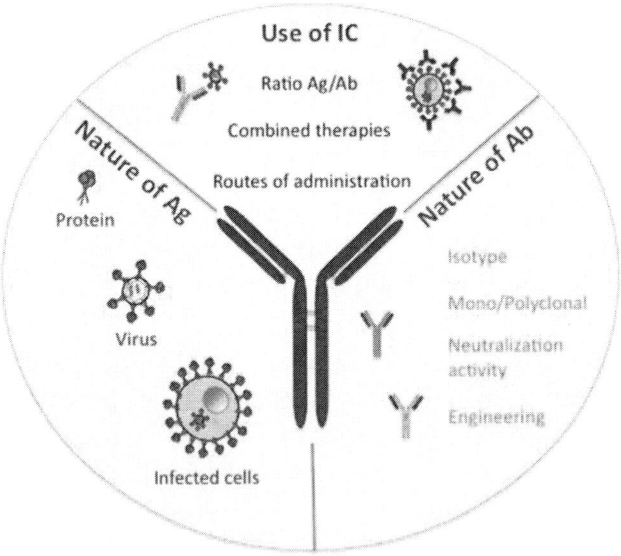

Figure 2. Parameters to consider for achieving optimal IC-mediated modulation of antiviral immune responses. The optimization of vaccine-like-effect-inducing protocols will require the consideration of several parameters such as the nature of the antigen (that is, purified viral proteins, whole virions and infected cells) and the antibody (that is, monoclonal vs polyclonal, nature of the isotype, engineered Fc domain with improved effector functions and so on) used to form the immunogenic ICs, as differences in these parameters might impact immunological outcomes. In addition, whether the optimized ICs are used alone or in combination with immunostimulatory molecules might also be of paramount importance. Several other parameters, including the IC dosage, the route of administration, the choice of adjuvant and the immunological status of patients, will also have to be considered.

MODULATION OF ANTIVIRAL IMMUNE RESPONSES BY ICS FORMED WITH ENDOGENOUS ANTIBODIES DURING THE COURSE OF VIRAL INFECTIONS

ICs formed with endogenous antibodies generated in virally infected mice have been shown to influence antiviral cellular immune responses in several models (Table 2). Notably, the highly neutralizing humoral response generated against the FrCasE retrovirus in mAb-treated-infected mice was demonstrated to limit the viral propagation and to enhance memory cellular responses long after the disappearance of the therapeutic mAb (which occurs within two weeks post administration, reflecting the natural IgG lifespan *in vivo*). IC-mediated activation of DCs upon binding to FcγR was key for this effect.[43] Similarly, in an influenza virus infection model, ICs formed with endogenous antiviral antibodies promoted more sustained antigen presentation by DCs, resulting in stronger $CD8^+$ T-cell proliferation.[64] Interestingly, such prolonged antigen presentation by DCs was dependent on virus-specific, isotype-switched antibodies that facilitated the capture and cross-presentation of viral antigens by FcγR-expressing DCs. In addition, serum antibodies can affect the virus-specific $CD4^+$/$CD8^+$ T-cell balance in an Fc-dependent manner during RSV infection.[65] An enhanced ratio of RSV-neutralizing to -non-neutralizing antibodies profoundly enhanced the $CD4^+$ T-cell response. In a murine lymphocytic choriomeningitis virus (LCMV) infection model, endogenous virus-specific antibodies could stimulate innate immunity and thereby positively affect both the induction and the maintenance of the virus-specific $CD8^+$ T-cell response. Notably, anti-LCMV antibodies limited viral replication in peripheral organs, but allowed replication of the virus in the marginal zone of the spleen, promoting $CD8^+$ T-cell priming.[66] Interestingly, anti-LCMV antibodies were also reported to be essential for long-term maintenance of the memory CTL response in infected mice.[67, 68]

Table 2 - Modulation of immune responses by ICs involving antiviral host humoral responses.

Murine models of infection	Immune outcome	Reference
FrCasE virus (MLV)	Enhanced memory cellular CD8+ responses	43
Influenza	Prolonged Ag presentation by DC; enhanced proliferation of CD8+ T cells	64
RSV	Modification of CD4+/CD8+ T-cell balance	65
LCMV	Innate immune activation; induction of virus-specific CD8+ T-cell response	66

Abbreviations: lymphocytic choriomeningitis virus, LCMV; murine leukemia virus, MLV, respiratory syncytial virus, RSV.

These observations, together with the *in vitro* studies described above, demonstrate that virus-specific antibodies can promote the acquisition, processing and presentation of antigens that are subsequently instrumental for priming T-cell responses and programming functional $CD8^+$ memory in an Fc-dependent manner. They strengthen the concept that antiviral antibodies can regulate the quality and function of antiviral T-cell responses through the formation of ICs. Moreover, they also provide a rationale for developing novel IC-based therapeutic vaccination strategies.

ENHANCEMENT OF ANTIVIRAL IMMUNE RESPONSES IN IC-BASED VACCINATION STRATEGIES

In 1961, Terres and Wolins[69] demonstrated the ability of ICs to induce higher antibody titers than antigens alone. Since then, the immunogenic potential of ICs, alone or in combination with different types of adjuvants, has been tested in several viral infection systems, including animal models of human infections, for example, those involving HBV, HIV, RSV or flaviviruses. The immunostimulatory are principally attributed to the ability of Fc antibody fragments to recruit the host immune system. However, evidence also implicates Fab fragments in modulation of the antiviral immune response, although the outcomes are less documented and were proposed to occur via alterations in antigen conformation and/or in the exposure of specific epitopes.

We describe the enhancement in antiviral immune responses observed in IC-based vaccination experiments below (Table 3).

Table 3 - Vaccine strategies based on immunogenic ICs.

Antigen	Antibody	Administration	Host	Adjuvant	Immunological/clinical outcome	Reference
Yeast-derived recombinant HBsAg	HBIG (purified from patients)	Intramuscular	Human (clinical trial)		Decreased viral load Higher titers of HBsAg Ab Increased frequency IFN-γ and IL-2 producing T cells	60–62
DHBsAg	Polyclonal Anti-DHBsAg	Intraperitoneal	Ducks	Bacteria-based solid matrix	Clearance of serum DHBsAg	70
HBsAg (HBV vaccine, GenHevac B)	mAb Anti-HBV (1B11)	Intravenous and subcutaneous	BALB/c mice	Aluminum hydroxyde	Enhancement of humoral responses	71
HBsAg (S, PreS1, Prs2 domain of HBV)	Polyclonal Anti-HBV	Intramuscular	C57BL/6 HBsAg-positive transgenic mice	DNA plasmid coding HBsAg	Decreased Ag serum levels Induction of CTL responses	72
WHVsAg	Polyclonal Anti-WHV	Intramuscular	Woodchucks	DNA plasmid coding WHBsAg	Reduction of viral load and antigenemia	73
HBsAg (plasma-derived HBV S protein)	Polyclonal Anti-HBV	Intranasal inhalation	BALB/c mice	Cholera toxin or ODN containing CpG	Mucosal and systemic Th1-polarized immune responses	74
Recombinant HIV-1 gp 120	Anti-CD4 (654-D mAb)	Intraperitoneal	BALB/c mice	MPL/DDA	Enhancement of humoral responses	75–77
RSV A2 strain	Anti-RSV (palivizumab)	Intranasal	C57BL/6 mice	—	Priming of virus-specific T- and B-cell responses	78

Abbreviations: antibody, Ab; cytotoxic T lymphocyte, CTL; dimethyldioctadecylammonium, DDA; duck HBsAg, DHBsAg; hepatitis B immunoglobulin, HBIG; hepatitis B surface antigen, HBsAg; hepatitis B virus, HBV; interferon, IFN; interleukin, IL; monophosphoryl lipid-A, MPL; oligodeoxynucleotide, ODN; respiratory syncytial virus, RSV; woodchuck hepatitis virus, WHV; WHV antigen, WHVAg.

HBV

ICs have been tested as vaccines to augment protective immune responses in different animal models of HBV infection. In ducks, ICs made with duck HBsAg and rabbit anti-duck HBsAg (DHBsAg/anti-DHB) were used as immunogens in the form of solid matrix–antibody–antigen complexes (SMAA). Such SMAAs contained killed *Staphylococcus aureus* as a solid matrix and mAb-opsonized viruses.[79]They were initially shown to induce both humoral and CTL responses against the paramyxovirus simian virus 5 in immunized mice.[80] Immunization of HBV-infected ducks with SMAA-based DHBsAg/anti-DHB ICs led to the viral clearance in 60% of infected ducks. Notably, the administration of DHBsAg/anti-DHB ICs lacking *Staphylococcus aureus* showed decreased immunization efficiency, suggesting that the bacteria-based solid matrix functions as an adjuvant.[70]

ICs have also been tested as a therapeutic vaccine against HBV infection in mice[63, 71, 72] and woodchucks.[73] BALB/c mice immunized with HBsAg/anti-HBV ICs produced the increased levels of virus-specific antibodies.[71] Moreover, administering HBsAg/anti-HBV ICs to BALB/c mice via intranasal inhalation induced both mucosal and systemic Th1-polarized immune responses, when administered with adjuvants such as cholera toxin or oligodeoxynucleotides containing immunostimulatory CpG motifs (CpG). This was not observed using HBsAg alone.[74] In addition, the administration of HBsAg/anti-HBV ICs to HBsAg-positive transgenic mice decreased the serum HBsAg levels and induced stronger CTL responses than HBsAg alone.[72] Notably, the co-administration of ICs and a plasmid coding for HBsAg increased the antiviral immune response induced by ICs, indicating the adjuvant effect of DNA in this setting. A similar effect was also reported in a woodchuck model of HBV infection: immunization of woodchuck hepatitis virus (WHV)-infected animals with WHV surface antigen/anti-WHV antibody ICs combined with a DNA vaccine resulted in a higher reduction of both viral load and antigenemia relative to ICs alone.[73] Interestingly, the WHV-infected animals were pretreated with lamivudine (a potent HBV antiviral drug able to enhance T-cell responses in chronically HBV-infected patients) before IC/DNA immunization, suggesting that combination strategies should be considered in treating chronic HBV infections (Figure 2).

The enhancement of antiviral immune responses by ICs *in vitro* and in preclinical models of HBV infection paved the way for the development of IC-based therapeutic vaccination strategies against chronic viral hepatitis B infection. A therapeutic vaccine composed of yeast-derived recombinant HBsAg/anti-HBV immunogenic complexes (YICs) has been tested in a series of clinical trials. This vaccine approach was initially shown to be safe and to induce higher titers of HBsAg antibodies, as well as to increase serum IFN-γ and IL-2 levels in a phase I trial.[60] Importantly, a subpopulation of chronic viral hepatitis B patients showed a decrease in serum HBV viral load and HBsAg levels together with an increase in anti-HBsAg antibody titers in subsequent phase II trials.[61, 62] From a mechanistic standpoint, recent data showing that the administration of YIC-loaded DCs to mice increased both $CD8^+$ and $CD4^+$ T-cell responses[63] suggest that the improved immune responses induced by YICs might account for the antiviral effect observed in a fraction of patients. In an attempt to enhance the immunogenic potential of YIC-based vaccines, a phase III trial tested the therapeutic effect of a higher number of IC doses. Unfortunately, overstimulation with YIC decreased the vaccine efficiency due to host immune fatigue.[81] This suggests that vaccination protocols must be optimized and must take into account both the nature and the dose of ICs, as well as other parameters such as the route of administration, the type of adjuvant and the immunological status of patients to achieve efficient protective immunization (Figure 2).

HIV

In 1988, a study immunized healthy volunteers with HIV peptides.[82] The authors found that compared with free antigen, recall immunization with ICs induced stronger T-cell responses through uncharacterized mechanisms. Other reports also describe alteration of the anti-HIV response by ICs.[75,76,77,83] In particular, the immunization of immunocompetent mice with ICs containing a recombinant HIV-1 gp120 Env glycoprotein and a mAb (654-D mAb) directed to the CD4-binding site induced a higher virus-neutralizing antibody response relative to free antigen. As described above, humoral responses were further increased upon the co-administration of ICs and monophosphoryl lipid-A/dimethyldioctadecylammonium adjuvants. Notably, the interaction of the anti-CD4-binding site mAb with HIV-1 gp120 induced conformational changes in the latter, leading to the enhanced antigenicity and immunogenicity of neutralizing epitopes localized in the HIV-1 V3 loop.[75] These observations highlight the ability of anti-HIV-1 antibodies to induce antigenic alterations in specific HIV-1 gp120 epitopes upon IC formation. Interestingly, further improvement in the immunogenicity of the V3 loop was obtained in ICs generated with gp120 mutants lacking site-specific N-linked glycans.[76,77,83] Taken together, these observations suggest that the ability of ICs to stimulate the induction of neutralizing antibodies is dictated by the nature of the antigen, as well as the specificity and affinity of the mAbs utilized. These results also indicate the potential contribution of Fab-mediated activities in the enhancement of antiviral humoral responses by ICs.

Flavivirus

Tsouchnikas *et al.*[84] investigated the influence of immunization with ICs on the specificity of antibody responses using the E protein of the tick-borne encephalitis virus as an immunogen. Mice were immunized with a dimeric soluble form of E (sE) alone or in complex with mAbs specific for each of the three domains of E. The antibody response induced by these ICs was compared with that observed after immunization with sE alone. Unexpectedly, immunization with

ICs did not change the extent of the overall antibody response in immunized mice. However, substantially different antibody responses were observed between the different ICs. These differences most likely reflected an epitope-shielding phenomenon and antibody-mediated structural changes that led to the dissociation of the sE dimer. Thus, such phenomena can profoundly influence the fine specificity of antibody responses to the same immunogen and must be considered in IC-based vaccination strategies.

RSV

As mentioned above, serum anti-RSV antibodies can affect virus-specific T-cell responses.[65] On the basis of this, Kruijsen *et al.*[78] tested whether ICs made with the commercial RSV-neutralizing mAb palivizumab could influence adaptive immune response priming after intranasal administration. Substantial anti-RSV T-cell priming and B-cell responses were observed in mice receiving RSV-ICs, resulting in predominant Th1-type $CD4^+$ T-cell response and IgG2c antibody responses. Importantly, the ICs also primed anti-RSV $CD8^+$ T cells. These data have important implications for the prophylaxis and treatment of pediatric RSV infections. Nevertheless, interactions between ICs and neonatal versus adult innate and adaptive immune systems still need to be investigated because mouse studies have revealed potential antibody-induced neonatal autoimmunity in certain settings.[85, 86]

ICS AND IMMUNE DYSFUNCTION

In the course of viral infections, the formation of ICs composed of viral determinants and the resulting host humoral responses can potentially produce deleterious effects. Persistent ICs are formed in a variety of chronic viral infections and may lead to unregulated and protracted FcγR signaling. This may lead to immune dysfunction instead of stimulating antiviral immune responses. In this regard, the high levels of ICs formed during LCMV infection interfere with FcγR-mediated activities.[87, 88] These endogenously formed ICs were shown to outcompete the effector functions of exogenously administered therapeutic mAbs, in particular binding to FcγRs expressed by immune cells. Persistent endogenous ICs are also linked to dysfunctional B-cell responses in HIV infection, including the suppression of antiviral IgA responses and impaired production of neutralizing antibodies (reviewed in Moir *et al.*[89]). The composition of ICs might also negatively affect the efficiency of the antiviral immune response. For instance, the composition of ICs has been shown to be dynamic throughout the course of HIV infections due to changes in both antibody specificities and virion levels. Notably, circulating ICs are initially comprised of antibodies that opsonize both infectious and non-infectious virions. This results in a decrease in the availability of antibodies able to blunt viral propagation. This phenomenon probably contributes to the reduced efficiency of the antibodies generated during acute infection.[90] Changes in circulating ICs have also been reported in HCV infections. The level of circulating ICs is low in acutely infected patients, whereas chronically infected individuals show a high proportion of immunocomplexed HCV, raising the possibility that ICs may have a role in the pathogenesis of HCV, namely liver damage.[91] Moreover, the formation of ICs with non-neutralizing antibodies may also lead to the antibody-dependent enhancement of viral infection of FcγR-expressing cells. This happens in several viral infections, including those by the dengue virus.[92, 93, 94, 95] Along this line, the binding of ICs to FcγRs on monocytes/macrophages can paradoxically suppress innate immunity, induce IL-10 production and bias responses from Th1 toward Th2. This in turn leads to the increased infectious outputs by infected cells via intrinsic antibody-dependent enhancement.[94, 96]

Finally, ICs have also been reported to have a role in increasing viral loads in the context of gene transfer-based vaccination strategies. In the STEP HIV-1 vaccine trial, which evaluated a replication-defective adenovirus type 5 vector vaccine, the ICs formed with pre-existing anti-Adv5 antibodies improved the environment for HIV-1 replication in T cells. This may have been due to the IC-driven activation of a DC–T-cell axis that induces the activation of $CD4^+$ T cells and leads to a permissive environment for HIV-1 infection. This environment probably explains the increased propagation of HIV-1 infection among adenovirus type 5-seropositive vaccine recipients.[97]

IMPROVEMENT OF POTENTIAL VACCINE-LIKE EFFECTS OF MAB-BASED IMMUNOTHERAPIES

Several approaches can be considered to enhance the immunomodulatory potential of antiviral mAbs, both alone and in the form of ICs, in particular through combining neutralizing mAbs and IC-based vaccination strategies with other therapies. A first possibility would consist of inhibiting immunosuppressive mechanisms in infected individuals by either depleting the Treg response, as suggested by Nasser *et al.*[45] or targeting immune checkpoints, the latter strategy having already led to improved immune responses against both viral infections and cancer.[98, 99, 100, 101] In addition, the combination of antiviral mAbs with different immunostimulatory agents can also be envisaged. Because the primary structure and glycosylation pattern of the Fc fragment are both essential for antibody effector functions due to their impact on the engagement of type I and type II FcR family members,[26, 27] Fc engineering might also represent another approach, not only to improve direct antiviral effects, but also to induce stronger vaccine-like effects. In this regard, identification of the main FcRs and FcR-mediated mechanisms involved in enhancing the antiviral immune response will be of utmost importance. Taking into account that the various IgG isotypes display different effector functions and interact differently with FcγRs, the careful selection of antiviral mAb subclasses is also crucial for enhancing antiviral immune responses. Finally, as FcγR polymorphisms have already been associated with differences in viral disease progression and the therapeutic efficiency of anticancer mAbs, it will be important to evaluate the extent to which such polymorphisms can affect the vaccine-like effects induced by mAb-based antiviral immunotherapies.

CONCLUSION

The therapeutic potential of antiviral mAbs is now widely accepted, and their use as antiviral drugs is increasingly under consideration. The diverse biological activities of these mAbs lead to the direct control of viral propagation and the modulation of antiviral immunity. This provides a novel rationale for their use in diverse prophylactic and therapeutic approaches. The improvement in both humoral and cellular responses achieved through the administration of mAbs, either free or in the form of immunogenic ICs, offers new therapeutic options. The challenge now is to improve our understanding of how ICs convert mAb-based immunotherapies from 'passive' to 'active' and to exploit the underlying mechanisms. This conversion will be crucial in reaching the goal of using antiviral mAbs to induce long-lasting protective immunity against life-threatening viral infections.

ACKNOWLEDGEMENTS

This work was supported by grants from the 'Ligue Nationale contre le Cancer', the 'Fondation ARC', 'Sidaction' and the 'Fondation pour la Recherche Médicale'. Jennifer Lambour, Mar Naranjo-Gomez, Marc Piechaczyk and Mireia Pelegrin are part of the 'MabImprove Labex', a public grant overseen by the French National Research Agency (ANR) as part of the 'Investissements d'Avenir' program (reference: ANR-10-LABX -53-01) that also supported this work. We are grateful to Drs Eric Kremer (Institute of Molecular Genetics of Montpellier, France) and Robert Hipskind (Institute of Molecular Genetics of Montpellier, France) for critical reading of the manuscript.

REFERENCES

1. Irani V, Guy AJ, Andrew D, Beeson JG, Ramsland PA, Richards JS. Molecular properties of human IgG subclasses and their implications for designing therapeutic monoclonal antibodies against infectious diseases.*Mol Immunol* 2015; 67: 171–182.
2. Vacchelli E, Eggermont A, Galon J *et al.* Trial watch: monoclonal antibodies in cancer therapy. *Oncoimmunology* 2013; 2: e22789.
3. Bornholdt ZA, Turner HL, Murin CD *et al.* Isolation of potent neutralizing antibodies from a survivor of the 2014 Ebola virus outbreak. *Science* 2016;351: 1078–1083.
4. Corti D, Misasi J, Mulangu S *et al.* Protective monotherapy against lethal Ebola virus infection by a potently neutralizing antibody. *Science* 2016;351: 1339–1342.

5. Corti D, Zhao J, Pedotti M *et al.* Prophylactic and postexposure efficacy of a potent human monoclonal antibody against MERS coronavirus. *Proc Natl Acad Sci USA* 2015; 112: 10473–10478.
6. Johnson RF, Bagci U, Keith L *et al.* 3B11-N, a monoclonal antibody against MERS-CoV, reduces lung pathology in rhesus monkeys following intratracheal inoculation of MERS-CoV Jordan-n3/2012. *Virology* 2016; 490: 49–58.
7. Qiu X, Wong G, Audet J *et al.* Reversion of advanced Ebola virus disease in nonhuman primates with ZMapp. *Nature* 2014; 514: 47–53.
8. Barouch DH, Whitney JB, Moldt B *et al.* Therapeutic efficacy of potent neutralizing HIV-1-specific monoclonal antibodies in SHIV-infected rhesus monkeys. *Nature* 2013; 503: 224–228.
9. Berry JD, Gaudet RG. Antibodies in infectious diseases: polyclonals, monoclonals and niche biotechnology. *N Biotechnol* 2011; 28: 489–501.
10. Both L, Banyard AC, van Dolleweerd C, Wright E, Ma JK, Fooks AR. Monoclonal antibodies for prophylactic and therapeutic use against viral infections. *Vaccine* 2013; 31: 1553–1559.
11. Corti D, Lanzavecchia A. Broadly neutralizing antiviral antibodies. *Annu Rev Immunol* 2013; 31: 705–742.
12. de Jong YP, Dorner M, Mommersteeg MC *et al.* Broadly neutralizing antibodies abrogate established hepatitis C virus infection. *Sci Transl Med*2014; 6: 254ra129.
13. Dejnirattisai W, Wongwiwat W, Supasa S *et al.* A new class of highly potent, broadly neutralizing antibodies isolated from viremic patients infected with dengue virus. *Nat Immunol* 2015; 16: 170–177.
14. Flego M, Ascione A, Cianfriglia M, Vella S. Clinical development of monoclonal antibody-based drugs in HIV and HCV diseases. *BMC Med* 2013;11: 4.

15. Flyak AI, Ilinykh PA, Murin CD *et al.* Mechanism of human antibody-mediated neutralization of Marburg virus. *Cell* 2015; 160: 893–903.

16. Flyak AI, Shen X, Murin CD *et al.* Cross-reactive and potent neutralizing antibody responses in human survivors of natural Ebolavirus infection. *Cell* 2015; 164: 392–405.

17. Gautam R, Nishimura Y, Pegu A *et al.* A single injection of anti-HIV-1 antibodies protects against repeated SHIV challenges. *Nature* 2016; 533: 105–109.

18. Hessell AJ, Jaworski JP, Epson E *et al.* Early short-term treatment with neutralizing human monoclonal antibodies halts SHIV infection in infant macaques. *Nat Med* 2016; 22: 362–368.

19. Krawczyk A, Arndt MA, Grosse-Hovest L *et al.* Overcoming drug-resistant herpes simplex virus (HSV) infection by a humanized antibody. *Proc Natl Acad Sci USA* 2013; 110: 6760–6765.

20. Marasco WA, Sui J. The growth and potential of human antiviral monoclonal antibody therapeutics. *Nat Biotechnol* 2007; 25: 1421–1434.

21. Tan Y, Ng Q, Jia Q, Kwang J, He F. A novel humanized antibody neutralizes H5N1 influenza virus via two different mechanisms. *J Virol* 2015; 89: 3712–3722.

22. Williams KL, Sukupolvi-Petty S, Beltramello M *et al.* Therapeutic efficacy of antibodies lacking Fcgamma receptor binding against lethal dengue virus infection is due to neutralizing potency and blocking of enhancing antibodies [corrected]. *PLoS Pathog* 2013; 9: e1003157.

23. Caskey M, Klein F, Lorenzi JC *et al.* Viraemia suppressed in HIV-1-infected humans by broadly neutralizing antibody 3BNC117. *Nature* 2015; 522: 487–491.

24. Lynch RM, Boritz E, Coates EE *et al.* Virologic effects of broadly neutralizing antibody VRC01 administration during chronic HIV-1 infection. *Sci Transl Med* 2015; 7: 319ra206.

25. Bruhns P, Jonsson F. Mouse and human FcR effector functions. *Immunol Rev* 2015; 268: 25–51.

26. Pincetic A, Bournazos S, DiLillo DJ *et al.* Type I and type II Fc receptors regulate innate and adaptive immunity. *Nat Immunol* 2014; 15: 707–716.

27. Euler Z, Alter G. Exploring the potential of monoclonal antibody therapeutics for HIV-1 eradication. *AIDS Res Hum Retroviruses* 2014; 31: 13–24.

28. Hessell AJ, Haigwood NL. Neutralizing antibodies and control of HIV: moves and countermoves. *Curr HIV/AIDS Rep* 2012; 9: 64–72.

29. Su B, Moog C. Which antibody functions are important for an HIV vaccine?*Front Immunol* 2014; 5: 289.

30. Nimmerjahn F, Gordan S, Lux A. FcgammaR dependent mechanisms of cytotoxic, agonistic, and neutralizing antibody activities. *Trends Immunol*2015; 36: 325–336.

31. Malbec M, Porrot F, Rua R *et al.* Broadly neutralizing antibodies that inhibit HIV-1 cell to cell transmission. *J Exp Med* 2013; 210: 2813–2821.

32. Bruhns P. Properties of mouse and human IgG receptors and their contribution to disease models. *Blood* 2012; 119: 5640–5649.

33. Getahun A, Heyman B. How antibodies act as natural adjuvants. *Immunol Lett* 2006; 104: 38–45.

34. Heyman B. Antibodies as natural adjuvants. *Curr Top Microbiol Immunol*2014; 382: 201–219.

35. Hjelm F, Carlsson F, Getahun A, Heyman B. Antibody-mediated regulation of the immune response. *Scand J Immunol* 2006; 64: 177–184.

36. Nimmerjahn F, Ravetch JV. Fcgamma receptors as regulators of immune responses. *Nat Rev Immunol* 2008; 8: 34–47.

37. Schwab I, Nimmerjahn F. Intravenous immunoglobulin therapy: how does IgG modulate the immune system? *Nat Rev Immunol* 2013; 13: 176–189.

38. Brady LJ. Antibody-mediated immunomodulation: a strategy to improve host responses against microbial antigens. *Infect Immun* 2005; 73: 671–678.

39. Pelegrin M, Naranjo-Gomez M, Piechaczyk M. Antiviral monoclonal antibodies: can they be more than simple neutralizing agents? *Trends Microbiol* 2015; 23: 653–665. |

40. Gros L, Dreja H, Fiser AL, Plays M, Pelegrin M, Piechaczyk M. Induction of long-term protective antiviral endogenous immune response by short neutralizing monoclonal antibody treatment. *J Virol* 2005; 79: 6272–6280.

41. Gros L, Pelegrin M, Michaud HA *et al.* Endogenous cytotoxic T-cell response contributes to the long-term antiretroviral protection induced by a short period of antibody-based immunotherapy of neonatally infected mice. *J Virol* 2008; 82: 1339–1349.

42. Gros L, Pelegrin M, Plays M, Piechaczyk M. Efficient mother-to-child transfer of antiretroviral immunity in the context of preclinical monoclonal antibody-based immunotherapy. *J Virol* 2006; 80: 10191–10200.

43. Michaud HA, Gomard T, Gros L *et al.* A crucial role for infected-cell/antibody immune complexes in the enhancement of endogenous antiviral immunity by short passive immunotherapy. *PLoS Pathog* 2010; 6: e1000948.

44. Nasser R, Pelegrin M, Michaud HA *et al.* Long-lasting protective antiviral immunity induced by passive immunotherapies requires both neutralizing and effector functions of the administered monoclonal antibody. *J Virol*2010; 84: 10169–10181.

45. Nasser R, Pelegrin M, Plays M, Gros L, Piechaczyk M. Control of regulatory T cells is necessary for vaccine-like effects of antiviral immunotherapy by monoclonal antibodies. *Blood* 2013; 121: 1102–1111.

46. Boyoglu-Barnum S, Chirkova T, Todd SO *et al.* Prophylaxis with a respiratory syncytial virus (RSV) anti-G protein monoclonal antibody shifts the adaptive immune response to RSV rA2-line19F infection from Th2 to Th1 in BALB/c mice. *J Virol* 2014; 88: 10569–10583.

47. Bossart KN, Geisbert TW, Feldmann H *et al.* A neutralizing human monoclonal antibody protects african green monkeys

from hendra virus challenge. *Sci Transl Med* 2011; 3: 105ra103.

48. Geisbert TW, Mire CE, Geisbert JB *et al.* Therapeutic treatment of Nipah virus infection in nonhuman primates with a neutralizing human monoclonal antibody. *Sci Transl Med* 2014; 6: 242ra282.

49. Jaworski JP, Kobie J, Brower Z *et al.* Neutralizing polyclonal IgG present during acute infection prevents rapid disease onset in simian-human immunodeficiency virus SHIVSF162P3-infected infant rhesus macaques. *J Virol* 2013; 87: 10447–10459.

50. Ng CT, Jaworski JP, Jayaraman P *et al.* Passive neutralizing antibody controls SHIV viremia and enhances B cell responses in infant macaques.*Nat Med* 2010; 16: 1117–1119.

51. Watkins JD, Siddappa NB, Lakhashe SK *et al.* An anti-HIV-1 V3 loop antibody fully protects cross-clade and elicits T-cell immunity in macaques mucosally challenged with an R5 clade C SHIV. *PLoS One* 2011; 6: e18207.

52. Schoofs T, Klein F, Braunschweig M *et al.* HIV-1 therapy with monoclonal antibody 3BNC117 elicits hoost immune responses against HIV-1. *Science*2016; 352: 997–1001.

53. Bournazos S, Klein F, Pietzsch J, Seaman MS, Nussenzweig MC, Ravetch JV. Broadly neutralizing anti-HIV-1 antibodies require Fc effector functions for *in vivo* activity. *Cell* 2014; 158: 1243–1253.

54. Halper-Stromberg A, Lu CL, Klein F *et al.* Broadly neutralizing antibodies and viral inducers decrease rebound from HIV-1 latent reservoirs in humanized mice. *Cell* 2014; 158: 989–999.

55. Celis E, Chang TW. HBsAg-serum protein complexes stimulate immune T lymphocytes more efficiently than do pure HBsAg. *Hepatology* 1984; 4: 1116–1123.

56. Zheng BJ, Zhou J, Qu D *et al.* Selective functional deficit in dendritic cell—T cell interaction is a crucial mechanism in

chronic hepatitis B virus infection. *J Viral Hepat* 2004; 11: 217–224.

57. Villinger F, Mayne AE, Bostik P *et al.* Evidence for antibody-mediated enhancement of simian immunodeficiency virus (SIV) Gag antigen processing and cross presentation in SIV-infected rhesus macaques. *J Virol* 2003; 77: 10–24.

58. Yamamoto T, Iwamoto N, Yamamoto H *et al.* Polyfunctional CD4+ T-cell induction in neutralizing antibody-triggered control of simian immunodeficiency virus infection. *J Virol* 2009; 83: 5514–5524.

59. Posch W, Cardinaud S, Hamimi C *et al.* Antibodies attenuate the capacity of dendritic cells to stimulate HIV-specific cytotoxic T lymphocytes. *J Allergy Clin Immunol* 2012; 130: 1368–1374 e1362.

60. Xu DZ, Huang KL, Zhao K *et al.* Vaccination with recombinant HBsAg-HBIG complex in healthy adults. *Vaccine* 2005; 23: 2658–2664.

61. Yao X, Zheng B, Zhou J *et al.* Therapeutic effect of hepatitis B surface antigen-antibody complex is associated with cytolytic and non-cytolytic immune responses in hepatitis B patients. *Vaccine* 2007; 25: 1771–1779.

62. Xu DZ, Zhao K, Guo LM *et al.* A randomized controlled phase IIb trial of antigen-antibody immunogenic complex therapeutic vaccine in chronic hepatitis B patients. *PLoS One* 2008; 3: e2565.

63. Liu H, Geng S, Wang B *et al.* Immuno-potentiating pathway of HBsAg-HBIG immunogenic complex visualized. *Hum Vaccin Immunother* 2015; 12: 77–84.

64. Leon B, Ballesteros-Tato A, Randall TD, Lund FE. Prolonged antigen presentation by immune complex-binding dendritic cells programs the proliferative capacity of memory CD8 T cells. *J Exp Med* 2014; 211: 1637–1655.

65. Kruijsen D, Bakkers MJ, van Uden NO *et al.* Serum antibodies critically affect virus-specific CD4+/CD8+ T cell balance during respiratory syncytial virus infections. *J Immunol* 2010; 185: 6489–6498.

66. Duhan V, Khairnar V, Friedrich SK *et al.* Virus-specific antibodies allow viral replication in the marginal zone, thereby promoting CD8(+) T-cell priming and viral control. *Sci Rep* 2016; 6: 19191.

67. Bachmann MF, Hunziker L, Zinkernagel RM, Storni T, Kopf M. Maintenance of memory CTL responses by T helper cells and CD40-CD40 ligand: antibodies provide the key. *Eur J Immunol* 2004; 34: 317–326.

68. Bergthaler A, Flatz L, Verschoor A *et al.* Impaired antibody response causes persistence of prototypic T cell-contained virus. *PLoS Biol* 2009; 7: e80.

69. Terres G, Wolins W. Enhanced immunological sensitization of mice by the simultaneous injection of antigen and specific antiserum. I. Effect of varying the amount of antigen used relative to the antiserum. *J Immunol*1961; 86: 361–368.

70. Wen YM, Qu D, Zhou SH. Antigen-antibody complex as therapeutic vaccine for viral hepatitis B. *Int Rev Immunol* 1999; 18: 251–258.

71. Basalp A, Cirakoglu B, Bermek E. Enhancement of the immune response to hepatitis B virus vaccine by antigen specific IgM. *Immunol Lett* 2000; 73: 1–6.

72. Zheng BJ, Ng MH, He LF *et al.* Therapeutic efficacy of hepatitis B surface antigen-antibodies-recombinant DNA composite in HBsAg transgenic mice.*Vaccine* 2001; 19: 4219–4225.

73. Lu M, Yao X, Xu Y *et al.* Combination of an antiviral drug and immunomodulation against hepadnaviral infection in the woodchuck model.*J Virol* 2008; 82: 2598–2603.

74. McCluskie MJ, Wen YM, Di Q, Davis HL. Immunization against hepatitis B virus by mucosal administration of antigen-antibody complexes. *Viral Immunol* 1998; 11: 245–252.

75. Hioe CE, Visciano ML, Kumar R *et al.* The use of immune complex vaccines to enhance antibody responses against neutralizing epitopes on HIV-1 envelope gp120. *Vaccine* 2009; 28: 352–360.

76. Kumar R, Tuen M, Li H, Tse DB, Hioe CE. Improving immunogenicity of HIV-1 envelope gp120 by glycan removal

and immune complex formation.*Vaccine* 2011; 29: 9064–9074.

77. Kumar R, Tuen M, Liu J *et al.* Elicitation of broadly reactive antibodies against glycan-modulated neutralizing V3 epitopes of HIV-1 by immune complex vaccines. *Vaccine* 2013; 31: 5413–5421.

78. Kruijsen D, Einarsdottir HK, Schijf MA *et al.* Intranasal administration of antibody-bound respiratory syncytial virus particles efficiently primes virus-specific immune responses in mice. *J Virol* 2013; 87: 7550–7557.

79. Randall RE, Young DF, Southern JA. Immunization with solid matrix-antibody-antigen complexes containing surface or internal virus structural proteins protects mice from infection with the paramyxovirus, simian virus 5. *J Gen Virol* 1988; 69: 2517–2526.

80. Randall RE, Young DF. Solid matrix-antibody-antigen complexes induce antigen-specific CD8+ cells that clear a persistent paramyxovirus infection.*J Virol* 1991; 65: 719–726.

81. Xu DZ, Wang XY, Shen XL *et al.* Results of a phase III clinical trial with an HBsAg-HBIG immunogenic complex therapeutic vaccine for chronic hepatitis B patients: experiences and findings. *J Hepatol* 2013; 59: 450–456.

82. Berzofsky JA, Bensussan A, Cease KB *et al.* Antigenic peptides recognized by T lymphocytes from AIDS viral envelope-immune humans. *Nature* 1988;334: 706–708.

83. Kumar R, Visciano ML, Li H, Hioe C. Targeting a neutralizing epitope of HIV envelope Gp120 by immune complex vaccine. *J AIDS Clin Res* 2012; S8: pii: 5512.

84. Tsouchnikas G, Zlatkovic J, Jarmer J *et al.* Immunization with immune complexes modulates the fine specificity of antibody responses to a flavivirus antigen. *J Virol* 2015; 89: 7970–7978.

85. Rival C, Samy E, Setiady Y, Tung K. Cutting edge: Ly49C/I(-) neonatal NK cells predispose newborns to autoimmune

ovarian disease induced by maternal autoantibody. *J Immunol* 2013; 191: 2865–2869.

86. Rival C, Setiady Y, Samy ET, Harakal J, Tung KS. The unique neonatal NK cells: a critical component required for neonatal autoimmune disease induction by maternal autoantibody. *Front Immunol* 2014; 5: 242.

87. Wieland A, Shashidharamurthy R, Kamphorst AO *et al.* Antibody effector functions mediated by Fcgamma-receptors are compromised during persistent viral infection. *Immunity* 2015; 42: 367–378.

88. Yamada DH, Elsaesser H, Lux A *et al.* Suppression of Fcgamma-receptor-mediated antibody effector function during persistent viral infection.*Immunity* 2015; 42: 379–390.

89. Moir S, Fauci AS. B cells in HIV infection and disease. *Nat Rev Immunol*2009; 9: 235–245.

90. Liu P, Overman RG, Yates NL *et al.* Dynamic antibody specificities and virion concentrations in circulating immune complexes in acute to chronic HIV-1 infection. *J Virol* 2011; 85: 11196–11207.

91. Riva E, Maggi F, Abbruzzese F *et al.* Immune complexed (IC) hepatitis C virus (HCV) in chronically and acutely HCV-infected patients. *Med Microbiol Immunol* 2009; 198: 13–18.

92. Acosta EG, Bartenschlager R. Paradoxical role of antibodies in dengue virus infections: considerations for prophylactic vaccine development. *Expert Rev Vaccines* 2016; 15: 467–482.

93. Halstead SB. Dengue antibody-dependent enhancement: knowns and unknowns. *Microbiol Spectr* 2014 doi:10.1128/microbiolspec.AID-0022-2014.

94. Halstead SB, Mahalingam S, Marovich MA, Ubol S, Mosser DM. Intrinsic antibody-dependent enhancement of microbial infection in macrophages: disease regulation by immune complexes. *Lancet Infect Dis* 2010; 10: 712–722.

95. Ubol S, Halstead SB. How innate immune mechanisms contribute to antibody-enhanced viral infections. *Clin Vaccine Immunol* 2010; 17: 1829–1835. |

96. Tsai TT, Chuang YJ, Lin YS *et al.* Antibody-dependent enhancement infection facilitates dengue virus-regulated signaling of IL-10 production in monocytes. *PLoS Negl Trop Dis* 2014; 8: e3320.

97. Perreau M, Pantaleo G, Kremer EJ. Activation of a dendritic cell-T cell axis by Ad5 immune complexes creates an improved environment for replication of HIV in T cells. *J Exp Med* 2008; 205: 2717–2725.

98. Bengsch B, Martin B, Thimme R. Restoration of HBV-specific CD8+ T cell function by PD-1 blockade in inactive carrier patients is linked to T cell differentiation. *J Hepatol* 2014; 61: 1212–1219.

99. Gardiner D, Lalezari J, Lawitz E *et al.* A randomized, double-blind, placebo-controlled assessment of BMS-936558, a fully human monoclonal antibody to programmed death-1 (PD-1), in patients with chronic hepatitis C virus infection. *PLoS One* 2013; 8: e63818.

100. Sharma P, Allison JP. Immune checkpoint targeting in cancer therapy: toward combination strategies with curative potential. *Cell* 2015; 161: 205–214.

101. Sherman AC, Trehanpati N, Daucher M *et al.* Augmentation of hepatitis B virus-specific cellular immunity with programmed death receptor-1/programmed death receptor-L1 blockade in hepatitis B virus and HIV/hepatitis B virus coinfected patients treated with adefovir. *AIDS Res Hum Retroviruses* 2013; 29: 665–672.

Index